THE ENTERTAINMENT
MARKETING REVOLUTION

ISBN 0-13-029350-4

9 780130 293503

FINANCIAL TIMES

Prentice Hall

In an increasingly competitive world, it is quality
of thinking that gives an edge—an idea that opens new
doors, a technique that solves a problem, or an insight
that simply helps make sense of it all.

We work with leading authors in the various arenas
of business and finance to bring cutting-edge thinking
and best learning practice to a global market.

It is our goal to create world-class print publications
and electronic products that give readers
knowledge and understanding which can then be
applied, whether studying or at work.

To find out more about our business
products, you can visit us at www.ft-ph.com

Pearson
Education

THE ENTERTAINMENT MARKETING REVOLUTION

Bringing the Moguls, the Media, and the Magic to the World

AL LIEBERMAN

WITH PATRICIA ESGATE

An Imprint of Pearson Education

Upper Saddle River, NJ • New York • London • San Francisco • Toronto
Sydney • Tokyo • Singapore • Hong Kong • Cape Town
Madrid • Paris • Milan • Munich • Amsterdam

www.ft-ph.com

Library of Congress Cataloging-in-Publication Data

Lieberman, Al.
   The entertainment revolution : bringing the moguls, the media, and the magic to
the world / Al Lieberman, with Patricia Esgate.
      p. cm.
   Includes bibliographical references (p.) and index.
   ISBN 0-13-029350-4 (alk. paper)
   1. Mass media--Marketing. I. Esgate, Patricia. II. Title

P96.M36 L54 2002
302.23'068'8--dc21

200216448

Production supervisor: *Wil Mara*
Cover design director: *Jerry Votta*
Cover design: *Nina Scuderi*
Interior design: *Gail Cocker-Bogusz*
Manufacturing buyer: *Maura Zaldivar*
VP, executive editor: *Tim Moore*
Editorial assistant: *Allyson Kloss*
Marketing manager: *Bryan Gambrel*
Composition: *Wil Mara*

©2002 by Financial Times Prentice Hall
An imprint of Pearson Education, Inc.
Upper Saddle River, New Jersey 07458

Financial Times Prentice Hall books are widely used by corporations and government
agencies for training, marketing, and resale.

For information regarding corporate and government bulk discounts please contact:
Corporate and Government Sales (800) 382-3419 or corpsales@pearsontechgroup.com

Printed in the United States of America

10 9 8 7 6 5 4 3 2 1

ISBN 0-13-029350-4

Pearson Education LTD.
Pearson Education Australia PTY, Limited
Pearson Education Singapore, Pte. Ltd.
Pearson Education North Asia Ltd.
Pearson Education Canada, Ltd.
Pearson Educación de Mexico, S.A. de C.V.
Pearson Education—Japan
Pearson Education Malaysia, Pte. Ltd.

FINANCIAL TIMES PRENTICE HALL BOOKS

For more information, please go to www.ft-ph.com

Thomas L. Barton, William G. Shenkir, and Paul L. Walker
  Making Enterprise Risk Management Pay Off:
  How Leading Companies Implement Risk Management

Deirdre Breakenridge
  Cyberbranding: Brand Building in the Digital Economy

William C. Byham, Audrey B. Smith, and Matthew J. Paese
  Grow Your Own Leaders: How to Identify, Develop, and Retain
  Leadership Talent

Jonathan Cagan and Craig M. Vogel
  Creating Breakthrough Products: Innovation from Product Planning
  to Program Approval

Subir Chowdhury
  The Talent Era: Achieving a High Return on Talent

Sherry Cooper
  Ride the Wave: Taking Control in a Turbulent Financial Age

James W. Cortada
  21st Century Business: Managing and Working
  in the New Digital Economy

James W. Cortada
  Making the Information Society: Experience, Consequences,
  and Possibilities

Aswath Damodaran
  The Dark Side of Valuation: Valuing Old Tech, New Tech,
  and New Economy Companies

Henry A. Davis and William W. Sihler
  Financial Turnarounds: Preserving Enterprise Value

Sarv Devaraj and Rajiv Kohli
  The IT Payoff: Measuring the Business Value
  of Information Technology Investments

Jaime Ellertson and Charles W. Ogilvie
  Frontiers of Financial Services: Turning Customer Interactions
  Into Profits

Nicholas D. Evans
  Business Agility: Strategies for Gaining Competitive Advantage
  through Mobile Business Solutions

Kenneth R. Ferris and Barbara S. Pécherot Petitt
Valuation: Avoiding the Winner's Curse

David Gladstone and Laura Gladstone
Venture Capital Handbook: An Entrepreneur's Guide to Raising Venture Capital, Revised and Updated

David R. Henderson
The Joy of Freedom: An Economist's Odyssey

Philip Jenks and Stephen Eckett, Editors
The Global-Investor Book of Investing Rules: Invaluable Advice from 150 Master Investors

Thomas Kern, Mary Cecelia Lacity, and Leslie P. Willcocks
Netsourcing: Renting Business Applications and Services Over a Network

Al Lieberman, with Patricia Esgate
The Entertainment Marketing Revolution: Bringing the Moguls, the Media, and the Magic to the World

Frederick C. Militello, Jr., and Michael D. Schwalberg
Leverage Competencies: What Financial Executives Need to Lead

D. Quinn Mills
Buy, Lie, and Sell High: How Investors Lost Out on Enron and the Internet Bubble

Dale Neef
E-procurement: From Strategy to Implementation

John R. Nofsinger
Investment Madness: How Psychology Affects Your Investing... And What to Do About It

Tom Osenton
Customer Share Marketing: How the World's Great Marketers Unlock Profits from Customer Loyalty

W. Alan Randolph and Barry Z. Posner
Checkered Flag Projects: 10 Rules for Creating and Managing Projects that Win, Second Edition

Stephen P. Robbins
The Truth About Managing People...And Nothing but the Truth

Eric G. Stephan and Wayne R. Pace
Powerful Leadership: How to Unleash the Potential in Others and Simplify Your Own Life

Jonathan Wight
Saving Adam Smith: A Tale of Wealth, Transformation, and Virtue

Yoram J. Wind and Vijay Mahajan, with Robert Gunther
Convergence Marketing: Strategies for Reaching the New Hybrid Consumer

CONTENTS

FOREWORD   xv

INTRODUCTION   xix

CHAPTER 1   PEELING THE ONION:
ENTERTAINMENT MARKETING BASICS 1

OVERVIEW 1
THE FOUR C'S OF ENTERTAINMENT 2
CONTENT 2
CONDUIT 7
CONSUMPTION 11
CONVERGENCE 12
RUBBER BRANDS: EXTENDING
  THE EQUITY 14
SUMMARY 18

CHAPTER 2   PEOPLE, POWER,
AND PLAYERS 19

OVERVIEW 19
MOLDING THE MESSAGE 20
DECISIONS, DECISIONS 23

TAILORING THE TEAM 26

MOVERS AND SHAKERS 30

MEMORABLE MOGULS 35

SUMMARY 40

CHAPTER 3   MOVIES: WANNASEE, HAFTASEE, AND MUSTSEE 41

OVERVIEW 41

TO MARKET, TO MARKET 41

RISKY BUSINESS 45

WANNASEE 50

INDEPENDENT FILMS 58

SUMMARY 63

FURTHER READING 63

CHAPTER 4   NETWORK TV, SYNDICATION, AND RADIO 65

OVERVIEW 65

NETWORK TELEVISION:
   "THE MOTHER OF THEM ALL" 66

LOCAL TELEVISION STATIONS 68

THE BASICS OF TV RATINGS 71

PROMOTION AND MARKETING 75

SYNDICATION 81

NON-COMMERCIALLY DRIVEN
   BROADCASTING 85

TV TECHNOLOGY 87

SUMMARY: NETWORK TV
   AND SYNDICATION 90

RADIO 91

DON'T TOUCH THAT DIAL:

THE BASICS OF RADIO MARKETING 91
THE BEAT GOES ON...AND ON 95
FOR FURTHER READING 99

Chapter 5 Cable Television and Direct
Broadcast Satellite: Basic, Premium,
and Pay-Per-View 101

OVERVIEW 101
THE BASICS OF BASIC CABLE 102
THE GROWTH OF THE INDUSTRY 107
CABLE'S MARKETING ADVANTAGE: REACH
    AND SEGMENTATION 111
MEDIA, MARKETING, AND MONEY 119
THE SEARCH FOR SUBSCRIBERS 122
NEW DIRECTIONS IN THE MULTICHANNEL
    ARENA 124
NEW TV TECHNOLOGY 125
SUMMARY 127
FOR FURTHER READING 128

Chapter 6 Publishing: The Printed Word 129

OVERVIEW 129
BOOKS 130
WHEN, WHERE, AND TO WHOM 134
MARKETING BOOKS 136
NEW WRINKLES IN BOOK MARKETING 141
THE FINAL FRONTIER: CHARACTER AS
    BRAND 146
THE CHANGING PUBLISHING ENVIRONMENT
    147
SUMMARY: BOOKS 154

NEWSPAPERS 155

SUMMARY: NEWSPAPERS 159

MAGAZINES 159

SUMMARY: MAGAZINES 162

ELECTRONIC GAMES 162

SUMMARY: ELECTRONIC GAMES 166

SUMMARY: PUBLISHING 166

FOR FURTHER READING 167

CHAPTER 7 MUSIC 169

OVERVIEW 169

MUSIC LABELS 172

THE ALL-IMPORTANT AIRPLAY 173

LIVE MUSIC 175

GETTING THE MUSIC TO THE MASSES:
    RETAIL DISTRIBUTION 179

MARKETING THE MUSIC 182

NEW NICHES 186

TECHNO TRENDS 192

THE GLOBAL MUSIC MARKET 195

BILLBOARD.COM: A CASE STUDY 198

SUMMARY 203

FOR FURTHER READING 204

CHAPTER 8 SPORTS 205

OVERVIEW 205

MAJOR LEAGUE SPORTS 208

THE IMPACT OF MARKETING 215

NON-LEAGUE SPORTS 221

SPORTS ONLINE: TODAY'S TECHNOLOGIES
    228

SUMMARY 231

FOR FURTHER READING 231

CHAPTER 9 TRAVEL AND TOURISM 233

OVERVIEW 233

PROMISING PARADISE 234

BUILDING THE PLAN 238

CREATING AN IDENTITY 240

DYNAMICS OF TRAVEL
, AND TOURISM MARKETING 247

RELATIONSHIP MARKETING 249

ADVERTISING, PUBLICITY,
AND PROMOTION 254

ALTERNATIVE DESTINATIONS 256

SUMMARY 267

FOR FURTHER READING 267

CHAPTER 10 LOCATION-BASED ENTERTAINMENT AND
EXPERIENTIAL BRANDING 269

OVERVIEW 269

LOCATION-BASED ENTERTAINMENT 270

OFF THE STREETS AND INTO THE MALL 276

EXPERIENTIAL BRANDING 279

THE ECONOMICS OF EXPERIENCE 288

BRINGING THE BRAND TO LIFE 289

THE 11 STAGES OF PROJECT DEVELOPMENT
291

SUMMARY 294

FOR FURTHER READING 294

CHAPTER 11 CHANGES AND CHALLENGES 297

OVERVIEW 297

GOING GLOBAL 298

MARKETING IN THE NEW MILLENNIUM 299

PIRACY 304

THE GLOBAL SNAPSHOT 308

SUMMARY 315

CHAPTER 12 CONCLUSION: WHERE DO WE GO FROM HERE? 317

INDEX 325

FOREWORD

One of the most interesting phenomena in the entertainment industry is that everyone seems to have an opinion—and an expert one at that! Perhaps it is because the industry is open and available for public review and critique. Professional journalists have a field day selecting the best and worst of film-making and television programming; business pundits advise which media conglomerates have the best and worst strategies for growth, acquisition, marketing, and global expansion. Frequently opinions are widely disseminated with little understanding of the intricacies of managing the creativity-based enterprise. In our business, there is often a thin line between artistic muse and commercial ascent.

The ability to describe both sides of that thin line, and to provide a thoughtful analysis of the key factors at play in determining success, is rare indeed. Al Lieberman has done that and more in *The Entertainment Marketing Revolution*. I met Al several years ago, a lifetime in the entertainment industry, where there is little time for long-term friendships. We met shortly after he became a Professor at the Stern School of Business, at New York University, at a time when he was creating a badly needed course curriculum to teach aspiring producers and studio executives about the business side of this often poorly organized and badly managed industry. He began with undergraduates in both the Business School and the world-class Tisch Film Program. The program was expanded shortly thereafter to include MBA and Graduate Film and Music students.

We talked at length about the benefits of merging business acumen and creativity in a pragmatic way. I later had the pleasure of conducting sessions of his marketing class, witnessing firsthand the impressive results of this merger. I have been consistently impressed with the students in Al's program—their interest in the business and creative sides of our endeavors and their insights into the importance of integrating both to be successful. Al was the pioneer who recognized the fact that creating this integration and enabling these synergies would, in fact, be the best preparation for the future leaders of our industry.

Now with over 20 courses in the Entertainment, Media and Technology Initiative, the program Al created has expanded its audience beyond aspiring producers and studio executives, to include students with an interest in all facets of the industry. Al now teaches five courses with over 275 students. He is a popular professor with a continuing interest in new trends; in the avalanches and earthquakes as well as the slight tremors which are easily overlooked, but can and do shake the entertainment industry to its core.

In *The Entertainment Marketing Revolution*, Al and his writing partner, Pat Esgate, have described what we in the industry have been living through for the past decade—change that is constant, challenging, exciting and enervating in nature—global and seismic in scope. This book accurately documents the power shifts and opportunities for new players in the business. In an example from my own world, it describes the increasing importance of independent film with its growing audience—a David and Goliath story of upstart entrepreneurs and studio behemoths vying for the hearts, minds and substantial box office dollars of the movie-going audience.

He has understood that no one chapter or even a whole book can capture every nuance or change, but instead a snapshot in time, providing the reader with a sure footing, a basis upon which to understand the future. In this sense, the book will be of value to every student aspiring to the business or creative side of the entertainment industry, to novitiates already in the growing workforce within the industry, as well as to the entertainment consumer, continually fascinated with the back stories and inner workings of this powerful segment of our society.

Over the past several years, Al has gained a wealth of information through bringing students and industry executives together to share lessons learned and answer probing questions. He has taken these shared moments of interchange with industry leaders, combined them with his own career experience with industry clients, and woven them together in a way that accurately captures the field of entertainment businesses, in constant and ever-changing motion.

In this book, you can anticipate a practical guide to the interplay of the various forces at work on the entertainment and media landscape, the plot twists and turns of a good novel, and considerable insight into an industry, which forms public opinion and determines popular culture, as much as it reflects them.

My colleagues and I wish Al much success with this honest appraisal, his valuable scholarship, and its contribution to the current and future generation of entertainment entrepreneurs, employees, and fans.

KATHLEEN DORE

PRESIDENT
BRAVO NETWORKS GROUP
DIVISION OF CABLEVISION SYSTEMS CORPORATION

INTRODUCTION:

"Let Us Entertain You"

P.T. Barnum was *the* master showman. He knew what the masses wanted, from lowbrow sideshow freaks to the highbrow culture of Jenny Lind, imported straight from Europe. Barnum knew that people craved entertainment—it gave them somewhere to go, something to talk about, something to take their minds off the humdrum days of their humdrum lives. He excelled at divining the desires of his audience and creating just the spectacles they'd flock to see. And, he knew that the buildup to a show was just as important as the actual performance.

Barnum knew that the right kind of promotion was critical to the success of the show—and that every event and every happening called for its own particular approach to its own particular audience. What P.T. Barnum knew best of all was that to pull in an audience, you have to reach out the hook and reel them in. You need the right hawker out there, enticing the crowd. You have to make them notice, make them wonder, and get them to follow their curiosity right into the tent. P.T. Barnum may not have heard of the term yet, but he was the Master of Marketing.

While the basic principles of marketing may not have changed drastically from Barnum's days, the global big top has increased dramatically in size. Entertainment drove more than $500 billion[1] in worldwide revenue in the year 2000—more bucks than Barnum could ever have ballyhooed his way. And, given that figure has been rising every year for the last decade, odds are that the dollars will continue to pile up.

---

1. Veronis, Suhler & Associates, *Communications Industry Historical and Projected Expenditures*, 2000.

Today, there are a lot more Barnums, many more tents, and innumerable hawkers out there shouting for our attention. In fact, the din has been raised to the point that, in order to lure us into the tent, entertainment marketing itself has turned into a form of entertainment all its own—a virtual sideshow of technology, celebrity, and bells and whistles. And the big top? Sometimes it seems as though we're destined to live under one tent, supplied by one fast food company, one software company, and one entertainment company. But for now, we're somewhere in between Barnum and *BizCorpGlobal*.

ENTERTAINMENT TAKES THE STAGE

Entertainment as an industry has shown steady growth since P.T. Barnum's day. While the first big kick occurred in the early part of the 20th Century, when movies appeared on the scene, the true explosion of entertainment came in the post-World War II era. Movie moguls enjoyed a relatively cornered market in pre-war times; Hollywood was the center of attention, given that technology had not yet reared its intriguing head in the form of television. The favorite at-home form of entertainment was radio, which had grown from crystal sets in the attic to decorative cabinets in the living room, with the family gathered 'round for an evening of music and programming.

Then the world turned upside down.

FROM V-DAY TO V-CHIP

Outside the palm-lined streets of Hollywood, the world was in transformation. While the United States slowly crawled out of the Depression through a series of government-related programs, other parts of the globe found themselves under different influences. The poor and starving in Europe and Japan turned their eyes toward leaders who promised a new and glittering future, born out of the rising of the masses, the extermination of undesirables, the acquisition of historic land holdings—whatever it took to build a power base.

It was only a matter of time before the global cauldron boiled over. World War II arrived, and with it, a sociological and technological upheaval unlike any that came before. Women worked outside the home en masse for the first time in modern history, tasting economic freedom. Backed by huge infusions of war-driven government dollars, industry and technology leapfrogged forward. By the time Johnnie came marching home, the wheels were in motion for a vastly different society than before the war. The economy stayed in overdrive: paychecks grew fatter, workdays shorter. In the midst of this economic growth, families boomed. And most important, the seeds of technology, sown in strategic advances in science and communication, spawned the beginnings of a technological revolution.

As usual in the history of humankind, these advances ultimately found their greatest source of revenue in the entertainment of the masses.

The tidal wave of the good life in America broke free from both coasts of the U.S. and sped toward Europe and the Pacific. Infused by the dollars of the Marshall Plan in Europe and a combination of American investment and Japanese vision in Japan, the economies of both theaters of war returned to and surpassed pre-war peaks. The advancement of technology was at first overshadowed by hard goods, but by the late 1950s and early 1960s, the roots of a technological revolution were in place.

The sociological revolution was already in full swing. Back in the U.S., Levitt and Sons Construction Company built the first mass-produced town[2] of 17,000-plus cloned homes, completed in 1951. Suddenly, communities were sprouting up where cornfields once stood. The "starter homes" soon included not only radios, but also the new technology: television. Right down the block, in the brand-new strip mall, a new cinema broke ground. Money was good, jobs became plentiful, and the masses, moving to the suburbs, more time and money on their hands, were eager to find new ways to spend both.

Entertainment exploded. The convergence of discretionary time, disposable income, and especially, advancing technology put the entertainment bandwagon into overdrive in the second half of the 20th Century. With time on their hands, money in their pockets, and a general sense of a great good life, the varied peoples of the American public demanded and received distraction.

The entertainment industry, sensing the moment at hand, kicked up another notch and cranked out movies, TV programs, and music, managing not only to bypass the barriers of Korea, McCarthy, and Vietnam, but to actually take advantage of them. The widening split between far left and far right—not to mention the mass in the middle—opened up huge new niches, and all areas of entertainment were quick to exploit the opportunities.

---

2.   Levittown, NY was such a success that Levittown, PA soon followed, built by the same construction company.

The individual entertainment segments thrived. Movies jumped from the silver screen to cathode ray tubes, at first simply showing up on network TV. Then, that quick-thinking upstart, Ted Turner, purchased the MGM film library for TNT and the rush was on. Movies became the staple content that drove the initial boom of the cable industry, through new concepts such as Home Box Office (HBO) and Showtime, later joined by offshoots such as American Movie Classics, Independent Film Channel, Bravo, Starz, and more. The home consumer gained control with Betamax, then video home system (VHS), then digital versatile disc (DVD), opening yet another channel of distribution, to be followed later by satellite TV, movies on-demand, and pay-per-view.

Television found the mother lode in the advent of cable, erupting from three networks to hundreds of channels, thousands of programs, and unlimited dollars, with the syndication of hit network series providing an afterlife for audience favorites. With the introduction of VHS players, then recorders, television became tied even tighter to the studios, which finally took the leap into developing their own programs, side by side with feature films.

Craving even more content, cable blasted sports from the sleepy backwater province of local stadiums to satellite transmissions, beaming one "America's Team" after another into cities, towns, and suburbs with no local heroes of their own. Sports figures became superstars overnight, with salaries to match. Leagues that simply provided a skeleton for competition became cultures, with fans fixated on licensed logo-wear. The NFL and NBA became icons, usurping baseball as a point of passion for millions.

And music? Set free from small venues and unchained from the scratchy airwaves of AM radio and vinyl records, music found new power in the surging market of compact discs (CDs) and superstar performers who mounted global tours with semis carting towers of speakers and tons of technology from one stadium to another, selling out wherever they traveled. The backlash to such over-abundance—alternative music—turned into its own powerhouse.

Even sleepy publishing, once the haven for a few magazine titles and that old-fashioned medium, books, suddenly sprang to life as publishers found that niche markets could provide a base of readership never before considered. In a few short decades, the magazine market grew to over 20,000 titles, as it seemed that every individual on the face of the earth could find some periodical that would focus on his or her own particular passion.

Then came the personal computer (PC), possibly the single most important advancement in the field of entertainment—although the full power of this technology is yet to be seen. PCs have made possible the electronic game industry, which now exceeds movies in yearly revenue. And the Internet—a whole new revolution in entertainment—is becoming the conduit for downloadable music (MPEGs, Napster), movies, and Web sites for every conceivable form of entertainment, driving even more revenue from youthful consumers who recently proclaimed that they would much rather spend their hours in front of their computer than a television. Why? Because it's interactive—because the consumer now has the power to communicate with the entertainment. No less an entertainment powerhouse than Time Warner discovered the strength of the Internet, when—unthinkable—AOL bought the company for $183 billion.

Finally, we have TiVo™ (a service that allows consumers to digitally record content for viewing at a later date, sans commercials), video on-demand, and digital movies replacing traditional film, allowing for the transmission of movies as well as live performances. The expansion of entertainment brands into branded entertainment destinations completes the cycle that started with local venues and grew to national and international distribution. It now returns to something that people can experience personally, one-on-one—not just in theme parks, but in facilities down the street and around the corner.

What has been the driving force between this explosion, this convergence, this intertwined knot of entertainment mediums that blends from one conduit to another? Mr. Barnum's basics: entertainment marketing. It has also been the realization that the public has a hunger for stimulation, a desire to identify with something larger, a need to feed themselves with images and sounds and sights—that vehicles must be created to take each individual product and catapult it above the din that engulfs today's consumer.

SERIOUS COMPETITION FOR SERIOUS MONEY

Competition for the consumer's interest has now reached Olympian levels. Traditional marketing channels such as TV, print, and outdoor advertising are becoming saturated; promoters are constantly in search of new ways to spread the word. As always, necessity has been busy mothering invention, so just when it seems there isn't one more square inch of turf that can be covered by ads—airport baggage carousels, supermarket floors, subway stations—technology rears its intriguing head. Advertisers can now insert a digital image overlay into the broadcast of nearly anything. So, for example, instead of relying on the local stadium camera to pick up the ad plastered over the box seats, promoters can now simply patch a digitized image wherever they want it, and change it in seconds.

Today's consumer is faced with an estimated 3,000 marketing messages daily. Therefore, the successful marketer must create a message that truly draws away from the pack. And, when it comes to entertainment marketing, the best way to do that is to create a message that becomes entertaining in and of itself—one that creates its own "wannasee," buzz, word-of-mouth momentum—reversing Marshall McLuhan's groundbreaking thoughts on the medium as the message in the span of one short generation.

The stakes in this race grow higher yearly. At the close of the Millennium, for the year 1999, the entertainment industries generated $250 billion across the eight major sectors to be covered in this book: movies, home video, broadcast, cable, music, publishing, sports, and electronic games (see Table A-1).

TABLE A-1   Gross Entertainment Revenues, 1990 / 1999 (in Millions of $)

SECTOR	1990 U.S.	1999 U.S.	1999 WORLD
Movies	$5.4	$7.2	$15.6
Home video, DVD	13.6	16.4	32.6
Broadcast/ Network TV	30.0	55.0	101.3
Cable	10.0	40.0	70.0
Music	7.6	14.2	40.1
Publishing	40.0	50.0	90.1
Sports	30.0	60.3	130.4
Electronic Games	2.1	6.8	16.4
TOTALS	**138.7**	**249.9**	**496.5**

As the second leading U.S. export, the entertainment industry sells an equal amount abroad, generating nearly $500 billion on a worldwide scale. According to Jack Valenti, president of the Motion Picture Association of America (MPAA), entertainment is the only U.S.-based industry in which there is a trade surplus, not deficit. Therefore, it is no surprise that today's entertainment moguls are focused on issues of fair trade, including NAFTA, the European Union, and China's recent entry into the World Trade Organization. In today's world, with information moving at the speed of light, both domestic and international distribution are critical—and marketing even more so.

THE 50,000-FOOT VIEW

Entertainment marketing left second-class status in its rear-view mirror decades ago, and as a result, created a heavily trafficked marketplace constantly faced with the collision of time, money, and changing trends. How does entertainment marketing differ from other forms of promotion? Consider these factors:

- Entertainment marketing is consumed with speed—there is little or no time to test-market before release, before one source or another gets word of the buzz on a project and broadcasts it to the world at large.
- Every film and CD is a new product, and each one is different: different content, different audiences, different deal structures. There may be two or three—or ten—of these products released every week, yet every campaign must hit the target on the money, on time.
- With film, any misfire—any hint of bad box office—must be counteracted immediately, since the window of first-run distribution is only three to four weeks.
- Budgets for entertainment marketing can be huge—the average marketing budget for a film that costs between $50 and $100 million to produce is between $25 and $40 million—but the burn rate extremely high, with much of the budget being spent during the six- to eight-week period just before and during the film's theatrical release dates.
- While entertainment marketing shares the search for the right genre with its more traditional cousin, the production of entertainment content is based totally on creativity; therefore, it is fraught with the possibilities of human frailties. Production and release dates can change with the sneeze of a

star. Bringing a product to market often combines a fine balance of crossed fingers and creative finagling.

- Entertainment marketing first focuses on selling an experience rather than an object. The audience must first buy into the event, before the sale of objects associated with that encounter—a highly desirable outcome, not to mention revenue stream—can occur.

- Entertainment is subject to the same whims and vagaries as fashion. Trends and styles change; with the pre-production planning and strategizing stretching out years before actual release, entertainment producers must strive to catch the wave before it crashes into the cliffs of consumer apathy.

- Award shows—not within the control of the marketer—can make or break entertainment products. Very few consumers may care what seal of approval a chair, a car, or a carton of eggs may carry, but the profitability—or failure—of a film, or an album, can rest on the opening of an envelope one evening each spring.

- The changing face of technology carries with it ever-expanding channels of distribution for entertainment products, many of which have their own particular following. Each of these channels must be addressed, and marketers must be constantly aware of the demographics involved in every new format.

- The marketing of entertainment focuses not only on the initial product itself—the movie, the CD, the program, the sports spectacle—but also on all the associated products spun off through licensing and merchandising. Each product can launch billions of dollars in revenue, if carefully handled and strategized across all channels. In fact, licensing and merchandising revenue can widely eclipse the revenue brought in by the original event.

- The global desire for entertainment requires a universal understanding of the language needed to promote the product, both locally and internationally.

Keep in mind that every single one of these factors impacts every single entertainment product—above and beyond all of this is the single biggest challenge facing every release and every promotion: competition from all other forms of entertainment.

Think about it: your blockbuster movie, weighing in at $150 million, is not being released into an entertainment vacuum. The scenario is much the opposite. Your baby is being thrown right into the

bathwater, along with that week's new CD release(s), big author pub-
lication(s), video game(s), must-see TV show(s), playoff game(s)—
oh, and the other studio's big behemoth. Each and every one of these
products is duking it out for the eyes, ears, and wallets of the consumer. Your job is to find a way to bring it to the very front of the
consumer's consciousness.

As a marketing professional, you have many weapons in your
arsenal: print, network TV, cable, radio, Internet, billboards, bus
posters, skywriters, and costumed characters roaming the street of
every city in the U.S., Europe, South America, Africa, India, and Australia. Most likely, if your baby truly is a blockbuster, you have a budget the size of a first-tier athlete's contract. If not, you're faced with
the opportunity to become the golden child of the industry by creating a guerilla campaign aimed at knocking the consumer's socks off.
In any case, you're about to join a long line of folks who have come
before you, eager to parlay their product into the season's big hit—in
any way they can.

THE MARCH OF MARKETING

Marketing money has been the fertilizer that has fed the entertainment industry for over a century. But entertainment promotion
wasn't always the prima donna it is today. The growth of entertainment—and the marketing of the same—climbed steadily in the last
half of the last century. Prior to that, peddling distraction to the
masses was a cottage industry. Part of this was due to the fact that
the consumer base was made up of people who had been born very
close to the introduction of electricity into the home, so the novelty
of the various diversions themselves, coupled with the public's desire
to be entertained, carried the entertainment industry along on its
own impetus. Even during the height of the Great Depression, people
flocked to the theaters, eager to relieve themselves of the grim dark-
ness that surrounded day-to-day life.

During this period of infancy, the concepts of branding, brand
promotion, and brand extension were hardly even a twinkle in the
eyes of promoters. There were no stars in Hollywood in the early
days—Mary Pickford, the first movie celebrity, was known only as
the "girl with the golden curls" until someone noticed that more people attended movies that featured that shining halo. If anything, the
studios themselves became known for the types of entertainment
they excelled at—MGM musicals, Mack Sennett comedies—and the

stable of stars under contract. The idea of individual idols controlling the destiny of a feature was several decades off.

The upshot of this was that producers spent their money on the development of the product and the distribution deal rather than any of the widespread media blanketing we see today. After all, the media itself consisted of newspapers, magazines, and radio, and each of these conduits was primarily local or regional in nature. A producer could rely on a few well-placed announcements prior to the opening of a movie to drive the audience into the theater. Even "word of mouth" carried less weight, given that these words stayed in the neighborhood, with very little in the way of rapid communication available to the mass public. The occasional bomb could actually be fine-tuned before it reached general release, with no one the wiser. Life was good for the movie moguls.

For instance, in the early days of the Golden Age of Entertainment—the 20th Century—radio and print somewhat peacefully co-existed from a marketing revenue perspective, blissfully sharing the budgets of local merchants. As entertainment mediums, each had its strong suit; print articles or ads, for instance, could be torn out, or at least carried along during commutes. While radio didn't leave anything physical in its wake, its content could be targeted to different parts of the day. So, radio and print rolled along, content in the knowledge that neither one was stealing much thunder—or advertising dollars—from the other.

Along came movies, and the stakes began to rise. Movies pulled people away from home radio and the printed page, but movies were not, in and of themselves, marketing mediums. In fact, they were a bonanza that worked and played well with the others. After all, theater listings provided a great source of ad revenues to print, as well as radio. Then there were all of those stories to be told about the stars of the day—great fodder for listeners and readers, and a great basis for a whole new genre of publications: fan magazines. A pretty happy little universe out there: Mom in the kitchen, listening to the radio while she did the dishes; Dad checking out the evening paper; the whole family taking in a movie on Friday night—in and of itself a new trend in socialization—and radio, print, and film sharing the marketing wealth. On the licensing side, studios began to realize the power of the brands their movies had become and started churning out tie-ins—and dollars—through licensing, creating a stream of consumables for every release: tee-shirts, toys, travel mugs—trinkets by the trillions.

Then came television, and with it a marketing battle for the wallet bulge that expanded with the introduction of every new medium, each leap in technology producing yet another industry fearfully looking over its shoulder, concerned that the revenue from advertising would be stolen by the new kid in town. Early TV programs started the trend as sponsors flocked to the new medium, just as they had in radio's early days.

Just when the movie marketers were feeling pretty content with their ability to get folks out of the house and into the theaters, the small screen started beckoning consumers back into their living rooms. "Free" TV, funded by the dollars flowing in from commercials and sponsorship, looked as if it might kill the golden goose of the silver screen. So, movie marketers started to crank up their efforts with giveaways, loyalty programs, more ads in print, and more spots on radio. They turned up the gossip just a notch or two as well—hey, sex always sells—oh, and they produced better quality films. Movie sales climbed back up, and the marketers breathed a sigh of relief.

Next it was TV's turn. While networks jumped from genre to genre—westerns, detectives, doctors, shows about poor people moving to rich neighborhoods and rich people moving to poor neighborhoods, game shows, soap operas—the American public seemed content to while away their hours switching between three networks. The networks were relatively delighted to split the ad revenue, although each did their best to make sure its portion was greater than the other two. Marketing for each of the networks pretty much relied on the usual suspects as needed—print, print, or print—along with a few spots on the network itself, utilizing undersold space.

Then came cable. "Hogwash!!" the industry shouted, "People will never pay for TV when they can get it for FREE!" No, and they would never buy sliced bread or trade in old Bessie for one of those horseless carriages, either.

Never doubt the consumer's desire for choice.

Suddenly, network TV found itself in the position of needing to lure viewers—and keep advertisers—and the entertainment marketing volume turned up another notch. The powers that be finally realized that the advertising plugs on their own networks were reaching viewers that were already watching and started looking for more innovative ways to reach the public—including better quality programming.

Ah, but cable TV found its comeuppance as well. It was not only the networks that fought back; VHS made inroads into the sacred cable turf of both recent-release movies and old favorites, and then came DVD. Now, cable was forced to push its way through the crowd of virtual pitchmen, trying to lure customers/viewers/guests to keep those subscriptions rolling in and the advertisers happy. Up went the marketing meter one more time, and with it the quality of the offering, as premium providers began producing their own movies and series.

Then, just when the consumer thought life was complete in the old recliner, remote in hand, 500 channels at the ready, stations streaming in via cable and satellite, SHAZAM!!—here came the home computer, followed by re-writeable CDs, downloadable digital music and Napster, and electronic games, which overtook movies in yearly revenues—all through the power of the positive pitch. Suddenly there were two small screens in the home battling it out for marketing bucks, with banner ads and hyperlinks crisscrossing Web sites all over the Internet.

Meanwhile, over in the music aisle, a flat-lining vinyl-based industry took a little bump from cassettes, but met manna from heaven in the form of CDs. Marketers shifted gears, pushing new releases of new music right alongside new releases of old music, surfing a wave of hype touting better audio quality and lifetime durability. Music executives, looking for ways to further increase revenues, began to drill further and further into niche markets, expanding the horizons into hip-hop, rap, country/western, blues, R&B, hard rock, heavy metal, Christian, world music, classical, jazz, new age—each and every niche accompanied by its own army of ads in every medium appropriate to the demographic.

And sports? Baseball felt the fire of the NFL on its tail; the NBA exploded in a mushroom cloud of teams; hockey dipped out of the cold northern climes and into such faraway places as Miami and Dallas; arena football, World Cup soccer, golf, tennis—all of it consumed the American populace until it seemed as though we were surrounded by one great slamma-jamma-smashmouth-empty-the-benches rivalry, fed and watered by the most competitive teams in our society, the ad agencies. And who could have predicted the World Wrestling Foundation, flexing its massive merchandising muscles?

So, here we sit, with the entertainment marketing volume turned to max, messages coming in through network TV, bus shelters, radio spots, online advertising, telemarketing, bulk mail, subway cards, giveaways, print ads, blimps, stickers, cereal boxes, sponsored music tours, branded arenas—everything but the bat silhouette streaking across the sky of Gotham City. Through all of this ongoing battle for every last cent the consumer has to spend, not one medium has gone out of business. Yes, there have been mergers, acquisitions, and realignments, but the bottom line is this: Revenues continue to grow in every single area of entertainment, including those for entertainment marketing, as everyone screams for our attention and mediums feed on one another in one great big consumer campaign for brand loyalty.

Much of this continued health and phenomenal growth can be traced to the ability of the marketing gurus to understand not only who their audience is, but who it might be. It isn't enough to simply plug, plug, and re-plug a product to the existing consumer base. Growth occurs only when that base can be expanded. Entertainment is the perfect industry for an expansion-based model—especially in a world with more time and income on its hands.

BROADENING THE BUSINESS

The shift from an industrial economy to a service-based economy had a huge impact on the domestic audience. More service-oriented businesses—not the least of which were the fast food joints springing up everywhere in sight—called for more workers. More and more of those workers came from younger age groups. More youth with more jobs meant more disposable income in the hands of a demographic—the 18- to 24-year-olds—that spend a higher percentage of their time socializing in the modern version of the mating ritual. And, entertainment destinations are the perfect place to take a date.

Marketing executives, poring over their research, recognized this trend and leaped on it. The content base of the message began to widen toward different age groups. It then widened even further as research brought to light the differing desires of males versus females as regards entertainment content. It grew further still as the research became even more sophisticated and began to focus on marital status, income, ethnicity, lifestyles, philosophical beliefs, diet—in short, slicing and dicing into hundreds of niches—each creating yet another opportunity to develop new and innovative marketing approaches. Action movie figure with your latte, sir?

As the public fed on the ever-widening buffet of entertainment choices, the appetite for inside information grew. What started out in the 1920s and 1930s as gossip, a la Hedda Hopper and Louella Parsons, has morphed into cocktail conversation and barroom banter. What was once a two-inch bit in the back of the financial pages, or a splashy story in some fanzine rag, is now the cover story for *Time, Newsweek*, and *US News & World Report*, the lead story on the business page, and a full-length article in the Sunday magazine. Fanzines have become an independent industry, with *People, InStyle, Entertainment Weekly, Premier, US, Rolling Stone, Vibe, Blaze*, and *Spin*; more than half a dozen movie screen magazines and five soap opera periodicals, all geared to lay bare the lifestyles of the rich and famous celebrities in every avenue of entertainment.

The spotlight is no longer focused solely on the stars, either. In fact, the line has become very fuzzy since the mogul has stepped out from behind the scenes. It's hard to say who got more press in the late 1990s: Julia Roberts and Tom Cruise or Michael Eisner and Michael Ovitz. The failure of any number of heavy-hitting films took a back seat to the barbarians-at-the-gate appeal of studio takeovers and media mergers. Entertainment is big business and big press, from regular reports of box office revenues to bestseller lists to weekly ratings of network TV shows. And, don't forget the expectations for seasonal success from video retailers and suppliers. All of this—and much more—is explored in the mainstream press as well as in trade publications such as *Variety, Hollywood Reporter, Billboard, Broadcast & Cable, Electronic Media*, and hundreds of other magazines examining every aspect of each of the sectors.

So here we are at the doorstep of the 21st Century, in a world that has been well-schooled in the pleasures of both in- and out-of-home entertainment, surrounded by a population that has grown used to having the ability to choose among hundreds of entertainment opportunities. The marketing professional of today operates in an industry consumed by louder, faster, bigger, and brighter to reach an audience on choice overload. In short, entertainment marketing is not a career for the indecisive, the incompatible, or the inexperienced. With over $500 billion in total revenue at stake, today's entertainment marketing professional must be fully aware of the mistakes of the past and the opportunities of the future, and be able to combine the knowledge of the two to produce something extraordinary.

But be warned: If you think the entertainment industry is a glitzy, fun business, full of ski-slope weekends and fabulous Mondays at Morton's, you're right—for about one-tenth of one percent of the population that makes up the toilers and scrapers of the industry. For everyone else, it's a shin-skinning climb up a greased power pyramid, each and every one of the contestants willing to do his or her worst to get to the top. And what do you do once there? Being at the top is the closest experience you can have to jumping out of an airplane without a parachute. It's high-stakes, high-speed, and high-risk—and for very few, high-rewards.

Still want to get into the tent? Well, step right up, ladies and gents. You pay your money, you take your chances.

1

PEELING THE ONION: ENTERTAINMENT MARKETING BASICS

OVERVIEW

Before we begin a detailed overview of each of the current entertainment niches, let's take a look at the core product itself. At the heart of anything that looks easy, there typically lies a basic structure that allows for a graceful manipulation of material or information to create something that speaks to the masses. In art, it's the golden rectangle; in digital media, it's one and zero; in professional wrestling, it's...well, let's move on.

The entertainment product shares some attributes in common with other products and services in other industries, especially in the extension of the brand. Licensing, merchandising, sponsorship—all of these occur in other industries. However, entertainment has some unique properties that affect the use and distribution of the brand.

THE FOUR C'S OF ENTERTAINMENT

The structure that defines the whole of the entertainment industry can be described in terms of four C's:

1. Content: The actual entertainment product, from the initial idea to the completed product, ready to be delivered to the consumer.
2. Conduit: The delivery of the product: theaters, bandwidth, coaxial cable, satellite, television receive-only (TVRO) dish, laser, wireless, ultra high frequency (UHF), very high frequency (VHF), digital transmission, location-based retail, etc.
3. Consumption: The form in which the consumer actually makes use of the product: film, high-definition television (HDTV), compact disc-read-only memory (CD-ROM), digital, set-top box, DVD, Web TV, personal digital assistant (PDA), cellular, e-book, PC, etc.
4. Convergence: How do the various media and technologies come together to affect the globalization of the entertainment industry: TV- or PC-centric, telephony, Internet, simulation?

In its broadest form, entertainment marketing touches each of these areas: what consumers may ultimately watch/listen to/read, how they may choose to hook into an activity, in what format they consume the product, and how they may utilize a convergence of all forms. Think in terms of the marketing behind a film, the video version of the same, and the pay-per-view cable offering of the movie or DVD viewed on the same computer utilized to play electronic games and download music from the Internet. Entertainment companies have a huge stake in all of these transactions; therefore, they are affected by the marketing strategies to reach each of them.

But in all cases, all conduits lead back to content. No content, no entertainment—unless, of course, you find the idea of watching static on a TV screen fun.

CONTENT

The simplest way to deconstruct content is to think of it as an onion: multi-layered and hard to peel one layer without grabbing part of the next. Content covers everything that happens to produce the actual entertainment product that is ultimately delivered, in one form or another, to the consumer. There are four elements that run across every industry sector in regard to content. They include:

■ The development of a CREATIVE IDEA, to prime the pump or start the production process.

■ The endorsement and utilization of TECHNOLOGY to help complete the production.

■ The importance of TALENT to act in or flesh out the idea and make it work.

But, what truly sets entertainment apart from other products is the fourth element:

■ The PERISHABILITY of the product, since time is always of the essence due to changes in consumer trends and tastes.

While the argument can be made that these four steps occur in any industry production cycle, what sets the process apart in entertainment is that these four steps do not occur in a linear fashion—far from it. Because of the perishability of entertainment—because it is a luxury, not a necessity, and must be available to the public when the public wants it, not a minute sooner or a second later—the steps occur in concert with one another. While content may come from the mind of one person, it takes an army of dedicated professionals to craft it into a product that hits the market at just the right time, in just the right form, with exactly the right buzz to grab the lion's share of the consumer's discretionary income.

In the early days of mass entertainment, when a much smaller investment might have been at stake, products were often carefully nurtured, strategies tested and retested. But in today's incredibly fast-paced world—where communication technology allows for only an instantaneous spread of word of mouth, of buzz, of product awareness—every entertainment product is in a race to the finish line from the moment the light goes green. The "wannasee, wannaread, wannawatch, gottahear" marketing produced for the launch of a product can mark the difference between success and failure; the promotions that create these compelling messages must simultaneously weave in and out throughout the process of production, distribution, and consumer transaction.

Content is the onion, and the first intertwining layer is the *creative* element.

CREATIVE

In entertainment, content—that which entertains—is king, the coin of the realm. Without the initial creation of Mickey Mouse, there would be no Disneyland, Walt Disney World, Tokyo Disney, EuroDisney, Disney Cruise Line, Disney Store, Disney on Broadway, Disney books, videos, interactive CDs, tee-shirts, coffee mugs, designer furniture, stuffed animals, or Happy Meal™ toys. No $500 million bonus for Mr. Disney, Michael Eisner. Somewhere along the line, there has to be the heart of the movie, the book, the script, the score—the creative idea. Oh, and if there's a cute little furry something that can be morphed into a billion products, so much the better.

In the old days, no one referred to any of this as "content"—at least, not to the face of the creator of the content. Before *BizCorp-Global* came to Hollywood, the industry still allowed for the illusion that the creative element was art—in some ways, it was part of the Hollywood mystique. The public liked the idea that the creative came from the mind of some non-business soul, toiling away over an old Underwood typewriter, hoping to hit the big time. It was the Great American Novel or Play. Often, it really was the Great American Writer: Robert Benchley, F. Scott Fitzgerald, Eugene O'Neill—all of them put in their time in the writers' bungalows of major studios. Once it passed from the creator's hands into production, it may have become a product, but in the beginning, it was art.

Fact is, that poor soul really still is toiling away over the creative, although in most cases, the soul isn't all that poor anymore. Nor is that soul necessarily creating the idea on his or her own. In today's entertainment world, the creative product is often an outgrowth of a strategic research process that has minutely identified a market, like a vein of ore waiting to be mined. The strategic development (SD) team at any major entertainment provider is often the initiator of what will ultimately become a new product/destination. Millions of dollars and thousands of hours of time may have been invested in a concept long before the actual creative process fully begins. SD, which typically has a full-time staff as well as outside consultants, will carefully examine the market demographics, competition, impact on brand identity, development cost, and ultimate return on investment in a search for new revenue streams.

This initial investment does not guarantee that a product will ever come to market. More times than not, a concept is shelved when the idea being researched proves to be either unprofitable or not profitable enough. Disney, for example, believes that a new product line (for example, a Disney Store or Cruise Line) must ultimately become a billion-dollar—that's right, billion with a "b"—revenue stream to be seriously considered. While some products and concepts may be launched because they extend the brand equity, each project is minutely researched, and may even come to fruition in terms of a product rollout, only to be shuttered if full-profit expectations are not met.

But none of this investment—either from a strategic development perspective or the simple act of a singular idea that slips in as a no-brainer product—would be worth a cent if it could not be protected in some way. Thus, we come to the second "C" of content: *copyright*.

COPYRIGHT

In the late 1970s, when the movie industry finally awoke from its glitz-induced slumber (probably from the sound of a thousand MBAs thundering up the road, swarming to save several bankrupt studios from complete annihilation), the new business-based management focused its full concentration on copyright. The bottom line was this: Without copyright, there is no entertainment industry—for there is no legally protectable product that can be bought, sold, licensed, leveraged, extended, and otherwise shaken by the ankles until every penny drops out of its pockets into the hands of the investors.

This focus on copyright dovetailed with the passage of the Copyright Act of 1976, which gave creators and their assignees exclusive rights to reproduce, distribute, and make the most of other uses of their original works. With the passage of this act, made necessary by changes in technology and global usage, copyright also applied to much more than traditional writings—it now protected motion pictures, videotapes, sound recordings, computer programs, databases, and many other original creations, including artwork and sculpture. Additionally, certain works were now exempted from copyright protection, in particular, works of the U.S. government.

And so, contracts flowing from the entertainment world, in all areas, now contain phrases such as "intellectual property," "work product," and "work for hire." All of these terms define the who, when, why, and where of idea or concept ownership—that an idea itself can be owned by a person or an entity (and not necessarily by the actual creator of the same), and therefore not copied in any form or fashion by anyone else—including that creator—either for fun or for profit. The ownership of ideas and concepts is a very complex and important subject, since copyright allows for the syndication of TV shows, the licensing of brands, the sale of sports paraphernalia, the inclusion of comic book characters on lunchboxes, and the endless string of movies sequels. Creative may be the soul of entertainment, but copyright is the key to the cash.

From a marketing perspective, the ballyhoo has already begun at the creative stage of content—whether it's news about what major star has been signed for what upcoming blockbuster movie, which must-read author has holed up to pen another tale, what software giant (or even midget) is working on the latest version of MurderPillageGorebots Meet Miasma—the machine is cranked up to whet the consumer's appetite. This part of the campaign may be relatively low-key—a PR placement here or there, maybe a mention in the back page of *People*—in case the project takes a turn.

Now that the creative and copyright elements have joined together to begin the content process, the product must now be filmed/animated/scripted/recorded, promoted, shipped out the door, and experienced by the customer. So, we move on to the next layer of the onion: production.

PRODUCTION

While the initial idea for the creative content may come from just one person, it takes an army of people to actually deliver the final entertainment product to the consumer's doorstep, TV, local theater, bookstore, or PC. The production phase includes everything it takes to produce the best book, movie, home video, music CD, network TV or cable show, radio program, electronic game, or any other of a myriad of packaged or pre-produced entertainment products. This would include the launch of a new ride or exhibit at a theme park, or the completion of a state-of-the-art movie (or live) theater.

Again, this is not linear—the project may swing back and forth from the creative element to production throughout these first two steps, whether for re-writes, legal challenges, or a change in players. This can be especially true concerning shifts in talent in film, since each new player that comes to the table may require a slightly different approach to his or her character—and that character's interaction with other characters—both of which are highly dependent on that new player's position in the Hollywood pecking order.

Marketing is in serious swing by this point in the project, especially as production moves closer to release. The idea is to build up the desire of the public to see/hear/read the product, so that by the time it's finally poured into its respective conduit, the public is waiting at the other end, in a lather and ready to be showered with the latest release.

CONDUIT

Conduit, the distribution of an entertainment product in a high-tech age, refers to two elements of the delivery process: the where and the how. In simple terms, the conduit is the actual process by which a product is distributed, as opposed to the consumption (coming later in this chapter), which is the final form in which the consumer receives the product. For example, think of a theater as the conduit and the exhibition of a movie as the consumable.

The retail distribution of films has gone through a variety of changes since the early days of the industry. From the early days of penny arcades until today, film emporiums have been the first-run conduits to the consumer. But, exhibitors have faced many ups and downs in their history, starting in earnest when film studios felt that distribution was far too random; the lack of control over how the film reached the consumer was a constant sore point for the major studios, which decided to take things into their own hands. Paramount, Warner, Universal, and Fox all bought movie theater chains and operated them as captive divisions. Thus, it was their theaters that got each of the studio's best film products.

Even then, the moguls understood that certain alliances could be profitable—and market corneringæso they often sent their so-called "A" and "B" films ("A" referring to the big productions with the big stars; "B" referring to less important films, usually utilizing second-tier or over-the-hill actors) to a few "friendly" competitors. As a result, independent and smaller theater chains were pushed out of the distribution flow, or received only the "C" or "D" films, which were of relatively poor quality. Since these theaters could only attract minimal audiences, they were often faced with bankruptcy, or fire sales to the studio chains. Many independents struggled to keep up by creating loyalty through giveaway programs, in which customers could collect an entire set of dishes—one dish at a time—by going to that theater once a week.

The government eventually stepped in to protect both the small theater owner and the consumer, knowing that production distribution and exhibition in the hands of a few moguls would lead to escalating ticket prices. In 1942, Paramount, the lead studio in anti-competitive practices, signed a "consent decree," ordering the studios to sell off their theater chains over a two-year time limit, and forbidding any obvious discriminatory distribution activities.

BRINGING THE MOUNTAIN TO THE MASSES

Big studios were not the only force in the changing panorama of entertainment distribution. The rise of "big box" retail and mixed-use real estate development also had a powerful impact. Early in the 1920s, the first so-called "shopping center" appeared in the U.S.: Kansas City's Country Club Plaza. J.C. Nichols, a visionary developer, saw opportunity on the outskirts of the bustling Midwestern city and began his project by building housing—housing designed with the use of automobiles in mind, at a time when the general population believed that automobiles were either a fad or a rich person's plaything. But not Nichols; he saw the future, and was the forerunner to the modern mixed-use development, including a destination retail/entertainment center close to his housing project. Nichols understood that to meet the needs of a community, it would be necessary to give them something to do with their leisure hours. He answered that need with Country Club Plaza, and a major trend of the 20th Century was born.

In short, mixed-use is the perfect embodiment of "If you build it, they will come." Fast-forwarding from Nichols to the end of the 20th Century (see all those strip malls, shopping centers, and mega malls flashing by?), we arrive at the modern version of County Club Plaza: the super center. Super centers feature all the products modern man and woman might crave, in a super-sized package: big box retail. Where the entertainment supply chain may once have ended at local bookstores, single-screen movie theaters, down-the-block record shops, and newsstands selling the day's press and a rack full of magazines, it is now firmly locked into superstores, megaplexes, and mass merchandisers who carry every entertainment product, often at deep discount. The Barnes & Nobles, Tower Records, and 24-screen Loews theater complexes with stadium seating have become the destinations of choice for a population that wants variety, volume, and velocity—get it here, get it now, and get it fast, all in one place.

The star of the super center concept in the 1990s was the multiplex. The key to successful retail is visitation: the number of times a customer shows up to shop, keeping in mind that impulse buying—stopping in just because you're there—is important to the bottom line. Developers, looking for ways to get people back more often, realized that entertainment was a great draw—and entertainment that changed once a week was a *really* great draw. Cinemas became the interchangeable software of the shopping experience; thus, the concept of the megaplex exploded.

Most of the areas in which the megaplexes appeared already had movie theaters. Usually, they had a single screen or even several, packaged in nice boxes somewhere nearby. Those theaters were often owned by the same chains that were building the multiplexes, but they were a little worse for wear and tear. So, the new theaters had to be something special to draw the consumer. Bingo: stadium seating, espresso machines, chicken tenders, and, in the case of Regal Cinemas, one of the fastest growing chains of the 1990s, entire family entertainment centers, with everything from indoor miniature golf to laser tag, all meant to lure the viewers away from their old hangouts. The film industry, by the way, applauded this strategy—anything to keep driving people out of their homes and into the theaters!

The strategy worked incredibly well. Theater chains exploded in growth—and in stock value as well—and within the span of a few years, they spread like kudzu in the Deep South. But kudzu, a lush green vine that overtakes everything in its path, eventually chokes the original vegetation to death, and so did the new megaplexes. The chains that had been the darling of the developers suddenly found themselves on the verge—or actually in—bankruptcy. Why? They built them, and the consumers came. But in doing so, they stopped going to the other theaters in the area, which left the chains with huge holdings on their hands: the existing theaters, complete with 10-, 20-, you-name-it-year leases. Oops.

Keep in mind that the importance of the megaplexing of America is one of the keys to the entertainment marketing revolution because films are often the starting point for many of the other products within the entertainment industry spectrum. Fortunately for film, the financial woes of the movie chains did not stop the consumer from going to the movies—in fact, box office is now up, thanks to all those comfy reclining theater seats. And, by the way, there are those who believe that the bankruptcies of some of the chains will merely allow the chains to come back stronger than ever, as they now have an avenue to divest themselves of those pesky leases they hold on properties that are sorely out of date.

As for the rest of the big boxes, the only victims of the saturation of big book, record, and video stores will be the smaller independents—the competition.

TRENDS IN TECHNOLOGY

Distribution is not limited to the where of location—at least not drivable locations. Technology-based distribution—the how—is the other side of the coin, and this is where the world is really in flux. Long gone are the days of a child's—or adult's—wide-eyed wonder at such a marvel as Dick Tracy's wrist radio, or even the choice between UHF and VHF, although both those modes of television broadcasting are still in play. The players today are coaxial and fiber-optic cable, satellite, TVRO dishes, direct broadcast satellite (DBS), laser, wireless, and of course, film. The consumers are presented with a vast array of choices and means with which to enjoy their entertainment experiences. Chief among these is the holy grail of bandwidth—a signal wide enough to carry multiple choices at one time, the path by which true video on-demand—any movie, any time—will be delivered into the consumer's home. In the meantime, coaxial (and fiber-optic) cable and satellite battle it out with one another to deliver entertainment to the home, while laser and wireless transmission are still in their entertainment technology infancy.

Then there's the Internet. Say what you will about the tumble of the dot-com industry, but the Internet is here to stay, and like every other technological revolution in communication, sooner or later someone will figure out how to use it not only to provide entertainment, but also to make large bundles of money off providing entertainment. In fact, one of the hottest issues facing the legal system today is the subject of copyright on the Internet—a global communication system, not adjudicated by any one-court system. Repeat after me: The creative element is the soul of entertainment, but copyright is the key to the cash.

The Internet has also challenged the traditional retail establishment by producing regional, national, and now global communities connected by e-commerce sites. Many in the retail community have created a "clicks and bricks" harmony within their own distribution channels, while extending their marketing reach through synergistic relationships with other Web sites. For example, Barnes & Noble has partnered with America Online (AOL) by creating a "keyword: BN" link within the AOL community, instantly transporting AOL members to the Barnes & Noble Web site. Others have not been so fortunate; E-toys, which appeared to be competing effectively with giants such as Toys 'R' Us and Wal-Mart in the sale of leisure-time products, filed for bankruptcy in 2001.

Even direct marketing catalogs, long a staple in the classic retailer's portfolio of consumer promotion, have been overshadowed by the instant gratification of Internet transactions. However, the classic direct-to-consumer clubs for books, magazines, CDs, videos, and leisure collectibles continue to be important for those consumers who have formed the continuity habit and are reluctant to stop.

Each and every one of these distribution channels is equally important to the distribution of entertainment marketing; the use of each, as well as the synergistic relationships that are quickly developing between them, will be discussed in a later chapter. However, neither content nor conduit is important without someone to consume the product.

CONSUMPTION

The consumption phase is the point at which the finished entertainment product has been offered to the public, through effective advertising as part of a fully integrated marketing program, resulting in a transaction—someone consuming the product. Remember that little description about the highly competitive entertainment market and all of the choices the typical consumer is faced with in any given week? The consumption phase is when the marketing rubber really hits the road, or the marketing executive depends on his or her ability to successfully lure the consumer.

The transaction may be buying a ticket at the local cinema, viewing a video, listening to a CD, clicking the channels on a set-top box, reading an e-book, or ordering the latest Patricia Cornwell book from Amazon.com. Or, it could be a visit to a live concert, where 100,000 fans are motivated emotionally and physically by pulsating laser lights, incredibly loud music, and the sense of sharing it all with their fellow devotees.

In the U.S., there are over 1500 television stations, nearly 120 cable programmers, 35,000 movie screens, 10,000 radio stations, 500 newspapers, and 20,000 magazines for people to consume. We have yet to identify the number of new, old, and classic CDs, books, newsletters, live concerts, Broadway shows, off-Broadway shows, summer theaters, nightclubs, and theme parks to enable the consumer to feed his or her entertainment habit. The typical American annually watches 1550 hours of television, listens to 1160 hours of radio, spends 180 hours reading newspapers, and 110 hours reading magazines.

CONVERGENCE

From both the technology and content standpoints, convergence is the true wave of the future. At the heart of convergence is the ability to create, transmit, and capture *all* information—movies, art, music, news—in a digital format. Once that information has been reduced to the 1s and 0s of the digital world, it can be transmitted over any available form of the new technology—cell phones, television, cable, CD-ROMs, PCs—via satellite broadcast or cable transmission. Wired or wireless, the ability to move information fluidly from point to point will create a new world of information, entertainment, and services.

Consider this scenario: You return home from the office—if, in fact, you have to leave your home for such a place—to find your dwelling perfectly prepared for your arrival—temperature, lighting, sound, and visuals. Your monitor presents you with your mail, including stills and videos of your parents, sent from their anniversary cruise in the Greek islands. Knowing that today is the actual anniversary, you video-conference to the ship to wish them well; having finished that, you double-check your e-reservations for tonight's performance of *La Traviata*, broadcast live from the Metropolitan Opera in New York and downloaded to your local theater tonight. You transmit directions to your friend's Palm Pilot, since he rarely visits that part of town, and alert your car service that you are ready to depart by sending email to the driver's cell phone.

What does all of this mean to the entertainment world, outside of the ability to move content digitally? Most important is the variety of conduit channels that are now available. As a simple example, consider the following statement: "I watched ESPN last night." Were you watching ESPN or ESPN 2? Were you watching it on your television, or were you viewing it on a closed-circuit broadcast at the ESPN Zone down the street? Or, were you viewing it on espn.com? Through convergence, the choices for the consumer will become almost limitless—and the challenges and possibilities for marketing professionals even more exciting.

There is little excuse for boredom during our free time, so is there any real basis to a complaint that "variety" is lacking? Budget restrictions in this age of affluence are a non-issue, and the worst criticism of all from the early days of black-and-white network TV— "Where is the quality?"—finds mass media fluff offset in every sector by intellectually stimulating and emotionally rewarding content. The real issue is choice—what the consumers select, voting with their feet and their pocketbooks to determine the winner of the weekend entertainment sweepstakes. The management of studios and entertainment conglomerates quake, stars rise, shooting stars are extinguished, and fortunes rise or fall on the measure of a weekend at the box office.

At the heart of this fame or misfortune are the entertainment marketing experts.

Riding the waves of discretionary time, disposable income, and expanding technologies, marketing teams build brands, develop audience awareness, and create need versus want. This attack is the heart and soul of entertainment marketing. As a textbook definition, marketing includes identifying unmet needs, producing products and services to meet those needs, and pricing, distributing, and promoting those products and services to produce a profit.[1] If the team is successful, its products will leave all the others in the dust—or at least coughing slightly as they try to catch up.

But, just as the creative cannot successfully become content without an army of professionals carefully preening each product, successful marketing is not accomplished by any one individual. It is the product of a carefully orchestrated attack, and often, in today's entertainment industry, that attack is coming from a multitude of

---

1. This is opposed to *advertising*, which is a paid form of communicating a message by the use of various media, generally persuasive in nature, or *public relations*, which is a form of communication primarily directed toward gaining public understanding and acceptance, usually dealing with issues rather than products or services.

directions, stretching the brand into a variety of products and revenue streams.

RUBBER BRANDS: EXTENDING THE EQUITY

First, start with a chain of movie theaters for stability, then add a movie studio, a book publishing company, a cable operator (with several major cable programmers), and a leading video retailer. Next, sell off the cable franchises, add a retail store, close the retail store, acquire a national radio network, and then add a billboard company and get a television network in the bargain. Finally, sell off the textbook division of the publisher, trigger the option on acquiring the majority share of another television network, then grab a wrestling franchise and incorporate it under the programming umbrella. What do you have? CBS/Viacom, the parent that originally spun off Viacom under the Play regime, is now the subsidiary.

In another case, a major conglomerate known as Gulf & Western sold off everything but its entertainment products and changed its name to Paramount Communications. Then, when it was taken off in a hostile, competitive battle with another suitor, it became the Paramount and Simon & Schuster division of Viacom.

In all of these changes, some basic marketing questions arise, not the least of which is how to keep the brand identity—and the brand equity. The real issue here is what happens in a simple matter of identity, since marketing is about presenting the clearest communication of the corporate mission, its products, and finally its name, logo, and various divisions. For example, Viacom decided to join many of its competitors in extending their brand out into the local marketplace through retail outlets. Disney had been very successful with the Disney Store, and Warner had opted for a similar strategy. Viacom threw its hat into the ring, but had disastrous results. Why? The public had no idea who or what Viacom was. If they made it into the Viacom retail outlet on Michigan Avenue in Chicago—and investigated the separate retail areas set up inside—the names Nickelodeon and CBS would have certainly rung a bell. But very few visitors had any interest whatsoever in Viacom itself, so retail sales were disastrous.

Then there is the tale of Harper & Row (now HarperCollins Publishers), a venerable and historic publishing company. It was acquired by NewsCorp. in 1995, followed soon after by the purchase of Collins, Ltd. (a leading UK publisher) and a few small global publishing companies. The command went out from Rupert Murdoch to the then-CEO, George Craig, to merge these companies, cut out the fat, and create an effective and prestigious corporate logo for the combined properties. Leading corporate identity consultants were called in to help with the identification and renaming process. The result was several bids at the multi-million-dollar level and a timetable reaching toward two years in fulfillment.

The evolution was effected by George Craig, precipitated by instructions from Murdoch, whose mindset and background as a factory accountant rebelled at both the price and timetable of the program's implementation. In a six-month period, with the front-running design strategy coming from Ivan Chermayeff, the new HarperCollinsPublishers identity (no spaces between words, and surrounded by the fire and water, blue and red logo) was presented, gained approval, and was implemented. Was this a big deal? No, because the team knew exactly what Murdoch wanted. However, the heavy lifting came from the development of an extensive and expensive design manual and the sell-in of the concept to each and every division around the world—the end game of corporate identity. Its importance to sales and marketing was the ability to link every single one of hundreds of imprints under the new corporate title and make it look like it belonged there forever.

Finally, no one does synergy better than Disney. Michael Eisner preaches it day and night at the company with incredible success. Synergy is all about marketing and the halo effect, which can enable one form of a product to morph into another. The original product, usually a film, can translate into as many different successful products as consumers will accept and purchase. Both *The Lion King* and *Beauty and the Beast* have been translated not only into hundreds of thousands of spin-off retail items, but into Broadway musicals as well.

Disney's success is not limited to feature films and animation. For example, Disney took a very successful cable channel, ESPN, and multiplexed that brand into ESPN2 as a platform for extreme sports and college games. Then they launched *ESPN* magazine, which is now considered a legitimate competitor to *Sports Illustrated*. The next step was to stretch the brand even further—into the local market—with the introduction of the ESPN Zone, a sports bar/restaurant experience that has sports fans reserving seats for major events, broadcast on cutting-edge technology throughout the facility. In a move that has its fans and protesters, Disney capped off its synergistic play by all but swallowing up a section of Times Square in New York with *The Lion King*, *Beauty and the Beast*, and *Aida* all playing in their own theaters within a three-block radius, joined by the flagship ESPN Zone, and, of course, a Disney Store.

LICENSING, MERCHANDISING, AND SPONSORSHIP

Whatever the approach, the ultimate payoff of synergy is the creation of the three most conspicuous revenue streams evolving directly from the entertainment and media businesses: licensing, merchandise retailing, and sponsorship. Each acts not only as a revenue stream, but also as a marketing strategy—marketing that more than pays for itself. As always, there are several ways to measure the success of these supplementary revenues, either as separate categories related to the entertainment and media sectors or as a percentage of all sales, both domestic and international.

For example, the total sales in the U.S., as recorded by the Licensing Institute of America at their last conference, was $89 billion in licensed products sold during 1999, continuing an upward growth trend established more than a decade ago. Entertainment and media-related licensing was nearly $60 billion—or about two-thirds—of the total. But synergy also happens through deals with companies outside the parent company's umbrella; the remaining $29 billion of licensing came from other forms, including household products, cigarette products, general merchandise, packaged goods, private-label store brands, and fashion designers.

In fact, the fashion industry is often represented as a close cousin to the entertainment industry. Fashion shows are staged like Broadway opening nights, with fabulous sets and the most current hit music driving the display of beautiful models—some of whom eventually realize their ambition to act in major motion pictures. The fashion business has also been well-integrated into the media, as it uses public relations, music videos, magazine covers, and product placement to burnish the brand—while adding to the bottom-line profitability of the entertainment product being utilized.

Fashion circles back around to join the entertainment industry in the growth of entertainment-related sponsorship sales. We find fashion icons like Hilfiger, Lauren, and Armani sponsoring major music concerts, film premiers, sports contests, product placement within network TV and cable shows, film festivals, and Broadway openings.

Continuing in a synergistic vein, consider the liquor, soft drink beverage, and fast food industries, which are certainly interested in their stockholders' satisfaction and aggressively chase sponsorship and its important promotion subset, product tie-ins. As only one small example of the need to appreciate vertical integration, synergy, and the careful nurturing and protection of brands, Disney's *The Lion King* stands out. *The Lion King* brand has generated billions in licensed product sales since it was launched.

Most important, revenue from licensed products can cover the sins of box office failures, protect the funds needed to invest in new properties, and maintain shareholder value in a highly volatile and competitive segment of the world economy.

Another lesson to be learned from this group of self-promoting, income-generating vehicles is that licensing, merchandising, and sponsorship have the added benefit of being marketing tactics in and of themselves. Any marketing professional alive would give a year's salary to have millions of consumers wearing his or her brand to schools, to the park on weekends, while shopping in the malls, lying on sheets, using towels, drinking from glasses—all with brand reminders. Buying and wearing products promotes the idea that Looney Tunes characters from Warner Bros. are fun, *Beauty and the Beast* is a wonderful Disney movie and video, and Donald Duck and Mickey Mouse are great family fare. They also look good on special-events ties, tee-shirts, and expensive jackets. These products are live billboards that provide an implied endorsement, maintaining brand awareness and credibility.

Branding is a serious program, and a commercial support system that is well worth the planning and involvement of marketing teams that can envision the future, even in the face of artistic criticism. Herein lies the separation between the art film or independent movie made as a statement of the director's life view as contrasted with a film that is made for pure mass audience engagement with the prospect of a huge return on investment. But, branding is not about momentary profits—it is a long-term strategy that can pay off handsomely over the years. A classic brand, sustained for 30 or 50 years, still as fresh and productive as when it was first invented, is a perfect example of value in equity. Franchises like Mickey Mouse, Bugs Bunny, Elmer Fudd, Peanuts, Superman, Batman, and many others are often the pillars of major media companies, or at least the support of a division. They can be expected to perform financially every time they are brought out and re-launched for a new audience.

The good times will continue to roll as long as there is disposable income to fuel the purchases and discretionary time to enjoy the ever-growing portfolio of entertainment choices. While movies themselves may be a relatively small part of the overall revenue stream in the entertainment industry, films are still the center of the entertainment universe, creating a launchpad for the remaining platforms: video, retail, DVD, books, magazines, electronic games, and more.

SUMMARY

Content, conduit, consumption, and convergence: These four elements form the basic structure of all entertainment products. However, since entertainment is generally based on a creative idea, the glue that binds the industry together is copyright, which gives the content-holder of same the ability to create protectable revenue streams, such as licensing and sponsorship, from the product.

Now that we've defined the structure—on with the show!

2

PEOPLE, POWER, AND PLAYERS

OVERVIEW

In an industry that depends not only on getting to market before a trend has passed—and in some cases, even creating the trend in the first place—what does it take to create big box office, platinum records, bestsellers, and first movers in the marketplace? The usual marketing questions are all present: where to market the product and to whom; how to price, package, and position; when is the best time of year to introduce the product; and, how to communicate the values, benefits, and availability of the product. In entertainment, the cycle is condensed. Entertainment products are of the moment. They are not investments, like cars or furniture. They are not consumables, like detergent or toothpaste. They are seasonal only from the perspective of blockbuster for the summer or family movie for the holidays. The content is ever-changing—and, when successful, ever-growing. This chapter will examine the people, the power, and the ploys necessary to bring an entertainment product to market.

MOLDING THE MESSAGE

If entertainment itself can be broken into four C's, the entertainment hierarchy can be defined by three P's: *people, power, and players*. While many of the broad issues in the entertainment industry are the same as they might be in almost any business, the speed at which a product must be delivered, coupled with the budgets associated with the product, demands players that can connect hundreds of dots in a very short time span. That level of play requires the power to make things happen, and people willing to do whatever it takes to make those things happen *in time*.

With no creative production lines and no linear progression from start to finish, marketing must ride the development process, supporting all the products associated with the core content: a film, music track, electronic game, theatrical script, novel—any intellectual property that will cover all the costs and make a profit. The marketing message must maintain crystal-clear consistency to reach these goals. Even the aspiring actor sweating under the Orlando sun inside a theme park character costume must deliver an experience that is harmonious with the consumer's expectation. While entertainment starts as a momentary fancy in the public's imagination, the role of marketing is to carefully feed and water that fancy until it grows into something much larger, more extendable, and more profitable.

The people who take responsibility for marketing entertainment are constantly faced with decisions that must be made in incredibly collapsed time frames. In most industries, decisions are made based on a fair amount of information, with short- and long-term planning objectives. Questions such as what are the other guys doing, how does the market seem to be responding, what price points have been covered, has the market reached saturation, and how will this year's new product introduction open the door for something slightly more radical next year may be answered in full detail, with reams of backup.

The entertainment executive, however, must understand the public's tastes and be able to guess where those tastes may be heading—often without the kind of research or precedents other industries count on. The executive must know in his or her gut when to give the green light, that final nod of approval—knowing full well that his or her head may roll if that gut feeling is wrong. The associated marketing campaign must absolutely recognize all the factors, all the trends, and all the tastes to best position and promote the product—while the product is still in the content phase. A wrong decision can destroy a major asset and the millions or billions of dollars in goodwill developed over decades.

Finally, the marketing of entertainment demands an approach that is entertaining in and of itself. Entertainment and marketing have become so incredibly intertwined that it is almost impossible to separate one from the other. Consider this: What is a tee-shirt with "Limp Bizkit" printed across the front? Is it a promotional item, or an extension of a revenue stream?

IN THE GOOD OLD DAYS...

Regardless of the industry, product, or service, marketing in any industry is about brand development, customers, and matching one to another while motivating the prospects to make a purchase decision. This has been the province of traditional companies—the Coca-Colas, Fords, and Microsofts—throughout the 20th Century.

During most of this time—certainly up until the 1970s—entertainment companies remained a cottage industry developed by entrepreneurs and wheeler-dealers who had little use for marketing, other than as an add-on once a film was ready for release. They spent money only on product production and the sales representatives they needed to close the deal and gain distribution. Entertainment and media had several things in common, but most importantly, they were all experiential businesses, simply giving the customers a good time or a break from their everyday problems. This was relatively easy, since the competition for discretionary time and disposable income was fairly uncomplicated. A simple announcement or awareness campaign would sell out movie tickets, sports events, rock concerts, Broadway shows, and most entertainment options. The three television networks made channel switching a minor issue, and counter-programming was but a twinkle in the strategist's eye.

By the early 1980s, major brands began to appear in the entertainment industry, some with access to a world market. Competition between products and leisure services began to intensify, even as the consumer's available time was compressed with new responsibilities, growing industry pressures, and the desire for personal time to self-educate, train, and learn new skills. The need to refine the marketing strategy within the various entertainment niches became more apparent as more products competed for the same dollars.

VIVA LA REVOLUTION!!

Entertainment executives, eager to hold on to—and increase—their market share, overcame their earlier reluctance to expend time and resources on marketing—in a big way. The pendulum now swung to enormous advertising and promotion budgets to attract and motivate consumer purchases. By 1999, the average marketing budget for a film that cost between $50 and $100 million to produce was between $25 and $40 million, much of it spent during the six- to eight-week period just before and during the film's theatrical release dates. Today, studios with 12 to 15 films for release in one year mount a marketing war chest of $500 to $750 million. They work with leading global advertising agencies or media buying services, supported by in-company creative units and directed by experienced marketing professionals.

Television networks have also thrown their hats into the marketing fray; having for years relied on free or unused airtime on their own networks to promote new programs, research showed that this form of promotion simply spoke to the same committed network viewers. Marketing plans for networks began to include the previously unmentionable or impossible idea of using print advertising in newspapers, magazines, TV guides, or even TV listing pages in local tabloids. They then expanded to using cable, outdoor billboards, and the ubiquitous subway and bus posters, where millions of urban workers spend their transport time to and from work.

Magazines—already in partnership with advertising agencies and advertisers—took some of their own marketing advice and developed dual-strategy marketing campaigns: one for the consumer to build awareness of upcoming magazine issues, and the other directed at the business community to announce growing circulations. This enhanced the quality of their reader demographics in terms of age, family size, income, and even spending habits. Marketing campaigns based on special promotions encouraged readership trials.

Even cable TV, long a free-rider on network TV's coattails, came to the conclusion that effective marketing was necessary to brand new channels, build awareness, and stand out from a universe of exploding channel growth—100 choices and still counting.

Radio, sports venues, electronic games, theme parks, blockbuster books, and unique imprints all rapidly joined this entertainment marketing revolution. Budgets expanded and new, sometimes outrageous themes and tactics were implemented to stand out in this fast-paced, perishable world of glamour, glitz, and blockbuster entertainment.

There are contingency budgets, teaser campaign budgets, tie-in product budgets, and (in the case of movies) budgets to encourage home video rentals and sales as well as pay-per-view cable viewing. The game of out-spending and out-marketing at the highest dollar level is played only by the leading studios, eager to take advantage of the various consumer viewing windows available to them in the entertainment universe.

But not everyone in the entertainment world is a major player with huge resources; companies with small or nonexistent budgets are becoming more mainstream. Every aspect of the industry—faced with politics, budget cuts, forced retirements, and fall-out from the vast quantity of consolidations—finds hundreds of talented youngsters and experienced professionals to create production companies and support businesses. These include advertising boutiques, public relations enterprises, media buying shops, and other opportunities built around the business.

From blockbuster extravaganzas to off-off-off-Broadway plays, the marketing team is an intrinsic part of the success, creating strategies focused on one goal: developing awareness for the product. It could be major stars meeting the press at a five-star hotel or stenciled messages on a New York sidewalk. Whatever it takes, entertainment marketers must focus the public's attention on their product above all others. Their ability to do so—and the budgets afforded their efforts—have led to a revolution in entertainment marketing.

DECISIONS, DECISIONS

Marketing professionals face a variety of decisions on each project, in no way limited to how much to spend, how to spend it, where to spend it, and defining the nature of the message. Some professionals pride themselves on seat-of-the-pants, nose-to-the-breeze, arbitrary guesswork, while others swear by the application of sophisticated analysis; in any case, there is very little margin for error. And yet, error and the unpredictability of slippage plague the release of each film. No matter how careful the planning, there may always be the surprise that makes winners out of weak entries and losers out of sure things.

Surprises may come from the constant stream of related decisions being made in other areas that affect a marketing program, decisions that are difficult to categorize or visualize until they are fully discussed, formulated, argued over, and weighed against the possible political repercussions. This keeps everyone on their toes, trying to predict the unusual or unpredictable—or at least being flexible enough to shift positioning if the circumstances require it. In the tightly wound world of entertainment, "positioning" could refer to the positioning of the product, or the personal position of a team member savvy to the politics of the industry.

In any case, decisions can be broken down into three categories:

- Large decisions
- Small decisions
- No decision at all

Small decisions include those that are recurring, consistent, must be made week after week, month after month, season after season, and usually look similar from studio to studio—or even from sector to sector. These decisions, formulated by the marketing team and signed off on by the executive in charge, include:

- What is the marketing budget?
- When will we launch it in the marketplace?
- Who is the hypothetical target audience?
- Will we spend the advertising budget in network, cable, and print or use some other media mix?
- What is our fallback plan?
- What are the key elements for the visual aspect of the campaign?
- Which service organizations will be used for research and advertising?
- Is there a seasonal message as part of the marketing push?

There are hundreds of these small decisions that must be made, some with a planning timetable of 6 to 12 months, and some which must be made very quickly to respond to the particular situation in the marketplace at the moment.

Large decisions, usually made by the leader or chief executive of the company with the brain trust of advisors and board members, include:

■ Should the company acquire a competitor or any allied company?

■ If there is a merger or acquisition, what will its impact be on the marketplace situation?

■ Will that merger or acquisition allow for a dominant share of market in the sector?

■ What will be the expected impact on the competition's marketing practices?

■ What will the government accept or reject?

■ Is there potential for expanding global marketing clout?

■ Is this potential ally going to provide access to a new audience segment?

■ Will it provide marketing efficiencies that create greater returns on advertising and branding investments?

These decisions are generally made over a much longer period of time—but may also appear very quickly on the radar screen, depending on opportunities in the marketplace. These types of decisions call for strong leadership, with good instincts in the industry as a whole.

The dreaded *no decision at all* can happen when a process has gotten out of control, costs have skyrocketed, finished product has been delayed, and no one wants to take the blame for a bad decision. In still-entrepreneurial environments, the practice of avoidance and the seeking out of scapegoats for potentially bad decisions or inactivity are signals that the marketing and management processes have broken down, the organization is frozen, and the leadership is failing.

RELYING ON RESEARCH

To avoid the *no decision at all* scenario, use research. Today, creating any kind of marketing plan without a carefully designed research program is a cardinal sin. This need for research extends to the introduction a new product, the re-launch of an old product, the extension of a successful product line, or the capture of leadership share for a corporation or division.

In the 1980s—and even into the early 1990s—the idea of a well-planned investment in research often led to incredulous responses from the most senior executives of the entertainment sectors. In the early 1990s, competition became intense, and it became too costly to guess incorrectly. However, even the most hardened of research professionals will admit that research in these arenas can only measure so many variables, and give limited but reasonable direction. Stories abound in the industry of long-term research, costing hundreds of thousands of dollars, that was ignored based on the final decision of the CEO—who simply went with a gut feeling. More often than not, these stories are only told when a project is ultimately successful.

For the most part, research is now the bedrock of the industry, shaping programs to meet market demand. The AC Nielsen companies provide the most comprehensive network/local television ratings and "share of audience" research systems, through diary panels and some recording boxes. Arbitron gives similar information for local and national radio stations, and Starch helps advertisers understand the influence of powerful ads in the magazine editorial environment. EDI-Neilsen is now one of two or three companies that specializes in the electronic transmission of audience ticket sales over a weekend, providing instant gratification—or the Maalox moment—to tension-stricken executives waiting for the results of a box office hit or bomb. Measurement has come out of the closet for music sales, cable audience penetration, and movie box office sales.

The availability of finely-tuned research has increased the number of decisions made in any entertainment sector. Product diversification, fragmentation, and a diverse, rapidly increasing population have led to a trend away from mass marketing and toward niche marketing. Just as Coca-Cola realized there are diet soda and natural fruit-based beverage market segments in addition to the classic cola segment, the entertainment industry has realized there are different demographic, age, gender, and other niche target markets for a variety of vastly different film, TV, sports, radio, and publishing genres. This trend is great for cross-media marketing, but certainly creates even more decisions in an already pressure-packed industry.

TAILORING THE TEAM

With the size of the budgets at stake, the number of decisions to be made, and the various sectors that may be affected, today's entertainment marketing team has become a key player in the development of the initial entertainment concept itself, molding concepts to fit demographic niches. The marketing team is now a standard fixture at the conceptual stage of product development in all entertainment sectors. The team's presence at this stage allows for additional time to develop a creative strategy, a marketing plan, a media schedule, and alternatives to each that take into consideration goals achieved, exceeded, or not reached.

There are those who sometimes decry the influence of the marketing team in the development stage, pointing to the reliance on research and data that can change quickly in today's fast-moving world. And, there are those who feel that content is better left in the hands of its traditional sponsor, the production team. On occasion, if the production team is under pressure to produce results, there is an adversarial atmosphere. In this case, if a movie is successful, it is the brilliance of the production team; if a film fails, it is the fault of the marketing team. In the best of all worlds, it is usually the excellence of the often hundreds needed to make it all come together. In this integrated environment, the questions of who is on the team, what they do, and how they work together tend to overlap in the process of creating a sustainable product that meets the marketing goals of the company.

The simplest way to explain the complex structure of the entertainment/marketing team is to make a distinction between roles and jobs. The job of a talent agent or business manager may include the responsibility of assembling and packaging a team of talent for the production of a creative product. The agent's/manager's role might also embrace the marketplace positioning of the product, through the particular relationships with the team members he or she has helped assemble. Regardless of the task, the agent's/manager's goal is to make the product a "must see," a "must read," or a "must watch."

The titles of the marketing professionals performing these roles reflect the intertwining of marketing and production. They may include the president of licensing and merchandising, head of home video sales, entertainment attorney (which could be a house counsel and/or law-firm attorney), chief financial officer, talent agent, literary agent, and the president of an independent production company. Then there are the heads of subsidiaries that could provide synergy and develop supplementary income streams. These would include the head of television production, the head of cable and DBS licensing, the head of theme park ride conception, the heads of the music and publishing divisions, as well as their business development and marketing executives. And let us not forget the head of publicity, an executive who has moved up through the ranks of public relations and owns the most rifled Rolodex in town.

All of these executives will not be found at every meeting. They are kept informed with daily and weekly updates on the progress of production, the market potential, and any audience research that has been done in the field. They are well aware of the usual "windowing" dates (the time gap allowed between the arrival of the film in theaters and the date on which the film should be released in each of the supplementary or ancillary distribution forms). They must know the final, or "drop dead," dates: which critical decisions must be made for the final and confirmed release dates of the entertainment products in production. Finally, they must be fully aware of the various synergistic products that may have been created to grow the concept: If the marketing plan involves a CD with a soundtrack from the film, or a PBS concert features a major pop or operatic world star about to release a video, then everyone, in all jobs and responsibilities, must collaborate on a consistent message and audience target.

In each sector, the nature and job description of the teams may differ, but there is no doubt that the planning, strategy development, implementation, and measurement of success—or the learning experience of a failure—separate a superior marketing team and secure its place in the corporate environs. However, all of this presumes that business is careening along as usual. When business becomes "unusual"—a star is replaced on a film; the script goes through rewrite number 33; the lead singer needs surgery on her vocal cords—the dates, the costs, and the marketing plans must be reworked.

In any case, keeping the marketing machine on track means managing a myriad of details, from concept to consumption. In some cases, major entertainment companies reach outside their own in-house teams for additional support and input. This often involves the use of an advertising agency.

THE ROLE OF THE OUTSIDE AGENCY

Of the over 2500 advertising agencies listed in the *Red Book* (a major reference source in the ad business, providing information on clients, geographic concentration, specialties, global coverage, billings, revenues, and senior executives), most do not list an entertainment company as a client—for a variety of reasons (see Table 2–1). For some, it is lack of experience; for others, it is the challenge of the industry's volatility; and for others still, the unbundling of services makes the industry unaffordable to service. Nevertheless, the reported spending for this sector of the economy totaled well over $10 billion in measured media for the year 2000. This spending level has increased consistently over the last 10 years as budgets have nearly doubled to support blockbuster films and new TV network and cable launches.

Agencies that have established a foothold in the industry find great loyalty and very little turnover of the account until there is a perceived client conflict or deep business decline. They also find a feeding frenzy when the mega-million-dollar media budgets and total marketing programs for Disney, Warner Bros., Miramax, and others go up for periodic review.

Entertainment companies also frequently access other suppliers through advertising agencies, including research firms, consulting firms, data suppliers, direct marketing companies, trailer houses, media planning and buying specialists, public relations firms, Internet agencies, and lobbying firms. Each of these serves a different purpose in the development of an integrated entertainment marketing plan and implementation program.

TABLE 2-1   Major Agencies Representing the Entertainment Industry[a]

AGENCY	CLIENT COMPANY
McCann Erickson	Columbia Pictures
DDB Worldwide	Universal Studios and Theme Parks
Western Media, Division of Interpublic	Disney Studios
Grey Advertising	Warner Bros. Studios, WB Network, *Entertainment Weekly*, *People* Magazine
TWBA, Division of Omnicom	ABC TV Network
Young & Rubicam	Showtime, Viacom, Blockbuster Video, Sony Electronics Game
Saatchi & Saatchi	News Corp

a. As of September 2001.

There are also a myriad of small and mid-sized agencies handling diverse creative and media projects for entertainment companies. These agencies are finding new ways to showcase their other clients through their entertainment accounts—and the entertainment companies are more than happy to help them out, through lucrative sponsorship, licensing, and, in growing numbers, product placement deals. In mid-2000, ABC announced it would reorganize its sales and marketing department, as the release read, "to form a unique marketing partnership with its advertising and promotion clients." Named ABC Unlimited, the new unit was designed to work with advertisers to help them reach targeted markets through the application of various ABC properties (and perhaps Disney, the parent company's properties as well). They cited the combination of the *Who Wants to be a Millionaire?* show with a special promotion for AT&T, and a giveaway promotion for the launch of Oldsmobile's new model Alero.

In the entertainment marketing industry, large budgets and intense time frames call for seasoned teams of marketing professionals who have the right instincts, the ability to make quick decisions, the knowledge of when to rely on research, and great contacts both inside and outside their own companies. They are faced with hundreds of decisions that can make or break a project. The majority of these decisions are made throughout the life of a project, in a very non-linear format, usually out of the public eye.

At the heart of the decision-making process stands the one person who may ultimately rise to the top, or fall on his or her own sword: the leader.

MOVERS AND SHAKERS

Regardless of who he or she has placed on his or her team, the leader bears the ultimate responsibility for moving the entire process forward to the end result: a transaction for money—in fact, *lots* of transactions for money. The successful leader accomplishes this task through a very fragile series of relationships and deals: some based on talent, some on money, some on power, and almost all, in entertainment, based on personalities. The people who rise to the top of the entertainment industry understand how to manipulate all of these factors to create a winning outcome.

FOLLOW THE LEADER

While teams of experts assist along the various steps involved in the marketing timeline—including awards presentations, deal negotiations, and contract completions—they can only *help* the boss navigate the precarious grounds in the attempt to avoid disaster: costs exceeding revenues, or the other side of the creative-based coin of entertainment, nothing happening at all. Delays can come from a strike by writers, a concession demanded by a star, even a hurricane—either in the form of weather or a disgruntled studio executive. In an industry based on human talent, the leader must be a consummate politician, a brilliant strategist, and a charismatic executive who can make things happen. He or she must lead, guide, direct, manage, support, compensate, build, and structure the creative process.

In the traditional business model, the president makes more money than his or her employees and usually has more benefits, more freedom, and the final authority to make decisions affecting the business and the employees. Not in this world. The president of marketing at a movie studio, the head of a talent agency, or the producer who finances and manages the marketing function makes far less money than the superstar. That star—who makes three pictures a year, each paying more than $20 million—is being paid well beyond most executives' compensation. In the entertainment world, money is the ultimate report card—a report card that is published not only in industry magazines, but also in consumer periodicals ranging from *The New York Times* to *People* magazine. What the consumer public may *not* see, however, is the other kind of capital that entertainment leaders possess—a kind of capital that allows them to make picture after picture, with greater long-term results for the leader.

When academics discuss the application of a model to the entertainment industry's management style, they talk about the development of value in the market. To develop value, it is important to make investments of three kinds of capital. The first—financial capital—are the funds needed to run a business. These funds are usually raised through public or private placements. The second is human capital—the individuals who create the ideas, make the decisions, and provide the professional services or selective experience to make a successful product launch through a disciplined marketing program. But it is the third form that entertainment leaders use for exploration, analysis, and even implementation. It is called "social capital"—the relationships that exist among the veterans of the industry wars.

In entertainment, there is little formula to fall back on, and even less insight to the rapidly changing tastes of the market. Yet the leader must make consistently successful decisions—while dealing with pop culture and fickle loyalties at the box office/retail outlets/ broadcast distribution points. No one can rely on history to assess and create the direction for tomorrow's projects. The only history available is the amount of money a project made or lost, under whose guidance. Often, regardless of whatever may have come to pass during the actual production of an entertainment product, good or bad, it is that final report card—the money made—that makes the next project happen—that, and the relationships maintained.

Relationships are more important than title or money in the entertainment industry. Relationships create power and authority through the ability to get things done. Even when a recent project may have failed, or a set of prior circumstances may not have been all they could have been, certain industry players can still get the green light based on who they know. Nowhere is the old adage "Be careful on your way up, because you never know who you'll meet on your way down" more true than in this industry. A poker game at an executive's home can often be as important as a major staff meeting at the studio. More than one major project has come about after a Friday night discussion of what movie to make, who to hire, and how to craft the financials.

These leaders are the professionals who manage the selection of the product and employ vast numbers of creative people at salaries and perquisites that range from union-required minimums to the extravagant levels that managers and agents can negotiate. The president of worldwide marketing and his/her colleagues holding the titles of president of production and distribution, as well as the CEO of the studio, must have the ability to develop marketing strategies and implement the marketing plan under minimum input situations. Often there is only bare-bones research and budgets, and timetables that are out of control. There may be little room for error, careers on the line, and tens or hundreds of millions at stake. Yet, decisions must be made and implemented—decisions that will make or break careers. When dollars are tight, some of these decisions may be affected by a true entertainment art form: the making of a deal.

DEAL ME IN

Deal-making is usually associated with the initial steps in formalizing a creative project and gaining financing. However, when it comes to creative marketing, deal-making proceeds as the producer or the director—or on occasion, the star—tries to usurp responsibility for the marketing message and even the selection of the media. If the team member has experience in this arena, and knows when to push the right buttons, it can go very well. If non-marketing professionals get involved with the marketing—to brandish their ego, burnish their image, or simply exercise power—the implementation can go wildly astray. This can lead to the wrong audience seeing a film. If that audience is disappointed and spreads negative word of mouth, a very big budget movie can become a very big financial failure.

However, the right use of the deal is critical to success. Getting a star on the right primetime talk show requires deals to be made at the highest studio and network levels, especially when a star from one network is promoted on a talk show owned by another. Here is where contacts, relationships, experience, and public relations savvy become very valuable in the integration of the marketing communications plan.

Nothing in deal-making happens as a reflex. It is not "the way it has been done in the past" or "the way we have always done it." Everything is negotiated, starting with the time an event should begin, the size of the budget, the people to be involved, the expected outcome, the titles or credits, and the friends who will receive some form of participation. Even the promotions department requires deals to be made to get sponsors or product placement people to provide items for free, funding for contests, sweepstakes, wardrobe, air tickets, limousine services, hotels, and catering. This is often where the true mettle of the marketing team member is tested: putting the package together with maximum effort and minimum cost.

Deal-making is also a specialty of the stars themselves. While big names can certainly have an impact on the green lighting of a project, some ventures are still considered too risky for studios to undertake. When this occurs, there are other considerations that go into the making of a decision. If Barbra Streisand wants to make *Yentl* or *Prince of Tides* or Madonna wants to star in a third remake of *Evita*, the studio may need to maintain good relations on behalf of their music division—and produce, finance, or at least distribute the project. It took almost 15 years for John Travolta, an acknowledged devotee of Scientology, to get a movie made from one of the books written by the deceased founder of the popular religion—a project that turned out to be a box office disaster.

The ultimate—and riskiest—type of deal-making is the grass-roots effort of an actor or actress who wants to promote him- or her-self in a personal project to increase his or her visibility. This is a very labor-intensive, frequently frustrating experience for actors whose goal is to build a star role or platform. The actor may write the script, find the financing, develop the marketing, advertising, and public relations, and then cause the movie to build an audience. *The Big Night*, written, produced, and starring Stanley Tucci, got Holly-wood's attention and built a fan base for Stanley, who soon after won roles in several movies. This type of self-marketing may include the occasional billboard, personal public relations, attendance at every possible function, film festival, and charity dinner, along with build-ing relationships with leading gossip columnists like Liz Smith, Rex Reed, and others. If it works, it's golden. If it doesn't, it's history, as may be the actor.

Generally speaking, the true artists of the deal—and the legends of Hollywood—are those superpowers that rise to the top of the industry through a combination of deals, talent, experience, and luck: the moguls.

IF THE MOUNTAIN WON'T COME TO THE MOGUL, THE MOGUL WILL GO TO THE MEDIA

In a world built on image, the leaders in charge of polishing the pedestals have found themselves atop their very own columns—gos-sip and otherwise. The people who once were legends within their own industries have now become incredibly public icons, often gen-erating more sustained publicity than the stars or projects they cre-ate. And, in the highly charged world of publicity, glamour, and ego, maintaining one's equilibrium is no small feat.

Starting in the late 1970s, as mergers and acquisitions became the talk of Hollywood, the entertainment industry became more visi-ble to the public at large. Suddenly, the industry was front-page news in the leading business magazines—and it was the business execu-tives who were the superstars, competing with their own employees, actors/actresses, and creative talent for importance, notoriety, fame, wealth, ostentatious lifestyles, and multiple marriages. These moguls began to generate a rock-star image as they strategized and syner-gized the process of growing their companies well beyond the small studios they once were. And, as often happens with glitz and fame, the pixie dust surrounding these luminaries began to rub off, even on the very research-oriented, pragmatic number-crunchers at major Wall Street investment houses. The mogul as a media presence was off and running.

Moguls have used this fascination to the advantage of their businesses and themselves. Invitations have flooded in, asking these media and marketing moguls to be keynote speakers at major media conferences, especially those in the new media or convergence crossroads. These conferences have become wonderful opportunities to market the moguls themselves, as well as the latest news about their companies. Hundreds of industry middle managers—as well as those interested in the industry—now pay ever-increasing admission prices, hoping to learn the secrets of success.

The leading trade magazine of the industry, *Variety*, in cooperation with Schroders (a private investment banking company with a respectable entertainment practice), have showcased their relationship in the industry with a one-day conference—*The Big Picture*—which has been playing to a full house for nearly 10 years. Keynote speakers have included leading entertainment and media executives and major players in the industry. Yearly meetings in the mountains of Colorado draw the brightest luminaries from throughout the entertainment industry and have become the focus of such mass-circulation periodicals as *Vanity Fair*. In an entertainment- and experience-focused age, the average person on the street has access to—and can discuss at length—the kinds of information once buried in tiny columns in the last page of the business section.

MEMORABLE MOGULS

Entertainment executives are people of importance and stature in a very visible industry. Like other moguls throughout the history of American business and economics, these entertainment figures are very charismatic, with their lives chronicled in books, newspaper articles, interviews, television portraits, and even C-Span presentations in front of Congress. The strategies and plots that have evolved into this cult of personality have become dinner-table talk for a population ever more interested in what goes on in the lives of the rich and powerful.

A few of the names emblazoned across publications such as *Time*, *Newsweek*, and *The Wall Street Journal* include the following:

BARRY DILLER

Diller was a young executive at the ABC Television Network when he met Charles Bluhdorn, the Austrian founder and builder of one of the first truly multi-dimensional conglomerates, Gulf & Western. The company was affectionately known as Engulf and Devour due to its acquisitive leader. Bluhdorn had just completed his purchase of Paramount studios, a film company (like so many others in the mid-1970s) having financial difficulty with very little fiscal control and no real business management in place. Bluhdorn contacted Diller to gain some advance knowledge of the pricing for licensing movies to television networks, part of Bluhdorn's plan of getting some additional, reliable cash flow for a studio starved for cash during a downturn in Paramount's movie-making fortunes.

Diller was the youngest programming executive at any network. He saw an enormous opportunity and made a mega-million-dollar deal to purchase a large package of current and future Paramount movies, slightly overpaying for the "B," "C," and "D" movies and vastly underpaying for the "A" movies. It was a good deal in a classic win-win scenario, unusual to most Hollywood executives who usually went for the jugular. It worked especially well for Bludhorn's Paramount, providing funding to make the next round of great movies. It was no surprise to find Barry Diller anointed as the youngest president of a studio, Paramount Pictures. He brought with him two very promising executives, Michael Eisner and Jeffrey Katzenberg.

After many years of successfully running Paramount, Diller was recruited by another mogul, Rupert Murdoch, who was looking for very specific skills. What Murdoch wanted was someone who could refurbish the 20th Century Fox studio, also purchased at fire sale prices, and use the production facilities to help build a fourth television network. No one believed the first assignment would be easy, and everyone believed the second assignment was impossible. The concept for a fourth network was laughable at the time, especially since everyone knew Murdoch carried an Australian passport and was surrounded by hard-drinking, tough-talking loyalists from Down Under.

Thus, Barry Diller became one of the highest paid and senior-most executives at News Corp, already a global corporation on its way to conquering another medium, network television in the U.S. However, Diller wanted equity—to be an owner, a respectable request. Since Diller had revived the studio, successfully started a network, and was at the top of his career as an employee, it was time to make a move. When Murdoch turned him down for an equity position, it was time for Diller to move on.

Diller had an Apple Powerbook, a mega-million-dollar severance and payout package, and dreams of owning major media he could run himself. To many of the sideline experts, it was unfathomable that he would buy a slightly down-market shopping channel called Quality, Value, and Convenience (QVC). To Diller, the loss of face was unimportant.

Diller went on to lose several opportunities (with the support of friends and bankers) to try to acquire his old stomping grounds, Paramount Communications—which Viacom eventually bought. He tried to buy CBS, and lost out to Mel Karmizan's Infinity Broadcasting. Eventually, the Robertson family, part owners of QVC, bought him out of that media position. Only when one of his greatest industry fans decided to sell off Universal's USA Network (now the largest audience cable network) did Diller begin to put his company together. Soon it included local television stations in several interesting markets, a substantial stake in Ticketmaster, and several independent film production studios that had been divested from the Universal-Polygram merger. Barry Diller returned to power.

MICHAEL EISNER

With the death of Walt Disney, the Walt Disney Company began to slip into a deep abyss of lackluster films and general creative inertia, soon finding itself on the verge of ruin. The Bass brothers, young oil billionaires from Texas, sensed a deal. They bought huge chunks of Disney stock on the cheap and hired recruiters to entice a senior executive from the movie industry to lead a revival.

The senior executive they came up with was Michael Eisner, who had risen through the industry at NBC, ABC, and Paramount, where he took over as President and Chief Operating Officer when Barry Diller ran off to join the Murdoch circus. Eisner brought two other highly talented individuals with him: Frank Wells, a perfect counterpoint and steadying influence to Michael's volatile creativity, and an energetic animation and marketing whiz, Jeffrey Katzenberg. Eisner—with only a four-year college education in psychology and literature—became the embodiment of the newly revived Disney empire.

Michael Eisner has risen to power and fame by almost single-handedly writing the book on brand leveraging. Eisner took a brand that was loved by millions and turned it into a property worth billions, building The Walt Disney Company into an entertainment powerhouse whose Magic Kingdom includes domestic and international theme parks, film, animation, television, publishing, new media, retail stores, a cruise line, and a long-term multi-million-dollar deal with McDonalds. Eisner has been well-compensated for his revival of the Disney brand, receiving a $550 million success- and contract-related bonus in 1995. Wall Street has rewarded him and the company shareholders with enormous share value appreciation, while other media and entertainment stocks have waned.

However, that path to success has not been smooth. Frank Wells—highly respected and much loved—died in a helicopter crash, leaving both an organizational and emotional hole in the company. His death also led to some very bumpy times for Eisner as a leader. Wells was not immediately replaced; Eisner shouldered the responsibilities of both positions. Other executives in the organization, believing themselves to be qualified to step into the job, grew increasingly impatient. Chief among these was Jeffrey Katzenberg, whom Eisner rejected as his second in command. Katzenberg moved on to DreamWorks SKG, and sued Disney for what he felt was just compensation for his contract. The battle was lengthy and very public, causing all parties embarrassment, and eventually costing the company millions.

In the meantime, Eisner also went through a fiasco with his then-friend and super talent agent, Michael Ovitz, hiring, disenfranchising, and then firing him as President after a brief 18 months. This mistake again cost the company millions in a buyout of Ovitz's contract, as well as further revolution in the executive ranks.

However, Eisner is still developing and expanding the company. Along with a newly announced theme park plan for Hong Kong, it appears that Eisner is working his way through the alphabet of entertainment, with the "Mouse That Walt Built" now owning ABC, Disney, ESPN, and most recently, the Fox Family Network.

GERALD LEVIN

Levin, an attorney by background, was the young man in charge of HBO, which grew into the leading premium cable network. Levin was the first to build a national cable television distribution system through satellite links. When it came time for the late Steve Ross to appoint his successor following the merger of Warner Communications and Time-Life, it was Gerald Levin who understood the new media. He became the senior executive in charge of making the merger of two very disparate corporate cultures come together.

While many believed that the mix of button-down white shirts and school ties would have difficulty working with the Hollywood culture, Gerald Levin made it happen.

Levin brought the movie company titans Bob Daley and Richard Semel to the table of the new organization. Levin had provided a new and very lucrative outlet for their Warner Studios movies in HBO's uncut, unedited movie channel. Years later, Levin had to choose between his heir apparent, Michael Fuchs, the then-powerful head of HBO, and the Semel-Daley team, the Co-Presidents of Warner Studios, for the management of the Time Warner music division, WarnerElectraAtlantic (WEA). The Semel-Daley team won and Levin was forced to ask for Fuchs' resignation. However, when Ted Turner sold his Turner Broadcasting company to Time Warner, Turner wielded his power and forced Levin to accept the resignation of the Daley-Semel team, which had a dismal profit/loss record with Warner Bros. Films.

As this book goes to press, the governments of the European Union and the U.S. have failed to block the next major step, an acquisition of Time Warner by AOL (creating the ultimate new media distribution system), but have succeeded in blocking the purchase of EMI as an addition to Warner's music label portfolio. Levin will leave a final legacy in the combination of new media, content, and classic media.

MICHAEL OVITZ

Ovitz was the head and founder of his own talent agency, CAA, and one of the most powerful men in the industry. He was known for brokering major talent packages and serving as advisor and consultant to leaders in multi-billion-dollar acquisitions, mergers, and sales of entertainment properties. In the mid-1990s, he left to become President of the Walt Disney Company, as Michael Eisner's number-two executive. He soon found himself left out of the inner circle, since no one was required to meet with him, follow his instructions, or act on his behalf. He may not have realized that he was leaving the frying pan for the fire of one of the most competitive companies in the business, joining an executive team that had been hungering for the opportunity to become Frank Wells' replacement following Wells' tragic death. That the job went to someone far outside the Disney ranks did not sit well at "The Happiest Place on Earth," and few bemoaned the loss of Ovitz when his tenure lasted only 18 months. It was a public and anticipated firing; even more public was the

Teflon-coated settlement Ovitz was given on his way out the door: a $100 million severance payout. Important as all such large severances are, it allowed Ovitz to set up new ventures once again.

Throughout these relationships, it is not only the moguls that ultimately affect the direction of the entertainment industry, but the people they mentor as well. Eisner and Katzenberg both stepped away from Diller's shadow, although Katzenberg ultimately had to separate from Eisner as well. David Geffen learned at the feet of Steve Ross; Sid Sheinberg had Lew Wasserman; and Steven Spielberg had Sid Sheinberg. There is a continuum in the industry that reaches far and wide; this network has become even more important as what once were studios have become conglomerates, and the conglomerates have begun to synergize into one great interwoven web of entertainment marketing and revenue. In many cases, it is the longstanding relationships of the moguls that bring these packages together.

SUMMARY

As the entertainment industry has grown and the synergy between sectors has increased, the ability to make things happen, to break logjams, and to have that final "can-do" spirit has become increasingly important. While the players of early Hollywood reveled in their power in the domestic film business, today's mogul extends his or her reach well beyond the movies themselves. Through distribution, licensing, and sponsorship, entertainment moguls now direct international campaigns that move with the speed of an ever-widening pool of new technology.

But at the heart of it all, there is still that flickering image on the movie screen.

3 MOVIES: WANNASEE, HAFTASEE, AND MUSTSEE

OVERVIEW

S amuel Taylor Coleridge called drama "that willing suspension of disbelief for the moment, which constitutes poetic faith." Most modern producers would probably call the act of financing and making a movie the willing suspension of financial sanity. Movie marketing is the hedge against disaster and the support system for success.

TO MARKET, TO MARKET

Consider this: On a movie that cost $100 million to produce, the average prints and advertising (P&A) budget can be as low as $25 million, or as high as $50 million. If the movie has legs (that is, has a long, successful run at the theaters) and can sustain a successful box office run, that number no longer has any anchor holding it to the ground. The entire budget can disappear in four weeks or less, depending on the length of the movie's run in the theaters and how wide the movie opens.

The process by which this happens is fairly simple. First, each print (also called a negative) with a soundtrack costs about $2,000 to dub, or duplicate, from the master. If a major film opens wide (meaning it is shown on more than 1,000 screens, and usually at least 2,000 screens), the cost of sending prints simultaneously to run on every screen can cost about $4,000,000—plus delivery charges. If the film is delayed for some reason—there is a need for re-editing or shooting additional footage, for example—airfreight and courier delivery services increase the cost. The film must be at the theater in time to play on opening night or the theater will go dark (be closed for the day the film was to have been shown). Of course, the theater could run a movie that has already closed, assuming those prints have not yet been returned to the studio.

Next on the ledger sheet is the advertising budget. Tiiu Lukk, in her excellent book, *Movie Marketing: Opening the Picture and Giving It Legs*,[1] describes advertising plans and budgets by genre, or type of movie, in-depth. Lukk interviewed hundreds of film producers and marketing executives on how budgets are assembled and segmented by media objectives.

Let's take a look at one of the films Lukk describes that had a high production and marketing budget and was reasonably successful at building and achieving its projected box office revenue. That film was *Golden Eye*, the first opportunity for the new James Bond, Pierce Brosnan, to show the world and, more importantly, the keeper of the film franchise distribution rights, MGM/UA, that he had what it took to maintain the successful 007 formula and continue to generate consistent box office returns.

The film was rumored to have cost over $70 million to produce, mostly because of exotic locations and the incredible special effects, explosions, and rapid scene changes, all part of the expected Bond entertainment formula. The marketing budget, as reported by Lukk (and obtained from the 1996 Competitive Media Reporting and Pub-

---

1.   Lukk, Tiiu, *Movie Marketing: Opening the Picture and Giving It Legs* (Los Angeles: Silman-James Press, 1997).

lishers Information Bureau), was about $23 million. That brought the total budget to about $100 million, or a ratio of one dollar of advertising to every three dollars of production.

Nearly $14 million disappeared in only four weeks of network and local television, with some small amount on cable for 30-second TV spots. Another $8.5 million was spent during the same time period for newspaper advertising. This probably included co-op arrangements with theater chains and local independent theater owners, in which the studio was billed for its share of all the local newspaper advertising showing the exact start time for the movie.

Golden Eye had box office domestic revenues of more than $100 million, providing a breakeven in the U.S., and another $200 million globally, which resulted in a handsome profit to the distributor. This did not include license fees for home video, network TV rights, cable and premium cable airing, let alone merchandising and licensing arrangements. In this case, the studio's belief in the franchise and the new franchise player paid off handsomely.

Most fortunate—and surely underscoring the belief in the seemingly golden Bond franchise—was the addition of $50 million or more to the marketing of a film that did not cost the studio or distributor a dime. Sponsors like BMW, Omega watches, Yves St. Laurent, and others used the Bond film as an advertising vehicle, showing 007 in their TV spots and in their four-color magazine ads, building an enormous "buzz" that created an aura of glamour, excitement, and world-class style. This mirrored the image presented in the film, and gained the broadest possible awareness at no extra expense.

While *Golden Eye* is a perfect example of how things are supposed to work, the formula doesn't always hold true for every film. It takes great strategy, carefully planned synergy, and a strong circulatory system to survive and thrive as a marketing professional in the motion picture business.

Big Box Office for Filmed Entertainment

From 1990 to 1999, revenue generated from movies grew from $12.8 billion to $24.9 billion. The most important revenue source was Domestic Box Office (DBO), even though it only accounted for 12% of total film revenues. DBO is what sets the benchmark for all other revenues that will be generated by a film, from videos to licensed products. This ancillary business often provides a major portion of a film's profits. In the short lifespan of a film's initial release, the most critical time period is opening weekend, since it accounts for 20% of total box office gross. Therefore, marketers have a very short window of opportunity to create a brand image for films—the image that will pave the way for all other business.

Oddly enough, it would seem as though marketers would be in an uphill battle to lure audiences into the theater to view any one of the 500 films released each year. With video cassette recorders (VCRs) in more than 65% of TV households, video stores on every corner, a rapidly declining price in DVD players, a shorter time window for releasing films to premium cable channels such as HBO and Showtime, pay-per-view on 10 or more expanded cable channels, and deals negotiated with network TV for advertising-interrupted "Monday at the Movies," there is no reason to ever have to enter a movie theater. In fact, given the ever-increasing price of going to the movies (with almost $10 per ticket, another $10 for popcorn and soda for two, another fistful for the parking lot attendant, and paying the babysitter, you're suddenly at $50 for what was once only a nickel), you might think that the theaters would be pretty empty.

Surprisingly, box office revenue grew 29% from 1994 to 2001. Although a small portion of that growth was attributable to inflation, most of the growth was due to consumers going to the movies more often. During that same period, consumers' visits per year increased 10%.

Why are people going to theaters? Probably the single most important factor in the increase in movie-*going* is the increase in in-home entertainment opportunities. While this might seem to fly in the face of out-of-home entertainment growth, the simple fact remains: people are social by nature. After a long spell of online competition to movies, chat rooms, email, and electronic games, people of all ages still follow their instinct to herd. Ever since Fred and Wilma first met by the tribal fire, people have sought out ways to congregate with one another. Entertainment is one of the primary opportunities to accomplish that goal, and in our present-day culture, movies still offer the chance to sit in the dark with 300 strangers and participate in laughing, crying, thinking, and generally being swept away by the experience.

Additionally, exhibitors (General Cinema, Sony Loews, AMC, and others) are focusing on movie-going quality in an effort to shift movie-going from a commodity that competes with all other viewing opportunities to a stand-alone experience. The movie theater has geared up for this battle by building newer, bigger, better, cleaner, multi-screen megaplexes all over the country, even in expensive center-city real estate locations. Stadium seating, snap-in food trays, credit card kiosks, fancy coffee bars, high-priced but filling comfort food, pleasant staff, free candy on the way out, bright clean bathrooms, larger inside waiting areas, and placement near other amusement areas for after-movie interests are all part of the arsenal of the leading theater chains. This focus on the experience has led consumers to become inelastic to ticket price increases—as evidenced by the recent 6% increase to $9.50 per ticket in Manhattan—with relatively little reaction from the public.

One of the key market segments still swept into the theater are teens and young adults—a heavy movie-going group. Based on projections from the U.S. Bureau of the Census, this segment of the population is expected to grow at twice the rate of the total population through 2005 (CAGR of 1.5% versus total population CAGR of .7%). Teenagers will always search for the one private place to congregate away from the eyes of parents, teachers, and other adults. Dating, hanging out, and privacy drives the 12–18- and 20–25-year-olds to movie theaters in droves. This has made the teen and young adult demographic the most sought after by movie studios and their marketing partners. The presence of this tempting, free-spending demographic has had a dramatic impact on movie content, as studios churn out what seems to be an endless string of action and special effect-driven films that may or may not actually contain meaningful content.

RISKY BUSINESS

The business of movie-making is extremely risky. For every blockbuster, there are a hundred near misses, misses, outright failures, and straight-to-videos. However, most studio executives are completely risk-averse, especially now that movie studios have become parts of large public entertainment conglomerates. Film divisions are important to conglomerates because they create lucrative assets. Each new release is added to a film library, which enhances the value of a conglomerate's cable and television channels. However, Wall Street analysts are very unforgiving when movie divisions have a string of box office flops. Studio executives try to reduce risk through creative co-financing deals, cutting costs, and creating movies that they know will appeal to the biggest audiences with the most dollars.

This recent paradigm of cost-cutting is drastically different from the way movies were made in the late 1980s and early 1990s. In the past, talent agents had more power and pulled the strings of studio executives. In addition, the explosive growth of home video drove movie revenue growth so rapidly that all studios were making money. Very little attention was paid to high expenses. This resulted in lavishly paid talent and a number of flops, for example, *Legal Eagles* with Robert Redford and *Waterworld* with Kevin Costner. In the past few years, the boom of home video has slowed and executives are feeling the pressure to take a closer look at the bottom line.

As studio executives cut the number of films in production, big names like Julia Roberts, Tom Hanks, and Steven Spielberg still command and receive multi-millions per project. Why? With fewer films in production, studios do not enjoy the benefit of cross-collateralized income, a phenomenon that occurs when a studio has a broad portfolio of films. Losses from one film can be offset by gains from another. With fewer chances for success, studio executives have increasingly relied on what has worked in the past. Films with big names attached to them are more "bankable." Studios are making more commercial projects with well-known talent that they feel will appeal to larger audiences with more discretionary income. This formula allows movie studios to simply plug in a potential genre and cast; if the models spit out a large enough revenue projection, the project will be pursued.

HIGH CONCEPT

The formulaic model typically used today in Hollywood is known as "high concept[2]." Defining the term is not easy, but Justin Wyatt's book,[3] *High Concept,* does as good a job as you will find anywhere. Among the distinguishing characteristics of a high concept movie are the following:

---

2.   The phrase high concept may well be traceable to Barry Diller, who used it as a programming executive in the 1970s. It later began to get common usage in *TV Guide* and eventually became a staple benchmark comment of the movie business. In a conflicting opinion, Disney's Jeffrey Katzenberg claims the phrase originated from Michael Eisner.

- Known stars and/or director
- Storyline can be rendered in a clear, simple sentence
- A recurring single-image marketing motif
- Connection to prequels, existing theatre, or established music
- Merchandising

Consider the movie *Jaws*. In addition to Richard Dreyfus and Roy Scheider in the cast, the film had a future marquee name in Steven Spielberg as director. The storyline came from a successful number-one bestseller novel by Peter Benchley. The single image used extensively in the print, trailers, TV commercials, and other media ads was a naked woman swimming and the open mouth of a great white shark coming up toward her—a strong contrast between good and evil in this clear and arresting image.

Jaws also enjoyed a full saturation marketing campaign in all media forms, aimed at not only building excitement, but also in maintaining it. *Jaws* opened at 409 theaters (which in 1975 was unusually wide) and grossed $7.61 million in its opening weekend. The movie went on to win three Oscars and become one of the top revenue-gaining movies of all time, according to *Variety*. The famous white shark eventually became a staple of the Universal Studios tourist attraction in California. Is it any wonder that a *Jaws 2* was inevitable?

When it came time for *Jaws 2*, there was once again a single unifying image and theme: "Just when you thought it was safe to go back in the water." It gave the movie-going public chills and set the box office cash registers ringing again.

High concept is in every way the ultimate Hollywood studio film expression, in that it usually takes any genre or idea, uses every extreme opportunity to push its point and image, makes absolutely sure it relates to as many diverse and broad-based audiences as possible, is packed with activity—not always just action, but rapid movement from scene to scene—and usually has at least one or more very high-profile or newly minted hot actors. It is a film that motivates repeat visits to the theater by mass audiences, followed by excellent word of mouth and great buzz. It is not always a blockbuster, meaning it does not have to cost over $100 million or have marketing budgets over $30 million. Some of the audience will see it

3.   Wyatt, Justin, *High Concept* (Austin, TX: University of Texas Press, 1994).

again in home video or on cable because it hits some emotional note or empathetic button.

Samples of high concept versus not high concept films are found in Table 3-1.

TABLE 3-1 High Concept Vs. Not High Concept Films

HIGH CONCEPT	NOT HIGH CONCEPT
Beverly Hills Cop, I & II	*Ace Ventura*
Titanic	*The Man in the Moon*
Mission Impossible, I & II	*Godfather III*
Lethal Weapon (all)	*Runaway Bride*
The Truman Show	
Godfather, I & II	
Pretty Woman	
James Bond (all)	

Of course, like all subjective definitions of a broad concept, high concept has many different interpretations and applications. Another synonym, or optional alternative description, for a high concept film is "tent pole" film. This simply means that the studio has decided a specific film will be its lead picture for a given year or season, and will place its production and marketing budget bets on this film and ride it as long and as far as possible. The expectation is that it will throw off huge box office returns, multiple supplementary revenue streams, and become an "evergreen" product, earning licensing fees around the world and returning for play several times over a decade. Only an animated film in this category or a made-from-a-comic strip film will also produce huge licensing and merchandising income for the studio.

However, even with experts conjuring up complicated models and "can't miss" formulas, accurately predicting movie performance is virtually impossible. There is no machine, computer, abacus, or psychic connection that can create the concept, script, and direction to turn an idea into a blockbuster financial success or critical artistic achievement. The industry's past, present, and future depend on writers, directors, actors, cinematographers, and all the other behind-the-scenes professionals—not the least of which are the individuals involved in marketing.

WHO, WHEN, AND HOW

The marketing of a studio's film is generally presided over by the president of marketing and his or her staff. However, many phases of marketing individual films are handled by the producer. "Producer" is a term applied to several different individuals connected with a film. Going one step further, the responsibilities of the position may differ depending on whether the film is produced by a studio or an independent.

A senior independent producer frequently options a property, book, or screenplay with personal funds, hires the writers, director, star and extras, or works with a talent agency to package the talent for the film. It is frequently up to the producer to develop the treatment or write the script to build up both momentum and credibility for the product. The independent producer is usually also responsible for the functioning of the film: the complete agreements for distribution, casting, collaborating, and managing the process.

Little of this work is performed by the executive producer, who usually gets this title because of a majority or significant financial investment in the production of the film. Sometimes a star obtains the title of executive producer, either for his or her bankable nature or need for ego-stroking.

In any case, ignoring the independent producer's role as marketer would be to describe the cinematographer's role as merely that of a cameraman, or the head of distribution at a studio as an order taker or sales clerk. A producer needs to be a marketing generalist, and is required to work with advertising professionals when the budget for marketing exceeds $10 million. The producer is involved with all aspects of marketing, including strategy development, trailer composition, selection of key visuals for print and poster advertising, and negotiating agreements with the stars to do publicity stills. The producer also works with the advertising agency or media buying service to ensure that the message is correct, and that the media is effectively purchased and targeted at the pre-determined audience. He or she also coordinates any licensing and merchandise contracts with the licensees, seeking an integrated communications image—an important goal, if the licensees are obligated by contract to spend advertising budgets in support of a new toy, publishing or music product, or other licensed item.

The in-house studio producer, on a "work for hire" arrangement as a salaried staff member, has restricted responsibilities primarily focused on controlling the budget, scheduling, and coordinating on-location staff with studio executives. Problems of any magnitude are usually discussed with the studio chiefs. The promotion of a film is overseen by the president of marketing.

Be assured that no one is surprised to see the involvement of the president, the CEO, and perhaps even the chairman of the studio when the initial production budget is $100 million or above and the marketing investment is $25 to $30 million dollars. And, when films spiral over budget, as they often do, there is a frequent need for top management to expand their share of voice against the competitive film offerings. When there is a summer of blockbusters, with five or more films at the $100 million level, management and the creative staff are in frequent discussion.

That discussion may turn to major conflict when things begin to go wrong. Yet in the highly volatile, content-driven, and risk-averse business of movie-making, the "suits" are often loathe to stop the creative process for fear that something magical will occur. Thus, there is no way to stop a *Heaven's Gate* or *Titanic* once they are in full production. These and many other films have far exceeded or even doubled their original budget. In the small town that is Hollywood, even as the odor is beginning to rise on the back lot, the major fear is that the creative team, the director and his/her crew, or even the star will never work with that studio or business executive again. When bad turns to worse, all the team can hope for is that an enormous success at the box office will redeem them.

WANNASEE

The marketing of a film can be the key to redemption. The movie marketer's challenge is to create "wannasee" among consumers—literally, creating enough buzz or word of mouth to drive viewers into the theater. It is the classic marketing technique of turning a want into a need. As mentioned earlier, marketers have a very short window of opportunity. To create strategies that will drive audiences, movie marketers, like consumer product marketers, rely heavily on consumer research. Focus groups, surveys, and in-depth interviews help studio executives make critical marketing and production decisions.

Like every other supplier in this age of risk reduction, studio executives want to be guaranteed that their films will appeal to wide audiences. While there is no such thing as a guaranteed success, consumer research can help ease the angst. At the end of the day, however, there has been more than one studio executive who tossed the research out the window and went on his or her gut instinct and possibly lived to tell the tale.

Regardless of the strategy or instinct, there are a variety of methods utilized in the marketing of a film. Some are actual processes; others are more conceptual in nature. The following are typical promotional strategies used in the marketing of movies.

TEST SCREENINGS

During the production and editing of a film, it is crucial to get a reaction from the target audience. This is effectively carried out via test screenings. Typically, passes will be randomly distributed in front of a movie theater. The pass entitles the respondent to see an unfinished version of a film. After the film, the audience is asked to fill out a lengthy survey, asking detailed questions about the characters, plot, and scenes.

While test screenings are a useful marketing tool, they have recently come under fire. Warner Bros. big-budget release *Wild Wild West* had a test screening that went so poorly, the audience actually booed.[4] The news quickly spread via the Internet on sites such as aintitcool.com. Even though the audience signed confidentiality agreements, the anonymity of the Internet made it easy to dish bad buzz about the uncompleted film. This proved disastrous. Further, the bad buzz was uncalled for since the film was not even completely edited yet. Unfortunately, Warner Bros.' effort to control the negative buzz was futile, and the movie was a box office failure.

SNEAK PREVIEWS

Studios only set up sneak previews if they are confident the preview audience will provide favorable word of mouth prior to opening. For instance, the Warner Bros. release *The Avengers* did not have any previews. Warner Bros. knew that a sneak preview would only generate negative buzz. With poorer quality films like *The Avengers*, studios open the "flop" as wide as possible, without any sneak previews. If the advertising campaign is successful, a significant audience will show up opening weekend to see the film before any of

---

4.   Svetkey, Benjamin, "Even Cowboys Get The Blues," *Entertainment Weekly*, July 8, 1999.

their friends. Inevitably, the negative word of mouth will circulate and the movie will be out of the theaters quickly—as was the case with *The Avengers.*

TELEVISION COMMERCIALS

Television is where most of the media dollars are spent. The goal of the commercial is to grab the audience's attention; whereas a trailer has a captive audience, a commercial has to fight to keep the audience from changing the channel. Because of this, most movie commercials rely heavily on good reviews and sexy images from the film—the type of content proven to keep viewers' fingers off the remote. Movie commercials are aired predominantly on Thursday evenings, when consumers are making their plans for the weekend.

Movie marketing strategies for blockbuster films—for instance, opening wide to over 2000 screens simultaneously—incorporate specific tactics. The media plan is developed over months of planning, with backup options in place for signs of success or weak performance. The strategy includes local TV and cable to capture specific target audiences: romantic films are advertised on Lifetime Channel, Romance Network, Food Network, and any other predominantly female show. Adventure films, spy stories, murder mysteries, sports films, and violent movies are advertised on ESPN, *Monday Night Football*, the networks, and adjacent to similar shows and movies on television. The prime movie-going audiences (12–18 and 19–25) are reached on MTV, VH1, BET, and on situation comedies (sitcoms) popular with that demographic: *Friends, Spin City,* and all the clones of these shows.

NEWSPAPER ADVERTISING

The local newspaper has always been the mainstay and underpinning for all movie advertising. The big marketing blitz for a perceived or actual blockbuster will get a double-page spread and a teaser campaign in every local newspaper city by city, as long as there are screens in that area. Almost all "A" movies (big-budget, big-star films with an expected four-week run or better) will get at least one full page in the Sunday editions. Most newspapers have either their own film reviewer or use nationally syndicated reviewers. If their evaluation of the movie is positive, they may even find their quotes picked up as part of the film's campaign. However, this tactic received a lot of press in the summer of 2001, when it was discovered that Sony Pictures had fabricated a reviewer, who, of course, gave great reviews to Sony films.

An important part of newspaper's support of the film industry are the special issues. As an example, *The New York Times* and *The Los Angeles Times* provide a series of special film issues each year. These may include the following: Spring Film Preview, Oscar Films, Summer Film Preview, Fall Film Preview, Holiday Film Preview, and the Hollywood Issue in *The New York Times Magazine*.

MOVIE TRAILERS

Although media and print are very important to a movie marketing campaign, the movie trailer (the short, punchy marketing vehicle shown in theaters prior to the feature film presentation) and television commercial are the most crucial elements. The best trailer tells a story and whets the appetite without giving the story away. The advertiser's challenge is to get people to see a film without telling everything about the film. Often, two trailers are produced. The first is called the teaser trailer, which is shown in theaters six months before the film is released.[5] The second trailer tells more of a story and is shown in theaters ten to eight weeks before the film opens.

Trailers can run a few minutes when shown in a theater, can be cut to a 30- or 60-second version for TV commercials, or can run as long as five to six minutes when placed as part of a rolling series of previews, or selling pieces at the beginning of a home video tape. While the home viewer can fast forward and skip this pre-sales material, most consumers consider it a quick way to learn about films either coming to the neighborhood screen or available at the video store.

Trailers have their plusses and minuses, depending on the movie as a whole and what's left on the cutting room floor. If handled by an expert, with the guidance of a movie marketing professional, trailers can hit a home run with the target audience. However, many studios allow the filmmakers to play a role in the marketing of a film. This can often lead to clashes because marketers are trying to deliver what the consumer wants, while filmmakers are concerned with the integrity of the story.

The marketer isn't always in the right, though; too much creative license can be disastrous. To capture the attention of the appropriate

---

5.   Lukk, (Ibid.).

segment of the audience, a trailer may focus on a certain element of a film, making the movie appear to be more of a solid representation of a genre than is truly deserved. The only slightly sensual, barely action-oriented, or vaguely funny comedy may utilize a trailer that exaggerates any of these elements. Consumers who have no other source of information will be disappointed when they actually see the movie, and thus negative word of mouth is created. There are also the rare occasions when the marketing team—faced with a truly weak movie or one that has no distinguishing characteristic—will pick up material that has been edited out of the feature film and use the footage in the trailer to build buzz.

Then there's the question of giving away the plot. There was some industry discussion that the trailer for the summer 2000 thriller *What Lies Beneath* gave away far too much of the plot. However, the movie had Harrison Ford, a female audience favorite, in the lead role. The target audience of women helped the film to a number-one spot at the box office—even though some complained, wishing they had known less of the plot twist. In actuality, while the trailer may have given away certain aspects of the plot, it threw viewers off the trail of the ending, while still creating enough excitement to get them into their seats, popcorn in hand.

There is also evidence that people want to see the very things that excited them in the trailer when they watch the movie on the screen. Another 2000 hit from Warner Bros., *The Perfect Storm*, showed the major special effect—a giant wave—in the trailer. Leaking the effect didn't keep the audience away—instead, it drove the movie to number one during its weekend box office opening.

The other strategy of the trailer as marketing device is played when garnering two different audiences for a movie that has a distinct, but potentially dual personality. *The English Patient*, an independent film acquired from a UK production company and distributed and marketed in the U.S. by Miramax, achieved this goal and built a mass audience for a niche-oriented film. Two very different trailers were made and cut into two very different commercials. The trailers were accurate in their use of footage from the film, but simply focused on the action, war scenes, and violent drama for the male audience and made the romantic scenes more prominent and expansive for the female audience. Neither audience was disappointed, since both were satisfied by the story, content, and elements each was seeking. The women brought the men and the men went willingly, resulting in a great marketing success.

MOVIE TIE-INS

Movie tie-ins give films added exposure through the company's ads and publicity, while films deliver the buzz to keep brands "hip." While studio executives try to find new franchises from which to launch toy tie-ins, they are also turning toward apparel companies. The most desired demographic is the teenage market. Teens are constantly bombarded with choices in a fragmented market. Teenagers think going to the movies is cool (92%).[6] Product tie-ins with a big hit film are a successful tactic to reach your target audience. Companies such as Tommy Hilfiger, Ray-Ban, and J. Crew have embraced movie tie-ins with great success. Burger King, McDonalds, and Taco Bell all report increased sales during tie-in periods.

Table 3–2 shows samples of successful movie tie-ins.

TABLE 3-2   Movie Tie-Ins.

MOVIE	PARTNER	PRODUCT	DEAL	TARGET
Mulan	McDonald's	Happy Meal	Part of ten-year deal	Kids and their parents
Armageddon	Swiss Army, Nokia	Product placement, specialty glasses, t-shirts	Trade for ads store mention	Teens
Lost in Space	Intel, Radisson, Long John Silvers	Themed meals, new product launch	Trade and payments	Various
The Mod Squad	Levi Strauss	Line of clothes based on those in movie	Trade for ads	Ages 15-24

---

6.   D'orio, Wayne, "Clothes Make The Teen," *American Demographics*, March 1999.

MOVIEFONE

The very familiar voice that is pre-recorded and compressed on software is part of yet another success story by a pair of young entrepreneurs who developed a business based on a perceived need and using what is now one of the oldest technologies, the telephone.

One of the most important elements in marketing film is the ability to communicate quickly and efficiently a brief description of the new movie releases, theaters closest to the consumer's home or apartment, and the times the film is playing. Andrew Jarecki and his partner, close friend, and college chum came up with the idea of Moviefone. The idea of dialing 777-FILM, or accessing Moviefone.com, a much used Web site on AOL, has become a national habit and is a useful alternative to scrolling through local newspapers.

AOL paid the two partners and their original investors millions of dollars for ownership of this very valuable marketing tool. This direct access to customers provides another media form and generates huge advertising revenues from major studios and film distributors who want to reach various segments of the movie-going public. The movie theater chains know how important this connection is and provide current movie viewing times at every theater for each movie. For the cost of a local call, there are ads supported by AOL and the leading metropolitan newspaper, for instance, *The New York Times*, in New York City. The humorous several minute commercials played in the theaters reach the very audience that Moviefone was created for, the moviegoer.

THE OSCARS®—A POWERFUL MARKETING TOOL

Everyone in the movie business knows the leverage a nomination at the annual Oscars can provide for a movie. The award ceremony itself is broadcast around the world, both live and taped for delayed broadcast, and is viewed by well over a billion people. This supports both DBO and foreign distribution.

Much has been said about the process of selecting the candidates for every award and the nature of the performance by the Master of Ceremonies, including Billy Crystal, Whoopi Goldberg, David Letterman, and Steve Martin. Additional coverage includes annual reviews of the acceptance speeches (which range from maudlin, tear-filled, and boring to hysterical, and occasionally, heartfelt or funny) and pre-shows that focus on the clothes and opinions of the stars.

However, the serious players in this event understand that a win, with careful promotion and competitive tactics, can add as much as $30 million to the DBO revenue and untold millions in foreign and supplementary revenues. *Life is Beautiful*, a subtitled Italian box office hit, after its Oscar award as best picture in 1998, was later released by its aggressive and clever distributor (Miramax) with a dubbed English track for those who wished to see it but disliked reading subtitles.

The Oscars has become a must-see for movie fans and those who want a quick review of films they should see if they have limited viewing opportunities. These films also have multiple visits by audiences captivated by award-winners. What would the film industry be without the obsessed? It is still a discussion of great wonder and envy that a proportion of *Titanic*'s female teen audience members saw the film more than 10 times and had memorized dialogue from the love scenes.

INTERNET

Most films released in the past decade have had a Web site. Some have been very imaginative and have engaged the audience to really get involved with the characters, the story, the unique ideas, or the links to related issues, including political, financial, and historical, or simply games requiring participation. *Sleepless in Seattle* was considered to have been a slow starter, with little going for it except two major stars, Tom Hanks and Meg Ryan. However, it moved to surprisingly strong box office due to many promotional gambits, including a sweepstakes promotion on the Internet offering a visit to the most romantic locations featured in the movie, New York City's Empire State building and the waterfront in Seattle.

The use of the Internet, however, has also backfired. In the case of *A.I.*, the Steven Spielberg/Stanley Kubrick film released in the summer of 2001, buzz for the movie was created through the creation of an interactive game that was placed on the film's Web site. The game achieved cult status, with buy-in from a very interested audience base. However, the game created a very high expectation— one the film failed to reach. Game players were very disappointed in the movie itself, and created negative word of mouth for the film, which failed to achieve its expected box office returns.

IN-FLIGHT MOVIES

At the opposite end of the spectrum from the hot, new theater-going experience is the in-flight movie. Typically shown on a screen the size of a paper plate, with audio supplied through earphones that approximate the experience of listening through down pillows strapped to your head, in-flight movies do offer some value to marketers. The film is highlighted in the airline's magazines, an additional exposure. The quality of the viewing experience itself may also drive additional pay-per-view or video rentals by those who decide they'd like to get a better idea of what it was they just watched. Finally, there is a modest revenue stream from airlines licensing for play.

TV programs also enjoy the exposure of the in-flight entertainment system, with trailers for popular shows, classic sitcoms, or quick cuts of current successful network TV programs.

In 2000, US Airways was the first U.S. airline to offer coach-class passengers an on-demand video system, offering 110 hours of programming on individual seatback screens. Parents can control what children see, while adults can watch the theatrical version of R-rated films, although films that deal with airline crashes or cause the use of those little paper bags are not shown.

INDEPENDENT FILMS

The cost of advertising a mainstream Hollywood movie has increased 105% since 1994 versus a mere 29% increase in DBO revenue. This trend makes the inherently risky business of filmmaking even more unappealing because the breakeven point is set so high. Bruised by big-budget box office flops such as *Speed 2* and *The Postman*, studio executives are salivating over the profit margins of low-budget films such as *There's Something About Mary* (cost: $25MM; U.S. box: $176MM) and *The Full Monty* (cost: $3MM; U.S. box: $46MM).[7] However, major studios find it difficult to turn a profit on genre/classics films because their overhead is much higher than independent producers. Therefore, studio executives opt to pick up

---

7.   Bannon, Lisa, "Beyond Star Wars, The Summer's Sleepers," *The Wall Street Journal*, April 23, 1999.

films produced more cost-efficiently by independents and make their profit as the distributor.

Optimally, producers should enlist marketing experts to consult them in every stage of production. The marketer should envision a marketing plan as soon as a project has the "green light." Some examples of the value that a marketer would add to an independent production are: (i) the incorporation of market research and industry trends, (ii) the use of focus groups to gauge audience perceptions of the film/scenes, and (iii) the formulation of an advertising and release strategy. This approach guarantees that films will not only have successful openings, but will go on to earn millions of dollars (they will have "legs").

This approach, referred to as the "studio model," is followed religiously by major studios. However, it is virtually shunned by independent producers. Independent producers are very different from mainstream producers in that they are INDEPENDENT from outside interference. Independent filmmakers will not change the way they tell their story and make their movie because some studio executive tells them to. Independent filmmakers only care about getting their movie made. Advertising and marketing are afterthoughts. Without better films, how can independent films take any market share from the majors?

The only viable strategy for independents to earn higher market share is to implement aggressive marketing strategies. Unfortunately, most independent distributors do not have large marketing departments with extensive budgets. Independent distributors are faced with the challenge of getting their message out to their target audience within a very limited window of opportunity.

MARKETING INDEPENDENT FILMS

Not all films are produced with lavish budgets, extensive promotional departments, audience testing, and second-guessing. A major segment of the motion picture industry is the independent film segment. Independent films are films that are made outside the studio system. However, the line between "independent" and "mainstream" studios has become blurred. The first successful independent film that had commercial appeal was *Sex, Lies and Videotape*, released in 1989. Miramax purchased the rights to *Sex, Lies and Videotape* for $1.1MM. Although considered a high price to pay for an independent film, *Sex, Lies and Videotape* proved a very profitable investment because the film earned $25MM in DBO.[8]

What has fueled the conglomerate's appetite for independent studios? Independent filmmakers are experts at making films on tiny budgets, a skill that eludes big Hollywood studio executives. Hollywood executives spend millions to make the most broad appeal films possible. The results are few hits with plenty of boring, bland misses.

The industry trend predicts that studios will increase their profit margins by cutting the number of films they produce, holding down production costs, and sharing more risk with financial partners. Although cost containment is nothing new to the industry, it is still a challenge to predict how the film-going audience will react to fewer high-budget mainstream offerings. Even a modest cut in output by the majors could result in about half a billion dollars in box office revenue for independents.

Table 3-3 shows some examples of cuts in major studio production volume.

TABLE 3-3   Cuts in Major Studio Production Volume

MAJOR STUDIO	HISTORICAL RELEASE VOLUME	RELEASE VOLUME AFTER CUTS IN PRODUCTION
Walt Disney Studios	30	20
Universal Studios	35	20
Fox	25	15-20
Warner Bros.	30	22

Independents can take advantage of this opportunity by making films that appeal to their target market.

Independent films represent about 40% of total releases, yet they only account for about 20% of total revenue. Why is there such a significant disconnect? First, independent films tend to have narrower audience appeal than Hollywood films. Second, there are also fewer screens dedicated to independent fare than to Hollywood films. Third, independent films may be of lower quality than major Hollywood releases simply because their production budgets are only a fraction of Hollywood releases.

---

8.   "The Biz," *Entertainment Weekly,* December 1997.

Independent films tell stories that might only appeal to a very narrow audience. Studios pass on niche stories that lack commercial appeal. Since the potential audience for independent films is smaller, it is even more difficult to get them into the theater. Independent marketers simply can't do a "Happy Meal" tie-in and expect to fill the theater.

One of the most unique aspects of the independent filmgoer is that he/she enjoys discovering a movie for him/herself. The independent audience does not like in-your-face marketing. Independent marketers are challenged to reach their audience without the audience knowing.

WORD OF MOUTH

Independent filmgoers rely heavily on word of mouth and reviews from film festivals as trusted sources. Marketers can capitalize on good word of mouth by staggering a film's opening. For example, *The Blair Witch Project* only opened on a handful of screens before opening wide two weeks later on July 30. Artisan knew the film would generate good word of mouth, so it opened the film in select key markets. The more people buzzed about *The Blair Witch Project*, the better its grosses were ($5MM in limited release).[9] In fact, the buzz was so strong, people camped outside to get tickets to the limited release. The lines themselves created such positive buzz that the *Wall Street Journal* called it "fierce."

INTERNET

Artisan also enlisted the Internet to generate buzz for *The Blair Witch Project*. Artisan favored the Internet because of its "discovery" aspect versus "in-your-face" television. Artisan felt that its target audience for *The Blair Witch Project* was online.

In addition to studios creating their own Web sites, there are countless Web sites with film reviews.

WILD POSTINGS

Another time-honored method to reach an audience is through displaying movie posters. While Hollywood studios pay to have their posters displayed on bus-stops and in subway stations, independent

---

9. Orwall, Bruce, "Small Studio Brews a Success Mixing the Web and an Edgy Film," *Wall Street Journal*, July 26, 1999.

film posters reside in places where you are not supposed to put posters (e.g., construction sites). There is an underground organization
referred to by independent marketers as the "poster mafia." Independent marketers must use these "snipers" to hang their posters
around a city. Otherwise, their posters would be torn down or covered immediately. Posters for independent films tend to be more
mysterious and cutting-edge than Hollywood movie posters, and certainly more subtle than studio posters.

INDEPENDENT SCREENS

Exhibitors are not ignoring the growth in the independent film
segment. In the past, exhibitors had fewer screens and would not
risk putting a specialty film on-screen. With the advent of large multiplexes, exhibitors are more likely to dedicate a screen or two to
independent films. Now, exhibitors are embracing independent films.
Loews Cineplex Entertainment, for instance, announced an "indie
(independent) screening series" with *The Shooting Gallery*. General
Cinemas is set to launch a chain of Sundance Cinemas to serve the
under-screened independent market. Using an outside research firm,
General Cinemas learned more about the independent filmgoer and
will capitalize on that knowledge to build theaters to cater to that
target audience.

THE INDEPENDENT MOVIE FAN

It is very important to know your audience for any type of marketing. The independent filmgoer is usually urban, median age of 33,
median household income of $56k. Independent filmgoers are also
more educated and hungry for culture. Since independent theaters
are concentrated in major urban areas, independent film devotees
are willing to travel to see independent films.[10]

All of these demographics and psychographics were reinforced
during a recent focus group, although one can learn almost as much
standing outside New York City's Angelika Theater listening to the
audience on line talking about independent film as they can from an
actual focus group. Out of 23 potential respondents recruited, almost
half were students or in the film industry. While this screening strategy works with consumer products, the audience for independent
films is really made up of film students and people in the media
industry.

---

10.   1997 SMRB and MarketCast, Inc.

The growth in the number of screens dedicated to independent films will create a huge supply. This supply of screens will create a demand for more independent films. This opportunity will create more competition in the independent film market. As a result, independent film marketers will have to be more aggressive to increase market share.

SUMMARY

The movie industry—both mainstream and independent—continues to be the central focus of the entertainment business. While other segments of the business may have surpassed movies in overall revenue, it is impossible to say how much those additional revenues depended on the marketing done for the original film. In any case, the product created and marketed as big-screen entertainment has supplemented the revenues of a wide variety of entertainment segments.

Among the segments affected by the movie industry, but also standing very much on their own, are network TV and syndication.

FURTHER READING

BOOKS

1. Abramowitz, Rachel, *Is That a Gun in your Pocket? Women's Experience of Power in Hollywood* (New York, NY: Random House, 1999).

2. Bart, Peter, *Who Killed Hollywood?... and Put the Tarnish on Tinseltown* (Los Angeles, CA: Renaissance Books, 1999).

3. Baumgarten, Paul A., Donald Fraber, and Mark Fleischer, *Producing, Financing and Distributing Film / A Comprehensive Legal and Business Guide* (New York, NY: Limelight Editions, 1998).

4. Cones, Jon W., Film *Finance & Distribution: A Dictionary of Terms* (Beverly Hills, CA: Silman James Press, 1992).

5. Lukk, Tiiu, *Movie Marketing* (Beverly Hills, CA: Silman-James Press, 1997).

6. Wyatt, Justin, *High Concept: Movies and Marketing in Hollywood* (Austin, TX: University of Texas Press, 1994).

7. Squire, Jason E., Ed., *The Movie Business Book,* (New York, NY: Simon & Schuster, 1992).

MAGAZINES TO DEVOUR

1. *Variety*
2. *Hollywood Reporter*
3. *The Industry Standard*
4. *Entertainment Weekly*
5. *Premier*

4

NETWORK TV,
SYNDICATION,
AND RADIO

OVERVIEW

B efore there was cable, premium cable, pay-per-view cable, direct broadcast, and the ability to use familiar euphemisms for the sex act, there was network television—and, of course, radio. Both of these mediums depended, for the most part, on revenue derived from commercial advertising, as opposed to subscription. While the argument regarding the quality of the content shown on network TV has raged on since the infamous "vast wasteland" days of Newton Minnow, the fact remains: network television still delivers the broadest mass reach of any of the mediums available today.

In this chapter, we'll take a look at the structure of the television medium, both national and local: the "Big Three" networks and the upstarts knocking at their gates; the systems by which audiences are ascertained, both in terms of volume and type; and the mechanics of marketing on network TV. Next, we'll investigate the second coming of hit TV series, also known as syndication, which has served both new networks and cable TV incredibly well in terms of providing content; then we'll take a quick glance at some of the newer technologies affecting broadcast TV. Finally, we'll shift our focus to radio, which is set up similarly to TV in terms of advertising, but has shifted towards drilling down into a niche listener base.

NETWORK TELEVISION: "THE MOTHER OF THEM ALL"

Revenues drive network television—and those revenues depend on a network gaining and maintaining a significant share of the available market. That share is captured through the development and broadcasting of content that will attract viewers—not just any viewers, but viewers in the specific target markets found most desirable by advertisers.

While network television has declined in percentage ratings and share (thanks to cable and direct broadcast), it is still a significant mass-reach medium. At least 75% of TV households have access to a network station as opposed to merely local stations; the ability of viewers to access these networks is mandated by the Federal Communications Commission (FCC). If a network can grab a 10%–12% share of those TV households, then ten to twelve million households are tuning into the content broadcast. Numbers of that magnitude continue to motivate advertisers to air their product messages on network television.

The three major networks have all had a turn at leadership in this very competitive arena, vying for the rapidly growing TV public with news, daytime programming, talk shows, and sitcoms. CBS, for instance, dominated the 1950s and early 1960s with number one-rated programs like *I Love Lucy*, *Gunsmoke*, and *The Beverly Hillbillies* until NBC's *Bonanza* and *Rowan & Martin's Laugh-In* took over through the rest of that decade early into the 1970s. Then CBS charged back with *All in the Family*, which held the number-one spot for five years. ABC, determined to reach the top of the pile, got serious with comedy in the late 1970s, when *Happy Days* and *Laverne & Shirley* helped propel the network to number one. CBS had the last laugh with *60 Minutes* and *Dallas*. ABC took the "If you can't beat 'em" approach, mimicking *Dallas* with its own *Dynasty*.

NBC finally got back on-board with *The Cosby Show*, which maintained its position as the number-one show for five years. When Bill Cosby bowed out, CBS's *60 Minutes* took the top spot until NBC's *Seinfeld* and *ER* dominated the late 1990s.

While this seesaw effect did little to encourage new and innovative programming, it did keep the attention of the viewers long enough to create significant revenue for the networks. The approach also opened the door for the competition, however. Viewers tiring of the relatively safe approach of the Big Three began to search out alternatives, and found them in the form of new networks eager to build share by targeting niches currently underserved by the mass approach.

THE UPSTARTS: NEWER NETWORKS

Fox (Twentieth Century Fox) was the first channel to challenge the entrenched trio; it was followed by successful entries into the market by WB (Warner Bros.) and UPN (United Paramount Network, a division of Viacom). Original material has been the consistent key to entering this market. Fox initially purchased proven sitcom series, but made its biggest gain with shows like *Married With Children*, *The Simpsons*, and sports events like college and professional football—the latter featuring insightful voices like that of former coach John Madden, along with innovative technologies like the computerized first-down stripe on the field and the information-laden scorebox in the corner of the screen. It also became a known part of the channel's identity that it would push the envelope on semi-nudity and language—at the time of its entry into network TV, those characteristics had been more consistent with some cable channels.

WB also started with the purchase of proven sitcoms, including reruns of *Friends*, *Cheers*, and *Sabrina, the Teenage Witch*. But to make its name, it soon started successful original content shows like *Buffy the Vampire Slayer*, *Hercules*, and *Xena: Warrior Princess*, which led to over 100 stations joining the network. WB followed the success of its originals with yet more slightly off-center content, leading some industry ad professionals to believe that the channel is oversubscribing to series that are written for a primarily younger audience.

UPN made its entry into the market behind an already robust following for professional wrestling in a skew pitched at an 18–49 largely male demographic. UPN has committed to more original dramas and comedies with a male edge. As one of the newer entries into the network fray, UPN would like to trade on the brand identity of Paramount, just as Fox and WB have with their parent studios. UPN, as a wholly owned division of Viacom, can also count on promotional help and assistance in building its affiliates from the company's other units.

The biggest gaining new network entrant, Pax (Paxson Communication), is partially owned by NBC. Pax is still establishing its market identity—without the support of NBC affiliates, at least in terms of carrying NBC content. An effort to rerun *Nightly News with Tom Brokaw* on Pax stations infuriated the affiliates, who showed their voting clout by successfully discouraging the idea. The affiliates wanted a new vision and programming identity for Pax, and rightfully so; simply rerunning NBC content could eventually affect revenues for local stations—and local stations, after all, are the engines that keep the networks humming.

LOCAL TELEVISION STATIONS

The networks sell their programming to 1,700 stations in America and 21,500 television stations worldwide.[1] While the viewing audience may think of their local network affiliate as being owned by the network itself, this is not always true. These stations are grouped into three primary relationships with the television networks: owned and operated (O&O), affiliates, and independents.

OWNED AND OPERATED

For the networks to ensure they can provide coverage to over 75% of U.S. TV households, they have acquired local television stations in major cities and leading U.S. markets with substantial TV household populations. These stations are referred to as O&O since they are, in fact, considered to be divisions of the networks and must carry the programming dictated by them.

Although the station's marketing management typically reports to the network's divisional marketing executive, the stations have a responsibility to create their own local marketing plans and put forth consistent efforts to brand their station within their market's (usu-

---

1. The National Association of Broadcasters' Information Resource Center (*www.nab.org*).

ally crowded) sphere of influence. This can mean having a helicopter that delivers local traffic conditions; weather, news, sports, and the occasional local programming; or syndicated programs, which the stations purchase on their own.

The stations share in the national advertising revenues generated by the networks, and, until recently, had no financial obligation to the networks except to show a consistent divisional profit. Now there is a movement afoot to have O&O stations pay for the rights to carry national programming, thus helping to defray some of the expensive marketing costs at the network level.

AFFILIATES

The next group of stations (totaling well over 800) is known as affiliates. Affiliates have contracts with each of the six network broadcasters that run for a period of years. In this relationship, the station has a responsibility—a commitment—to run programming supplied by the network, giving the network the increased TV household population it requires to fulfill FCC requirements. In return, the station benefits from the promotional efforts of the network on a national level, driving viewers locally.

On occasion, when a network goes through a pre-season exercise to gain clearance for a soon-to-be-televised new national program, an affiliate can decide not to carry or clear that program. It could be for any reason, including having an important local program to put in its place, or a concern over content that may not be acceptable to local viewers. The network, requiring coverage on a national basis, can then go to an independent, which is not affiliated with any network, to see if it wishes to carry the program in direct competition with its own affiliate. Sometimes a single episode of a national program might be pre-empted to allow for a locally produced program, such as a town hall meeting or a local retail-supported event.

INDEPENDENTS

The third group of stations, known as independents, consists of two types of station ownership: corporate (or group) ownership and "mom-and-pop" entrepreneurship. These stations have no contractual relationship with any network and are solely dependent on their own programmers to fill the stations' airtime with programs that appeal to viewers in their own market. They are in direct competition with in-market O&O stations as well as affiliate stations.

Station groups balance the cost of programming against locally generated advertising revenues by using original programming in several markets. They can also make advantageous license or rental agreements for syndicated programming in multiple markets. Single stations, or "mom-and-pop" stations, usually operate on tight budgets in much smaller markets. They are often good takeover targets for corporate groups eager to assemble the maximum population coverage, enabling them to become strong affiliate contenders when groups switch their alliances.

An example of an alliance switch took place in 1996, when a group of CBS affiliates who had reached a contract renewal period (in those days, every three years) decided to join with Fox on what they decided would be a more advantageous and productive basis.

LOCAL PROGRAMMING

Regardless of how well it may market and promote itself, every television station's success is directly attributable to the quality of its programming. Today's growing number of channels provides a home for a wide variety of content, servicing a range of niche audiences. Not only does this diversity make the audience happy, it provides a direct path to certain viewing groups that marketers may find desirable.

Local programming typically consists of news, documentaries, and sports. In most markets, one or more independent stations produce a daily newscast, which must compete with at least two daily newscasts from the ABC, CBS, and NBC affiliates. There is significant preparation necessary for everyday newscasts, which generally run for a half-hour to an hour for early-morning, noon, afternoon, and evening program slots. Many stations also provide five-minute local cut-ins. Viewership of local news is strong: at 17% for Americans under the age of 30, and 50% for those over the age of 65. Specialty cable news channels only garner 32% of public viewership.

Some local stations' news departments also produce weekend news programs, news magazines, news/talk shows, public affairs programs, and documentaries. Today, 31% of Americans watch news magazine shows regularly. Coincidentally, the same percentage of viewers also watch television talk shows, such as *Oprah*, which made its initial appearance as a local show called *Chicago A.M.*

Local sports programming is somewhat limited. Professional football and basketball are only sold to networks on a national basis, making it difficult for local stations to provide coverage. The NBA, however, also sells rights for local coverage to individual stations. Baseball is sold similarly to basketball. College football may be broadcast on both national and local stations, provided they are not aired at the same time. Amateur and community sporting events are usually aired on local stations.

When it comes to commercially driven TV—network or local, O&O, affiliated, part of a group, or a mom-and-pop operation—content is king. It is content that attracts and holds viewers, and holding viewers is crucial to market share, the guiding force behind the revenue generated from advertisers. How is that share determined? Through ratings. And when it comes to television ratings, Nielsen is the "Emperor of the Universe."

THE BASICS OF TV RATINGS

Ratings are essential to commercial television. Ratings are the root of all advertising dollars; they are the starting point for negotiations between networks and local stations for the price of commercial time.[2] When you mention ratings in respect to advertising-supported media—television and radio—the name most often mentioned is Nielsen Media Research.

Nielsen (*www.nielsenmedia.com*) was founded in 1923 by Arthur C. Nielsen, Sr. It was one of the first research companies to measure the audience for the burgeoning radio broadcasting and advertising industry. The company has flexed with the times and now also rates cable TV and the Web; for now, we'll focus on the mechanics of network TV.

HOW NIELSEN RATINGS WORK

Nielsen uses a recruited sample group of 5,000 households, representing 13,000 people (an average of 2.6 people per home), to get a perspective of viewing habits in the over 100 million homes with TVs in the U.S. Nielsen does not accept volunteers for its ratings service; "Nielsen families" are recruited through random selection to be statistically accurate. Every household in the U.S. has an equal chance

---

2.   According to Nielsen, approximately $44 billion per year is spent on national and local advertising.

of being selected, no matter where it is located. The random nature of the sample ensures that people of all backgrounds and ages can be included; however, it can only happen from Nielsen contacting them.[3]

Every effort is made by Nielsen to ensure that a thorough cross-section of ethnic and income groups is represented. In 1991, Nielsen expanded its monthly national reports to include data specifically on the viewing of African-American households, and in 1992, it expanded its reports to include specific Hispanic ratings. The firm also checks its samples against U.S. Census Bureau data. On occasion, Nielsen even does special studies it calls telephone coincidentals, in which the firm seeks to double-check its data against a random sample of direct telephone calls to homes.

To confirm exactly what shows are playing and when, Nielsen tracks more than 1,700 TV stations and 11,000 cable systems so it can properly credit viewing habits. In some specially selected homes (in the 48 largest markets), Nielsen technicians install metering equipment directly on TVs, VCRs, cable boxes, or satellite dishes, with all the meters connected to a centralized computer. The data collected through this system gives advertisers a clear picture of who is watching and when, helping guide the decision of where to best spend their dollars.

KEY TERMS

Nielsen uses the following terminology to describe ratings data:

- Sweeps: Periods in which local markets are simultaneously measured. Nielsen surveys all 210 local television markets during what are known as "sweeps months": November, February, and May; in July, Honolulu, Fairbanks, and Juneau are excluded. The data collected during sweeps is the basis by which local stations and cable systems make program decisions and set local ad rates.
- Designated Market Area (DMA): Nielsen's research divides the entire country into DMAs, or non-overlapping areas used for planning, buying, and evaluating TV audiences. Each DMA consists of a group of counties in which stations achieve the largest audience share. Each county in the U.S. is assigned to one DMA.

---

3. www.nielsenmedia.com/FAQ/"How do I become a Nielsen family?"

- Metro Area: The central part of the DMA, or the most densely populated portion of the market. Metro areas are helpful geographic breaks for local advertisers, since Nielsen provides detailed ratings and demographic information on metro areas as well as DMAs.

- Households Using Television (HUT): The percentage of all TV-owning households that have at least one TV set in use during a specific time period. During a typical weeknight, HUT levels tend to peak at about 60%–70%, meaning that 60% to 70% of TV-owning households have at least one set in use.

- Rating: A Nielsen rating point flexes with the population (i.e., number of households owning TVs). Early in this millennium, the number crossed the 1,000,000 household mark, and will continue to grow.

- Household Rating: The estimated percentage of all TV-owning households (or persons) tuned into a specific station or program at a given time. For example, if an episode of NBC's hit series *Friends* achieves a household rating of 12.5, this means that 12.5% of households owning TVs are tuned into this program.

- Share: The percentage of HUTs tuned into a specific station or program at a given time. If a *Friends* episode achieves a 25 share, this means that out of households with a TV in use, one-quarter of them are tuned into *Friends*. This would correspond to a HUT level of 50%, since the HUT level is simply the rating divided by the share.

KEY DEMOGRAPHICS

When considering where to place their advertising—and therefore, their dollars—decision-makers focus on what programs/time slots are most frequented by the particular demographic group to which they wish to sell. For example, placing an ad for a product mostly used by 18- to 24-year-old females in the middle of *Monday Night Football* probably isn't going to give an advertiser the best bang for its buck. While the advertiser might get a lot of eyeballs viewing the ad, the bodies connected to those eyeballs will not be likely to rush out to buy the product. Demographics are the key to matching the right wallet with the right product.

Demographics are also key factors in the concepting and production of the programming available on both network and cable TV. In the age-old chicken-or-egg argument, networks search for content that will lure advertising dollars to their coffers. The producers of this content are more than happy to oblige. With any luck, the viewing public happily tunes in, week after week, presumably unaware that their favorite show has been developed from a carefully crafted formula, not so much to enrich their minds or entertain them as to sell advertising space or drive subscriptions. After all, it is a business.

Network TV, with its broad base of viewership, tends to focus primarily on two key audience demographics:

- Adults, men and women, 18–24
- Adults, men and women, 25–49

Cable TV, however, is a different story. The ever-growing number of cable channels creates a scenario in which niche marketing is much more successful than mass-reach. Cable programming tends to drill down even further into particular age, race, gender, and economic variables. In fact, certain channels—Lifetime (women), BET (Black Entertainment Television), ESPN (sports)—are devoted to particular audiences to drive subscriptions and advertising. Niches are also divided into even tighter age segmentation. For example, a product looking for the 18- to 24-year-old market should not pass Go, but head directly to MTV.

TIME SLOTS

Simply having the content and knowing who wants to watch is not enough. The third important variable in selecting spots is knowing who is available to watch the programming at what time of day. Sections of the advertising clock are divided into what are known as dayparts. The key demographic for daytime TV is women, 25–54. Prime time tends to be adults, 18–49.

The principal dayparts used in TV ratings are:

- Early Morning (5 a.m.–9 a.m.)
- Daytime (9 a.m.–3 p.m.)
- Early Fringe (3 p.m.–5 p.m.)
- Early News (5 p.m.–7 p.m.)
- Access (7 p.m.–8 p.m.)
- Prime (8 p.m.–11 p.m.)
- Late News (11 p.m.–11:30 p.m.)
- Late Fringe (11:30 p.m.–1:00 a.m.)
- Prime time on Sundays runs from 7 p.m. to 11 p.m.

It is difficult to match a "typical" audience profile to each of these dayparts because the demographics are driven by the programming. For example, the typical audience watching UPN or Fox at 8 p.m. may be very different from the audience watching a PBS station. Programming is created to capture the audience for the advertiser, not vice versa.

Of course, the goal is to wrap all of the elements—age, gender, interest, economics—into programming that will attract the most viewers to the advertisers willing to spend the most money. To do that, the programming typically must be made available during the time of day when HUT levels are highest, the aptly named "prime time": 8 p.m. to 11 p.m. Among the six broadcast networks (NBC, ABC, CBS, FOX, UPN, and WB), NBC has been recently most profitable, in part because of its success in reaching the key 18–49 demographic during this essential time slot.

PROMOTION AND MARKETING

Networks, local stations, and radio must promote themselves along with promoting their individual programs and series. To attract advertisers, ad agencies, and media buying services, a network or station must be able to maintain and build its audience. While a certain amount of this viewer loyalty will come through the content aired, networks and stations as individual entities must also recognize the need to build and promote their own specific brand. Audience share and viewership numbers justify advertising prices. It is those numbers that keep growing despite the decline in absolute audience numbers.

Viewers that buy into the holistic messages of "Must-See TV" or "Come Home to CBS" can add incrementally to those already loyal to particular shows shown on the network. Local station affiliates also layer on additional viewers through self-marketing. The end result is the creation of a base of regular viewers. Network television remains a powerhouse because of its ability to deliver a mass audience of 5 to 10 million viewers for most shows, 20 million for the best shows, and nearly 50 million for specials like the Super Bowl or Academy Awards. Each and every one of these viewers must be wooed by more than just the actual broadcast of the event or show.

NETWORK SELF-PROMOTION

Self-promotion takes many forms and utilizes all available media. A drive down any highway will lead to sightings of billboards touting local radio stations, television sitcoms, news broadcasts, or the launch of a coming season's new shows. Or, turn on the radio and you're likely to hear a sound bite from a television show to be aired that evening. It's even common to see radio personalities in television commercials so listeners can catch a three-dimensional glimpse of people they have only known as voices. Banner ads on Internet sites focus on the audiences most likely to tune in at particular times to particular shows. Taking that medium one step further, every network has its own Web site, where fans of particular programs can log in to get the latest news on their favorite series, as well as news of other programming offered by the network.

Networks have also learned that to build audience share for a program, they must steal those viewers from other networks or cable program choices. Since networks do not permit advertising from competitive networks, careful selection of basic cable shows with compatible audiences become an important part of the network's media plan. This is also an enhanced revenue source for cable programmers and operators that is often synergistic, because the show being promoted may someday become a syndicated property for that very cable network.

ON-AIR SELF-PROMOTION

Self-promotion also takes the form of advertising aired on the network or station itself. Airtime on television networks is perishable; if it isn't sold to advertisers, it runs the risk of simply disappearing into the ether. Rather than have this happen, unsold time is utilized in a variety of ways, all of which build goodwill for the network or station in one form or another. Public service announcements (PSAs) are given to not-for-profit organizations. Government institutions may also benefit from unsold time, an act smiled upon by the FCC. Commercials touting the benefits of not smoking, just saying no to drugs, and not burning Smokey the Bear out of his habitat fall into this category.

The remainder of the available time may be used for promotion of the carrier itself. This is not "free time," but it certainly is more economical than spending promotional dollars on other media. Every minute of available advertising time has a dollar value attached to it. However, as networks and stations build their sales forecasts and operating budgets, they build in certain amounts of time they know will be used to carry their own message. Broadcasters will always prefer to sell any and all time over and above that which they have budgeted for self-promotion or PSAs, for it is the sale of that time that makes self-promotion possible and keeps the broadcaster profitable.

But why use on-air promotion to ask viewers to continue watching a station to which they are already tuned? To remind them to STAY tuned—to not touch that dial, or remote, in this day and age. All forms of media are interested in holding their audience, and doing it in the most economical way possible. As is true in any sales process, it is always easier and less expensive to harvest existing customers rather than to grow new ones. The existing customer only needs a focused reminder now and then, while the new customer warrants an all-out attack, utilizing other forms of media not necessarily controlled by the station or network.

VERTICAL, HORIZONTAL, AND STANDARD CROSS-PLUGS

On-air promotion takes the form of TV spots, usually running 30 seconds (known as promos) and, on occasion, 10 or 15 seconds (known as IDs). Networks also implement strategic devices that build off of successful shows in specific time slots. These can include vertical cross-plugs, which are commercials touting the show in the next time slot. The show receiving the promotion is usually new or has a similar demographic but weaker audience share. Vertical cross-plugs can hold viewers who are known to surf stations and may be willing to give the next program a trial viewing.

If the show of choice seems to be losing its Nielsen share or ratings, or if it is so strong that there is a chance of capturing new tiers and making fresh viewers loyal to the program, a standard or horizontal cross-plug provides a quick snapshot of the next program in the series. This is similar to a movie trailer or a "coming attractions" format, which maintains interest and builds buzz. This is most frequently used for daytime series and weekly primetime sitcoms.

INTRA-INDUSTRY MARKETING

Where each of the media really rolls up its sleeves and sells is when it sells within the industry itself. Trade magazines, promotion booklets, direct mail, and program sales conventions like the National Association of Television Programming Executives (NATPE) and MIFED (international film) or MIPCOM (international TV, video, cable, and satellite markets) are all vehicles through which the industry markets itself. It is here that network and station executives are treated to clear outlines of consumer advertising campaigns, including the media schedule, station clearance line-ups, and the size of the marketing budget in minute detail.

RELATIONSHIP MARKETING AND THE HALO EFFECT

What takes a program from mere flash-in-the-pan popularity—or on the flip side, utter unwatched disaster—and turns it into a long-running hit and syndication star? The answer is loyal fans. An audience that reserves the time slot every week so that they can become one with their program. In the best of all possible marketing worlds, the relationship these fans have developed with the program extends to the products, services, and brands offered during the commercial breaks. This is known as a *halo effect*; taking advantage of the halo effect is known as relationship marketing.

Most people who hate a program switch the channel or turn the set off, the advertising just a distant dream in some media buyer's brain. On the other hand, loyal viewers of *Friends* or *ER*, for example, may never move from their seat during the entire program. It is the hope and intention of the advertisers that the fan will not only see the commercial, but also associate it with their preference for the show. The goal is to create a consistent relationship between the program and the consumer.

Within the entertainment industry, relationship marketing is often called the development of a fan. Fans are frequently known to purchase merchandise or licensed products that relate to stars and programs in almost any medium. Viewers of *Jeopardy* have purchased enough copies of the software version of the show to justify bringing out *Jeopardy 2*. They have also boosted the sales of consistent advertisers like Volvo.[4] Fans are considered to be amenable to listening to advertising messages, and, in the world of network television, this is often the deciding factor in whether a show continues for six weeks, a season, or seemingly forever. In recent years, *M*A*S*H* lasted for 11 seasons (1972–1983), *Cheers* also lasted for 11 seasons (1982–1993), and *Seinfeld* ran for 9 years.

Some sense of the audience following for these shows can be seen by the viewership of the final episode of each:

---

4.   Alex Trebek explained that of all the automobile manufacturers approached about the idea of giving away a free car, only Volvo responded favorably. Later, several American automobile manufacturers insisted on the opportunity to also give away free cars on the show.

- *M*A*S*H*, 1983; Nielsen rating: 60.2; 77% share; 105 million viewers
- *Cheers*, 1993; Nielsen rating: 45.9; 72% share; 80 million viewers
- *Seinfeld*[5], 1998; Nielsen rating: 41.3; 58% share; 76 million viewers

SEND IN THE CLONES

Every network is looking for the next *Seinfeld*. The success of a new program or format can have a decided impact across the airwaves. ABC's *Who Wants to be a Millionaire* (*WWTBAM*) game show is a great example of how quickly a concept can catch on, and to what effect it can be used, reflecting the power of consumer interest. *WWTBAM*, originally produced and broadcast in Great Britain, was reformulated for American audiences using Regis Philbin as host. The show caught on like wildfire and catapulted to the top of its time slot almost immediately. Seeing the incredible results of the program, ABC grabbed the brass ring and ran, running the program several nights a week.

By doing so, ABC managed to have several spots in the Top Ten list for weeks on end, driving new ad revenue for a network that was sorely in need of a hit. The bonus, of course, was that ABC was now able to charge a premium for the spots, due to the high viewership of the program. Additionally, the *WWTBAM* franchise has now spread worldwide, with versions available in almost every major international market.

Once broadcasters find a successful formula, they have to maximize its success immediately and invest in a marketing budget to expand awareness and maintain loyalty: two classic marketing techniques. But, beware the semi-clone that attempts to trade on the popularity of a concept. Borrowing on the public's seeming fascination of becoming a millionaire, Fox took a slightly different angle with *Who Wants to Marry a Millionaire*, a program that caused embarrassment, potential lawsuits, and a decline in credibility for Fox—and risked a negative halo effect for advertisers.

---

5.   The Nielsen rating was highest in New York City, the setting for *Seinfeld*, at 49.1; in contrast, the rating in Memphis was 22.9.

THE FALL LAUNCHING SEASON

When shows are launched each fall, with nervous executives standing by with their fingers crossed, enormous effort is made to create a huge opening audience tune-in, setting the tone for the early purchase of advertising schedules by advertisers. This is known as a "strong up-front." Network marketing departments are in full swing, working with their own in-house team as well as external agencies to fashion the season's marketing plan, create the advertising message, and provide the rationale for placing percentages of the marketing budget in cable, print, outdoor billboards, radio, Internet, and promotions.

On-air advertising activity falls into its own category. Print advertising includes full-page ads in local newspapers, seeking tune-in for the networks as well as affiliate stations, and the use of standard ads in entertainment-oriented magazines like *Entertainment Weekly*, *US*, *Rolling Stone*, *People*, *InStyle*, and many others.

JUST LIKE IN THE MOVIES

Networks have learned from movie advertising—no surprise since ABC, CBS, WB, UPN, and Fox all have movie studios as sister divisions. Only NBC has no movie company with which to create close-up learning, but the strategy is readily discernable from observation.

This movie-based strategy includes the use of significant promotion and merchandising events. For example, CBS has created effective promotions and tie-in programs with major advertisers such as Kmart, Coca-Cola, and McDonalds. The product-specific sweepstakes and contests developed with these synergy partners have driven consumers to participate with both the program and advertiser's products. ABC was one of the first networks to utilize mall promotions that presented daytime television stars up-close and personal. Fans were able to meet them and get autographs; the stars often participated in fund-raising for local charities, driving further goodwill.

ABC's soap opera supermarket magazines—following in the long tradition of movie monthlies—are particularly effective. The magazines provide inside gossip on the daytime shows stars, helping fans stay involved while building interest in additional daily tune-in. The magazines also generate revenue.

Finally, in another strategy often employed in the movies, product placement has built additional revenues for programs while also creating a halo effect for advertisers. Viewers see products consumed or used by the characters of their favorite drama or sitcom and (hopefully) make a mental note to rush right out and purchase them.

SYNDICATION

If network TV is the "Mother," "The Daughter of it All" is syndication, providing a continuation of the progeny of networks in the licensing and distribution of what were formerly known as reruns. Reruns have been the vehicle through which new classic television networks have emerged, including Fox, WB, and UPN. However, syndication also includes new content created specifically for non-network television, specifically existing and new cable channels.

Network television channels are like a program supermarket with empty shelves. They wait for the manufactured goods to provide hungry consumers with their daily fare—in this case, entertainment. If programs are not available, the shelves are empty. Or, if the programs are not successful in attracting or holding the interest of the consumers, they are taken off the shelves (the channel, in this case) and are replaced quickly, often in the midseason of the schedule, with a new product offering. The phrase "content is king" is most applicable here. While there is a never-ending flow of programs to the networks, they must still match the interests of the audience to the shows.

Shows are produced by independent production houses, network production divisions, or movie studios with television production arms. They may also be produced by foreign companies, producing for their own networks and interested in licensing the concept. *Survivor* and *WWTBAM* are examples of foreign-produced concepts that have moved to the U.S. market. Finished programs from English-speaking networks like the BBC, Canadian Broadcast, or Australian Television networks are another example of internationally produced content.

Regardless of where they are produced, programs fall into three categories: off-net, first-run, and syndicated product in-auction.

OFF-NET

Off-net programs are created based on a successful pilot, usually costing in the area of $1 million. They are thoroughly researched and appear for the first time on network television during a 13-week schedule. If the show successfully grabs a large enough audience—like *Friends*, *Cheers*, *ER*, and others—it may run for several years. The content for the successful show will always be original programming, made on a tight, often stressful production timetable, and costing from $500,000 per episode and upwards.

Of course, once a show becomes a solid, long-lasting hit, star talent may begin seeking salary increases, which, of course, affects the cost of the show dramatically. On occasion, the star(s) may have partial ownership of the program. In the case of ABC's *Spin City*, Michael J. Fox, a star and part owner, found it necessary to resign from the show due to an increased onset of Parkinson's disease. He had final decision-making authority on selecting Charlie Sheen to replace him in the show, with every step of that process reported in the press and leading late-night talk shows. This coverage was good for both the goose and the gander: *Spin City* received additional exposure in the marketplace, and Fox received visibility for the new foundation he had set up to explore cures for this tragic disease.

Off-net shows, once having run on the networks, are available for licensing as reruns. There was a time when rerun product was considered an undesirable and dated product, to be shown only during the summer months by networks and stations that needed to fill an empty program slot. However, this changed when the Fox network discovered that no more than 30% of the TV viewing population had ever seen every first-run show of each series—even the successful shows. Since these shows had been massively popular in their first incarnation, it followed that there was an audience that was eager to catch those shows the second time around.

Stations now had a very simple way to fill empty time slots: off-net programs in rerun mode. It was the beginning of syndicated programming as a viable business—in fact, more than viable: When *The Cosby Show* went into rerun license, the total package of programs sold for over $800 million, making Cosby one of the wealthiest actors in television and giving the Carsey-Werner production company the initiative to try the same thing again with *Roseanne*. This production company is now a leader in producing shows either for eventual or immediate syndication.

FIRST-RUN

First-run programs are shows that are developed directly for syndication for local stations. The best example of shows developed specifically for syndication to local stations include *Hercules* and *Xena: Warrior Princess*, which have great appeal to a very attractive audience, young males and females 18–24. *Oprah, Entertainment Tonight,* and *E!* are all first-run shows that provide local stations with fresh, never-before-seen programming, which can build an audience and retain loyalty for several seasons in a row.

On occasion, some television pilots for well-considered network shows fail in audience research or are yanked out of the line-up in midseason due to poor ratings. These would still be considered (under the original definition) first-run programs, but are never commissioned for a full season. Instead, the programs are brought to the attention of local stations, eager for new, unexposed programming and given a second life. If this "almost first-run" programming builds audience interest, full 13-week schedules are purchased and sold to the thousands of television stations across the country that need to fill time slots on empty dayparts.

One of the most successful examples of an almost first-run syndicated show is *Baywatch*, now seen around the world. It continues to run after nearly a decade of seasons, and has spawned several look-alike shows based on the production companies' belief that imitation is the sincerest form of flattery. *Baywatch* originally aired on NBC, was dropped after one season, put into syndication, and has never looked back.

SYNDICATED PRODUCT IN AUCTION

The purpose of syndication is to maximize the income and returns to the syndicator, whether it is the production company, the network, the studio, the participating stars, or all of the above. With certain programs, the potential outright purchase price of the syndicated rights may seem too low. These programs may be placed into auction by the syndicator's representative or sales agent, similar to what happens in the publishing industry with a particularly tasty concept—Hillary Clinton's memoirs, for example.

If the program is hot enough, the auction typically entails a rash of bidding or an escalating price war, with the rights going to the highest bidder. In the business, this is a way of separating the seriously interested parties from the lesser stations. It clearly places deep-pocket stations at an advantage, and motivates station groups to bid for all of their stations as a package. The result is a higher price and greater profit for the syndicator.

There is a marketing implication, however: The higher the cost of the syndicated product, the more important targeted and effective marketing becomes to reach and motivate the viewing audience, building ratings and audience share.

STRIPPING

When a program becomes extremely popular—a talk show, or a personality show with a growing local or national audience following—then it is sold as a strip. Strips have segments, usually one half-hour every day of the week at the same time. *The Martha Stewart Living Show* is an example of stripping; her show runs every day on local channels around the country. If there is a major blockbuster TV hit like *The Cosby Show*, with several seasons of completed show segments, a local station or station group might decide to lock up an important time slot by stripping, or scheduling a segment every night during prime time. This provides continuity, important in the process of securing a major advertiser to sponsor the program.

SELLING AND LICENSING PROGRAMMING

The process of selling or licensing programming to local stations has several recognized methods of transaction, including all cash, barter, or a mix of cash and barter. Few people need an explanation of cash, but, as mentioned earlier, in some of the major auctions where five or more successful seasons are available for syndication, the stakes are very high and growing all the time. For some programs, the package price will soon reach billions of dollars—making some entertainers and producers very wealthy. However, these programs still need marketing to remind viewers of the program offering and their availability, or to remind them of what they may have missed the first time around.

CASH DEALS

When the deal for a license to run a show is all cash, the production company or studio that has developed, produced, and syndicated the show usually provides commercials and print ad slicks at no additional cost to the station. On-air promotions, which run as much as $30–$50,000 for a 30-second commercial plus residual costs, are covered by the production company as a form of co-op advertising. After all, it is just as important to the production company as the station that the program be successful; success means more sales of the program in other markets, as well as the enhanced reputation of the production company. The licensee runs TV spots on its own station(s) and works out a separate barter arrangement with local newspapers. The newspaper gets free advertising spots on the station; in exchange, the newspaper runs strips on their television tune-in page, promoting the local syndicated show, as well as providing some full-page ads at the beginning of a new season. Everyone wins, and very little cash changes hands, except to the original syndicator.

BARTER

In the case of small-market, cash-poor television stations, a programming schedule might be negotiated through a barter arrangement. Barter is based on the station's ability to sell local advertisers for supporting the show. The originator of the program contracts to receive half the income from the advertising time slots, with the local station receiving the balance. However, the owner of the program receives the owner's funds from the first sales. Once the originator has been paid his or her share, the balance goes to the station. In this way, a poor advertising season or selling performance does not jeopardize the producer's possibility of getting paid, and the station has not lost anything except the airtime provided. A combination of cash and barter is usually preferred, even from small markets, so the downside risk is minimized.

NON-COMMERCIALLY DRIVEN BROADCASTING

There is still one small island in the sea of commercial- and subscription-driven content: the Public Broadcasting Service (PBS). However, in the last two decades, PBS channels have come to resemble their competitive network TV counterparts more and more.

PUBLIC BROADCASTING—THE EVOLVING PICTURE

PBS has its roots in the FCC's Sixth Report, issued in 1952. The Sixth Report focused on the allocation of stations in the UHF and VHF frequencies, in an attempt to ensure that all communities would have access to the airwaves—not just the powerhouse networks. At the same time, the FCC also allocated one-tenth of the assigned channels to non-commercial TV. Communities with one or two VHF stations currently in operation automatically won an educational television frequency. This was the beginning of government-supported public television (PT), which led to the organization of PBS in 1969.

The evolution began in the 1980s when Lawrence Grossman became President of PBS. Prior to that, public television was known not only for government-supported, commercial-free broadcasting, but also for an eclectic program mix that varied from station to station. This mix led quite naturally to smaller, though loyal audiences—but loyal as they were, they were untouched by advertising in any way other than the sponsorship companies might provide to certain programs.

Of the four basic types of PBS stations (state, university, school, and community), the community stations became national leaders in the 1970s by contributing to the production of critically acclaimed original series such as the *National Geographic Specials*, *Nova*, and *Evening at the Pops*.[6] Grossman's arrival on the PBS scene marked the arrival of the "core schedule." PBS now began to focus on consistent evening schedules, which were nationally advertised. Furthermore, promotional campaigns led to PBS having a clearer identity and an expanded audience.

With government support dollars eroding, becoming inadequate to the needs of local stations, PBS learned to reach out for viewer support dollars, market by market; some began to take on barely conspicuous advertising.

On the national front, the unity of the PBS platform kicked in as a marketing driving force with several key marketing strategies:

- Signaling value: The use of consistent taglines nationwide, such as: "Public television is made possible by the support of viewers like you."
- Branding: The use of the Hal Riney & Partners agency and the application of a gradually increasing marketing budget. Through the use of press releases, PBS mounted a national branding campaign in the 1990s to reinforce its consistent

---

6.   Stations like WNET in New York, KCET in Los Angeles, WTTW in Chicago, WGBH in Boston, WETA in Washington, and WQED in Pittsburgh.

and educationally entertaining content. PBS logos were consistently positioned beside those of local stations, with taglines such as: "If PBS doesn't do it, who will?"

- Pop-ups: One or two programs a year were chosen to get premier promotional pushes.

- Maintaining and expanding viewership: The addition of support programs that rewarded contributors with program mailers, mugs, cloth bags, tee-shirts, videos, and other tokens of appreciation that signaled product loyalty. External promotions: The introduction of national direct mail, common-carriage advertising in *TV Guide*, public radio advertising, and Web sites to provide additional content.

On the marketing research front, PBS identified the Discovery Channel, Arts & Entertainment (A&E), the History Channel, and the Learning Channel—all supported by commercial advertising, but focused on educational content—as chief competitors. PBS has fought back with quality original programming, including the well-received Ken Burns' series on the Civil War and baseball. Even details such as viewer turn-off during lengthy post-program credits were considered; those credits have been shortened considerably. In short, PBS has rolled up its sleeves and gotten competitive, and continues to do so by emphasizing itself as a leader in technological shifts that include multimedia, HDTV, and the newest trends of education, information, and entertainment.

TV TECHNOLOGY

As with the rest of the world around us, the march of technology is leaving fresh footsteps on familiar places. Our viewing habits—from the perspectives of when we view, how we view, and at what level of quality we receive the content—are changing rapidly as new ways to receive programming appear.

HDTV

HDTV is a television display technology that provides a picture quality similar to 35mm movies with a sound quality equivalent to that of today's CDs. Some television stations have begun transmitting HDTV broadcasts to users on a limited number of channels. HDTV generally uses digital rather than analog signal transmission, although analog transmission is possible, as has been demonstrated in Japan.

HDTV compares with standard-definition television (SDTV) in that it has a higher quality display, with a vertical resolution from 720p[7] to 1080i.[8] This is at a frame rate of 60 frames per second, or twice that of conventional television. Another obvious contrast with conventional television is its wider aspect ratio[9] of 16:9. HDTV has a pixel number range from one to two million, as opposed to SDTV's range of 300,000 to one million. The audio quality of HDTV is Dolby Digital 5.1. For the non-geek reader, this translates to the following: an incredibly clear picture, noticeably different from what you're used to; a "frame" that allows for the entire shot to fit onto the TV screen, instead of needing to crop it; and sound that will make you look like the guy in the classic Maxell audio tape ad—your hair blown straight back from what's coming through the speakers.

For a program to be broadcast in HDTV, the television program must be filmed in the high-definition format. The viewer must have a high-definition television to receive it. Finally, the FCC has assigned channels for HDTV transmissions. Because of the digital nature of the transmission, researchers[10] are experimenting with Internet HDTV. However, the technology is still emerging in the mainstream and the price point for HDTV sets has still not trickled down enough to encourage mass-market usage.

MSN® TV

When Microsoft first bought WebTV Networks for $425 million in August of 1998, the future of this new medium seemed blessed. But, heading into the new millennium, the progress of Web TV—now

---

7. The "p" stands for progressive scaling—each scan includes every line for the complete picture.

8. The "i" stands for interfaced scanning—each scan includes alternate lines for half a picture.

9. The width and height ratio of the screen.

10. For instance, at Stanford and at the University of Washington's Computing and Communications Department.

known as MSN® TV—has been marked by as many steps backward as forward. The big question now is: Can it survive?

Developed in 1995, MSN® TV is a system that enables a user to watch television and, with a push of a button, check the weather on the Internet, examine incoming email, or look up movie listings. MSN® TV can be accessed through a set-top box about the size of a VCR, which attaches to an existing television, utilizing a telephone jack and software. Or, it can be accessed through an existing cable line, as offered by World Gate, @Home, and Media One. In any case, there is a fee for online services of approximately $20 per month, just as with an Internet connection.

However, the receiver/system does not have its own hard drive, so it is unable to run software that might be used normally to process Web stock portfolios (such as Quicken), nor does the system have a disk or CD-ROM drive. Printers can be connected, but the typical methods of storing information obtained from the Internet are not possible. Another hiccup is that from the normal eight to ten feet of TV viewing distance, the letters on the screen from Internet pages and email are often too small to read.

The marketing dilemma of MSN® TV is that it must have advertising to survive, and most major advertisers are not willing to divert resources to a medium with less than 5% the number of AOL's 11 million subscribers. Most digital electronics media experts agree that to survive, MSN® TV needs original and unique applications and programming, the way the initial appearance of Milton Berle jump-started network television so many years ago.

However, the television industry has become increasingly aware of the younger viewer's growing preference for the interactivity of computers versus the passive experience of TV viewing. There is new synergy between network TV and the Internet as both players search for ways to capture the interest—and dollars—of younger, more tech-comfortable viewers. For instance, in November 1999, a Web-cast of *The Drew Carey Show* drew two million viewers, a number that rivals that of some cable TV channels. However, the experience itself was extremely primitive, with slow downloads and often flickering images.

There is also international interest in MSN® TV. British Telecom is working to co-develop a low-cost asymmetric digital subscriber line (ADSL) model with Microsoft, Compaq, and Intel. The company is also working with the Universal ADSL Working Group, which is trying to establish a standard for DSL Lite, a lower cost version of

ADSL technology that can work faster than standard modems and operate through existing copper-based telephone lines. That technology was targeted for release by 2002.

TiVo ™

Building on the technology of the VCR, many consumer electronics manufacturers (e.g., Sony, Panasonic, and Philips) have already released digital network recorders with TiVo service. These recorders are capable of being programmed to record up to 30 hours of television programming. However, with TiVo technology, shows are automatically recorded on a unit's multi-gigabyte hard drive rather than tape. TiVo will search for programs of interest to the viewer and record them. TiVo allows a viewer to watch a recorded program while recording something else. And, in possibly the slickest move of all, TiVo allows the viewer to hit the Pause button, step out of the room, and then resume watching a program at the point he or she left it, even while the program is being broadcast.

TiVo-compatible recorders entered the market at a $300–$500 price point, with expectations of trickling down. The service itself is purchased through TiVo, either online or with a toll-free call. The initial price options were $9.95 a month, or $199 for a lifetime subscription per receiver. The service provides the program information the receiver needs to function, allowing the consumer to set up automatic recordings and receive free software updates.

There are plenty of TiVo marketing tools available to subscribers, such as *TiVolution*, an onscreen magazine, and Network Showcases. TiVo can also combine available local stations into an on-screen programming guide. A viewer can give thumbs-up or thumbs-down to programs he or she likes and tailor viewing to selectively recorded programming. The ultimate marketing pitch for today's custom-service consumer is: "Watch what you want, when you want."

SUMMARY: NETWORK TV AND SYNDICATION

Whether broadcast via the networks, local stations, or MSN®TV, or recorded on VCRs or TiVo, content remains king. Marketers continue to seek out programming that will deliver loyal audiences in the largest numbers available, ensuring eyes on the prize: the commercial message. Therefore, the mass reach of traditional broadcast-ing still offers the quickest path to the most viewers. New technology that allows commercials to be bypassed may someday have a much larger impact on the traditional forms of broadcast advertising—once the technology is affordable and functional—but for the time being, commercial messages are alive and well in TV land. If anything, such technology will only drive the marketer's message further into the actual content, through product placement.

RADIO

Radio is alive and well on the national marketing scene, although it certainly has gone through its changes since the days of *The Shadow* and FDR's *Fireside Chats*. While network radio still exists, a trend toward niche audiences has virtually eliminated mass market-ing. Today's radio programming is often syndicated or sent out to hundreds—if not thousands—of radio channels around the country, focused on listening audiences interested in very specific types of programming, such as country music, rock, or news/talk.

DON'T TOUCH THAT DIAL:
THE BASICS OF RADIO MARKETING

Regardless of the type of programming, the mechanics of mar-keting a radio station are fairly standard, and not dissimilar to the marketing of a TV station. In fact, today's radio marketer has the same kind of rating information in his or her toolbox as his or her not-so-distant TV relative.

The marketing manager or promotion director at a radio station is responsible for some of the traditional marketing mechanics as they fit this medium—for instance, establishing market position. An example would be establishing an image-oriented market position by heavily promoting commercial-free time blocks. The station may actually have more commercials than other stations, but the lis-tener's perception is what he or she has been repeatedly told.

Today's radio marketer is also responsible for organizing and implementing event-driven marketing opportunities and other non-traditional revenue sources (NRS). In short, the marketer's job is to gain new listeners, keep regular listeners tuned in, recycle the audience (for instance, by mentioning upcoming weather reports, road conditions, or features of interest to the listeners), and run promotions that give advertisers motivation to buy airtime.

Promotion can be community events, call-in contests, publicity, word-of-mouth campaigns, on-site broadcasts at events, giveaways (CDs, tee-shirts, mugs, and bumper stickers), and cross-promotion between daytime and evening audiences as well as between commonly owned (sister) stations. A recycling strategy means generating more listeners for a specific time slot from those already loyal to another of the station's time slots.

The object of promotion is to increase the overall time spent listening (TSL). Each station has a cumulative rating (cume), to which it can best add by gaining new listeners. A standard radio industry measuring tool is that of average quarter-hour ratings (AQH). How this works, for instance, is that stations with a high cume rating but a low AQH rating because of short TSLs need to work to keep listeners from shifting away as quickly as they have been.

In addition to the merchandising, contests, giveaways, buying spots on other media forms, on-air promotions, and event marketing, a station desperate to grow its listenership may resort to more expensive direct marketing and telemarketing techniques, using both the traditional telephone method as well as email.

The larger story in radio, from a marketing perspective, is who is listening to what, and how are they receiving the medium.

AUDIO DIVERSITY

The big change in today's radio is the evolution to niche marketing. According to the monthly report issued by the FCC, there are well over 12,500 radio stations in America,[11] compared with over 44,000 radio stations worldwide.[12]

But the mass marketing capabilities of such stations has been fragmented by the focused radio formats of the stations in the U.S.

---

11. The FCC numbers were current as of September 30, 1999 (see also: National Association of Broadcasters at *www.nab.org*).

12. The National Association of Broadcasters' Information Resource Center has compiled this number using the *CIA World Factbook* as its primary source.

The Radio Advertising Bureau's tracking of 10,394 of these commercial radio stations in America as of 1998[13] indicates the niche breakdown of U.S. radio stations, AM and FM, shown in Table 4–1.

TABLE 4-1   Commercial Radio Stations in America, by Format, as of 1998.

FORMAT—# OF STATIONS	FORMAT—# OF STATIONS
Country—2386	Classic Hits—192
News/Talk/Business—1131	Urban R & B—171
Adult Contemporary (AC)—844	Contemporary Christian—164
Oldies—799	New Rock, Modern Rock—145
Adult Standards—561	Urban AC—127
Spanish—493	Alternative Rock—96
Contemporary Hit Radio (CHR)—379	Jazz—88
Soft AC—368	Modern AC—79
Religion (Teaching, Music)—356	Ethnic—77
Classic Rock—282	R & B Oldies—56
Adult Hits, Hot AC—28	Gospel—45
Southern Gospel—273	Variety—43
Rock—266	Classical, Fine Arts—40
Sports—251	Easy Listening—39
Black Gospel—238	Children's—37

The listeners of the 2300+ country and western music stations are faithful fans. But, before giving country music the outright crown for most radio stations, consider that some of the aforementioned categories can be combined into broader groups, including rock and religious stations.

---

13. Radio Advertising Bureau (*www.rab.com*).

IDENTIFYING TARGET NICHES

The proliferation of niche radio has had a decided impact on the once-robust practice of mass marketing. This raises the obvious issue of how to identify and reach today's more diversified target markets. Godfrey and Ashley Herweg, in their book *FutureSell: Radio's Niche Marketing Revolution*, discuss several tactics appropriate to researching and identifying target markets.[14] For radio stations to have better relations with advertisers in an era of shrinking ad budgets and increasing means of advertising, the book makes a strong argument that mass marketing techniques are dead, and that today's success story is built on better information and the implementation of that data.

Among the techniques they encourage are:

- Know your audience: Supplement rating information with surveys by mail, by phone, and through focus groups.
- Listen and analyze: Seek to establish a more realistic picture of a station's audience (e.g., more accurate age, interest, and income ranges), and establish the what, when, how, and why listeners tune in to a station.
- Use better data: Utilize acquired data to adjust programming and skew, to pitch accurate and documented information to advertisers, and to copyright ads designed to best use the station's strength.
- Partner up: Seek effective partnerships with ad agencies and dedicated advertisers—for example, have on-site promotions, seek survey information, and offer specials at bookstores, car dealerships, or at any other advertiser that can provide a two-way marketing advantage.

For advertisers, following these steps may mean that the job is easier if you're selling Coca-Cola or pickup trucks (big with that big country number), but the going gets tougher with products that must span across several niche types.

CASE IN POINT: AMERICANA RADIO

"Americana" radio stations offer an intriguing case in point on the subject of spanning niches. Americana stations are those that

---

14.   Herweg, Godfrey W. and Ashley Page Herweg, *FutureSell: Radio's Niche Marketing Revolution* (Boston: Focal Press, 1997).

offer a mix of alternative country music, often showcasing regional or emerging talent. Of the over 2300+ country radio stations hitting the airways daily, at least 91 qualify for the Americana label. Three of the better-known examples are: KFAN (Fredricksburg, TX), KPIG (Monterey, CA), and KHYI (North Dallas, TX). The actual music mix may vary from one Americana station to another—thereby grabbing different demographic groups station-by-station—but each of the stations reflects the cadence of their geographic region.

Gavin,[15] a radio trade magazine, describes four sub-groups within this particular niche:

- Older country stations, with up to a 30% mix of the newer alternative sounds.
- Non-commercial stations, usually college-oriented or listener-supported, featuring an eclectic mix that may lean toward insurgent country sounds such as Steve Earle.
- Outright Americana stations, like KNBT (New Braunfels, TX).
- Adult Album Alternative (AAA)/Americana mixes—AAA sounds with varied mixes, usually non-commercial radio.

This quick breakdown of the Americana audience provides an intriguing snapshot of the types of listeners tuning into the commercial messages offered. One of the chief marketing thrusts of Americana radio stations remains word of mouth. Performers showcased on the stations as well as faithful fans rigorously promote the stations; advertisers on these stations could very well benefit from the halo effect. Americana stations have been around since the 1970s, but have gained a lot of their marketing momentum through Internet radio.

THE BEAT GOES ON...AND ON

In the early days, individual listeners sat in attics, headphones pressed to their ears, searching for faint signals from primitive stations. A few decades later, as America took to the highway, late-night drivers were treated to the occasional phenomena of stations from thousands of miles away suddenly coming across loud and clear. However, radio was a relatively geographically bounded medium; the

---

15. Also available on the Internet at *www.gavin.com*.

reach of radio's commercial messages depended solely on a station's broadcasting power.

Radio has found an important ally in the emerging technologies of the new millennium. Today, listeners around the globe can tune into the content delivered from stations in the tiniest markets, exploding the reach of this warhorse of a marketing medium. Chief among these allies are Internet radio, radio on TV, and satellite radio.

INTERNET RADIO

While Web TV may still be facing its challenges, radio has benefited tremendously from the new synergy between the Internet and an audience hungry for content. Just as e-retailers like Amazon.com have opened the doors for listing an array of CDs not found in every store, Internet radio links provide radio stations with a listener base far outside the reach of their traditional broadcasting capability, and far beyond their geographic boundaries. Internet radio now supplies a listening audience that is truly global.

FROM AIRWAVES TO I-WAVES

Altavista.com lists connections with over 1,500 Internet radio stations; Web sites like Kerbango.com offer numerous others. One of the biggest Web resources for Internet radio, Broadcast.com (with its own host of stations and tracking 660,000 hits per day), merged with Yahoo.com for an even greater presence. There are, at this writing, somewhere between 1,800 and 2,000 Internet radio stations, with the figure increasing rapidly enough to make tracking difficult—although Nielsen will be among the leaders in this effort. This fast-growing part of radio represents the realized potential of marketing media-mix.

Internet radio has some obvious advantages: lighter demands on advertising dollars for operation and no current FCC regulation. For those with sophisticated computer speaker systems and a dedicated phone line, the sound is digitally clean. But to date, this isn't the kind of radio a user can pack along for use at the beach—nor do Internet radio stations play well on home systems with normal speakers or connections that aren't high-speed enough to avoid normal broadband traffic jams on the information superhighway. Buffers can also cause signals to stutter, and servers can go down.

The driving force in Internet radio is an eclectic offering available to listeners who, in mass, have shown themselves ready to surf to sounds on the Internet. Stations like Skyjazz.com round out offerings with featured performers, background information, and opportunities to purchase CDs. This is an evolving technology likely to work out its own wrinkles and become an additional facet of the growing excitement about the Web.

I-MARKETING

The chief marketing and promotional challenge for these Internet radio stations is to not get lost in the shuffle. The same marketing issues apply to them as to other e-business ventures: linking to get traffic, using meta-tags[16] to better facilitate searches, using cross-media promotions within existing traditional airwave stations and through external promotion, and capturing the always hard-to-measure word-of-mouth advertising that has proven so vital to the explosive presence of other Internet music sites such as Napster and MP3.

RADIO ON TV

Over 100 radio stations are currently making their way into households today through an entirely different conduit— cable. Among the benefits are: clear, static-free, commercial-free, digital-quality sound on today's higher quality home entertainment systems; the name of the artist, label, and song scrolling on the TV screen; and focused listening selections from music channels specializing in jazz, rock, country, alternative country, Tejano, salsa, metal, classics, oldies, and many more. Each channel offers music not often available on commercial radio stations. This music is sometimes packaged as a unique program.

Music Choice of Horsham, PA is the outsourcer to which Time Warner, PrimeStar, and DIRECTV subscribe. In fact, Music Choice reaches 13 million households through 469 cable systems. It also features chat rooms, where fans of like music tastes can discuss their common interest, as well as get a chance to download music or buy CDs through CDNow, the company's retail partner.

---

16. Meta-tags are hidden HTML labels buried in index pages of Web sites to clearly identify sites to Internet search engines.

SATELLITE RADIO

Satellite radio is an emergent broadcast medium expected to do well early in the new millennium. Driven by subscriptions of just under $10 per month, this format will depend on radios equipped to receive signals through an antenna dish no bigger than a half-dollar. CD Radio/Sirius and XM Radio are two of the companies launched in 2001, with an initial offering of 50 music stations and 50 news/talk stations.

CD Radio found an important partner in The Ford Motor Company, which began releasing vehicles offering reception of the medium in 2001, including the Ford, Lincoln, Mercury, Mazda, Aston-Martin, Volvo, and Jaguar lines. Meanwhile, GM is installing XM Radio-receptive radios, putting it in a support group that includes DIRECTV and Clear Channel Communications. Retail electronics stores such as Best Buy and Circuit City offer the radios for installation in cars already on the road.

Programming offered on XM Radio includes CNN, BBC World Service, C-Span, BET, Radio One (which offers six African-American channels), Bloomberg News Radio, Salem Broadcasting (the number-one Christian broadcaster), and Hispanic Broadcast Corporation.

CD Radio plans to be commercial-free, while XM Radio will have a limited amount of advertising. Initial market projections indicated interest by up to 50 million people in this new technology. One possible glitch: the chance that satellite radio will disrupt existing cell phone traffic. Research offers no conclusions on this subject at this time.

SUMMARY: RADIO

The traditional medium of radio broadcasting, often counted down as a marketing medium but never out, has gone from a mass to a minor market over the last century. However, the new technology of the Internet, along with cable and dish, has opened the door for radio once again. Combined with this new ability to offer mass reach, radio's continued focus on niche markets offers marketers new ways to reach target-specific audiences—not unlike cable TV, whose ever-spinning web of niches will be discussed in the next chapter.

FOR FURTHER READING

BOOKS

1. Blumenthal, Howard J. and Oliver R. Goodenough, *This Business of Television* (New York, NY: Watson-Guptill, 1998).

2. Eastman, Susan Tyler, Douglas A. Ferguson, and Robert A. Klein, Eds., *Promotion and Marketing for Broadcasting and Cable, 3/E* (Boston, MA: Focus Press, 1999).

3. Herweg, Godfrey W. and Ashley Page Herweg, *Futuresell: Radio's Niche Marketing Revolution* (Boston, MA: Focus Press, 1997).

4. Litwak, Mark, *Dealmaking in the Film & Television Industry: From Negotiations to Final Contracts* (Los Angeles, CA: Silman-James, 1994).

5. Parsons, Patrick R., Robert Frieden, and Rob Frieden, *The Cable and Satellite Television Industries* (Boston, MA: Allyn & Bacon, 1997).

6. Resnik, Gail and Scott Trost, *All You Need to Know About the Movie and TV Business* (New York, NY: Fireside, 1996).

7. Walker, James R. and Douglas A. Ferguson, *The Broadcast Television Industry* (Boston, MA: Allyn & Bacon, 1997).

MAGAZINES TO DEVOUR

1. *Broadcast & Cable*

2. *Electronic Media*

3. *Entertainment Weekly*

4. *TV Guide*

5

CABLE TELEVISION AND DIRECT BROADCAST SATELLITE: BASIC, PREMIUM, AND PAY-PER-VIEW

OVERVIEW

First there was local reach (with the range, say, of an old old-time crystal radio); then there was mass-market reach, as in network broadcasts; and more recently came niche reach, the specialty of multichannel television, including cable TV (CATV), DBS, and multichannel multipoint distribution service (MMDS).[1]

---

1. MMDS is a form of wireless cable service that transmits signals at high frequencies, and is often called "wireless cable." With analog signals (in the manner of traditional antenna television), MMDS can handle 33 channels of television. When the signal is compressed and sent as a digital signal, it can send as many as 300 channels.

While the basic package of channels includes the broadcast networks, local O&O channels, market affiliates, and the large number of independents mostly available in large metropolitan cities, these products differ from network television chiefly in that they are subscription-based. Yet, because of the variety of programming they offer, as well as the improved picture and sound quality in antenna-poor reception areas, they represent one of the highest growth entertainment areas in the U.S.

As recently as 1980, CATV and DBS were barely worth Nielsen's time to track. But, they now command 40% of all viewing shares, and at times, the combined cable channels gain more viewing shares than the combined major network channels. It is estimated that three out of four homes in America now receive some form of multichannel television.

Viewer subscriptions to these services generate significant revenues for networks and service providers nationwide. However, the ad-supported portion of multichannel TV is proving it can generate significant advertising revenues as well—most interesting when you consider the fact that this segment of the industry was once thought of as "commercial-free" TV.

Today, multichannel TV networks are not only often ad-supported, but are among the fastest growing advertising media in the U.S. According to the Cable Television Advertising Bureau (*www.cabletvadbureau.com*), the advertising on cable channels has grown from $58 million in annual ad revenues in 1980 to $11.2 billion by 1999—not bad for something that grew out of sheer frustration.

THE BASICS OF BASIC CABLE

Back before there were fiber-optic cables crisscrossing the mountains and plains of America, the average TV viewer depended on roof-mounted antennas to receive signals from broadcasters. Sometimes they worked, and sometimes, due to any number of obstructions between the antenna and the signal, they didn't. In the late 1940s–early 1950s, in the tradition of can-do inventing, a diverse group of what might now be called techno-geeks—engineers and entrepreneurs—began experimenting with running cable from their TVs directly to towers erected in their areas.

From these seat-of-the-pants beginnings, an industry was born, leading to organized community approaches to the challenge, which came to be known as Community Antenna Television (CATV). Local entrepreneurs (sometimes local appliance retailers, seeing an opportunity to increase television sales) organized consortiums, erected towers, ran cables, signed up new housing developments as customers, beat the drums, blew the horns, and built businesses that eventually made many of them millionaires many times over when they sold out to the big dogs.

The FCC had no jurisdiction over these local CATV systems. The city or town granted the franchise to go through public or private property and gain access to the homes of prospective subscribers. In return for the franchise, the cable operators made a commitment to maintain the lines, paid a franchise fee in lieu of taxes on the start-up, and provided public access channels for local news and town meetings. The early systems were also expected to provide a conduit for anyone who had the time and inclination to go to the broadcasting office and speak about issues. The early take on CATV was that it was an electronic soapbox and no threat to the networks. The product itself became known as "basic cable," a term still in use by today's mega-operators.

EARLY CABLE MARKETING

For a single subscription fee, the early basic cable systems promised perfect reception and good programming on a variety of channels. The early marketing was simple and rudimentary. When a "new build," as it was called, announced to a community that cable was available, sign-ups began almost immediately. In traditional marketing terms, preliminary marketing was an appeal to the early adopters, who had the desire to be among the first in their community to have this new entertainment provider—whether they needed it or not. As usual, these trailblazers set the tone for the later adopters, who usually follow rather than lead the bandwagon.

As the demand for cable grew, the original entrepreneurs either sold out to larger organizations or grew their businesses into the mega-operations that rule the cable landscape today. Time Warner, TCI, Cablevision, Comcast, Cox Communications—all of these are known as multiple-system operators (MSOs), each of which control cable TV in relatively specific markets. There is little or no competition in most market areas. As these MSOs have invested more money in the technology and distribution of cable, their need and desire to generate more revenue has increased. To meet these goals, the MSOs must have more (and arguably better) programming than the networks to attract subscribers.

CABLE: CONTENT AND CONDUIT

The world of cable television can best be described in terms of content and conduit. On the conduit side are the cable operators. The operator is usually the enterprise that owns the hardware. Operators own franchises to broadcast, invest, and own the cable wire, the head-end from where the signal is sent. They also have the responsibility for installing the set-top boxes and maintaining the connection—the conduit—to the programs.

The programmers are the actual niche networks handling licensing or producing original content directed at their respective audiences. The various channels they provide to the operator represent genres of entertainment similar to the genres in the music, film and publishing sectors. There are vertical channels like CNN—all news all the time—and ESPN where sports are the primary menu. Horizontal channels like A&E, Bravo, and TBS provide a diversity of programming that includes movies, documentaries, panels, industry-specific news, talk shows, and other formats.

THE CRAWL TO THE HERE AND NOW

Marketers of early cable faced the challenge of a skeptical consumer base—certainly not unique to this industry. Some examples of the thoughts running through the minds of potential customers included:

- "You have to be crazy to pay $10 per month to watch free TV with a cable." —Los Angeles, 1975
- "No one will watch pornography, even soft core at home on television."—*Playboy* reader, 1985
- "$30 a month for cable is enough, they are raising the rates and now they want to charge $3.95 for a movie without commercials. I can wait to see it in my neighborhood theater, or I will order HBO." —Chicago, 1992
- "500 channels. I can't figure out what to watch with 65 channels." —Miami, 1995

How did the industry overcome these objections and expand at the rate it has? To put the issue simply: it developed new and original material.

Basic cable channels all found ways to lure the consumer. Made-for-TV movies found a real home in multichannel systems, where movies could be viewed in an uninterrupted fashion. Then there were comedy specials, featuring stand-up comics in full half-hour and hour shows. Nickelodeon came up with original cartoons, Discovery Channel had first-run, original nature programs, and A&E featured original dramas as well as humor. Soon, the content on multichannel TV was meeting and exceeding the quality broadcast by the networks, driving subscription campaigns for basic cable. Next, operators focused on extended revenue streams in the form of premium and pay-per-view channels.

PREMIUM CABLE CHANNELS

As movie tickets continued to climb in price—along with the price of popcorn, soft drinks, babysitters, and transportation/parking—urban and suburban movie buffs became intrigued by a new offering from their local cable provider, a channel called HBO. Initially marketed as "All movies, all the time, for the whole family," HBO advertising stressed cost savings and family togetherness. This approach worked fine with everyone but teenagers, who saw the movie theater as a place to get away from the watchful eyes of parents. Very few potential subscribers could deny the cost savings: one monthly subscription fee for all the movies their eyeballs could absorb.

Once again, one group led the charge to sign up. This group was even more selective than typical first adopters, since there was an additional monthly fee and the only programming offered was first-run movies, shown at least three or more months after they had completed their run in theaters. This form of cable channel was first called pay-TV, but changed to "premium" cable to avoid confusion with the new technology providing pay-per-view. These customers profiled as film buffs or movie addicts, financially capable of paying the extra fee, and sold on the combination of value and convenience.

Today's cable packages offer a plethora of premium viewing, with several choices of all-movie channels, as well as selected children's channels offered by most cable operators, either individually or as a package for a discounted fee. These include HBO, HBO2, HBO3, Showtime 1, Showtime 2, Cinemax, Disney, Encore, Starz, The Movie Channel, Sundance, and the Independent Film Channel (IFC). In some markets, the two "arts" movie channels, Sundance and IFC, are offered as premium channels because of the often violent or sexual nature of the movies. Since most newspapers do not carry listings for adult entertainment cable, the Playboy Channel and Spice are marketed discretely, through adult entertainment magazines, or to those viewing pay-per-view soft porn films in hotels.

PAY-PER-VIEW

Pay-per-view (PPV) movies were originally designed for the hospitality industry: to entertain a tired business executive, the family of five whose beach trip was ruined by rain, or the clandestine-affair couple looking for a little titillation in the form of soft porn. All of this continues to be made possible through Screenvision, the company licensing and distributing movies-on-demand. Screenvision's product generates income (especially the soft porn, which costs more to view) for the motel/hotel owner, the video company, and the studio; however, the studio garners the smallest share.

When it came to direct-to-consumer distribution, studios and distributors—the owners of filmed content—were not content to be in the backseat profit-wise. Having discovered high profits in alternative distribution methods, including home video entertainment rentals and sell-through, these entities were quick to take control of the first-run PPV business when it debuted on cable. Since they were not willing to lose the chance to enhance their own profitability, the content providers began to make deals directly with the cable operators, who were already connected to consumers with basic cable. Cable operators were enthusiastic; they envisioned an easy sale of the occasional PPV option to 65 million basic cable TV households. PPV was also offered as an exciting reason to connect to cable for those not yet subscribing, and was initially offered as a promotional benefit.

To this day, the "easy sale" has not quite come of age. The major competition to cable PPV movies has been the home video retailer. The major chains created arrangements with the movie studios, guaranteeing in-stock, in-depth on all new and major blockbuster titles, free home delivery and pick-up, in-store snacks to-go, and huge lists of categorized titles. The chains stopped relying on the "If you build it, they will come" syndrome, and spent millions of dollars on TV advertising, newspaper retail co-op ads, and promotions of a very generous nature, including sweepstakes, gift cards, and five-day rentals for a one-night price. These factors had a decided impact on the success of PPV sales.

The major weakness of the PPV movie offering is that the films are generally shown on the half-hour, and once started, run until finished. With encryption protection disallowing copying of the film, and beverage, bathroom, or phone call breaks as an interruption, the PPV movie is not very user-friendly. In addition, marketing by the content provider for PPV is relatively light and discreet, so as not to endanger relationships with the home video retailers—who account for nearly two-and-one-half times the revenue of theater box office receipts. It is also often difficult to round up members of the family and friends to efficiently watch a PPV film together.

All in all, the "golden goose" of PPV has laid an egg of a non-golden variety. What has redeemed PPV and provided a profitable use of the otherwise empty channels on the cable operator's box are sports. The best boxing matches, with sold-out venue audiences buying high-priced tickets, enable cable programmers to sell $35 front-row seats to millions of fight fans. These "seats" are purchased by consumers as well as by owners of sports bars and pubs, who feature the events to attract diners and drinkers. The offering now extends to all forms of sports and sport specials.

The PPV movie opportunity is awaiting near-video on-demand (NVOD), which will allow the viewer to start a film at any time, pause, return, and watch in snippets when interrupted by other events. This technology is now available; it will be interesting to see how the industry rolls it out, including a marketing campaign to build consumer awareness.

THE GROWTH OF THE INDUSTRY

Once basic cable became a staple of the American household, and premium channels and PPV had their hooks into viewing habits, the industry began to take off on a revenue skyrocket. As with most growth industries, there were entrepreneurs who took advantage of the opportunity—and organizations and individuals who took advantage of the customer—or at least, so some customers thought. As is typical in such situations, the government stepped in.

TELECOMMUNICATIONS ACT OF 1996

Prior to 1996, the FCC felt restrictions on broadcast station ownership would provide greater competition, and therefore a greater diversity of voices and programming choice. This was determined to be in the best interests of the public and suggested the possibility of an increase in the quality of entertainment offered. The Telecommunications Act of 1996[2] was the first update to telecommunications law in 62 years—amazing given the rapidity of change within the industry. The implications to the cable and satellite TV arenas were significant.

With the passage of the Act, the networks were able to expand their O&O stations from coverage of 25% of U.S. households to 35%. This 10% increase encouraged some consolidation and motivated significant station sales. The changes wrought by the Act included allowing for multiple radio station ownership in a market and cross-ownership of several media in one market, such as newspapers, radio, and TV stations.

Significant to this discussion of cable, the Telecommunications Act eliminated the long-standing restriction on network ownership of cable television systems. This opened the door for media companies with multiple stations to blanket a local audience on behalf of their advertisers with efficient cost-per-thousand media planning offers. Media companies could now provide both in-depth coverage of a local audience and synergy between their properties, making for enormous competitive clout.

Continued support of the first amendment's "Freedom of Speech" enabled the cable industry to enjoy enormous freedom in selection of content, as well as adding services that would be governed by free-market competition. By providing a strong force for deregulation, the Act also set the groundwork for the combination of cable operators and Internet suppliers. Companies could now plan the marketing and sale of converging media vehicles.

Furthermore, the Act allowed for interactive programming and the ability of cable and telephone companies to offer voice and video transmission on the same wire. It also required any sexually explicit service to be scrambled to prevent reception by non-subscribers, but allowed this content to be available between 10 p.m. and 6 a.m. Most important to the cable companies, the Act eliminated any control over the rates for service tiers, packages or single-channel services, or discounted rates for multiple dwelling units, as long as it was not construed as predatory pricing designed to push all other competi-

---

2.   A complete copy of the law can be downloaded in Adobe PDF format at the Federal Communications Commission's Web site (*www.fcc.gov*).

tors out of the market—this, in an era of rate regulation of public utilities.

While some subscribers may disagree with the MSOs' ability to rein themselves in when it comes to monthly fees, one case did prove the public's ability to inform the operators who was boss when it came to content offering.

CASE IN POINT: CAN A THREE-FINGERED MOUSE ARM-WRESTLE?

One of the most telling stories in cable TV programming occurred when Time Warner decided to flex its muscles. Unfortunately, it decided that the subject of said muscle-flexing would be Disney—not exactly the 98-pound weakling of the entertainment world. The result was the perfect demonstration of cable operator versus cable programmer at the "Big Brand" level.[3]

The principles in this public laundering of power plays were Robert Iger, President of Disney, Michael Eisner, Chairman of Disney, Gerald Levin, Chairman of Time Warner, Joseph Collins, Chairman of Time Warner Cable, and Richard Parsons, President of Time Warner. By extension, other participants in the struggle became Steve Case, Chairman of AOL, and Orrin Hatch, Chairman of the Senate Judiciary Committee.

Like many a brawl, there was bad blood that led up to the incident. Time Warner, after all, owned a stable of cartoon characters (including Bugs Bunny, Elmer Fudd, Sylvester, and Tweetie Bird) in direct competition with the likes of Mickey Mouse, Donald Duck, and Goofy. Time Warner also owned the Six Flags theme parks, direct competitors to Disneyland and Walt Disney World. Time Warner had even gone so far as to negatively advertise against Disney with a campaign showing a dog behind a chain-link fence labeled "Disneyland."

Negotiations between Time Warner (cable operator) and Disney (cable programmer) had broken down just prior to the May 2000 sweeps period. What had started out as routine negotiations for the renewal of the Disney-owned ABC network turned argumentative, then ugly. With the sweeps timing as a pressure point, Time Warner

---

3.   For much more detail, see Stewart, James B., "Mousetrap: What Time Warner didn't consider when it unplugged Disney," *The New Yorker*, July 31, 2000.

wanted more money from Disney; Disney wanted Time Warner to carry SoapNet, a soap opera channel, in addition to the 12 Disney-owned stations already carried by Time Warner (including ESPN and The Disney Channel). When negotiations broke down, Iger had ABC lawyers write to Time Warner, asking for an extension of an April 30 deadline. Instead of an extension, Time Warner cut off transmission of ABC. Viewers tuning in to watch ABC saw only a message that read: "Disney has taken ABC away from you."

Disney, never one to leave the gauntlet lie, countered with a test battle in Houston, where they took out full-page advertisements in the *Houston Chronicle*, warning that cable subscribers were at risk of losing ABC in the area. Disney employee Preston Padden even took the case to the mayor and newspaper editorial boards. In a grand expletive-deleted gesture, Disney then offered free satellite dishes to the Houston public, giving away 18,000 vouchers for them in three weeks.

The battle now turned even uglier for Time Warner. The still-pending merger between Time Warner and AOL took a hit when Orrin Hatch wrote to the Federal Trade Commission (FTC), expressing concern over Time Warner's ability to restrict consumer choice to gain market leverage. Time Warner, in this action with Disney, appeared to be running afoul of the Cable Act of 1992, which provides for broadcasting consent agreements, rates, and a willingness on the part of cable systems to accommodate new channels. Faced with tremendous pressure about its monopolistic powers—and a huge outcry from subscribers—Time Warner's President, Richard Parsons, eventually acted as diplomat. With Levin's blessing, Parsons met with Iger to arrange an extension, and subsequently a new agreement.

But the damage had been done. In hindsight, Time Warner learned that its customers didn't care about legal issues—but they did care about *Who Wants to be a Millionaire*, among other ABC shows. Furthermore, the battle awakened both the public and FTC to the peril of the power cable companies have over television. Time Warner may not have heard the last of this issue—proving once again that it is important to know when one's reach may exceed one's grasp.

CABLE'S MARKETING ADVANTAGE:
REACH AND SEGMENTATION

And speaking of reach...

The heart of cable marketing is its reach and ability to cozy into niche markets. Before we describe the channels by category and examine their marketing philosophy, consider the range of coverage provided. Cable offers advertisers the opportunity to reach over 280 million men, women, and children in about 100 million television households. Once seen as an exclusively mass audience with a singular mentality and a plain-vanilla entertainment orientation, cable channels deliver advertisers a diversity of age, race, religion, country of origin, intellectual leanings, and genre of entertainment. In terms of general categories, cable offers a doorway into some very specific and desirable markets:

- The executive or family that has a strong interest in the financial markets, managing their own portfolios, or staying ahead of the vast quantity of business news has a choice of CNBC, CNNfn, MSNBC, and Bloomberg via DIRECTV. In addition, each of these channels offers constant connectivity through their own Web sites and email streaming to hard-core viewers.

- Women are at least 50% of the U.S. workforce and are major decision-makers in the purchase of new homes, cars, family market-basket products, and clothing. While they are certainly a part of the audience watching any of the general-interest cable channels, they will also be found viewing the Food Network, Lifetime, Better Home and Gardens, and the Romance Channel.

- Teenagers, who form an audience with significant discretionary time and disposable income, are drawn to MTV, VH1, Nick at Night, and the various movie channels. All are strong platforms for the 16- to 25-year-old demographic, with Comedy Central expanding the upper end to 35+ years of age with some of the more sophisticated and graphic language programs.

- While broadcast television has an obligation required by law to provide a certain amount of educational programming for children, basic cable provides the Cartoon Network, Animal Planet, Discovery, Fox Family, and Nickelodeon. Premium cable provides The Disney Channel for an extra charge.

- Adults from ages 25–45 who are interested in quality entertainment and entertainment with an edge are drawn to A&E. A&E was one of the first cable channels to recognize that the consumer who watched the once government-supported PBS stations would be pleased to have advertising commercials pay for quality programming.

- If you want to reach males 18–49—or almost anyone with a sports interest—advertise on ESPN. Clearly one of the very valuable properties Disney obtained in the acquisition of ABC, ESPN has been one of the most widely watched basic channels and a leader among sports channels in general. Others have followed in ESPN's financially rewarding footsteps, including the Golf Channel, Fox Sports, Madison Square Garden Network, and Sports Channel from the Rainbow Programming division of Cablevision.

MINORITY REACH

One of the defining characteristics of cable television is that it can attract and appeal to the ethnic and minority segments of television-viewing households. The Hispanic and African-American populations represent two specific focus points for the cable industry:

- Hispanics, one of the fastest growing populations in the U.S., will soon represent one-third of all television viewers. Hispanics have an acknowledged high interest in entertainment. Many family members speak predominantly Spanish, and, taken as a whole, the national demographic of Hispanics has a significant gross disposable income as well as a household budget in the billions-of-dollars range. The population growth is selectively in major metropolitan areas from parts of Texas, to California, Florida, and New York. Univision and SIN networks provide quality programming from Mexico, Latin America, and Spain. These networks use Spanish-language newspapers, magazines, and public transportation posters to identify Spanish soap opera stars and historical documentaries for their countries of origin.

- Robert Johnson launched his dream in 1980 with a cable station dedicated to entertainment skewed to an African-American audience: BET. By the year 2000, the station was reaching 60 million total households in the U.S. and had twice been ranked by *Forbes* among "America's best small companies." The April 22, 2000 issue of *Billboard* was dedicated to the network's 20th anniversary. Why would a music magazine honor a cable TV network? As one record label put it, because BET brought "vision to our music."[4]

What are the implications for marketers in attempting to reach ethnic and minority segments? Understanding the slang or language is a necessity, as it is in any global marketing. Additionally, the use of obviously ethnic and minority actors and actresses or distinctive voiceovers in radio, television commercials, and print advertising is the difference between success and embarrassing failure.

More and more communication companies have developed specialty advertising and public relations agencies whose management and staff are from minority groups, speak the language, and understand the mores and culture of these valuable audience segments. Young & Rubicam (Y&R), now part of a global communications company based in England, has two such specialty units. The Bravo group works only on Hispanic advertising to run in targeted media; they educate their non-Hispanic advertisers eager to reach these markets about the difference between Mexican, Cuban, Puerto Rican, and other sub-segmented forms of the Spanish culture. Chang and Lee, another Y&R unit, specializes in advertising to various Asian audiences on cable channels that reach Chinese, Japanese, Korean, and other important national groups.

CASE IN POINT: VIACOM TAKES THE BET

The success of minority-focused cable channels did not go unnoticed by the Big Brands. Within months after BET's anniversary celebration, it became clear the network was about to change ownership. The announcement that Viacom—the third largest media and entertainment conglomerate—had plans to purchase BET and turn it into a powerhouse brand was met with mixed reviews. The primary concern was a backlash from BET viewers, given that the largest African-American owned and operated media company was about to be acquired by a predominantly white company.

In acquiring BET, Viacom saw an opportunity to provide proven marketing success in the ethnic audience sector and expand BET's distribution. The marketing synergy and understanding of this demographic were based on current success within the various operations at Viacom. CBS had the highest ratings of any network in

---

4.   Interscope/Geffen/A&M Records ad, BET insert, *Billboard*, April 22, 2000.

black households, UPN had an entire evening of black-themed shows, and Showtime had made a commitment to African-American programming.

Viacom, with many cable programmers under its umbrella, could provide clout in marketing BET to the MSOs and independent cable operators in ethnic communities. It also provided the resources needed to develop quality programming for a rapidly growing middle- and upper-class African-American community. The advantage of Viacom, for BET's consumer marketing, was the use of its varied media ownership, including billboards, radio stations, broadcast networks, and other cable programmers.

The bottom line in the Viacom/BET story is this: African-Americans represent 13% of the U.S. population, but it is reported[5] that only 1% of advertising spending targets these customers. Viacom saw a tremendous opportunity to reach an underserved market, while balancing existing synergy within all its brand units—an excellent long-term strategy.

ALL THE RIGHT MOVES

Strategy is an important element of the cable industry. With so many niches to service, operators and programmers alike find themselves in a constant chess game. Part of the game includes a classic marketing technique: brand extension.

There are several examples of this maneuver in the cable industry. For example, A&E created *Biography*, an internally developed product directed at a segment of the basic network audience. From research of the unique interests of their viewer constituency and the acquisition of book club lists, A&E identified an enormous population of history buffs. This led them to the next successful brand extension, the History Channel. Now they could target programming directly at consumers who purchased war films, played at war games, were in the military, retired from the military, or simply fascinated by the activities of the warring nations captured on black-and-white documentary footage, or simulated in docu-drama style. It also presented an opportunity to cross-promote these new channels on the mother channel, A&E.

Bravo focused on a menu similar to A&E, but added town meeting discussions with actors and actresses in their Actors Studio pro-

---

5. *Variety,* Nov. 6, 2000.

gram, especially geared to film buffs interested in anything about movies. When Bravo management within the parent company at Cablevision established this Actors Studio brand, Kathy Dore, President, and her marketing executive, Ed Carroll, set to work building their own line extension. The rumor that Sundance Institute was planning or searching for a home for its own independent film cable channel motivated Bravo to quickly launch its own, IFC. Sundance Channel arrived on the cable spectrum soon after.

ESPN also recognized that discrete audiences existed within their loyal sports-addicted viewership. Thus, ESPN2 and ESPN Classic were born to meet the demands of special audiences, including college football, basketball, international soccer, the WNBA (women's basketball), and the newest teenage craze, extreme or X-sports. Sponsors were prepared to advertise and market their products to these special audiences. For instance, Pepsi's Mountain Dew brand built an impressive soft drink market by becoming the lead sponsor of extreme sports competitions.

THE UNIVERSAL AUDIENCE

Cable is certainly not entirely focused on niches. There is a strong universal audience, as basic cable reaches over 60% of television households. Many viewers simply shift their allegiance from network to cable. They have become a displaced mass audience shared by TBS, American Movie Classics, TNT, Fox Family, and the other basic channels.

One of the major breakthroughs in cable was the launch of USA Network, with Kay Koplovitz as the CEO. Koplovitz, one of the first women to reach a senior management position in the cable industry, came from a strong programming and marketing background. She was one of the first to capture valuable programming from the syndication auctions by the broadcast networks and ran many seasons of *Murder, She Wrote, M*A*S*H*, and other mass-appeal products. She also gained a significant male and teenage audience with expanded coverage of the World Wrestling Foundation.

One of the difficulties—and strengths—behind USA's growth was its ownership, divided equally between Universal and Viacom. In only a few years, USA Network became the leading cable channel, with over 26 million viewers at the height of its success. In its search for channel expansion, USA management recognized the value of a special-interest audience that would allow them to use their marketing muscle and cable affiliate relationships. From information shared by their Universal parent, USA Network's marketing management became aware of the strong following for *Star Wars*, *Star Trek*, and other science fiction films. It was no surprise when USA Network launched the SciFi Channel and built it a great audience following by marketing to "Trekkies" and readers of science fiction literature.

Brand extension, however, is not an automatic given. Channels must fight the continuing battle for the cable version of "shelf space." Regardless of the discrete audiences attracted to an individual station or a group of stations, it is important to note that every channel competes with every other channel. With this competition in mind, how can the cable channels survive and thrive? The answer seems to be that it's difficult—unless they have the media equivalent of a "Sugar Daddy."

INDEPENDENT FILM JOINS THE CABLE FRAY

In 1981, Robert Redford founded the Sundance Institute, a non-profit organization dedicated to the support and development of filmmakers and other artists. The Institute runs year-round "labs" for independent filmmakers, screenwriters, composers, and theater artists. Modeled on theatrical workshops, the labs encourage experimentation on the principle that out of failure comes true artistic growth. The Institute's approach worked and acclaimed films like *El Norte* and *The Trip to Bountiful* began to emerge from its labs.

But in the early 1980s, there weren't many outlets for these kinds of films. One of the few places for exposure was Park City's U.S. Film Festival, founded in 1978. By 1985, the festival had grown so large, thanks in part to the many films originating at the Institute, that year-round staffing and programming became necessary. The Sundance Institute stepped forward to handle these responsibilities and incorporated the film festival into its slate of programs.

The story of the Sundance Film Festival (it was officially renamed in 1991) is, in many ways, the story of contemporary independent film and its steady rise in influence and market power. In 1989, Steven Soderbergh's *Sex, Lies, and Videotape* premiered at the festival; it went on to gross $25 million domestically and permanently altered the cinematic landscape. Suddenly, people began to believe that independent films were viable financially as well as artistically, and the place to see them—and discover new talent—was the Sundance Film Festival. Among the commercial and critical hits launched at the festival are *Four Weddings and a Funeral*, *Hoop Dreams*, *The Brothers McMullen*, *Shine*, and *The Full Monty*.

Independent film also benefited from the advent of home video, which created additional demand for new film product. The results have been impressive:

- Independent films accounted for 18.2% of U.S. box office revenue in 1998.

- Of 1998's top 100 video renting titles, 21 were independents.

- 60% of the 1998 Oscar nominees and 5 out of 6 of the winners in the top 6 categories were independents.

Approximately 1,300 films were submitted to the Sundance Institute for the 1999 Sundance Film Festival, an increase of 50% in four years. It's a scenario not unlike the one the Institute faced in 1985: a lot of films without a lot of places to go—and potentially a lot of people who'd like to see them...which brings us to Sundance Channel.

The mid-1990's saw the rise in recognition of independent film's audience potential. Seeking to broaden access to the genre, two competing cable channels were developed: Robert Redford's joint venture with Showtime Networks Inc. and Polygram Filmed Entertainment, Sundance Channel, and the Independent Film Channel (IFC). Since their inception, the two channels have amassed a very respectable audience of over 35 million television households.

While Sundance has the credibility of Redford's name, along with the association with the Sundance Film Festival, the IFC has marketed its brand on the premise of its freedom to associate with all independent film festivals, including Sundance. Additionally, the IFC has maintained credibility through its advisory board, which consists of many well-known actors, directors and players in the "indie" industry. Both channels stay true to their roots by their involvement in the making of independent films, including financing. Launching a premium cable/satellite network, even one with Robert Redford's name attached, is not easy. For one thing, space on cable systems is very limited. Cable operators have to want the service, which means that viewers have to want the service, and to want it, they have to understand what it is. A strong brand is needed in a crowded environment.

Thus was forged an unholy alliance between art and commerce. After all, both IFC and Sundance Channel are commercial enterprises devoted to quality independent films. The question is how to "sell" art without compromising it, keeping in mind that you're not doing art a favor if you can't get it to an audience. It's a constant balancing act.

But every so often, the interests of art and commerce coincide and a film that happens to be very good happens to sell like crazy. One outstanding moment of such divine congruence was Fine Line's *Shine*, a wonderful film that grossed pots of money and received seven Oscar® nominations, winning one for Best Actor (Geoffrey Rush). *Shine's* success, along with other films, caused the studios to take note; several began their own art film boutique divisions, through acquisitions (Disney/Miramax, Warner Brothers/New Line/Fine Line) and new banners (Sony Pictures Classics, Fox Searchlight). Expectations rose as films like *The Brothers McMullen*, *Il Postino* and *The Full Monty* (not to mention the juggernaut known as *Pulp Fiction*) generated huge profits in proportion to their budgets.

However, the fortunes of independent film have not yet been cemented in success. Complicating the situation is the fact that there aren't enough movie screens to go around. Event movies—such as the latest in the *Star Wars* series—from the major studios can command six screens at a ten-plex. Independent films can disappear after one week, long before word of mouth can build. Additionally, the executives at Fine Line, Miramax, October, Regency and the rest created a monster: the mainstream film in independent clothing. The real independents—films without a well-known lead that don't have major studios behind them—are left out in the cold. Both IFC and Sundance Channel help ameliorate this situation by giving edgier or less conventional films a shot at long life and broader audience exposure. At the same time, these films help the channels remain dynamic.

The marketing of the genre continues. In 1997, Sundance Channel joined with Starbucks Coffee and U.S. Satellite Broadcasting (USSB) in a national marketing campaign that allowed independent film fans to host viewing parties in 11 cities across the U.S. It included screenings of past Sundance Film Festival offerings and live coverage of that year's closing night activities. It was a promotional opportunity that gave access to greater independent film fan populations across the country.

Sundance Channel and Blockbuster Video, a sister division under the Viacom umbrella, joined forces to expand both their markets. In Blockbuster stores, posters announcing "Sundance Recommends" direct shoppers to a section specifically for independent films premiered on the Sundance Channel. Sundance marketing professionals use Blockbuster's consumer database to reach their target audience through direct mail campaigns. TV monitors in the video stores offer news about upcoming Sundance events.

IFC has taken a different approach to consumer marketing. In the late 90's, the network created IFC Productions, a film financing arm, and IFC Films, a distribution company like Sony Classics, Fine Line and Miramax. More than a dozen films are released into theatres each year with the IFC brand attached, expanding IFC's brand awareness as well as its reputation as a source of high quality film.

As consumer choices multiply, a network's first line of defense is to build and maintain a solid relationship with its audience. The best way for Sundance Channel to do that is to continue bringing viewers quality films they can't see anywhere else, along with information and behind-the-scenes insight they crave. As long as the programming is unique, the viewers will stay with the channel.

MEDIA, MARKETING, AND MONEY

Control of the airwaves is just as important on cable as it is on network TV. The difference is that on cable, a media conglomerate may develop and control many different channels, as opposed to one network. Successful media marketing in the cable industry is driven by MSOs that can package a variety of channels—reaching a variety of audiences—so that advertisers can expand their reach beyond the mass appeal of networks.

CABLE CARRIAGE

Think of it this way: A network may have 20 primetime shows hitting four demographic groups in the course of a week, in perhaps five primetime slots. The theory behind cable niches is that advertisers can hit those same demographics all day, all night, all week by buying a package of channels. Since repetition is the soul of advertising, MSOs that can offer these kinds of packages find themselves in the driver's seat of cable revenue, making it difficult for independent channels to get a share of the revenue.

Consider Time Warner: Its cable MSO, Warner Cable, has many cable programming niches in-house, including HBO, Cartoon Network, InCourt, CNN, CNNfn and CNN, and Sports Illustrated. Warner Cable is therefore in a position to leverage their audience clout in favor of their own new cable start-ups. Similarly, Viacom and Disney have vertical and horizontal integration that promotes this kind of power play.

Operators are reluctant to take on new channels unless they provide access to a brand-new audience. It usually takes a new channel about 36 months to reach breakeven (income equals cost of operation). When Fox News launched, the Murdoch-owned channel bent the rules to get carriage on as many operators as possible; instead of waiting to reach significant audience levels, they paid a "slotting," or "carriage," fee to gain entrance. While the early cable dream may have included easier access to the airwaves for start-ups, the realities are the same as in any other business: He who has the gold gets the goods.

In the case of cable, the goods are the subscribers, the advertisers, and the programmers. A serious subscriber in a major metropolitan market can be worth between $500 and $1000 each year he or she remains connected. This comes from a combination of monthly charges, including $35 for a basic package, another $12 for a three-channel premium package, and about $250 over the year for selected movies and sports events on PPV. In addition, the programmers pay the operators for each subscriber they can authenticate as connected and tuned in to their channels, as reported by the Nielsen surveys. BET, for instance, pays about 11 cents per subscriber per month, and collects about 50% of the advertising dollars that are attributable to their programming. Programmers also earn revenue by licensing their programs to other channels via syndication or international sales. Operators also derive income or participate on a per-inquiry basis with the television direct sales packagers of music compilations of catalog recordings, or collectibles, gifts and gimmicks sold via info-commercials. Operators collect advertiser revenues on each basic channel that provides commercial airtime as well.

The most profitable carriage for an operator is the "selling up" of a subscriber to take a premium package and/or call in for PPV, since the operator receives nearly 50% of the monthly fee. Since there is no advertising on these channels, the revenue split is of necessity greater than with basic channels.

However, to create revenue streams from any of these sources, a virtual maze of marketing must first take place. The cable industry must market both internally and externally, just like the networks. Cable programmers must sell their wares to cable operators as well as to viewers; cable operators must market their programs and services to their subscribers. Both must market themselves to that critical source of revenue, the advertiser.

MARKETING CONTENT: CABLE PROGRAMMERS

Each cable category and channel has a designated target audience. The marketing strategy for these channels is usually three-pronged:

■ First, they must convince the viewers that the channel will provide them with exactly the information and entertainment that suits their lifestyle, their interests, their values, and their entertainment requirements.

■ Second, the channels must maintain a market presence with cable operators all across the U.S.—and in some cases, around the world—to ensure carriage and basic cable package support.

■ Third, in anticipation of each programming and advertising planning season, they must convince current and prospective advertisers and their ad agencies that they can deliver viewers of the greatest value to this business community.

Cable channel sales and marketing professionals must support their ability to attract the customers of greatest demographic appeal to the advertisers, providing customer viewer profiles developed through proprietary or omnibus research.

The efforts of the programmers to reach their specific targets—viewers and advertisers—flow into the greater stream of the conduit itself, the cable operators. The operators provide the mass reach that allows for niche marketing, which is the heart and soul of cable.

CONDUIT MARKETING: CABLE OPERATORS

Since cable TV, unlike network TV, is a service to which one must subscribe, it is at some level directly marketed, whether by a salesperson or through an individual's contact with one of the nation's nearly 12,000 local service providers—the operators. These operators target new subscribers, existing subscribers, and advertisers. Many of these 12,000 providers are owned by MSOs such as Time Warner, AT&T, Cable Cox Communications, and Cablevision. These companies possess the resources to mount slick campaigns featuring print, audio, and video media use.

In the late 1990s, this advantage became increasingly more apparent as MSOs began to build brand images, one of the best modern-day ways to increase satisfaction and product loyalty. The MSO brand images focused on reliability, customer service, and technological leadership. MSOs also developed distinctive branding techniques as well as promotional strategies that included cooperation with frequent flyer programs, fast food industries, and cross-promotions with radio and network television stations. The target of these strategies is the subscriber, both new and existing. Dealing with subscriptions means dealing with "churn" (turnover). Remember that as with any marketing, it is easier and less expensive to retain an existing customer than to acquire a new one.

THE SEARCH FOR SUBSCRIBERS

Almost 100% of all homes in America have easy access to cable, which means all households are potential cable consumers. Those not already subscribing to cable represent the greatest growth area. This includes new housing developments. Then there are those who already have access but are not currently using cable, split by cable salespeople into "nevers" and "formers." The nevers have, as the word implies, never before subscribed to cable, even though the hookup may be already installed in their dwelling. Formers include transient users, such as apartment dwellers.

To reach potential subscribers, the cable and satellite industries use direct marketing, outdoor billboards, radio spots, door-to-door salespeople, and network television spots. While TV networks and stations don't accept advertising from direct competitors, they do willingly take the advertising dollars cable companies offer.

Small and independent cable operators that have resisted being bought out depend on their relationships within the community for marketing to their customers. Their major marketing efforts are directed at maintaining the goodwill of the customers they have, reducing churn, connecting new homeowners, and massaging the programmers who pay them for carriage of programs by selling their content.

The local operator bombards the community with coupons in local newspapers and "penny-saver," free-circulation tabloids (sometimes owned by the local cable company), offering free hook-up. One of the most important aspects of their marketing program is "selling up"—marketing premium and PPV services to customers with basic cable. Bill stuffers, sent out in every monthly billing invoice, offer one month free of a premium channel or one or two free PPV movies to build trial.

The MSO uses many similar marketing tactics, with two major differences: bigger audiences in each of their locations and bigger marketing budgets. On occasion, an MSO simply un-encrypts their premium channels and announces that this is their gift to loyal customers—another form of trial, without request. A certain percentage of basic cable viewers may then "convert," purchasing the premium package. MSOs also frequently send out glossy, four-color booklets announcing upcoming movies and special programs, engaging the customer and building a "must have" sensibility.

However, MSOs have had one specific hurdle to cross in building their subscription base. The early days of cable conglomerates saw a distinct lack of service, turning off many subscribers and, in part, forcing the passage of the Telecommunications Act of 1996, deregulating the cable industry to put pressure on the MSOs. In response, the leading cable operators focused on the service side of their business, both from the marketing and results standpoints. The results were lower churn and longer retention rates.

On the advertising side, the media company that owns the MSO can offer packages that include a cable media plan, magazines ads, radio commercials, posters at theme parks, ads on home video cassettes, and ads in cable bill enclosures. If the company owns a broadcast network, that too is factored into the package offering.

There are ways for small, independent operators to gain a share of the market: the marriage of cooperation and competition known as co-opetition.

CABLE COOPERATIVES

On occasion, a number of independent and MSO systems in a given regional territory may band together and form a marketing co-op. An example of this strategy is the Metro-Cable Marketing Co-Op, covering approximately 40 or more cable operators in the neighboring states of New York, New Jersey, and Pennsylvania. In their first joint effort, the co-op took advantage of critical mass to develop cost-effective mailing pieces offering a package of specials during one or two annual marketing periods. Potential subscribers were then called to action with a 1-800-OKCable phone number.

Funding for this offer came from the combined pool of independents and MSOs. While the average yearly budget for an individual operator might be as low as $10,000 and as high as $200,000 for a larger system or MSO affiliate, the co-op budget initially totaled over $1 million. This pool was matched by the programmers, with funds and film footage. The combined budget then grew to over $2 million.

The 1-800-OKCable calls were fielded by one bank of telemarketing personnel, who received the calls and dispensed the orders to the appropriate members. The marketing effort was totally accountable, measuring both cost per inquiry and cost per actual subscriber.

In the first three years, the co-op membership saw year-over-year growth of 15% in basic cable subscribers, and some systems added nearly 20% in premium and PPV revenues. The marketing budget has since grown to over $5 million. This case was reviewed at the annual Cable Tactical And Marketing (CTAM) conference; many of the strategies and marketing materials were acquired for use in other regional co-op markets.

NEW DIRECTIONS IN THE MULTICHANNEL ARENA

Strategies such as cooperatives will continue to be important in the cable industry as the framework in which it exists continues to change, driven by both new technology and subscriber demands.

WIRELESS AND UNPLUGGED

Because cable networks depend on both subscription and advertising fees for revenue, reaching 100% of television households is the Holy Grail. More households equal more subscriptions—and higher advertising rates, due to a larger demographic. But how can they reach the remote areas of the country? Digging trenches and setting cable wires hundreds if not thousands of miles across prairies, desert, and sporadically settled mountain ranges is unaffordable. The alternative can be reduced to three letters: DBS.

In the early stages, unwired households purchased large 8- to 10-foot-wide dishes known as TVRO. These dishes picked up cable programming as well as HBO and other premium channels—at no monthly charge. The large dish size was necessary because the transmission was via the relatively low-powered C-Band. The programs were sent via an uplink to the satellite's transponders, and then retransmitted back to earth. The signal was received by any downlink to the TVRO dishes within a particular geographic footprint. While the dishes did allow a certain percentage of non-wired households access to cable stations, the dishes themselves required a fair amount of yard room and investment.

The next step in transmission technology took care of these drawbacks and also allowed the satellite distribution system to be turned into a business. Higher powered satellites were developed, which made small, 18-inch diameter dishes viable. These were called "pizza pans" in the cable trade due to their size, shape, and potential ubiquity. They could be mounted on apartment terraces, window-sills, or house roofs.

USSB and DIRECTV were the earliest to launch proprietary sat-ellites, which distributed encrypted programming, allowing the pro-viders to control reception of over 100 channels. By 1997, more than eight million television households owned satellite dishes, receiving full cable packages at various subscription prices. Today, USSB, a division of Hubbard Broadcasting, primarily focuses on marketing premium multiplex packages from HBO, Showtime, and other monthly movie channels as well as offering extensive pay-TV options, all at competitive pricing. DIRECTV, a division of Hughes Electronics, competes more directly with cable operators, offering every basic channel and a complete menu of premium and pay-TV. The unique aspect of their marketing is to provide customized chan-nel combinations at various price configurations; even the cost of the basic channel package can be reduced by taking fewer channels.

Primestar offers a 39-inch dish at no cost to the consumer, but it requires a substantial installation fee. Primestar's early consumer marketing was through cable operators, who wanted a competitive offering to USSB and DIRECTV for those households not passed by cable wire. More recently, Primestar has created a relationship with Radio Shack. The retail outlets provide Primestar with greater geo-graphic coverage and a broader consumer target segment.

NEW TV TECHNOLOGY

There's more to the unfolding cable story than transmission trends. New technologies on the receiving end are opening doors for paradigm shifts in the role of television in today's household.

A BRIEF MENTION OF CONVERGENCE

Most major MSOs are now offering the sale of cable modems for easy access to the Internet and telephony services—a huge marketing opportunity in this era of deregulation. These offers are being tested with direct marketing efforts, telemarketing outbound calls, and tie-ins with local appliance stores. The promise of one-stop communications—information, entertainment, data, and transactions available through cable with just one bill—is still in its infancy. However, cable operators are mounting marketing campaigns to sell these other services. They do not wish to be left behind the combinations of AT&T and TCI or AOL Time Warner.

Cablevision, an MSO based on Long Island, New York, acquired 22 THE WIZ entertainment hardware and appliance stores to provide cable modem sales and installation at the neighborhood retail level. The success of this innovative sales and marketing effort is still undetermined.

INTERACTIVE TELEVISION

The opportunity of the home viewer to be an interactive participant with television has been a promise on the horizon of the broadband age. Interactivity suffered a few setbacks as the cable industry attempted to keep Microsoft from dominating set-top box technology. Companies like FutureTV were early pioneers in two-way television, which allows a user to buy movies, songs, do email, surf the Web, and watch sports events all from the same easy chair. However, firms like Liberate Technologies (funded by investors such as AOL, Comcast, Cox Communications, Oracle, and Sun Microsystems) and Open TV have now entered the arena, providing software for Internet-enhanced content and applications for the boxes.

Liberate has also partnered with Diva and SeaChange to provide video-on-demand. Open TV has ported to the Motorola DCT-2000 (the most widely deployed set-top box terminal box), and has also ported to the advanced model, Motorola's DCT-5000. Meanwhile, Microsoft has demonstrated its competitive slant with a suite of programs available through its Partner Programs.

DIGITAL TV

The television technology the public has known since it first appeared on the entertainment scene has been analog—that is, oscillating waves transmitted through airwaves to antennas, or through copper-based lines to sets. Recent technology allows these same kinds of signals to be digitized and transmitted with less resistance and static through fiber-optic lines. This digital technology offers clearer pictures and sound levels equivalent to CDs. Simply put, digitizing reduces signals to the plus and minus (or 1s and 0s) signals used by computers. Just as DVDs provide an enhanced level of home entertainment, digital television broadens its capabilities and consistency of delivery.

Of course, the television itself must be capable of receiving a digital signal, and a conduit, like a fiber-optic cable, must be present to carry it. But, both the ability to incorporate the full strength of multimedia and interface with the newer digital content through the standard of SDTV are expected to make continued major gains, and have been welcomed as educational as well as entertainment breakthroughs. As soon as the price points of home hardware, ongoing coalescence of improved transmission conduits, and original material prepared in digital format come to their expected crossroads, this may become the standard mode of all television of the future. It has already led to breakthroughs in related industries, like HDTV and Internet TV.

SUMMARY

As with the other entertainment media, multichannel marketing executives in cable and the newer technology, satellite TV, are continuing to explore ways to reach further into the discretionary time and disposable income of today's marketplace. While their content beginnings played off the success of old stand-by movies, today's multichannel media boasts some of the best original content on the airwaves, driving both advertising and subscription revenues, and challenging programmers to continue pushing the envelope.

Before we explore the marketing of some very important entertainment content—sports and music—let's examine the first mass media: publishing.

FOR FURTHER READING

BOOKS

1. Blumenthal, Howard J. and Oliver R. Goodenough, *This Business of Television* (New York, NY: Watson-Guptill, 1998).

2. Eastman, Susan Tyler, Douglas A. Ferguson, and Robert A. Klein, Eds., *Promotion and Marketing for Broadcasting and Cable, 3/E* (Boston, MA: Focus Press, 1999).

3. Litwak, Mark, *Dealmaking in the Film & Television Industry: From Negotiations to Final Contracts* (Los Angeles, CA: Silman-James, 1994).

4. Parsons, Patrick R., Robert Frieden, and Rob Frieden, *The Cable and Satellite Television Industries* (Boston, MA: Allyn & Bacon, 1997).

5. Resnik, Gail and Scott Trost, *All You Need to Know About the Movie and TV Business* (New York, NY: Fireside, 1996).

MAGAZINES TO DEVOUR

1. *Broadcast & Cable*

2. *Cable World*

3. *Cablevision*

4. *Electronic Media*

5. *Multichannel News*

6. *TV Guide*

6

PUBLISHING: THE PRINTED WORD

OVERVIEW

S hortly after Johannes Gutenberg pulled the first Bible off his printing press, publishing became a mass-market medium—but never so much as today. For all the hype about the paperless society, there seems to be no shortage whatsoever of books, newspapers, and above all, magazines—which appear to be the fraternal twin of cable TV in terms of filling the needs of the niche audience. All of these media have felt the effect of big companies getting bigger, especially with the shift to the "Big Box" bookstore. But publishing no longer means just paper; part of the information overload of the day includes a shift to growing new markets for multimedia products, scores of new software games, and books offered electronically on the Internet.

BOOKS

Book publishing covers a wide landscape: hardbacks, paperbacks, pocket-sized books, and coffee table books (not to mention books that could serve as coffee tables, given their size); also, professional publishing, religious publishing, and educational publishing (texts, professional references, workbooks, and support materials developed specifically for elementary, high school, and college). In the entertainment field, the two most common types of books are trade books and mass-market paperbacks.

TERMS OF THE TRADE

"Trade books," as defined by the Association of American Publishers (AAP), refers to books produced for general bookstore sale and for public library circulation. Adult trade includes fiction, poetry, literary comment, biography and history, the arts, music, theater, cinema, popular science and technology, cookery, home crafts, self-help, business, how-to books, popular medicine, sports, travel, gardening, nature, social issues, and public affairs. Many of these books are reprinted in lower priced editions called trade paperbacks or quality paperbacks. Often their original or only appearance is in a paperback edition.

The AAP defines "mass-market books" as reprints of fiction and nonfiction books, original fiction (some are published only in this format), and original nonfiction. Mass-market books are often sold though the channels that distribute magazines.

The fiction category of books represents the greatest percentage of books sold in any category. These are books identified as appealing to a mass audience and providing relaxation, and engrossing reading. They are often described as "mental transportation"—escapism in a small package. As an entertainment, fiction will be the focus of the book portion of this chapter

SOMETHING FOR EVERYONE

Within trade and mass-market publishing, books are further defined by the audience they serve. The term "genre" is used across the entertainment world to describe particular categories of writing, music, movies, television, and radio content. It helps content providers in all areas to understand and measure the popularity of one genre against another, as well as to strategize marketing plans for the audiences they serve. In publishing, the tracking of genres guides the decision-making process for allocating scarce resources, especially when it comes to paying advances or creating marketing support.

Some literary critics have been quick to attach a stigma to the marketing-driven concept of genre. Writers like Raymond Chandler and Dashiell Hammett created original, high-quality works, but were never widely considered to be "literary" by American critics of their day—though others[1] have ranked them in the top 100 American writers. Publishers catering to mass audiences and pop culture seem to care little for literary appellations, given that genre publishing has been very good to the whole industry.

Many genres have no clear-cut single descriptive, but instead have major and minor sub-categories. There is science fiction (sci-fi), which splits roughly between futuristic (Herbert's *Dune*) and sword-and-dragon fiction (Tolkien's *The Lord of the Rings*). Mystery books also fall into several popular and even niche sub-genres. These include cozy reading (Agatha Christie, Mary Higgins Clark), noir (Jim Thompson, James Ellroy), hard-knuckle (Mickey Spillane), and a number of other categories of distinction. Westerns still have their own shelves. Also, books of humor, poetry, plays, African-American, and gay literature find room on separate bookstore shelves, reaching for separate and distinct audiences.

CASE IN POINT: ROMANCE PUBLISHING

When the term "romance publishing" comes up in conversation, the imprint most people think of first is Harlequin Romances—and with good reason. The Toronto, Canada-based romance mass-market paperback empire Harlequin Enterprises acquires and releases over 700 titles annually to supermarkets, drug chains, mass merchandisers, and some of the major book retail chains. The umbrella of Harlequin Enterprises' yearly releases includes at least six titles from Harlequin, several from Silhouette, Steeple Hill (Christian Romance), Mira (longer brand-name romances), and Gold Eagle, an action-adventure series described as romances for men.

Harlequin began as a pure romance imprint, with formula-written books by a multitude of largely unknown authors who frequently contributed their first novel and never wrote again. The concept was developed by Canadian publishing executive Richard Bonnycastle in 1949. The single imprint was sold in bookstores and supermarkets as

---

1.   Jorge Luis Borges, for instance.

a small but growing genre directed at women predominantly living in suburban and Middle American communities. The acquisition of a small, established publisher from the UK, Mills & Boon, helped build international sales for the Harlequin line. By the end of the 1970s, Harlequin was the leading publisher of romance fiction.

The American Bookseller's Association (ABA) suggests that one out of every six mass-market paperbacks sold in the U.S. and Canada is either a Harlequin or a Silhouette Romance, giving the company a big 16% slice of the $1.8 billion mass-market paperback pie. However, while the romance genre hit a peak in the 1980s, with almost every major publishing house carrying its own romance imprint, the genre has hit a decline in the last decade.

This has happened for a variety of reasons, not the least of which was the changing roles of, and opportunities for, women in the late 20th Century. Coupled with a growing availability of spicier content across the media buffet, today's younger women, once the base for romance readers, are now demanding more from their "guilty pleasure" reading. According to the Romance Writers of America, 60% of all current romance readers live in towns of 50,000 people or less, and are usually 50 or older.

The charge for the next decade is to bring the Harlequin Romance brand into the 21st Century. This must be done without turning off the hard-core romance reader, who wolfs down three to six romance books weekly.

HARDBACK VERSUS PAPERBACK

In times past, it was common to bring a book out first in hardback, and if it did well, it would appear about a year later as a paperback. By late in the 20th Century, it had become more common to bring an emerging author to the public through a series of paperbacks before shifting to hardback status. Many emerging authors no longer have their first books come out as hardbound, but must earn that status.

For example, Laura Lippman is a Baltimore author of detective novels. Lippman, whose day job is as a reporter for *The Baltimore Sun,* has paid her dues by having her first four Tess Monaghan mystery novels released as mass-market paperbacks by Avon. Though Lippman's novels have won a significant number of awards (an Edgar, an Anthony, a Shamus, and a Macavity), her sales didn't ignite until after an October 1999 appearance on CBS *Sunday Morning.* Carrie Ferron, the Avon Executive Editor who has handled all of

Lippman's titles, saw to it that Lippman's next titles, *The Sugar House* (2000) and *In a Strange City* (2001), came out as Morrow hardbacks under the Avon/HarperCollins program.

FORECASTING

Before a publishing contract is extended to any author, someone has made a considered study of the proposed book to determine the return on investment (ROI). The acquisition editor, the person who most often signs an author, considers several cost factors, including plant costs (overhead of running the business), physical costs (such as PPB—printing, paper, binding), author royalty, and marketing. Increasingly, one of the key ingredients of this study is whether the product will bear its own marketing cost. All of this is factored against the discounts that must be extended to wholesalers and retailers. The editor then makes a calculated guess as to whether a proposed book will meet or exceed sales goals based on the company's capacity to sell within a reasonably defined market.

But how does the editor know the size of each book's market? Trade and mass-market book editors do not have the luxury of a somewhat predictable market segment, as in some educational or technical/trade markets. In college textbook publishing, for instance, the market segment is decided by how many students are sitting in classes that focus on that subject. In addition to this total size of the market, the college text editor must know the competition—the other books currently used in that market segment, their strengths and weaknesses, and whether the author or authorial team has the background, credibility, and knowledge to author a book able to displace that competition. In short, there is a relatively forecastable market with some finite and promising parameters.

This is not the case for the riskier area of trade or mass-market books. An acquisition editor of these books must consider the author's reputation and quality of the manuscript. If the author's name is Stephen King or John Grisham, the reputation part is a no-brainer. But, if it is an emerging author, like Donna Tartt, who received a $100,000 advance from Knopf for her first book, *The Secret History*, then the quality of the writing must speak for the book's potential.

How does a manuscript even reach the stage of consideration for publishing? In years past, publishers had staff employees called "readers." Their job was to screen manuscripts, many of them unsolicited. In the 1980s, to cut overhead costs, publishers dispensed with the role and began to return unsolicited manuscripts unopened. The "readers" were replaced by authors' agents. The agents, at no cost to the publisher—but with the speculation of 10%–15% of an author's royalty—screen manuscripts for quality and anticipate marketing considerations of the appropriate publishers of each manuscript. A successful agent follows the publishing industry, usually focusing on a particular segment or two. They know the patterns, trends, and personalities of the publishers. Some agents even act as packagers of books, going so far as to deliver a book ready as a specific type or genre to an appropriate publisher.

WHEN, WHERE, AND TO WHOM

The publishing of trade books happens in selling seasons. The Spring release of titles anticipates the selling window of July through September, and is heavily weighted to beach reading and light summer reading. The anticipation of Christmas season sales leads to a Fall release of books. The Fall list is heavier, especially in the nonfiction genres and specialty books arena. Each year, the NPD Group, an international provider of marketing information, makes available a *Consumer Research Study on Book Purchasing*, which is published by the ABA. This report confirms that most books are sold in the second half of the year, and that the Christmas sales window shows the most aggressive growth. However, some publishers are even going to three-season and monthly selling.

The NPD report also confirms a demographic shift in book buying. The Pacific region and Mountain region combine for almost 30% of all books sold, while the New England states, including Boston and New York, command only 5%. Even with 15% more sales from the Mid-Atlantic states, the East coast must bow to the West when it comes to book sales.

Who is the average book buyer? Not surprisingly, it is someone with disposable income. The greater proportions of books were purchased by those individuals with the largest incomes, most of whom are Baby Boomers. The increasing number of individuals receiving college degrees since the 1960s has encouraged book sales, while also contributing to the information explosion that led into the new millennium.

Once a book is ready to release to the public, it must find its way to consumers, whether through retail, a book club, or the Internet.

DISTRIBUTION CHANNELS

The distribution chain has seen great changes in the last decade, as Big Box retailers (such as Barnes & Noble and Borders) and the continuingly non-profitable Amazon.com have come to the forefront in the public's purchasing awareness.

In the past, wholesalers such as Ingrams and Baker & Taylor were the prominent middlemen in the distribution chain. Because it consumed too much time—and too many inventory dollars—to keep books in stock, retailers would order and reorder from the wholesalers. However, by the turn of the century, Barnes & Noble, Borders, and Amazon.com were ordering most of the books stocked directly from the publishers, thus enhancing their margins. This became true of a great number of independent bookstores as well. Today, wholesalers are being used increasingly for quick replenishment only. They have yet to diminish in importance, though.

Those retail outlets thought of specifically as "bookstores" are not the only news in book distribution. Anyone who has visited a Wal-Mart, Sam's Club, Target, or a host of other such stores has seen whole skids of books available at tremendous discounts. Grocery chains have sections dedicated to books; gourmet groceries have health and cookbook sections. In mass marketing terms; it's easy for people to buy books in a place where they already shop. Drugstores and supermarkets are naturals for mainstream entertainment products, and now handle a majority of all trade books sold.

What do the huge purchases of books by all of these retailers mean for publishers? A greater *laydown* (the number of copies of a book that can be presold and ready to ship the day of the book's release) for books already destined to succeed, primarily. Buyers committing discount resources to this kind of product tend toward the no-brainer books—those by Stephen King or John Grisham, or books already enjoying long-term status on *The New York Times'* bestseller list.

But getting a book into distribution does little for its sale, unless the public has been thoroughly made aware of its presence.

MARKETING BOOKS

The marketing of each book usually depends on a marketing professional who's intimately aware of the best and most cost-effective methods for a publisher, in a marketplace that is changing rapidly.

THE BOOK RELEASE

As with many entertainment products, the debut of a new product is trumpeted through a release process.

Until recently, trade shows and book fairs were highly significant events in the release cycle. The ABA's annual event was once a premier launch spot, as were the Frankfurt, Bologna, and Peking book fairs. But the one-fifth drop in small store membership in the ABA—caused by the impact of the newer retailers—lowered the impact of these events, since buyers at major chains and wholesalers are handled by specialized representatives of major publishers. The cost of attending such meetings is high; in some cases, it becomes more economically feasible to merely court the big buyers of chain stores directly. Book fairs such as BookExpo America and regional festivals like the New York City Book Fair continue to have an impact on a book's release, but have nowhere near the drum roll of previous days.

Since bigger, entertainment-savvy companies have begun to show dominance, the publicity and promotion of a major book release has come to resemble the release of a movie, with a fanfare of reviewing, space ads, and high-profile signings in large cities. But you don't have to visit many bookstores to figure out that not every book is a bestseller. In fact, a significant portion of the trade book business, including profits, is composed of mid-list and other levels of books. Like books that sell in bigger numbers, books that sell only a few thousand copies also have to be marketed. Momentum-building is even more important for these books, but must be accomplished on a smaller budget.

In any case, there are several marketing approaches that are common to all types of books.

THE CLASSIC APPROACH: SALES CALLS

A portion of book marketing has been consistent through the years. Major publishers staff sales representatives who call on bookstores before a book is released. These reps seek to reach an expectation about each book's laydown. For the large chains, there is often a separate, more-experienced rep assigned the task of dealing specifically with their needs.

A marketing staff or marketing manager supports the sales reps' effort by considering the market position of the book, examining the competition (whether direct or nearly direct), and preparing a tip sheet about the book that reduces its salient features to a selling format. These tasks may have already been anticipated at signing by the acquisition editor; in that case, the marketing manager acts as a facilitator and communication link to the sales force.

In the case of trade books, the tip sheet is often composed of the same sorts of comments a reader sees on the back cover or inside the dust jacket of hardbound copies. The marketing department is responsible for the preparation and dissemination of all such book descriptions, as well as press releases (where appropriate). Marketing also coordinates the timing of the book's release with events like meetings, festivals, a breaking news story, a film release—any event that can substantially support the book.

DIRECT MARKETING

Direct marketing, while one of the most expensive ways for publishers to market, can be effective if the target marketing is accurate, the numbers are significant enough for the advantages of a bulk mailing, and the price point is high enough to make the return hit a breakeven point as early as possible. Direct mail typically is now done only on niche books, and those are almost exclusively high-price books since a good response rate can be in the area of 2%.

However, books purchased through direct marketing account for a higher profit margin because customers pay list price and no discount is needed for a wholesaler or large retailer. An additional advantage for the publisher is that sales of the book through regular channels will also benefit, since a mailing will help drive those sales through regular retail and Internet channels. These additional sales usually offset any concerns by vendors or reps who do not receive commission on books sold through direct marketing means. In fact, a direct mailing can be billed to reps as an additional advantage to their sales effort.

Some of the best ways to identify a target market for direct marketing is through magazine subscription lists, which have usually already identified a niche that corresponds with the book's subject. In the case of a nonfiction mainstream title, there may be meetings, conferences, or special interest groups (SIGs) that can be approached by mail. A number of companies have tried to reach audiences through email contacts, but the chief issue there is some concern about the potential target's reaction to "spamming" (the Internet term for junk mail). Some states, like Washington, have banned unsolicited email marketing. Even without such legislation, the trend was already turned toward "permission marketing," in which the e-vendor first asks if it is okay to send such emails, and provides easy means to be removed from lists for such solicitations. The hassle and stigma aside, email marketers have often reported response rates equal to or higher than regular mail approaches, for considerably lower costs.

BACKLIST SALES

Backlist books (those formerly published by an author) can become another very important marketing tool. The moment a new book by a well-known author is released, the distribution machinery goes into gear. All of the author's former novels are re-released— often with new covers—and either packaged as a set or displayed next to each other.

This strategy is based on a critical tenet of successful entertainment marketing: *No one can see or read everything when it is first available*. Thus, every entertainment product needs multiple "windows of opportunity" to be seen and enjoyed by the widest possible audience. The Titanic story and the number of Agatha Christie reissues provide proof that some people revisit their favorite entertainment icon more than once.

For example, John Irving's *The Cider House Rules* became a backlist jackpot following the release of the movie. The Morrow hardcover original of the book accounted for 300,000 copies in 1985 when the book was released, making it the 12th bestselling book that year. After the movie garnered Academy Award attention early in 2000, the book shot back up in the charts to the number-one position, with a new total of 915,000 copies in print from 17 printings.

THE IMPORTANCE OF REVIEWS

When the subject of book reviews is mentioned, *The New York Times'* book review always seems to come to mind first. For years it has enjoyed a prominence that belies the fact that, according to U.S. Deptartment of Commerce Bureau of the Census information, more books are now sold on the Pacific coast that in all the New England

and Mid-Atlantic states combined. Almost every Sunday paper offers book reviews in a Living or Entertainment section, and free-circulation papers (those that thrive on advertising dollars while listing local entertainment) also include book reviews. *The Los Angeles Times'* book review has also established itself as a pillar of early insight, while whole magazines are dedicated to books, among them *Publisher's Weekly,* which also provides advance book reviews.

But, it is *The New York Times'* book review list that has become the "no-brainer" marketing signal for vendors to buy—and buy in quantity. As such, it receives a stupendous proportion of advance copies, or "cranes," of all books published. This advance version of a book is sent to newspapers, magazines, and Internet review sites before the book ever rolls off the printing press and is bound in its final form. In some cases, the advance copy is nothing more than a bound manuscript copy, often with errors still in place. In other cases, "folded-and-gathered" sets of galley proofs or page proofs are bound and sent, these too often containing errors that the authors and editors hopefully weed out before the book is published. The object for a publisher is not only to gain momentum, but also to get lines from the reviews—"blurbs"—that can appear on the jacket of hardbound and paperback copies.

Blurbs can also be requested from other established writers. There is usually an honorarium (paid fee) associated with these, although some authors are quite willing to promote their fellow authors. A blurb also helps the reader decide to buy a book—if Stephen King liked it, then I will. That became so true that Stephen King now draws an almost unflinching line against doing any more blurbs.

New to the review game are the populist reviews found at Web sites such as Amazon.com. Posted by actual readers of the book, these can sometimes be fair, sometimes dicey—but always influential. Publishers live in fear of a flamingly negative review that kills a book. The reverse is also true; many publishers work hard to get five-star reviews on the site.

THE POWER OF PUBLICITY—THE TV TALK-SHOW CIRCUIT

Book promotion helped supply content for early television talk shows—Jack Parr's hour-and-a-half version of *The Tonight Show* being one of the first. Authors, willing to sit with Jack and shamelessly promote their books, provided great conversation and food for thought for readers. When Johnny Carson took over, and the show was reduced to an hour-long format, authors still played a role in the lineup. But, by the time Jay Leno took over the desk, book authors rarely appeared, with the exception of top names like Stephen King and John Grisham. Book conversation is now limited to film and TV personalities plugging their own works.

The format grew even more limited as the networks concentrated on their own stars. However, other talk shows emerged. Always hungry for content, new shows reverted back to the author interview, providing a new outlet for promotion. An established author—or one with a unique spin—could sit with Phil Donahue, Rosie O'Donnell, or Charlie Rose and build the audience's awareness of the author's work. The talk-show format lends itself well to this type of promotion, since the author's appearance also constitutes an endorsement by the talk-show host or hostess.

For example, of all the talk shows with ties to book marketing, *Oprah* has probably done the most for book sales in recent history. Since initiating a book selection program in 1996, Oprah Winfrey has demonstrated TV's Midas touch. In 1999, eight of her book club choices tallied 171 weeks as bestsellers, or about 22% of all available slots (complete list available at *www.oprah.com*). TV's power of promotion was also proven when previously unknown Brad Herzog was a contestant on Regis Philbin's *Who Wants to Be a Millionaire*. Herzog won only $64,000 as a contestant, but his book, *States of Mind*, shot all the way to #7 on Amazon.com's list and lingered in the top 25 for weeks. This was for a book with an original print run of 5,000 copies.

However, shows such as *Oprah* have a very narrow window of opportunity for the number of guests per year. Therefore, publishers tend to promote only their top books on the show. This makes local and regional shows a much more commonly used media for the majority of the business.

RADIO INTERVIEWS

One proven way to get exposure for a book is for the author to be a guest on a radio talk show. The audiences for these shows fill particular niches, each with its own interest in reading material. Howard Stern has a slightly lower income following; Don Imus' audience is in a higher income bracket and is better educated than listeners of National Public Radio; Dr. Laura Schlesinger reaches over 20 million listeners on more than 450 stations.

Radio stations are ubiquitous, and those with an all-news or talk format are always hungry for guests. Regional format shows are often eager to bring a local author's work to light. But how to cast beyond that? A good publicist will be aware of all promotional opportunities, and will include radio among the early targets for exposure and momentum-building. A great example of the power of radio is the phenomenon of *Chicken Soup for the Soul*, which was first advertised in *Radio-TV Interview Report*. It climbed to number one on *The New York Times*' bestseller list, and has engendered a family of clones the likes of which publishing has not seen in a while.

BOOK AWARDS

Awards sell books. A few of the publishing awards given each year include the Booker Prize, the National Book Award, the Caldecott Medal, the Newberry Medal, the National Book Critics Award, the Circle Awards, the PEN/Faulkner Award, the Macavity, the Edgar, the Anthony, and the Shamus (the last three are all given to books in the mystery genre). Oddly enough, the Nobel Prize in Literature seems to mark the death knell of a writer—many who receive this distinguished award rarely ever write another significant book. However, the sales of all that author's books get a boost that usually exceeds beyond the author's lifetime.

Can a publisher help an author win an award? In most cases, the integrity of the award dictates that the nomination and decision process be made by impartial judges, members of the award-granting organization. But a top-flight trade acquisition editor knows when he or she has signed a book capable of winning an award, and will take every step possible to see that copies of the book reach those who nominate or judge such annual award events.

Some emerging publishers have cut several steps from the process by using a contest to select books for publication, and then promoting the book with the publisher's award. This is a particularly — ahem—novel concept, but only one of many new approaches to entice readers.

NEW WRINKLES IN BOOK MARKETING

Just as MBAs have swelled the ranks of other entertainment sectors, so too has contemporary publishing seen an influx of the business-minded. Combined with the impact of the digitalization and globalization of the industry, and a flurry of mergers and acquisitions, the old game has seen some new twists.

THE AUTHOR AS MARKETER

Small publishers, some emerging publishers eager to fill niches left behind as too mid-list by larger houses, and even the larger houses themselves are encouraging authors to become part of the marketing push. Today's authors are often asked to:

- Initiate book-signing tours
- Create Web sites with hot links to the publisher or booksellers
- Utilize their agents or a publicist[2] to help coordinate events and promotion

These publishers either make their preference for proactive authors clear early, or bring up the subject during the book-signing process. In some instances, however, the authors themselves may become the focus of the publisher's marketing spotlight.

BRANDING THE GENRE AND THE AUTHOR

As in most entertainment sectors, niche marketing has played a role in expanding the business of publishing. For example, westerns, action-adventure, and spy novels have always been a hit with a male audience from 25–65, while romance books, both contemporary as well as historical (known in the business as "bodice-rippers") have appealed to women readers from 25–65. Mystery books, with many sub-genres, have some crossover appeal to both men and women. In the past decade, vampire novels (Anne Rice) have become a rage with a consistent following within the category, including line extensions or follow-stories arising from the original story line.

So, how does a publisher build an "evergreen," or sustained revenue stream, in these reader favorites? The answer is through marketing—more specifically, through brand marketing.

Many imprints have grown an identity that has become part of the public's brand sense of that line. Knopf and St. Martin's have carved names for themselves as publishers of solid mystery fiction.

---

2. A "publicist" fulfills a different role than an agent, and is often more responsible for promotion, including the building and maintaining of momentum. Self-published authors and authors of books published by small presses can find the hiring of a publicist a huge boost, though the significant cost may offset some of the advantage.

When Otto Penzler first formed Mysterious Press, he wanted to leave no room for confusion about the brand focus of that imprint. Likewise, TOR made its brand presence known with a focus on science fiction.

However, it is usually the author rather than the imprint that becomes the brand. A customer falls madly in love with an author's style and storytelling technique, building a need to read another of the author's books. The beauty of this phenomenon is that older titles gain as much as do new releases; once a reader gets hooked on an author, he or she will search out all of that author's work.

The responsibility of the publisher is to manage the production or writing of the popular author's next book, and to build awareness among the readers that a new book is on its way. All of this is performed successfully when a publisher builds the author into a celebrity, surrounding the author's books with a blockbuster halo and building the author into a recognizable and ever-present brand.

The author as brand is similar—though not identical—to the movie or TV star as brand. In either case, the audience finds sufficient areas of appeal and the desire to spend time and money on products attached to the star brand. These industry icons are described as "bankable": having the ability to take a subject and turn it into a money machine rather than a loss leader. Ian Fleming, John Le Carre, and Robert Ludlum are spy-thriller series brands; Stephen King and Dean Koontz are giant horror series brands; Janet Dailey and Nora Roberts are superstars of the contemporary romance novel; while Larry McMurtry and Louis L'Amour are primarily best-selling western writers; and Elmore Leonard and Sue Grafton are detective brands.

The marketing of author as brand is still in a developmental stage. It includes the occasional purchase of relatively inexpensive 30-second local market spot television, using the author's story line as a mini-movie. On occasion, a simple voiceover on a still frame of the book cover with some tantalizing copy, a few reviewers' raves, and a reference to other successful books from the same author can build a groundswell.

Cable TV advertising allows for more direct, targeted access to the audience for a given genre. It is relatively inexpensive to reach the perfect female audience with Lifetime, the Food Network, and the Romance Channel. The male audience is available through ESPN, CNBC, or the local transmission of any major sports event.

The branding approach is not foolproof, however. As with any product, once an audience has been groomed to a brand's particular attributes, those attributes cannot be toyed with. In the case of publishing, authors occasionally write in several genres, either under a pen name (pseudonym) or using their own name. Ed McBain, author of the 87th Precinct novels, also has a separate literary reputation under his real name (Evan Hunter) with books like *The Blackboard Jungle*. The most important objective is to avoid "unselling a brand" by confusing the fan of one author/genre with other works by the same author in another vein. For example, someone like Loren Estleman risks unselling his brand by earning separate reputations in both the western and detective genres.

MORE MOVIE TIE-INS

While all books do not convert comfortably to other media, the ones that do can enjoy repeat sales when a picture of the star of the movie replaces the original cover. Tom Cruise on the cover of *The Firm*, Julia Roberts on the cover of *The Pelican Brief*, and Danny DeVito on the cover of *The Rainmaker* all built additional sales for author John Grisham. Harrison Ford graced the covers of some Tom Clancy books, and Clint Eastwood was on the cover of the bestseller *Absolute Power*. All served to build the identity of these authors as stars—and brands—in their own right.

However, branding is certainly not limited to authors. Returning to the highly successful genre of romance publishing discussed earlier in the chapter, one well-known line created a model for publisher-as-brand in the second half of the 20th Century.

CASE IN POINT: SILHOUETTE ROMANCES

In the U.S., Simon & Schuster CEO Richard Snyder noted the success of the Harlequin line and decided to hire a group of non-publishing marketing and sales professionals to build a competitor. The new team developed a strategy for Silhouette Romance, which was to grow far beyond the boundaries of the competition. The challenger imprint took a leaf from classic marketing and created line extensions and flanker brands for new readers in broader economic and geographic demographics.

Silhouette Romance, the basic line with new authors, exciting cover graphics, color-coded title designations, and distinct romance category racks, was published and distributed to leading retailers, including supermarkets, drug chains, discount stores, and mass merchandisers like Wal-Mart, Kmart, and Target stores.

While this original line was directed at the senior or older female demographic, new sub-brands were soon introduced. Silhouette Desire was directed at the 25–45-year-old woman and was written with a more contemporary, sensual story line. Silhouette Special Edition offered a longer novel (365 pages) in contrast with the typical formula romance of 196 pages, at a slightly higher price. This found an audience of hard-core romance readers that wanted to linger over a longer book rather than finishing too quickly. Silhouette Intimate Moments had at its core a Christian or religious message coupled with fairly tame but well-written love stories. Silhouette First Love was directed at teenagers, already used to a category of books called Young Adult, and combined tame love stories based on high school crushes and disappointments with friends and parents. First Love provided problems/solutions under the umbrella of romantic entanglement.

The result was 30 different Silhouette Romance books released every month under various line extensions with separate color-coding, cover art, rack or display designations, and specific television and print advertising directed at distinct female audiences. Well over 60 million books were shipped to every possible type of retail outlet known to carry paperback books typically catering to women shoppers. Research, monitoring, major promotions, couponing, sampling, book clubs, tie-in programs, highlighted activities at major book-selling conferences, and exposure on talk shows for multiple published authors like Janet Daily, Nora Roberts, and others built a groundswell of consumer interest and multiple Silhouette book purchases. The average sale was a minimum of two books at each purchase and there were many sales of six or more Silhouettes at any one time.

Over the next three years, after confirmation through extensive localized research, an international sub-rights team developed licensing agreements in 16 languages for distribution in over 50 countries worldwide. Retail sales on a worldwide basis reached over $350 million dollars, making the romance category the best selling genre in the world. When the Silhouette division of Simon & Schuster was finally sold to TorStar Corp, Toronto, Canada and combined with Harlequin sales, the total revenue was well into three-quarters of a billion dollars—enough to inspire romance in any business-minded MBA.

THE FINAL FRONTIER: CHARACTER AS BRAND

While many fictional characters have served as stars of entertainment content—Snow White, Winnie-the-Pooh—most of these have become star brands over long periods of time, moving from the page to the screen as entertainment sectors found that the content they represented could be stretched into other profitable areas. However, few characters represent the modern-day approach to the whole of entertainment marketing—books, film, licensing—as well as Harry Potter.

CASE IN POINT: HARRY POTTER

On a train trip from her small village in the countryside of England to London, seeking employment, a single mother began to daydream about a young boy with big eyes, round glasses, a very high IQ, a quirky sense of humor, and the ability to use magical powers to make exciting things happen. With the launch of Harry Potter's first book, a paradigm shift occurred in children's book publishing.

A small UK publishing house secured the first rights to the first novel. Barely realizing what it had in its hand, they offered the U.S. and worldwide rights to Scholastic, Inc., the leading global children's book and educational materials (newsletters, classroom newspapers, text books, early readers, video and audio tapes) publisher, including stakes in some highly acclaimed children's theatrical and home video films.

While typical hardback or trade format fiction books sell under 200,000 copies, blockbusters (Clancy, Turow, Sheldon, Collins, Fleming, Le Carre, etc.) sell close to a million copies or slightly more, Harry Potter hardbound books one through four sold in excess of three million copies each. Young Mr. Potter has repeated or exceeded those numbers in the paperback versions. A focus on the contributions of great marketing explains why and how this happened.

First, as soon as the book went into circulation among the literary agents and those knowledgeable about children's publishing, the marketing machine was set to work. An all-points alert went out to every possible promotional opportunity available, including global talk shows and interviews with the still-dazed-but-delighted Ms. Rowling.

Second, the popularity—as built through marketing efforts—of the brand reached a near frenzy with the publication of book four. Demand was built by artificially limiting the supply for a sold out or possibly unattainable product. This created an atmosphere of "must have." The launch date was a pre-announced event, and the books were rationed by geographic area and store location, thus putting into place a master marketing tactic. The need—or perceived need—for advance orders or prepaid reservations for the book was trumpeted with stories in national consumer, business, and trade press, including *Time, Variety, Publisher's Weekly,* and a cover story in *Newsweek*. Seemingly overnight, Harry Potter became a brand in the same children's book solar system as Dr. Seuss, Maurice Sendak, and even classics like the Hardy Boys and Nancy Drew.

The third marketing hurricane was the decision by Warner Bros. studio to option the book for a film and start a global search for the young actor to play Harry Potter. Meanwhile, the studio's licensing, merchandise, and sponsorship magicians went to work. They strove to make the Potter character a marketing icon that would shake Disney's ownership of the licensing marketing crown and provide a true battle for domination of the children's entertainment sector.

THE CHANGING PUBLISHING ENVIRONMENT

"There may just be two or three publishers in the future, the way they're gobbling each other," someone said in one of the booths at the annual ABA meeting. Attendance was down at the meeting as well, in part because membership is down. The ABA has trimmed to one-fifth its former size, dropping over one thousand members. In contrast, book superstores like Barnes & Noble and Borders more than doubled in number. Independent booksellers continue to lose the fight with chains, and the erosion is only accelerated by the addition of Internet sellers like Amazon.com. But what does this dramatic shift in bookstores have to do with publishing mergers and acquisitions?

The math is simple. Trade books are sold with what is known as a *long discount*. That means wholesalers and major retailers demand 50%, 55%, and even 60% discounts to handle trade books. Most independent bookstores must buy their books from major wholesalers, like Ingrams and Baker & Taylor, and the discount the independent stores see is less than if they bought direct. Some are beginning to buy their larger quantities directly; but for smaller quantities, they rely on wholesalers. But it is not discounts that killed the independent; it was the inability of independents to put enough books into their bookstores (too little cash flow, no access to large capital markets) and their linked inability to discount to the customer—along with what was often a 1960s temperament about business and business management.

In addition to larger discounts, the bookstore chains can also benefit publishers with high-volume returns, as they did in the 1990s. Mid-sized and small publishers were less able to recover in this area, and many were acquired or folded. Several other companies were gobbled in the mergers and acquisitions frenzy late in the 20th Century.

But what slow evolution in trade publishing happened roughly between 1950 and 2000 and caught the eye of the moguls? Once again, the C's of content and conduit.

MOGULS, MERGERS, AND ACQUISITIONS

Back in the second half of the 20th Century, over 10,000 small, independent bookstores were scattered across America. Barnes & Noble was a small New York City entity, specializing in *remaindered* titles—ones that hadn't sold well enough through regular channels and had been sold in warehouse-clearing lumps at below the cost of printing them, just to recover some investment by the publishers. Borders was a single bookstore just off the campus of the University of Michigan in Ann Arbor.

The publishing side at mid-century was considered a gentlemen's game. Most of the typically male editors and publishers at the hundreds of imprints and not-very-large publishing houses (Random House, Simon & Schuster, Harper & Row, McGraw Hill, and Doubleday, to name a few) had generally graduated from good schools with an English or History major. They were paid poorly, and usually came from well-to-do families with no urgency for making a great deal of money.

However, the perks were extraordinary. Editors spent their working day reading, rubbing shoulders with erudite and intelligent authors, and discussing the latest manuscripts or recently published bestsellers with like-minded colleagues. Then they went off for a wonderful expense-account lunch or dinner with a current or soon-to-be author. A sort of college atmosphere was created in the office:

wooden shelves filled with books and paneled conference rooms where tea or brandy was served to mostly men in tweed sports coats with leather patches at the elbow. Experimentation and risk-taking were considered on a subjective basis, accounting for the early stock at remainder dealers like Barnes & Noble. These were the heady days of Max Perkins at Scribner's and the pipe-smoking Bennet Cerf at Random House.

The book industry, however, carried no advertising. Revenue came solely from the retailers who carried the volumes and the readers who were addicted to reading a "good book." All of this was to change with the growth of the entertainment conglomerate and the recognition that books were also content—and the basis of ideas from which movie scripts could be abstracted.

What eventually caught the attention of moguls and investors were the success stories—the *Gone with the Wind* sorts of stories. Much like the film industry, it is the entertainment portion of publishing (compared to the more deliberate educational, professional, or other nonfiction segments) where the breakaway success stories most often occur. It was this potential jackpot that made trade publishing attractive to investors, especially the content-driven entertainment conglomerates.

Dovetailing with an interest in content acquisition was the increasing impact of computers and digital information. Suddenly there was value in investing, owning, and publishing information—far greater value than in older, slower days, when the spread of information was primarily through printed matter. That which was once printed could now not only be converted into entertainment media—TV and film—but into bits and bytes that could encircle the globe at the push of a button. The "Information Superhighway" was born, and with it a new desire by the conglomerates to control the supply chain. Mergers and acquisitions accelerated in the 1980s with such notable events as Rupert Murdoch's acquisition of Harper & Row, Bertelsmann AG's acquisition of Dell and Doubleday, and Paramount and Times-Mirror's emergence as global media players.

The new empires began their global reach with books, which contained content that could be of interest to people around the world. Sub-rights divisions were created in each of the publishing houses to extend the publishing rights and protection of intellectual property from the U.S. to the global marketplace. These sub-rights divisions also obtained licensing agreements to extend that revenue stream internationally. At first it seemed to simply be an ego enhancement for the author, but it soon became apparent that the term "bestseller" would translate nicely into hundreds of languages. As their global influence intensified, the film industry and some of the larger publishers realized the need to establish their claim over talent, intellectual property, and electronic rights, in the face of growing power from new forms of delivery and distribution.

By the 1990s, Viacom had stepped in to buy Paramount, which now included Simon & Schuster. Disney bought Cap Cities/ABC for $19 billion, Westinghouse got CBS for $5.4 billion, and Time Warner acquired the Turner Broadcast holdings for $8.5 billion. What deals of this magnitude most demonstrated was that content, particularly in the print industry, as well as with audio and video media, was the most viable product of the day.

At the tag end of the millennium, Penguin merged with Putnam, Random House combined with Bantam Doubleday Dell, and Harper-Collins took over Morrow and Avon. What did all that mean in terms of sales numbers? In 1999, five corporations accounted for 85% of all the books dominating *Publisher Weekly's* hardcover charts, and those same five companies were responsible for 85% of the paperback list's top titles as well. Random House alone was responsible for 40% of all hardbacks on the list and one-third of all paperback bestsellers.

And what was the impact of a global marketplace? International sales account for as much as 40% of most good publishers' income. Additionally, the growth of e-tailing (which accounts for as much as 30% of most publishers' domestic income) has forced global pricing into the book business. No longer is a book published in the U.S. at $30 and sold in Europe at $90; the Internet has leveled pricing.

SMALL PUBLISHERS IN THE MIX

While big publishers get bigger and the big bookstore chains do the same, there are still a number of small publishers and small, independent bookstores fighting the good fight. Several small press magazines and the Small Publishers Association of North America (SPAN) serve the growing number of small publishers, which includes traditional imprints, university presses, and newer imprints that have surged to fill the niches left uncovered by publishers grown too big to sign marginal or mid-list titles.

In fact, given the tightening focus of major publishers, many niches are left open as new frontiers for entrepreneurial publishers with start-up companies. Whether it is the intention of these companies to rise to become major forces themselves or to merely create enough of a presence to tempt the acquisitions unit of a major house remains to be seen. But, for many, the opportunity to grow in a robust market is aided by new digital technology that assists the small business.

DIGITAL DAYS: THE IMPACT OF THE COMPUTER ON BOOK PUBLISHING

The arrival of the PC and the shift to digital content have had tremendous impact on publishing in all media forms. Early in the transformation, publishers were able to save the keystrokes of authors and, in some cases, even get camera-ready copy (digitally prepared and ready to print) for books, thus saving significantly in plant costs.

Recently, the two largest benefactors of digitization in the publishing industry have been *electronic publishers* (a topic covered later) and *print-on-demand* (POD) publishers. POD is a significant step since it reduces inventory costs for publishers, including taxation for those not in the non-profit sector.

In an era of increasing customization, printing books only as they are ordered makes sound business sense. True, the PPB costs run higher for each book, but this is more than offset by eliminating waste, returns, taxes on inventory, warehousing costs, and a number of other expenses related to bulk printings. Digital publishing has even become pivotal to the decision process. As John Conley, V.P. of Strategy and New Business Development at R.R. Donnelley & Sons put it, digital publishing also allows a publisher to do pilot or test-market programs while lowering print runs against returns to better manage risks. Soon, almost every book printed may also be available as an e-book.

Preparing a book on a computer, often with what-you-see-is-what-you-get (WYSIWYG) pages almost ready to publish, has inspired a number of authors to consider the next step: having the book bound and handled on a POD basis, or converted to be digitally read and offered directly to the public.

SELF-PUBLISHING

Anyone with enough money, time, and a smattering of book publishing knowledge can take a manuscript to a printer in camera-ready form and end up with a bound book. In Henry David Thoreau's time, self-publishing was the norm. Thoreau claimed that a large part of his own library was composed of copies of his own books. Marketing is everything.

There have been vanity presses (such as Vantage Press) for years. But recently, as the bar was raised at most publishing houses, authors' groups and printing presses across the nation had a collective surge of interest in self-publication. This also came at a time when the ability for the private individual to make acceptable camera-ready copy suitable for publication was made easier by affordable software and hardware—the latter including printers with 600 dots per inch (dpi) output.

Though it's easier these days to prepare a book, it's not easier to market one. Most people able to write and prepare a manuscript run into an obstacle when trying to decide how to launch and implement a fully-realized marketing program, not to mention how to address order-fulfillment problems related to selling a book. Internet vendors and a few local independent stores can help to a degree. But, in many cases, self-publication is an education of its own about the importance of marketing. That education has been eased by new support from local and national authors' associations and Internet magazines such as *Self-Publishing Magazine* (*www.self-publishing.com*). Fortunately for some early authors, electronic publishing (e-publishing) is gradually emerging as a legitimate alternative.

ELECTRONIC PUBLISHING

At the 1999 Seybold Conference, 35,000 attendees of this core meeting for digital publishing heard the resounding message: "Publishing will change more in the next five years than in the past 500."

For some time, publishers had considered the plusses and minuses of publishing on the Internet. The big plus was that most production processes led to having a manuscript in digital form. Most manuscripts these days arrive at the publishing house in one digital form or another, a few readily susceptible to e-publishing or conversion. But, the big minus was that no one had yet found a way to make money by publishing books on the Web.

The bulk of the mass market was quite accustomed to holding a book while reading it. Even today, most people don't care to read significant blocks of prose on their computer screen. The early publishers of e-books found that publishing them in Adobe Acrobat format suited their purposes best because people could download Acrobat Reader for free from the Adobe site, or, the purchaser of an Internet-published book could download and print a copy. But, anyone who has held a 700–900-page manuscript printed single-sided on paper knows that it's not the sort of book to read in the tub or on an airplane trip. In paper and toner alone, the cost is sometimes higher than just buying a hardback or paperback, even though Internet publishers lowered their price points to as acceptable a level as they could.

Still, the novelty of certain books published on the Internet—available nowhere else—drove some sales. Internet publishers, regardless of the format they were publishing in, soon were posting sales increases that caught the attention of mainstream publishers. But, as with any new conduit, a standard needed to be set that would ensure the downloadability of the content. The standard that emerged is known as Open e-Book Standard (OEB). The OEB format, based on the Internet core languages HTML and XML for the widest possible acceptance, is intended to ensure that texts can be read on any sort of electronic device: desktop and laptop PCs, handheld devices such as the Palm Pilot and Handspring's Visor, and dedicated electronic book display devices such as NuvoMedia's Rocket eBook or the SoftBook. [3]

E-publishing was on the rise. The sheer growing interest in Internet commerce, in addition to more computers in homes, drove an increase in sales that soon caught the eye of other entertainment publishers. In 1999, Barnes & Noble bought into an on-demand publisher, iUniverse. As recently as April 2000, Random House became the first major publisher to buy a share of an e-publisher when it took a 49% stake of Xlibris, based in Philadelphia. An interesting aspect of that purchase was that much of the list at Xlibris was made up of self-published books. Speculation was made about Random House's intentions—whether they were mining for author lists or attempting to acquire the tools for e-publishing.

While some start-up and established companies rushed to enter the e-publishing market, others hesitated. What made them wait was searching for a model of someone, anyone, who had made significant money at publishing books on the Internet. The Internet was dotted with companies like Electron Press (*www.electronpress.com*), whose main business was, like other small publishers, to release titles by authors who had not attracted the attention of major pub-

---

3.   Hilts, Paul, "Publishers Hail E-Book Standard," *Publishersweekly.com*, October 4, 1999.

lishers with their sidestepping of emerging and mid-list authors. But, a success story in e-publishing was in the wings waiting to emerge.

Chris MacAskill, CEO of Fatbrain, through a Web creation called Mightywords (*www.mightywords.com*), offered thousands of titles within months of launching that site. Aggressively pursuing the market, Fatbrain tried to negotiate with Stephen King for rights to a short story. Simon & Schuster and the author chose other arrangements. That King short story, *Riding the Bullet*, was eventually released through an arrangement between Simon & Schuster and several e-book publishers, one of which summed up the arrangement by saying: "This little horror puppy isn't going to be available in print. Ever!" In fact, the book was encrypted to ensure that copies could not be printed, a measure underscoring an ongoing concern about e-piracy. King's story was e-released on March 14, 2000 and became an instant e-bestseller, with at least 400,000 copies downloaded in the first 24 hours.

Among the beneficiaries of the Simon & Schuster arrangement to release King's story were Glassbook, netLibrary, Nuvomedia's Rocket eBook, Peanut Press, Crowsnest Book, Softbook Press, and Softlock.com. The use of the latter is particularly significant, since Softlock has become a virtual Ingrams (or e-wholesaler) of e-publishing, facilitating the conversion to e-book format that allows any retailer with a Web site to have access to the story.

Other authors, such as Mary Higgins Clark, are also making appearances in e-format. With these bigger names comes the kind of credibility that will make e-publishing even more viable in time.

SUMMARY: BOOKS

Content and conduit are the two key words that describe the evolution in book publishing in the latter half of the 20th Century. As content gained value in the eyes of entertainment conglomerates, book publishers became targets of acquisition. Furthermore, the niche approach to book content allowed for the introduction and expansion of several genres as readers' tastes became more focused. Finally, the evolving technology associated with both digitalization and the Internet promise to create new opportunities for both the publishing and marketing of books.

NEWSPAPERS

The lights dim and the smell of fresh-popped popcorn permeates the dim theater as black-and-white images flicker across the big screen in newsreel fashion. Orson Wells fills the screen as Charles Foster Kane in the 1941 movie *Citizen Kane*, still widely acclaimed as one of the finest films ever made. Yet the movie, with its coverage from sled to Xanadu, is a thinly veiled tour of the life of one of the first media moguls, William Randolph Hearst.

The newspaper industry experienced a dramatic renewal of interest for moguls late in the 20th Century. The dynamic shift occurred as a multitude of small daily papers competing for circulation in the mid-to-late 19th Century evolved, along with Sunday and free-circulation papers, into the huge news groups and cooperative efforts that dominate the 21st Century. And all of this came about because of the new king of newspaper revenue: advertising.

THE BEGINNING—MEDIA MOGULS

Newspapers were the first of all media forms to attract and foster moguls in America. To name just a few of the moguls who, beside Hearst, left a legacy of an entire newspaper group: James M. Cox (*Evening News*, Dayton, OH), Charles H. Dow, Edward D. Jones, and Charles M. Bergstresser (*Wall Street Journal*), Frank E. Gannett (*Times-Union*, Rochester, NY), James McClatchy (*Sacramento Bee*), Frank Munsey (*New York Sun, Herald*), General Harrison Gray Otis (*The Los Angeles Times*), Joseph Pulitzer (*Post-Dispatch*, St. Louis), Eugene C. Pullium (*Indianapolis Star*), Henry J. Raymond and George Jones (*The New York Times*), Edward W. Scripps (*Penny Press*, Cleveland, OH), and Charles and Michael De Young (*San Francisco Chronicle*).

It was Hearst who, after establishing the *San Francisco Examiner* in 1887, went on to grow one of the nation's first newspaper groups, which today includes Seattle's *Post-Intelligencer* and the *Express-News* of San Antonio. But the nation was not always a cluster of news groups. At one time, small, independent papers literally covered America, some barely big enough to cover a city or county, others bigger metro dailies fighting for the city's readership. At that time, the money to be made came from circulation—copies delivered at the door or sold on the streets. That was soon to change.

THE REVENUE REVOLUTION

A series of progressive steps marked the cycle of change in the newspaper industry, including:

- The saturation of dailies marked by slower gains in circulation
- An increase in Sunday papers as a product diversification
- The formation of groups, or chains, of newspapers to better control costs
- The mergers of competing big-city newspapers
- The creation of labor unions
- An increase in the importance of advertising
- The formation of more weekly and free-circulation papers
- The shift from hot-lead to digital off-set presses
- A shift from a purely vertical format to more horizontal stories
- A more visually and color-oriented public precipitated by TV

Of all these changes, it was the increase in revenues from advertising that most made the newspaper industry glitter in the eyes of moguls and huge entertainment groups late in the 20th Century.

For example, the advertising revenues of newspapers increased from $2 billion in 1950 to $36 billion per year by 1995. An earlier dependence on circulation decreased in significance until it accounted for only 15% of most newspapers' revenue. In fact, of all advertising dollars spent in the nation, newspapers command the biggest share of all, about 23%.

CHANGING COMPETITIVE ENVIRONMENT

In the heady days of early competition, newspapers battled for scoops and occasionally fought on the streets. The micro-marketing scene was home delivery, sales in newsstands, even the crier out hawking "extras." The most important part of a paper was "above-the-fold," the portion of the paper uppermost on a stack or seen in the now ubiquitous coin machines. The above-the-fold section (top half of the first page) had to grab the eye of the potential reader, similar to the screaming headlines of tabloids.

But the days of multiple papers scrapping for business in the same big town were numbered. The circulation of daily newspapers peaked in the 1970s, although there were still some small daily papers serving tightly regional areas. Many of these had been absorbed by growing chains. On the macro-marketing scene, there were morning papers, evening papers, dailies, and Sunday papers.

Papers like the *Wall Street Journal* expanded on the strength of sound financial coverage. The Gannett group responded to the public's visual and color orientation—as well as shorter attention span—by coming out with the color-rich and easy-to-read *USA Today*. The *New York Times* took advantage of the digital ability to print simultaneously from various locations to present its traditionally thorough and well-written coverage to remote corners of America. Tabloids like the *National Enquirer* found a consumer interest and leaped to exploit it.

At the same time, free-circulation papers were emerging on a wide scale. These presented deeper coverage of local entertainment venues, want ads, or whatever niche needed serving to carry the advertisements that supported them. Each paper had some kind of niche, with the larger ones competing only in an umbrella overlap manner. But the big story remained the increasing advertising revenues and climbing plant costs that resulted in many papers being made part of a group.

THE GROUP TROOP

By the early 21st Century, over 75% of all newspapers were part of some group, as media moguls had been quick to spot the increasing revenues from advertising.

The initial move toward chains of newspapers came in the face of cost issues, like fluctuating prices in the bulk paper market, rising labor costs, and the increasing costs of new technology. Bigger city papers could no longer afford to compete, and in many cases, merged. The advantages of shared technological resources led to many chains of smaller newspapers; some of these included different niche coverage as well, like weeklies, Sunday papers, and free-circulation papers.

One of the most important and historically significant leaps by a chain was the 1982 debut of the Gannett group's *USA Today*. Originally a chain of small and mid-sized New England papers organized into a group by Frank E. Gannett, it grew under the direction of Gannett's successor, Paul Miller. Miller built it into the largest chain of newspapers in America, a task carried on by Al Neuharth. The graphically rich and innovative *USA Today* responded to a visual trend with more and color art, while the paper's stories tended to be shorter, more suitable to a lowering national attention span. While some in the industry dubbed it "McPaper," it became an ideal source of news for travelers less interested in regionally focused news, finance, lifestyle, and sports. It also offered affordable national advertising.

It was that rebirth of interest by media moguls that led to the current newspaper landscape. In spite of any rumors of its slipping stature, the newspaper industry continues to sell more than 60 million copies every day, and generates over $45 billion per year. Those kinds of numbers put the cash register glitter in the eyes of moguls with money to invest.

The collapse of inner-city competition and the combining of smaller papers in the face of rising plant costs started the movement toward chains. The combined ability to offer advertisement deals helped moguls from other media heighten and accelerate the trend. Just a few of the billion-dollar plus groups involved in the industry are Capital Cities/ABC, Cox Enterprises, Dow Jones & Co., Gannett, Hearst, Knight-Ridder, New York Times, E.W. Scripps, Thomson (Canadian), Times Mirror, Tribune (Chicago), and the Washington Post. Many of these corporate names should ring a bell in association with other entertainment media.

NEWSPAPERS ON THE INTERNET

A national poll conducted by Princeton Survey Research Associates announced in May 2000 that the Internet "has matched or superseded other media to become even more important in users' lives than TV or newspapers."

This is the kind of story that led author Michael Crichton to label newspapers as "mediasaurs." But, before anyone rings the death knoll for newspapers, a quick trip to the World Wide Web (WWW) discloses that almost every newspaper already has a presence on the Internet. This raises the question: Why give something away for free that you charge for elsewhere?

An Internet presence by a newspaper is, if done correctly, a marketing strategy. Not only is it an expanded location for advertisements, but it can also draw readers to print versions of the newspaper. For example, *The Los Angeles Times* first appeared on the Internet through an agreement with Prodigy, but later formed its own Web presence. For a company using nearly 500 tons of newsprint covered by 700 gallons of ink a day, having a readership on the Internet actually saves big money. Though more than 20,000 people subscribe to the Internet version, the print version continues to sell over 600,000 copies per day.

SUMMARY: NEWSPAPERS

The economics of the late 20th Century, combined with the desire of media conglomerates to build vertical businesses, resulted in a trend toward newspaper groups. There has been a gradual evolution toward serving customers' needs through well-defined newspaper niches such as morning or evening, paid circulation or free, national or tight regional coverage.

Focusing on the special interests of readers is even more an issue in the following coverage of the magazine scene.

MAGAZINES

Magazines, perhaps as clearly as any other form of publishing, exemplify market segmentation by niches. If media executives could determine by demographics, geography, occupation, or any of the other determinants of special interest that demand for a magazine on underwater basket weaving existed, you can bet one would be woven right into the fabric of the market.

MANY ARE PUBLISHED, BUT FEW ARE PLAYERS

There are by some counts over 20,000 magazines published annually, although the Gale periodical directory lists fewer. There are regional magazines, non-for-profit magazines, trade magazines, special-interest magazines, magazines for men, for women, for seniors, for people with hobbies, people who plan to marry, have children, or already have children, or for people who like sports, news, politics, and countless other subjects.

Of all these, approximately 160 magazines account for 85% of the revenue generated by this industry. The names of the companies generating the most revenue from magazines include Time Warner, Hearst Corporation, Reed Elsevier, Advance Publications, International Data Group, Thomson Corp, Ziff Davis Publishing, Reader's Digest Association, News Corp, and Meredith Corporation.

Among the giant media companies mentioned earlier in the chapter, Capital Cities/ABC, Tele-Communications, Inc., CBS, Inc., Gannett Co., General Electric Co., New York Times Co., Viacom,

Knight-Ridder, Cox Enterprises, and Turner Broadcasting all have stakes in the magazine industry.

Of course, not all of these publish just to the entertainment area; several have technical and informational magazines that generate significant revenues.

REVENUE AND RETURN ON INVESTMENT

The chief sources of revenue for a magazine include circulation (mail delivery or newsstand sales), advertisements, mailing list rental, reprints or book spin-offs, advertorials (special multi-page sections dedicated to one advertiser), as well as a number of smaller revenue sources like special issues.

Magazines have a heavy dependence on advertising. Newsstand or subscription sales count for little except to substantiate the reading population; editorial content balances with advertising to carry a magazine, with circulation more necessary for generating advertising rates than for generating revenue.

The magic measurement of a magazine's success is cost per thousand, or CPM, which gives the clearest view of the potential ROI for a new magazine in a competitive niche. To get the CPM, you divide the total magazine circulation by the cost of a full-page black-and-white advertisement. These numbers are readily available for most existing magazines, since they list their ad rates as well as circulation—the latter for those who wish to buy (rent) the magazine's mailing list for their own marketing strategies.

A number of factors affect the profitability of a magazine. The standard practice among magazines is to have a ratio of advertising pages to editorial of 40% to 60%. As ad pages are added to each magazine release, editorial pages can be added. Circulation numbers are examined at the CPM rate, at the cost of acquiring new subscribers, at the cost of rolling a new subscriber into becoming a regular subscriber (an acquisition), and at the cost of renewing current regular subscribers. The "churn" of customers letting subscriptions lapse, and the much higher cost of getting new subscribers, can be major cost factors for a magazine. From an editorial standpoint, the magazine must consider its editorial cost per page in relation to its direct sales cost of each ad page: salaries, commissions, and other direct and indirect costs.

Just as with newspapers, many of the costs associated with magazines are associated with the actual printing and delivery—making the Internet an intriguing publishing possibility.

ZINES: INTERACTING ON THE INTERNET

Why on earth would a magazine already making money through circulation and newsstand sales offer a magazine for free on the Internet? The answer is similar to the case of newspapers—because there is more money to be made from advertising, and Web advertising dollars do not cannibalize advertising dollars from the printed magazines because the advertiser is frequently a different, more Internet-oriented advertiser.

Every year there are more PCs, hand-held devices, and other links to the Internet. Every year magazines continue to deal with the same concerns they've always had: Is it worth cutting down trees and slapping ink on pages? What do we do about rising labor costs? What do we do about rising postage costs?

Many of the industry's challenges are eliminated when it comes to publishing a "zine"—an electronic magazine. Zines offer a wealth of advantages: no expensive color printing—in fact, no printing at all; no inventory of paper and ink; no postage; no geographic limits to whom a magazine can serve. However, there certainly are costs associated with Internet publishing: graphic design, Web architecture, and most important, the staffing necessary to update the magazine more often than if it was printed once a week or once a month. Internet readers rely on Web sites because they like their information current—that day, that hour. Successful zines can generate tremendous traffic. When Ziff-Davis' *PC Magazine* and *Interactive Week* first came onto the company's ZD Internet site, that URL quickly ramped up to an average of three million hits a month.

One of the first things established magazines learned about releasing a zine version was to use the strength of the Web—offer an animated version of a sidebar, give a sound bite instead of a printed interview, and feature a three-dimensional (3D) or virtual look at something in a way no print magazine can do. Zines also offer the ability to extend the brand at a fraction of the cost of developing a new print version. For instance, *Smithsonian Magazine* not only made the conversion to the Internet with a Web version (*www.smithsonianmag.si.edu*), but it also developed a special kid's castle (*www.kidscastle.si.edu*).

Doing business on the Internet means the magazine must follow standard approaches to get traffic, or "hits." Having an easy-to-identify domain name helps. Getting listed on browsers such as Yahoo, Google, and Altavista is essential, as is embedding meta-tags, which are keywords that relate to the magazine buried in invisible HTML code on the home page. Search engines will read these meta-tags and list the magazine in the results provided by the browser. An Internet magazine can register hits from every passing browser, and then parlay those into new advertising revenues.

The biggest advantage that the Internet offers in the way of building brand loyalty is interactivity. Viewers/readers of zines that are formatted to use the strengths of the Web find that they have options not available in print versions. They can read summaries of stories, or view in-depth versions; they can give immediate feedback via email; and they can take part in polls and see immediate results. Zines that utilize these techniques can build strong audience loyalty to their sites.

SUMMARY: MAGAZINES

Magazines continue to be the leader in niche marketing opportunities as regards the entertainment sector of publishing. With an estimated 20,000+ titles in the marketplace, there are few audiences that cannot be reached via this medium. Furthermore, the expansion of magazines onto the Internet will continue to offer opportunities to reach an even wider audience.

ELECTRONIC GAMES

At the Electronic Entertainment Expo held in Los Angeles in May 2000, Douglas Lowenstein, President of the Interactive Digital Software Association (IDSA), predicted that software games would be the entertainment of the future. "Given a choice between the passive experience of watching TV and playing video games with the family in the living room, increasingly people are choosing games," he said.

ONLY A GAME?

The software game industry accounted for $6.1 billion of entertainment business in 1999 (compared to the movie industry's $7.5 billion box office during the same period), and the big players in that arena expect to compete for even bigger dollars in the future. The software game industry grew 11% in 1999 alone. According to a study made by the IDSA, 36% of U.S. household heads list video and computer games as a primary activity in their homes, almost twice the number that picked television as their primary entertainment form. A separate study, made by Peter D. Hart Research Associates, Inc. in Washington, D.C., determined that 145 million Americans, or approximately 6% of those six years old and older, play some form of interactive game.

The software game industry was not yet 30 years old at the turn of the century, but it had come a long way since the early Tandy games. From more sophisticated joysticks to the look and feel of almost lifelike graphics, gaming software has rapidly improved. One side-effect of these improvements has been the rapid downturn of the arcade-style video game. Since home consumers are able to play newer, more advanced versions of the same games they once found in arcades, the out-of-home entertainment industry has seen a rapid decline in the once flourishing family entertainment center sector.

Nintendo has long been a leader in gaming software and hardware, with *Pokemon*, the *Mario Brothers*, and its solid-selling Game-Boy product line. The GameCube, released in November 2001, was a direct response to Sony's PlayStation 2, which sold four million units before the middle of 2001. Microsoft finally entered the market in 2001 with XBOX, creating even more competition in a rapidly evolving industry.

NEW GAME FRONTIERS

The survivors of the next level of play in the software game competition will be those who master games with interactive components on the Internet, as well as wireless games.

Sony, for instance, anticipates that digital subscriber lines (DSL) and cable communication lines will be available all across America within 10 years. The company is actively seeking to partner with other big players to bring high-speed Internet to the gaming world. Sony is also looking at wireless networking as an alternative connection to Internet interactive play.

Sega of America, a unit of Japan's Sega Enterprises Ltd., offers an Internet service to promote online gaming with its new SegaNet. Another indication that online gaming is growing in popularity is AOL's alliance with Electronic Arts, Inc., a leading software game maker. Their intention is to offer a family of games. AOL's CEO Bob Pittman confirmed that, "The lines are blurring. This will be a world of tremendous alliances."

Nokia Corp., a cellular phone manufacturer, introduced a service that allows game application developers and online content publishers to create interactive entertainment for mobile devices. The technology behind Nokia's move is the Wireless Application Protocol (WAP). The company expects that by the end of 2003, more people will access the Internet by mobile handsets than through a PC. Cellular usage increased in Japan immediately when networks deployed NTT DoCoMo's iMode, a service similar to what Nokia intends to offer. However, the limit of 9.6kbps data bandwidth for WAP, as well as the black-and-white bitmap graphics, means shorter games with such game-enabled devices until a new generation of phones become available.

TARGETING THE MARKET

The increasing sophistication of hardware interfaces with the existing game market is one indication that young males with pimples are not the only users of the medium. According to the ISDA, most games are purchased by young adults, ages 18–24. But adults 25–40 follow closely, while women account for 43% of all games sold. This last statistic is one marketers should consider closely. Many of these women are likely mothers buying software for their families. While the tendency may be to target the end-user, moms still hold the purse strings when it comes to family purchases.

CROSS-MARKETING

There will be more alliances between software game companies and cable and networking companies with their ability to turn set-top boxes, consoles, hand-held devices, and other hardware into replacements for play stations. Additionally, expect to see other forms of cross-pollination taking advantage of the burgeoning revenue stream from software games.

The software game market has already benefited from the sale of supporting books and magazines featuring new products. In the near future, George Jones, Editor of *Computer Gaming World*, predicts that the software game industry will create closer and more effective ties with Hollywood. In the past, according to Jones, if a game carried a movie or TV title, it was to sell an otherwise weak game. Today, the opposite may be the case, with movies and TV series benefiting from a loyal game-playing audience.

For instance, Simon & Schuster (S&S) Interactive expects to release a software game title based on *Sabrina the Animated TV*

Series, as well as *Daria's Inferno*, based on the MTV series. Along with its sports parodies and other products, it will release Mac and PC versions of *Star Trek: Deep Space Nine*. Other S&S cross-media deals include an agreement with the Mars candy company for a children's math program based on the M&M candy characters of the TV commercials. More than half of Fox Interactive's new game titles have established mass-market recognition that have more appeal to the game-buying public. Activision's Ethisham Rabbani, Vice President of Global Brand Management, said that 10 of its 22 new titles stem from licensed agreements from movies or television. With DVD hardware becoming more accessible to a wider audience, more entertainment industry synergy seems inevitable.

MARKETING HURDLES

One challenge for the software gaming industry to overcome is the issue of violence in software games. Following the disclosure that the two teenagers who killed 15 fellow students at Columbine High School in Colorado had been avid players of games like *Doom* and *Quake*, the industry faced public relations problems. But that did little to slow the 11% growth of the industry in the year that followed the incident.

Another pressing issue for the software gaming industry is the same challenge that plagues the music and movie industries—piracy. Much like the headline-grabbing Napster, which allowed online users to search each other's computers for the common MP3 format of most music files, the software industry fights against programs like Gnutella. The program has no respect for copyrights and downloads songs, images, pirated music videos, and illegally decoded DVD movies. It was a rogue product originally developed by Nullsoft, a subsidiary of AOL, and though it was quickly pulled from the Internet, countless copies and variations were already circulating.

In a fast-growing frontier, even if answers are found to combat programs like Gnutella, others will rise in its place—each more sophisticated than the last. Companies like BMG Entertainment and Sony Music Entertainment were among the first to offer online versions of digital entertainment with technical safeguards preventing copying. In the battleground that is technology, these skirmishes should continue for some time. But who could be better suited to fight them than the makers of software games?

NEW CHANNELS OF DISTRIBUTION

Software games were originally sold across America in computer stores, where huge screens showed the games in progress and customers tried out the games on state-of-the-art hardware. But just as books have become a revenue staple of groceries and discount chains, so has software become a popular mass-market item in the same venues. Even gas stations and convenience stores are getting into the act. But the *Caveat Emptor* remains: Check the compatibility, since many of the programs remaindered or sold in mass are there for a reason; they are not upwardly compatible with newer hardware.

SUMMARY: ELECTRONIC GAMES

The software gaming industry is the darling of the entertainment media industry. With sales double those of movie box office, games are on the rise as an at-home alternative to old destination-driven locations such as malls and arcades. Advancing technology in this industry will continue to offer marketing professionals new avenues of promotion, as well as new opportunities to reach a young, affluent, and interactivity-prone audience.

SUMMARY: PUBLISHING

The impact of the digitization of publishing in all forms, combined with the increasing sense of global community and the segmentation of special-interest markets into niches, continues to cause the big to get bigger. As media and entertainment conglomerates look for new ways to develop content, the field of publishing will continue to be a focus for acquisition. Finally, the long-term impact of the conglomerates will be an increased synergy between entertainment sectors, offering intriguing marketing opportunities.

Content over packaging continues to be a dominant trend in publishing, creating intellectual property concerns as well as marketing opportunities. The same holds true for the field of music, which is discussed in the next chapter.

FOR FURTHER READING

BOOKS

1. Daly, Charles P. et al., *The Magazine Publishing Industry* (Boston, MA: Allyn & Bacon, 1996).

2. Forsyth, Patrick and Robin Birn, *Marketing in Publishing* (Bethel, CT: Rutledge, 1997).

3. Albert N. Greco, *The Book Publishing Industry* (Boston, MA: Allyn & Bacon, 1996).

4. Kleper, Michael, *The Handbook of Digital Publishing* (New York, NY: Pearson, 2000).

5. Picard, Robert G. and Jeffrey H. Brody, *The Newspaper Publishing Industry* (Boston, MA: Allyn & Bacon, 1996).

MAGAZINES TO DEVOUR

1. *Editor & Publisher*

2. *Electronic Media*

3. *Electronic Publishing*

4. *Multimedia News*

5. *Publish*

6. *Publisher's Weekly*

OTHER RESOURCES

1. *Gale Directory of Publications & Broadcast Media* (published each year by Gale Research).

2. *LMP: Literary Market Place: The Directory of the American Book Publishing Industry* (published each year by Bowker).

3. *Publishers, Distributors & Wholesalers of the United States* (published each year by Bowker).

4. Ulrich's *International Periodicals Directory* (published each year by Bowker).

7 MUSIC

OVERVIEW

S ince the earliest priests chanted in front of an open camp-fire—accompanied by a drumbeat on hollow logs or on tightly stretched animal skins—music has been a focal point of religious inspiration, festive occasions, and social interaction. More recently, music has served a wider spectrum of interests, ranging from idol worship by teenagers to intellectual stimulation for symphony fans. Avid followers of all ages attend live music performances, purchase and collect recorded music, and remain loyal and sometimes frenzied fans. This is the core of today's $40 billion recorded and live concert music industry.

A QUICK SNAPSHOT OF THE MUSIC DEVELOPMENT PROCESS

As in every sector of the entertainment industry, each music career has its own crossroads. However, the typical path to the top of the heap looks something like this:

- Aspiring singer/songwriter writes a few hot songs for a hot genre.
- He/she/they form a band—or work solo—and build a loyal fan base at music clubs and festivals.
- He/she/they hire a manager and/or producer.
- He/she/they make a basic demo and send it to music labels and scouts; they perhaps hire a freelance public relations (PR) person.
- An A&R (Artist & Repertoire) professional hears the demo, likes it, makes a recommendation to produce a quality CD, and puts the act in front of a music label executive with decision-making authority.
- A senior executive at the label agrees to go forward and commits to a budget to move the act forward.
- The label either hires or uses staff engineers, studios, back-up artists, songwriters, and an in-house producer to polish the work.
- A CD is mastered and a major marketing push is developed.
- A music video is made, a publicist arranges talk shows, a tour manager books major concerts, magazine covers are planned, national radio play is organized, and the music video is aired on MTV or VH-1.
- Shipments go to wholesalers, major music retailers are sent details on marketing push, signage is put up in stores, and a media and publicity campaign is implemented.

From that point on, only the market will tell if the artist at the eye of this storm will be a one-hit wonder, a major superstar, or a comfortable career-type. Regardless of the star's status, he or she will become intimately familiar with the ways of the business—starting with the importance of intellectual property (IP).

THE RIGHTS STUFF

Once again, in the beginning, there is "C": content. As in every other sector of entertainment, music content must be protected carefully. The music industry was one of the first to recognize the need for organizations that protected the IP rights of artists.

Two early pieces of legislation influenced the decision to create organizations that would protect these rights. In 1897, the U.S. granted performance rights to authors of non-dramatic musical works (prior to this time, the performance had to be for profit), but an author of a musical work was hard-pressed to check up on every performance of his or her output. This was the rationale behind the 1914 formation of the American Society of Composers, Authors and Publishers (ASCAP); the belief was that the author's rights could be protected better collectively. ASCAP became increasingly more powerful in the U.S. until 1939, when radio broadcasters, unhappy with ASCAP's monopoly, formed their own organization: Broadcast Music Inc. (BMI). BMI has become the other major performing rights association in the U.S., also representing composers, publishers, and songwriters.

ASCAP and BMI employ a blanket license, granted for a given period, which permits various institutions to perform any work in their repertoire. They then distribute royalties to members based on the popularity of their works. This allows the author to avoid handling each infringement of the copyright on an individual basis—a tremendous cost savings to the artist. It does, however, mean that these organizations must closely police the use of the works. Many a bar owner has discovered this when a representative from BMI has shown up to take a look at the jukebox.

IP continues to be a hot potato in this segment of the industry, with the Internet and "sampling" (the use of certain portions of an author's work included in someone else's new composition) examples of two challenges recently facing composers. In another controversy, the Recording Industry Association of America (RIAA) led an effort to change the U.S. copyright law that designated sound recordings as "works for hire." The controversy began with language in the 1999 Satellite Home Viewer Improvement Act that might have prevented artists from reclaiming ownership of their master recordings. The RIAA worked with the Artist's Coalition (led by Don Henley, formerly of the hit group, the Eagles), the National Academy of Recording Arts and Sciences (NARAS), the American Federation of Musicians (AF of M), the American Federation of Television and Radio Artists (AFTRA), and the Music Managers Forum to create language that would have a long-term effect on the future IP rights of musicians.

Because of this successful effort, these groups have expressed the intention of continuing to work together, along with international organizations such as BUMA (Holland), GEMA (Germany), SACEM

(France), and the Performing Rights Society (PRS, UK) on an International Joint Music Venture (IMJV) aimed at heading off music IP issues brought on by the Web and globalization of the music marketplace.

Continuing with the C's of entertainment, the music sector also deals with conduit. At the head of the conduit flow are the music labels themselves.

MUSIC LABELS

Music is a hit-driven business, pure and simple—the more hits, the more money. The average projection says that for every several hundred CD releases, there are 20 to 25 gold (500,000 units sold) or platinum (1,000,000 units sold) releases. One way to acquire more hits is to invest in more new artists—but the easier way is to simply buy a label that represents artists with proven track records. This theory of "bigger is better" has led to Universal gobbling up Polygram for over $10 billion and WarnerElectraArista Music (WEA, a division of Time Warner) combining with EMI, the only major record label of the "Big Five" record companies (Warner Music, Sony Music, Universal Music, BMG, and EMI) not associated with a larger, consolidated media player.

INDEPENDENTS

This consolidation in the industry has resulted in many new independents springing up. These new labels may join forces with a few disenfranchised or new talents, using CDs or cassette sales at concerts and free performances—or over the Internet—to cover the costs of their start-ups as they struggle to create the next important mini-label.

However, independents as a whole are far from being small potatoes. Independent labels (as a group) generally have the largest share of pre-recorded industry sales promoted by Sound Scan and released by NARM (National Association of Recording Manufacturers). These sales can represent anything from a garage band making its own CD for limited release to companies like Rhino Records, TVT, and others who generate between $50–$100 million in sales. Many of these larger independents give the artist great creative freedom—and a greater share of the total revenue pie, including tour receipts, licensing, and merchandise.

PRIVATE LABELS

While the big get bigger and the mini-labels look more and more maxi, there is still room in the music industry for the self-promoter. Ever since the early days of recording, there have always been those pioneering souls who had a 45 pressed—or today, a CD burned—thrown them in the car, and made the rounds of the radio stations. For instance, country western singer Lucinda Williams got her start selling her own CDs on street corners and at gigs in Austin, TX. She was eventually "discovered" at an annual South-By-Southwest (SXSW) music festival held in Austin.

Or, take the case of a genre-specific rising star like Mike Blakely. His music is best described as alternative adult country western, with the emphasis on western. A successful novelist of historical westerns such as *Comanche Dawn*, he also sings lead in a group doing gigs across America. The label "Swing Rider Records" was formed to promote his CDs. Recent recordings *West of You* and *In the Dust* were recorded at the LA-Z-L Studio in Kingsland, TX; the cost of properly recording, mixing, and producing such a CD runs around $20,000.

An artist like Blakely, clearly aware of his niche, usually promotes his or her CDs to the weekly music trade magazine *Gavin*, which covers the American radio industry. *Gavin* collects and compiles the playlists of more than 1,300 radio stations; it also offers a mailing service, doing bulk CD mailings to the niche radio genres specified by the artist. In Blakely's case, these mailings would probably be directed to Americana stations.

Building momentum is harder for a small label than a large one, since advertising budgets, a full-time publicist, and a major tour manager are not part of the picture. The advent of sales through Internet e-tailers and wider music play on eclectic Internet stations are providing emerging artists an opportunity that did not previously exist. But, before we make the jump to the Information Superhighway, let's take a look at the more established path to listeners.

THE ALL-IMPORTANT AIRPLAY

Part of the standard promotion for any group's or individual's success is getting airplay on radio stations. This poses a variety of challenges, as radio is an advertising-driven medium. Stations want to play the songs that are most likely to attract listeners to their format, the playlist of which has been carefully mapped out to grab the particular demographics advertisers are after. However, MTV's successful formula of 80% new to 20% older tunes has encouraged some stations to provide more airtime for newer songs.

To get airtime, the label's promoter must first get the new singles and albums in the hands of the appropriate stations. Advertising budgets can help in this regard; a mega-budget often signals to station programmers that a song can merit more playtime to the benefit of a station and its advertising.

However, there is more to getting airplay than just demographics and advertisers. Radio revenues are also dependent on independent promoters, the people who act as middlemen between record labels and radio stations. These "indies" offer a variety of payments to the stations to play certain songs—for instance, cash and promotional items—with the money to pay for such enticements coming from the record labels themselves.

These payments are not to be confused with "payola"—the term that grew out of the scandals that wracked the radio world in the 1950s, when disc jockeys (DJs) like Alan Freed were found to have received payments to play certain songs. Payola is only illegal when the listener is not made aware that payments are being made. The fact that indies are bona-fide businesspeople providing a "service" to the industry—up-front—keeps the practice from falling to the wrong side of the law.

Fredric Dannen's book, *Hit Men: Power Brokers & Fast Money Inside the Music Business,* [1] offers an intriguing insight into the practices—good and bad—of the music promotion business. As described in *Hit Men,* in the early days, the enforcers or distributors—financially supported and acknowledged by the labels—would buy "radio play" from DJs at radio stations all across the country

---

1.   Dannen, Fredric, *Hit Men: Power Brokers & Fast Money Inside the Music Business* (New York, NY: Vintage, 1991).

with cash, drugs, and sex. When charges of racketeering and corrupt practices were brought against individuals at the labels and radio stations, the business cleaned itself up. Legitimate businesses were created under formal contract, with the labels to maintain constant contact with the radio stations, studio managers, DJs, and program directors, using full-blown marketing kits and promotional items to gain airtime. These practices include legitimate agreements to promote co-op advertising dollars to gain strong "airplay" support.

But what about the public, you might ask, and their desire to hear certain songs? Certainly those "request lines" lighting up must have some impact on airtime? The answer: maybe yes, maybe no.

THE BOGUS REQUEST SCAM

In the 1990s, country music radio stations in particular were plagued with floods of requests programmers soon began to suspect weren't genuine.[2] The calls came in clusters; hip DJs soon identified several specific labels they felt were responsible for hiring agencies to make bogus calls. This sort of promotion, unethical and as much a possible source of harm to performers as a help, began again in the new millennium, but radio stations were quicker to spot the patterns.

Because station programmers may skew their mix based on requests, a motive might have been to ensure more hits for a label's products. Some DJs retaliate by boycotting all products from these suspicious labels. Record labels are quick to deny the allegations, often claiming over-zealous fans. Radio stations, however, ultimately distrust labels associated with the practice, and a resulting diminished skew can result. This practice is much more difficult to perpetuate with Internet-generated station requests, since email-submitted requests may be more readily screened.

While it may be hard to identify "real" listeners over the airwaves, it certainly isn't difficult to do at the heart of the music experience: the live performance.

---

2.   Stark, Phyllis, "Bogus Request Calls Hit Country Stations," *Billboard*, April 22, 2000.

LIVE MUSIC

Live music happens in venues across America: Madison Square Garden in New York City, blues bars in San Francisco, the Newport Jazz Festival, honky-tonk dance ballrooms in Oklahoma, stadiums, outdoor amphitheaters, beach boardwalks, bandshells, and open-air plazas. While some may prefer their music in intimate settings—where they can actually see the artist—others crave the experience of being surrounded by thousands of other rabid fans.

The modern-day P.T. Barnum who brings this circus to town knows how to build interest, anticipation, and deliver a fanfare. The three rings in this particular case are the act itself, the associated retail sales of tee-shirts, CDs, and full-color programs packed with photos, and the sponsorship dollars built on synergy with brands anxious to bring their message to the artist's audience. These revenue streams enable the producer/promoter to gain a return on the significant investment necessary to stage these modern-day spectaculars. The promoter's marketing program will utilize local newspapers, local spot television, and heavy promotional radio featuring ticket giveaways to call-ins from listeners.

However, live music presentations have become more and more expensive due to the cost of venue rentals, housing for talent, equipment, special-effects, laser shows, special lighting, and large-screen projection. It has become essential to locate sponsors who can fund the bulk of the expense. Kool cigarettes became the founding sponsor of the Kool Jazz Concerts in New York and Newport, while Tommy Hilfiger supports new boy groups like N'Sync. Budweiser, Pepsi, and Coca-Cola all support warm–weather, outdoor concerts and provide seed money as well as outright sponsorship funds, balanced by obtaining exclusive pouring rights (the only brand of beverage poured at the event).

Hundreds of these sponsored events go on around the U.S. every year, driving sales for both the artist and the sponsor and giving live-music fans a chance to feed their craving. However, nothing gives the true live-concert fan an experience like the "big top" of the music world: the megatour.

MEGATOURS

There are only a few megatours each year, bringing groups and artists like The Who, The Rolling Stones, Clint Black, Ricky Martin, and Madonna to the largest possible venues in the U.S. and around the world. These events are timed with the release of a new album and are supported by enormous marketing funds and PR machinery, all in the name of reaching for double platinum-level sales.

CASE IN POINT: KISS AND SELL

A classic example of megatouring is the marketing of the rock band Kiss in the 1970s.[3] During the early years of music touring and the development of major tent or stadium shows, audiences expected to be shocked, excited, even surprised. Crazy costumes, over-the-top make-up, smashing guitars on stage, laser light presentations, smoke machines, and a huge variety of special-effects were used to lend sizzle to rapidly rising rock & roll stars. Kiss was the perfect example of the early megatour band.

One of the highest earning rock groups in the world—approaching over $1 billion in sales of records, concert tickets, and merchandise over its illustrious career—Kiss seemed especially aware that the frontier of their era was visual impact, tied to an audience that grew up with eyes glued to television sets. With outrageous costumes that followed the androgynous style of Mick Jagger and David Bowie, and tongues out in blatant counter-cultural fashion, the group captured the fancy of a growing following. By mid-decade, the group had been signed by Frank Zappa to appear on his label (owned by parent company Warner), and had acquired eight gold or platinum albums.

But you can only have so many explosions, smash so many guitars, and chomp so many carbon-based life forms before the glitz no longer glitters. The music industry rewards talent on the way up, maximizing sales, supporting marketing efforts on a grand scale, and then, just as quickly, abandons the group not able to maintain fan loyalty, sustain personal touring, or maintain the hype necessary to stay in the public eye. Kiss faded in popularity in the 1980s, only to rise later from deep decline to once again be ranked as one of the hottest bands in the land. The group's phoenix-like rebirth was one of nostalgia for those early frontier days of rock popularity, and lasted only briefly.

A megatour is a high-water mark of success for a star or group, and indicates a high level of trackable interest—the ability to fill the largest venues throughout America and the world. A promoter

---

3.   Lendt, Chris K., *Kiss and Sell: The Making of a Supergroup* (Watson-Guptill Pub., 1997).

orchestrating such a tour must make certain assurances regarding the artist's responsibilities, while the venue must also be able to assure the promoter that the seats will be filled. A typical tour contract is loaded with "riders," which ensure both sides other comfort levels. For instance, details may include the exact number and size of lights, sound capabilities, even the specific food or other entertainment that will be available to the artists.

Megatours are the perfect example of the medium becoming the message—while the music itself is the main draw, the message of the star's bankability that comes from such an event only serves to more firmly place that artist in the firmament of top performers. In today's technology-driven world, however, megatours are not the only way to keep a performer in the eye of the audience. The big splash for an artist often comes in the form of the release of their music video.

THE IMPACT OF MUSIC VIDEOS AND MTV

The "Father of Music Video," MTV (a division and major brand of the CBS/Viacom corporation), was launched in August 1981. Robert Pittman, Vice President of MTV Programming from 1981 to 1986 and today President and CEO of AOL/Time Warner, was determined to create a medium that would be innovative, creative, and get people recharged about music—as well as offering record labels very strong promotional weapons for their product. Pittman was 110% successful. MTV is now recognized as a launchpad for new music and a considerable ally to music marketers.

From the beginning, the creators of MTV recognized the power of combining music and technology to form a conduit straight to the rapidly growing 15- to 34-year-old market. John Lack (MTV's creator) and his company, Warner Amex Cable (the original owner of MTV), decided on a strategy that would convince cable operators to carry the channel on their still uncrowded line-ups. They endorsed a unique advertising and promotion campaign inviting millions of young people to call their local cable operators and state: "I Want My MTV." This put MTV into over 40 million TV households, creating a permanent fixture in every teen and young adult household. Despite immediate competition from the TV networks and TBS (the first cable "super-station"), MTV prospered throughout the early 1980s and eventually launched a sister station, VH-1. This was a classic marketing tactic known as launching a "flanker brand." VH-1 was based on the same concept of playing music videos, but this time, it was geared to reach the wider and older audience of 25–45+-year-olds. It was projected that this audience would enjoy nostalgia music as well as middle-of-the-road pop and early rock & roll.

The need for resources elsewhere at Time Warner resulted in the sale of MTV and VH-1 to Viacom. The music cable channels began to change, launching original shows such as on-location college spring break programs as well as music star interview shows. This new and successful format created a different image for MTV, establishing it as a successful programmable vehicle and a cable channel with longevity. This helped provide a platform from which MTV Europe, MTV Asia, and MTV Latin America were launched, proving that music was truly a universal language, not to mention a global marketing vehicle.

Teens worldwide responded to American and English music. In November 1989, MTV went on-air in East Berlin and 48 hours later, the Berlin Wall fell. Needless to say, many political changes had been under development during the prior decade, but MTV seized on the coincidence with a publicity campaign that expounded the role of the channel in spreading capitalism and Western pop culture.

By the early 1990s, MTV was accepted as an established cable channel with a strong and loyal audience that replaced itself with each new generation. Marketers of all types recognized MTV as the youth conduit; in 1992, during its coverage of the 1992 presidential campaign, Bill Clinton appeared on an MTV interview show playing a cool saxophone and wearing dark glasses. Clinton won the young voters as well as the election, and MTV gained the reputation of speaking to the new and next generation of opinion leaders.

Eventually, MTV joined the Internet race and began to develop a dual-channel personality—and a dominant one. The Internet version, mtvi (mtv.com), was registering 4.2 million hits a month in early 2000, compared to 3 million hits a month for its nearest follower, MP3.[4] MTV continues to stay ahead of the technology and trend curves as it evolves and yet retains its core audience. MTV's more recent full-page ads in Billboard reflect its continuing marketing posture: "Our Corporate Identity—100% Youth: To connect with viewers aged 15–34 years."

The success of MTV has also influenced the growth of other cable music video stations such as Black Entertainment Television's (BET's) Black Star Power and Country Music Television's (CMT's) Great American Country for country music fans.

---

4. Media Metrix Home/Work Combined Panel, February 2000.

GETTING THE MUSIC TO THE MASSES: RETAIL DISTRIBUTION

Firing up the interest of the music consumer hopefully leads to the consumption phase: the purchase. The front line between the record manufacturers, distributors, and consumers has always been the retail outlets for music—from the early mom-and-pop store to the chains.

MOVING THE MERCHANDISE

The music business has always carried enormous clout and cachet due to its high margins and excellent profitability for all participants. In addition, like the publishing industry, the music business also provides fully guaranteed sales with almost total return privileges on all unsold merchandise (within a stipulated period of time). Therefore, should huge shipments (based on the anticipation of large retail sales) result in huge returns, the major injured party is usually the talent, who simply receives royalties on the net sales.

The labels have discovered a way to limit their liabilities, constrain the returns, and expand their points of distribution by reaching out to the big discounters—in effect changing the dynamics of the business. The youth audience, attracted by low music prices, makes chains like Best Buy and Circuit City salivate, since the 18–25 audience also buys new audio and entertainment equipment. Mass outlets such as Wal-Mart and Kmart sell pre-recorded bestsellers at greatly discounted prices—in some cases, below cost—and have gained nearly a 25% share of the music retail industry.

In the meantime, Musicland, Trans World Entertainment, Wherehouse, National Record Mart, Spec's Music and others have gone through reorganizations and shuttered many of their money-losing, poor-location stores to try and recoup lost business. However, much of the impact on these stores—which focus primarily on music as opposed to equipment—has come from the megastore market.

LIKE A VIRGIN

The earliest form of music retailing was the mom-and-pop record store, a now-quaint fixture in the local community, that featured racks of 45s and LPs. Along one wall, the store usually featured "listening booths"—small glass-enclosed rooms with a turntable and headphones. These stores are now gone from the face of the industry, replaced not only by the discounters mentioned previously, but also by the "superstores." The first steps toward super-storedom were taken by Sam Goody and Liberty Records, in 5,000–7,000-square-foot venues. Then came the slightly larger Tower Records, and its equal, Richard Branson's Virgin Records (which was eventually sold to EMI). Another retail challenger from the British shores, HMV, positioned itself between the elegance of Virgin and the tackiness of Tower Records, providing a funky, underground, contemporary design.

As the music market continued to heat up and retailing in general saw the success of "big box" stores, Virgin upped the ante with the addition of 100,000-square-foot Virgin Mega-Stores in locations around the U.S. and throughout the world. Virgin literally made a fine art out of the megastore by locating one of their outlets in the Carousel retail area of the Louvre in Paris. To further capitalize on the physical presence of New York's 14th Street store, Virgin borrowed a bit of New York history from 42nd Street by creating a continuous billowing puff of smoke that emanates from the façade of the building, high above the sidewalk—not unlike the old Camel spectacular in Times Square.

Each of the Virgin stores uses layout, design, ease of selection, sampling opportunities, sheer size, and depth of product as powerful marketing tools at the most precious point in the transaction, the point of sale. The same beautifully organized genres of music, sound studios, and attendant rooms filled with licensed products and merchandise are present in each location.

While the megastores of today bear little resemblance to the mom-and-pop stores of yesteryear, they do share one thing in common: the ability to listen to new music before you purchase. Given that there are over 25,000 new CDs released every year, listening posts are still required accessories at the retail level. But, the ability to try before you buy isn't the only holdout from the early days of music retailing.

MUSIC BY MAIL

There are very few music fans alive that haven't been seduced by the "free CDs" (or albums, depending on your generation) offered by music clubs such as Columbia House and BMG Direct. Owned by leading labels, both clubs have slowly grown over the years to gain an almost 15% share of all music shipments, cutting into the retail music store business. Music clubs have operated on the theory of providing "the store in your home," allowing consumers to review the offerings at their leisure. The clubs are typically marketed through direct mail, tabloid and magazine advertising, and TV commercials; they may occasionally offer free CDs for recommending a friend or for buying a certain number of CDs, a ploy generally overlooked by most music retailers.

The arrival of the Internet brought competition to music clubs. Sites such as CDNow.com and Amazon.com offer the same "shop in your home" service, without the annoying "negative option" mailings that most music clubs (as well as book clubs) employ. Negative option is the practice of automatically mailing an order card for a new item to a member each month and charging that member for the then-shipped item—unless the card is returned within a specific amount of time. Additionally, overnight shipping generally satisfies the delivery needs of consumers who use Internet sites.

Retailers have fought back against music by mail by providing their equivalent of the book retailer's autograph signings, free performances by up-and-coming artists, and Ticketmaster kiosks, which provide additional drivers to bring the target market through the door.

MARKETING THE MUSIC

With a global audience always searching for a new beat, music offers marketers a tremendous ability to reach niche markets. Marketing the product to these eager ears can take many forms, from pushing the personality to creating new mediums of delivery.

DADDY, WHAT'S AN LP?

One of the most amazing stories in music marketing occurred when the business reinvented itself with CDs, replacing the 33 1/3 LP (long-playing) record, which took over sales from the 45s and 78s that preceded it. While the introduction of LPs drove some incremental business (as music was re-mastered from 78s, especially during the shift from high-fidelity to stereo), that hardly compared with the gold rush that occurred with CDs.

The CD was invented by Royal Philips Electronics, a Dutch company based in Amsterdam, and best known for the manufacture of light bulbs and lighting accessories—in effect, the General Electric of

Europe. Philips had fashioned itself as a media and entertainment company, building and acquiring labels to achieve a 13% share of the pre-recorded music market. The company had also purchased a few small independent film production companies in an attempt to mirror the successful U.S. models of integrated entertainment. The CEO, Alan Levy, a wiry and lively Frenchman, was given a mandate to grow the company. Like many business leaders in the late 20th Century, he found a path to that growth in technology.

Philips' CD was a major breakthrough in the music industry. With the advantage of digitally recording the music on nearly indestructible CDs, the product offered a long-wearing carrier, extremely high-quality sound reproduction, and cost efficiency at large-quantity runs. While the initial patent was secret, it became too hot to hold back and was released to great fanfare.

As always, this new software required new hardware, making needle-activated stereo equipment outdated and useless. Within a few years, quality CD players were available from Sony, JVC, and Panasonic at a $1,000 price point. Multiple CD players were averaging $2,000–$5,000. But as usual, the price of the hardware dropped quickly as the market grew; before long, consumers were able to purchase boomboxes and portable CD players for under $100. With strong marketing of this new revolution and readily available hardware at affordable prices, it was no surprise that CD sales expanded the music market by nearly 30%; LPs declined to a share under 1% of sales. Today, LPs are relegated to nostalgia record shops.

This new medium also created a variety of new products. Plastic "jewel boxes" replaced the cardboard sleeve; new storage systems appeared in every music retail outlet. As technology raced forward, re-writable CD drives became standard accessories for new computer systems, allowing consumers to record their own "favorite hit" CDs. CD players replaced cassette decks in many automobiles, although upper-end models still offer both. While the new size—6" x 6"—offered space-saving advantages to both consumers and retailers, the jewel boxes were also easily pocketed by fast-fingered shoppers. Magnetic theft alarms became ubiquitous at retail outlets.

The burst of sales growth provided by the introduction of CDs gave the major labels the confidence to increase marketing budgets to drive more hits—not to mention very attractive profit and loss statements. However, all good things must come to an end. Once consumers finished their initial rush to replace older LPs with the new product, sales began to slip back to the kind of volume normally associated with the sales of new releases only. The industry awoke one day to find that the gold rush was over, and peered into the uncertain future in search of a new technology to recreate the boom. In the meantime, marketers continued to focus on tried and true methods of piquing consumer interest.

MARKETING PERSONALITIES

Possibly more so than in any other entertainment sector, music depends heavily on the marketing of personality—especially as it relates to those artists who perform live. The hype attendant to any on-stage appearance of a performer is part of the experience machine—getting the audience in a lather before they even enter the auditorium, creating a concert rush that energizes both the performer and the fan. Careers today are built on this phenomenon—careers that may end in a year, or continue on to achieve the same evergreen status as a Barbra Streisand or a Frank Sinatra. The Ricky Martins, Britney Spears, Christina Aguileras, and N'Synes of today are all superstars of 2001—but will they continue to sell out concerts with 100,000 seats in advance and possibly cross over to movies, TV, books, and other entertainment media? Or, will they flame out and disappear into the abyss of stars abandoned by fans and promoters? And, how do they get to their current status in the first place?

For the most part, they get there via the marketing machine that only the major labels can mount, selectively employed when everyone on the team believes this is "IT"—a superstar in the making, under contract. All the tactics required to achieve hit status will be employed with support from the top of the company. Multi-million-dollar budgets, staffs of professionals in publicity, A&R, advertising, touring, and venue relationships build an enormous opening for a tour touting a new album. Those appearances are backed with a no-expense-spared music video for multiple plays on MTV or VH-1, countless talk show interviews, leading magazine cover stories, organized fan clubs, and TV specials. The executive in charge of gaining distribution will send his or her sales force and distributors to major record chains and mass merchandise outlets, filling the pipeline with shipping orders. Finally, when the star's performance/marketing blitz is launched, a groundswell of hype, buzz, and CD purchasing hysteria leads to the reward: the record goes double platinum and pays for all the thousands of non-hits released by the label that year.

CASE IN POINT: DIXIE CHICKS TAKE FLIGHT

Consider the case of the Dixie Chicks' first headliner megatour. This Grammy-winning trio set out to prove that Garth Brooks isn't the only country talent capable of packing the biggest venues. Simon Renshaw, the group's manager at Senior Management, organized a 70-city tour that reflected the aggressive style needed to build on a group's presence in today's music business. With three different promotion groups and an advertising campaign of over $3 million, the effort demonstrated a classic music marketing campaign.

The group had done its initial touring in a supporting role for other high-profile events, such as the George Strait Country Music Festival, Lilith Fair, and Tim McGraw. After paying their touring dues, the performers felt they had sufficient new material for their own headliner tour.

GSD&M, an advertising agency in Austin, TX, was commissioned to begin the drum-roll of an advertising campaign with TV, radio, print, and outdoor promotion. The TV spots focused on the group's unfamiliarity with being a headliner group—the classic "We're number two, we try harder" approach. Each city on the tour was bombarded a week before each show and at least a week after —the logic being that positioning and profiling goes on even after the last note fades from the arena. Meanwhile, Sony collaborated with Wherehouse retail in a sweepstakes, and Gaylord Digital's new country Web site, MusicCountry.com, came onboard as the tour's sponsor. Other media got on the bandwagon, including the CMT country music cable network.

The highly visual presentation of each show focused on top sound, staging, and lighting, and immediate plans were made for follow-up tours in Australia and other international venues. Pricing and guarantees were let out on a bid basis to allow the marketplace to determine the still-emerging group's value. Ticket sales were additionally enhanced with one dollar out of each ticket going directly to the World Wildlife Fund. In short, the group left no stone unturned in a concerted effort to maximize exposure in building and maintaining its momentum.

The reward of the tour was a targeted gross of $35–$40 million, which built on the success of a debut album—*Wide Open Spaces*—that sold over six million units. The Dixie Chicks' follow-up, *Fly*, sold four million.

This type of multi-million-dollar sale allowed Sony to recoup their investment and justified their total support in the next round. If sales had been flat, the world as the artists knew it would have changed. As an example, Sony's Columbia Records division spent nearly $10 million just for advertising to launch Michael Jackson's *Hero* album, with all stops pulled out to advance the star's product to the top of the charts. Unfortunately, adverse publicity due to Jackson's controversial lifestyle, plus poor sales, resulted in Columbia abandoning future opportunities.

CROSS-PROMOTION

Other methods widely used in the marketing of music are cross-selling, tie-in programs, and music brand sponsorship. For example, offering CDs or cassettes from top performers at a bare bones price of $5.00 with the purchase of a burger and fries at any major fast food outlet is an effective promotion—and everyone wins. The labels get huge sales on a catalog of already released music; the talent receives a more modest royalty on the large volume sold; the fast food house builds traffic; and the stars receive enormous advertising and display marketing. The ROI is very acceptable and it leads to formidable sponsorship deals with stars, their managers, and labels.

The Country Music Association (CMA), in connection with Gaylord Entertainment and the Nashville Cable Network (now owned by CBS), holds an annual Country Music Marketing program where deals are brokered. The group helped Trisha Yearwood gain a multi-million-dollar deal with Discover Card and Brooks & Dunn with Lee's Wrangler Jeans. Garth Brooks and other country music stars "tie up" and receive concert and music video support in return for the endorsement of beverages, cereals, apparel, and automobiles. Music talent and sponsorship agencies put together these highly profitable and successful arrangements; marketing strategies and tactics are borrowed from one high-powered deal to the next. Like all such deals, success breeds higher financial commitments and bigger programs.

NEW NICHES

Music truly is the universal language—but it has still maintained specific fan bases, regardless of crossover appeal. As marketers discovered the power of niche products throughout the entertainment universe, the various sectors of the music world saw heightening popularity for a variety of different styles and tastes. Once music labels realized the vein of gold running through these segments, they began to mine them for all they were worth—a considerable sum, as it turns out.

THE LATIN CRAZE

According to *Sound Scan*, the U.S. Latino recording industry closed a record year in 1999 with 22.2 million units sold—ahead of 1998 sales figures by 41%. In pursuit of a niche marketing strategy, music labels have developed and promoted superstars such as Marc Anthony, Elvis Crispo, Ricky Martin, Enrique Iglesias, and Gloria Estefan & the Miami Sound Machine. The labels have benefited from the growth of the Hispanic demographic in the U.S., the nostalgia for music in their own language, and the recent phenomenon of cross-over—the widespread acceptance of Latin music by the non-Hispanic population. Marketing has included *Billboard* magazine's Latin Music Awards, held in Miami, Florida and broadcast on cable television's Telemundo network.

Imminently danceable, Latin music gave birth to the Brazilian sound (Bossa Nova), the Argentine sound (Tango), the Mexican sound (Mariachi), the Portuguese sound (Fado), and the Central and South American sounds (Mambo, Merengue, Salsa, and Lambada). Today, no one doubts the longevity of Latin music and the export potential of these stars. Sony music alone has invested tens of millions to market Ricky Martin and Marc Anthony with wildly expensive music videos airing on MTV, accompanied by major concerts at Madison Square Garden and Radio City Music Hall.

BLACK URBAN MUSIC

The urban ghettoes and talent inherent in the African-American population gave birth to hip-hop and rap, and expanded the roots of reggae, blues, and gospel. These styles were supported by major new fan magazines that were also marketers of the sound, including *Vibe* and *Blaze*. In addition to over 400 radio stations nationally featuring African-American music, another huge impact on the growth of this niche was BET, created by Robert Johnson out of Washington, D.C. in 1980 (covered more fully in Chapter 5).

Rhythm & blues (R&B), jazz, gospel, hip-hop, and rap music are showcased on various air and cable waves. But, of all these, rap music has captured the most recent news headlines for songs that often feature dicey language and encourage violence. Rap captured the eye of Congress, setting off a fray that focused on the age-old debate over art versus gratuitous indulgence and first amendment issues. In spite of this tussle, black music remains one of the high-growth areas in the business.

OPERA GOES POP

Placido Domingo, Luciano Pavarotti, and Jose Carreras had each developed fine and productive careers with performances in major opera houses around the world. They were mainstays at New York's Metropolitan Opera House and La Scala in Milan, singing arias in French, Italian, German—and rarely in English. They were accompanied by other members of the inner sanctum of the opera world, along with prominent divas of equal talent and girth. The stage settings were elaborate and the costumes spectacular. On occasion, each of the three would accompany a popular singing star on a CD, such as the collaboration of John Denver and Placido Domingo. But these were seen as deviations from the norm; their major sales were on classical labels, performing opera standards sung previously by such historic stars as Enrico Caruso.

It was only when a producer/presenter convinced the three they could realize worldwide presence and huge personal revenues if attired simply in tuxedos performing in front of a world-class orchestra led by a star conductor like James Levine or Zubin Mehta that "The Three Tenors" were born. The results of this talent combination surprised even the most knowledgeable music promoters and marketers. Appearing in concert, singing arias from their favorite operas or classical hits in English from shows like *West Side Story* and *Cats*, they achieved fame and fortune even beyond their wildest dreams. Performances in Athens, Paris, and New York resulted in platinum CD sales, gold VHS sales, licensing fees for HBO presentations, and public broadcast TV and radio fundraising events, which further increased sales of related merchandise.

While no one has the exact figures, it is rumored that the year 2000 generated more than $1 billion dollars in total revenues for The Three Tenors. There have been discussions of crafting other such combinations, including leading female opera stars, but nothing has been presented to challenge the Tenors' leadership. It has also enhanced opera in the eyes of consumers not usually comfortable with this genre.

Recently, Andreas Bocelli, a blind opera star from Italy, and Charlotte Church, a 12-year-old girl from Wales—both with magnificent operatic voices—have expanded this popularization of a classic métier.

CASE IN POINT: THE CHURCH PHENOMENON

Charlotte Church is a part of opera's resurgent story; but to a greater extent, she represents the music industry's effort to cultivate younger consumers.

Church's meteoric rise began in an only-in-the-movies manner. An English TV talent show, *Richard and Judy*, reached out for new young talent and eight-year-old Charlotte called them. The screener asked her to sing something over the phone, and Charlotte belted out *Pie Jesu*. She was told to get herself down to the studio. Church had a subsequent appearance on the *Big, Big Talent Show*, where she stole the show. After that came live concerts at an impressive string of venues, including the London Palladium and Royal Albert Hall, and the opportunity to open for fellow Welsh singer Shirley Bassey in Antwerp, Belgium.

When impresario Jonathan Shalit met her, he was so impressed he contacted Sony Music's UK Chairman Paul Burger, who listened and immediately signed her. His enthusiasm was justified when her first CD, *Voice of An Angel*, was released in 1998 and went double platinum in the UK in five weeks. Sony pushed the international envelope and the album went gold in Australia, New Zealand, and Hong Kong long before Charlotte would ever visit any of those places. Sony's wide international exposure, with divisions like Sony U.S. and Sony Japan, made further globetrotting sales and momentum not only possible, but inevitable.

As Sony has crossed media to bring out a video, *Voice of an Angel in Concert*, based on a well-received PBS special, and an audio book, *Voice of An Angel: My Story* (released Fall 2000), it is clear that the marketing posture of the teenager's promotion is quite different from the "teeny pop" handling of talents like Britney Spears or Christina Aguilera on MTV.

Charlotte has dominated a category *Billboard* calls "Classical Crossover" as a sustained number-one hit. Much of Charlotte's appeal rests in what Sam Sutherland, Amazon.com reviewer, calls "the unapologetic sweetness of her music and the unforced girlishness she flashes between songs." The obvious precocious talent, combined with a virginal enthusiasm for traditional, classical, and patriotic music, offers a refreshing contrast that has led to as many parents buying Charlotte Church products as the targeted teenagers.

JESUS SAVES AND ALSO SELLS

To the surprise of many in this age of high-profile, over-sexed rock stars, religion is the driver behind one of the fastest growing music genres: Christian music. Live and pre-recorded, it is unabashedly dedicated to Christianity and the celebration of Jesus. Christian/gospel music sales were up 11.5% in 2000 over the previous year, with sales totaling 49.8 million units. These numbers make it the fifth largest selling genre, according to the Gospel Music Association (GMA), as quoted in *Billboard* magazine, May 6, 2000.

On major TV stations and local channels—especially on Sunday mornings and during Christian holidays—fresh-faced, wholesome, conservatively dressed, and respectful young adults sing rock & roll, middle-of-the-road, pop, and other contemporary rhythms and lyrics that praise Jesus and thank God for all that is good. Lead singers are attractive stars in their own right, while the back-up singers are more a reflection of a church choir than a typical star's musical entourage.

This category of music is sold as major CD issues through chains of Christian book and religious gift stores throughout the country, driving huge increases in sales revenue. *Billboard* tracks the "Top Contemporary Christian" albums, including re-entry items such as Elvis Presley's *He Touched Me: The Gospel Music of Elvis Presley*. There are few returns to the labels—usually smaller, specialized companies like Word and Spring House (though big labels such as Atlantic do weigh in now and then in the category with hits as well)—since the music is evergreen and has no fad or timing issues. It is unique in the music industry to have a non-perishable product. In addition, the singers are frequently paid very minimal salaries, and do much of their own marketing and promotion in the service of the church.

While the strongest sales are in the Bible belt, or Southern Baptist strongholds, national Christian shows like *Crystal Palace* build sales of the music across the country.

REPACKAGING AND COMPILATIONS

What late-night TV viewer isn't familiar with the constantly scrolling, heavily over-voiced commercials touting music compilations? "EVERY RECORD EVER RECORDED!! Yes, you can have every record ever recorded all for the low, low price of..." But seriously? It's a serious business, with companies such as Rhino Records and TVT Records grabbing revenues of up to $100 million. While reissues were once considered the lowest end of the record industry—compilations slapped out quickly from old inventory—these concepts turned out to be highly and relentlessly profitable.

Entrepreneurs such as Richard Foos and Harold Bronson (Rhino) and Steve Gottlieb (TVT) purchase the rights to or license for reuse a variety of music, then repackage it in themes: Hits of the '70s, '80s, '90s; Romantic Love Songs; Party Music; Beach Songs. There is something for everyone, regardless of age, race, or gender. Rhino has taken the concept one step further by offering videos and books as well as films that are creatively packaged collections of materials from the past. They have since used a strategic partnership to expand the market by joining with a giant label, WEA, owner of the Atlantic label's catalog of classic R&B.

Legacy, a division of Sony Entertainment/Columbia Music, has discovered the formula of reissue and repackaging, and has zoomed to a level of major success in the field utilizing the Columbia Record catalog. Jeff Smith, Steve Lebowitz, and Adam Block have created a formidable entrepreneurship in-house at the multi-layered and often bureaucratic Sony; they have also gained access to other catalogs and created joint reissue agreements with major labels that are sitting on vast underutilized properties. Legacy has reissued division multi-CD sets featuring Frank Sinatra, Miles Davis, Louis Armstrong, Dave Brubeck, Billy Holiday, the great ladies of early jazz, and many more. While the marketing behind these releases is minimal, the basic tactics are always vibrant, and the loyalty of customers to the basic brand pays off handsomely.

SOUNDTRACKS

The soundtrack explosion owes its success and shares its parentage with the movie industry, though it also requires cooperation from the music business to flourish. Usually the process begins with the post-production of a film and falls into the following categories:

■ Non-musical film, utilizing music to heighten the tension or underscore the action, explosions, and random special effects; genres include action-adventure, horror, science fiction, and romance, using music from the public domain or composed by leading film music professionals, such as multiple Oscar winner John Williams. Some of the hundreds of examples include classics such as *2001: Space Odyssey, Armageddon,* and *Sleepless in Seattle.* A more recent example is the carry-over theme from the long-running TV series *Mission Impossi-*

ble, remade for the two Tom Cruise *Mission Impossible* movies.

- Musical film, featuring singing and dancing with new or already written songs to fit the characterization of the acting. This usually consists of films made from Broadway shows like *Carousel*, *Oklahoma*, *Porgy & Bess*, *Evita*, and *The Phantom of the Opera*, or animated movies like *The Lion King*, *Beauty and the Beast*, and *Tarzan*.

- Movies featuring a leading singer such as Whitney Houston in *The Bodyguard* and *The Preacher's Wife* or Dolly Parton in *The Best Little Whorehouse in Texas*. These movies have songs written or re-orchestrated specifically for the picture and go on to sell millions in CD form. During his early musical heyday, Kenny Rogers' musical signature *The Gambler* enabled him to create a gambler persona in a series of films.

- Blockbuster films that feature unique soundtracks. For example, the *Titanic* soundtrack, which consisted primarily of bagpipe music and featured one song by Celine Dion, became a surprise platinum CD success with worldwide sales of over 20 million copies. The widespread distribution of the CD, the radio play of the theme song, and the huge displays in retail music stores helped to promote and market an extended run of the film.

Soundtracks have become a large revenue stream and an excellent promotion and marketing opportunity, including the use of film clips from movie trailers on MTV and VH-1. This enlarges the simultaneous marketing of the film and music CD.

To take advantage of this opportunity, most film studios work closely with their music division; for example, Warner Bros. Studios with WEA, Sony Entertainment with Columbia Music, and Universal Studios with Universal/Polygram Music.

On occasion, music producers or A&R professionals are hired by film producers to locate or develop saleable and marketable music produced years earlier that evoke a certain nostalgia for a period or historical movie.

TECHNO TRENDS

There are few sectors of society that have remained untouched by the introduction of the PC and the Internet—and music certainly isn't one of them. Having boomed throughout the 20th Century with records, cassettes, and CDs, the industry suddenly came to the fork in the road created by the digital engineering of music.

A thorough understanding of music on the Internet requires some in-depth study of the wonders of digitization. For the purposes of this survey of entertainment marketing, we'll leave the study of the subject up to you. However, suffice it to say that the ability to send clear, downloadable music files has created new opportunities in the industry.

The transmission of music through high-speed Internet connections has spawned a variety of new conduits, including Internet radio and downloadable music files. In the case of Internet radio, computers have created the 20th Century version of late-night radio—when radio wave transmissions would carry incredibly long distances, much to the delight of late-night drivers. Many travelers could tell the tale of picking up the signal for a Pittsburgh station in Arizona, or a San Francisco broadcast in Oklahoma. With Internet radio, stations that utilize the technology can be heard around the world, 24 hours a day, clear as a bell—as can their advertising.

While the advantages of this global transmission are still to be fully determined, the concept is opening intriguing doors for revenue, both for stations and labels. It is believed that labels can now invest directly in Web radio ventures (such as clickradio.com) to get some of the advertising budgets from the stations that play their music. Clear Channel just purchased SFX to control promotion and band line-ups. "There will be lots of different business models out there," says Richard Bressler, TWDigital Media Chairman.

This same transmission of digitized files also allows for downloading—the actual transference of the sound file from the Internet into a file that can be stored on a PC—or on this century's version of the transistor radio, the MP3 player. This transfer is done via Motion Picture Experts Group (MPEG) files, an industry combination that develops standards for audio and video compression. MP3 compresses voluminous audio and video files to very slim and manageable playback content. Hundreds of MP3 files can fit on a single CD; 10 times this quantity can fit onto a computer hard drive. A fast, high-quality cable modem connection (128 kilobytes per second) enables consumers to gain access to volumes of music—for free.

And there's the rub. There is considerable concern in the recording industry regarding the protection of IP rights—which, of course, translates into revenue. Consumers who are downloading music files from Web sites such as MP3.com, real.com, listen.com, scour exchange, and others are doing so without paying anything for the privilege. While there are those who would pose the rebuttal that downloading MPEG files is no different than recording songs off the radio onto cassette, the fact of the matter is there is a huge difference. MP3 files are the same types of files used to create CDs; therefore, the consumer is able to get high-quality files, as opposed to the second-hand sound that comes out of recorded cassettes.

There is an advantage to musicians and aspiring rock stars, however; the free music downloaded from Web sites can serve to spread word of mouth about the sound, and can often result in consumers buying the entire CD, now that they've sampled a cut or two. Plus, with the portability of MP3 players such as the Diamond Multimedia Rio 500, Creative Labs Nomad, and Hewlett-Packard Jornada 540, the listener base is extended—affording a greater audience for the artist's work, and a greater risk that the artist might go unpaid for his or her creation.

PIRACY—A NEW LEGACY

From the street corners of Manhattan, to the alleys of Hollywood, to the back-street stalls of Beijing, to the beautifully appointed department stores of Sao Paulo, counterfeit CDs are carefully reproduced, artfully packaged, and sold at greatly reduced prices—with no revenue going to either the original music labels or the artists. The lack of IP protection or copyright enforcement in many countries around the world has resulted in the loss of billions of dollars to the music industry.

These days, though, there's talk of piracy on the high C's—the "C" standing for computer. In spite of copy protection procedures, music pirates are testing the waters of digitized music. The greatest controversy in this area was raised by the launch and widespread use of Napster. By registering at Napster.com, consumers could freely trade music files stored on various Napster users' hard drives, creating a huge Internet trading post of music that had been downloaded from owners' CDs. Napster took the position that since the original consumer had paid for the CD, it was now theirs to share any way they might like to. Artists and labels took the opposite position: that in this age of high-quality transmission, new rules were called for, especially considering the worldwide reach of the Internet.

In April 2000, Metallica became the first rock group to take legal action against Napster, claiming the software distributor had distributed Metallica MP3 tracks while making no compensation to the band. This $10 million copyright infringement suit, in which Metallica was joined by E/M Ventures and Creeping Death Music, echoed the sentiments of many other music performers and groups who felt their material had been wrongfully offered through Napster. Metallica's manager, Cliff Burnstein, claimed that over 100 tracks of the band's music, including portions of the not-yet-released *Mission Impossible 2* soundtrack, were found on the Napster site. After months of testimony, Napster awoke to the news that the court had found for the opposition.

But Napster wasn't the only new technology under scrutiny. MP3.com's Instant Listening Service allowed customers to access their music at any time on any device connected to the Internet, whether it was a hand-held computer or a telephone. Sony Music Entertainment Inc., Warner Music Group, Arista Records Inc., Atlantic Recordings Corp., Bertelsmann AG's BMG and EMI Group, and Capitol Records Inc. were among the companies that sued MP3.com in January 2000, claiming copyright infringement. In May of the same year, U.S. District Judge Jed S. Rakoff ruled that MP3.com had infringed on copyrights when it purchased tens of thousands of popular recordings and then copied them onto its computer servers so it could replay them for its subscribers.

On June 9, 2000, major news releases announced that San Diego-based MP3.com had reached settlements with Warner Music Group and BMG Entertainment to include licensing agreements that would allow music from both companies to be stored on the service. The licensing agreements would allow consumers that already owned Warner Music Group or BMG CDs to store copies with MP3.com. The record companies shared an undisclosed amount of money received in the settlements with their artists. Warner Music Group has a roster of more than 1,000 artists and includes The Atlantic Group, Elektra Entertainment Group, and Rhino Entertainment labels. BMG Entertainment owns more than 200 record labels in 54 countries, including Arista Records and RCA.

THE GLOBAL MUSIC MARKET

The universal nature of music enables American music labels to sell American CDs around the world with no change in music composition or language, played and distributed exactly as created. This does not, however, preclude the frequent licensing of published songs to foreign music distributors for use by local pop stars in Japan, Hong Kong, Korea, and all through the European countries. However, as markets have been conquered by foreign firms, countries have grown in economic, social, and cultural pride, and the local population has become more and more introspective and even nationalistic.

Thus, in markets like China, Hong Kong, Taiwan, Singapore, Japan, and the smaller Asian countries, there is a growing desire and support for developing local musical talent. The new Asian pop stars receive the same adulation, support, and marketing intensity as each and every local hero. The support usually comes from local or global labels that recognize the importance of having their own native pop stars. CDs, audiocassettes, tour groups, nightclub and concert hall performances, window posters, and TV appearances in those countries develop the brand image of the stars.

The following offers a glimpse into the expanding global music scene:

- Japanese music labels experienced expansion into the Taiwanese market because of a loophole in copyright law that allowed counterfeiters to get away with pirating albums not released in Taiwan within one month of their Japanese release. Japanese companies responded with limited releases in Taiwan to capitalize on the "J-pop" explosion caused by Japanese small- and big-screen acting stars. Also, Japanese branches of international music companies like Sony were in prime position to take advantage of expansion possibilities in the burgeoning music market in Korea.

- Chinese audiences have been some of the biggest downloaders of music from MP3, in part because of limited airplay provided for international repertoire on local radio stations, even in Hong Kong. As a result, the Internet has become the primary outlet.

- In New Zealand, Prime Minister Helen Clark announced an almost doubling of the amount provided for government funding for the local music industry. In the past, touring in Australia had been too expensive for most groups, while touring in America had often been out of reach. For New Zealand to have its impact on the growing global scene, the Labour Party intends to see that New Zealand artists get every opportunity.

- In Berlin, German-speaking hip-hop groups like Spezializtz have hopped the barrier from underground to mainstream music, with artists able to rewrite the counter-culture social trends that give the music its edge. Black music stations like JAM-FM give heavy airplay to music that gives a healthy sign of future global potential to all music forms.
- London's Zomba Group, with labels like Jive Records, featuring stars such as the Backstreet Boys, Britney Spears, and N'Sync, expanded on its presence in the European market by opening new wholly-owned affiliates in Italy, Spain, Norway, and Denmark.

In short, the international music scene is becoming an ever-growing marketing opportunity, and the media conglomerates are moving to take advantage of it.

CASE IN POINT: VIVENDI UNIVERSAL

As he maneuvered for advantage in Europe, Vivendi Chairman Jean-Marie Messier got a call in late 1999 from Edgar Bronfman, Jr., the President and CEO of The Seagram Company, Ltd., who was vacationing in Paris. Arriving in shirtsleeves for an informal breakfast, Bronfman asked about Messier's Internet plans and talked about some of Universal Music Group's Internet strategy. For example, Universal recently set up a joint venture with BMG, Get Music, to create a series of music Web sites. It wasn't until the end of breakfast, Messier recalls, that Bronfman remarked: "Your strengths and our strengths just naturally seem to go together." Messier said he began talking seriously with Bronfman about a deal in early January, making frequent trips to New York. The talks culminated with Universal, one of the largest media and record label conglomerates in the world, merging with Paris-based Vivendi SA and its entertainment division, Canal Plus SA, to form Vivendi Universal.

Breathless briefings, big headlines, and grand visions—will the deal live up to all the hype? "We've created a global leader," Messier said jubilantly, relaxing for a moment in the back seat as his car veered through the darkening Paris streets. And, added the cherubic-looking boss, "We're going to make the Internet swing." This tycoon in the making is a driven, hands-on manager, a relentless dealmaker who's as comfortable on Wall Street as he is in his sumptuous office overlooking the Arc de Triomphe.

Like other media moguls, Messier figures 21st Century consumers expect to be entertained and informed in new ways. They will still go to movies, watch television, and buy CDs—and Messier now has plenty to offer, from Universal Pictures' hit *Erin Brockovich*, to top-rated Canal+ soccer coverage, to Universal Music Group artists such as Elton John, hot rapper Eminem, and country singer Shania Twain. He can leverage those holdings on both sides of the Atlantic as well. For example, Seagram's partly owned USA Network might bring Ticketmaster and Home Shopping Network to Europe, while Hollywood movie projects could draw on European talent and financing.

Consumers want much more, and Vivendi Universal promises to give it to them digitally—anytime, anywhere, thanks to the magic of the Internet. How might it work? Through Vizzavi, a portal that appears as the default home page for the combined 80 million subscribers of Vodafone, Canal+, and Cegetel, who will eventually have Internet access via cell phone or digital TV. Strolling down the street, subscribers will be able to download songs from their favorite artist onto their cell phones. At home, they will punch a command into their digital TV set-top boxes to order back-episodes of a series. At their computers, they will take part in an online Q&A session with a sports star. Unlike AOL, subscribers will get Vizzavi free of charge. Revenues will come from advertising and click-throughs to paid services such as music downloads and live transmission of sports events. The addition of Seagram's entertainment properties gives Vizzavi a big boost; Vodafone Chairman Chris Gent says: "It will be very attractive, especially to younger users."

BILLBOARD.COM: A CASE STUDY

John Lerner is Vice President and Director of Operations for VNU eMedia, which is part of VNU USA. Lerner has been running the Web division of the parent company for the past five years and is one of the original founders of the electronic media group. In the following, Lerner shares, in a full case study, *Billboard*'s transition to the Internet, the challenges facing the brand, and its successes on the Internet.

Background: The *Billboard* brand name has been the premier source of music and entertainment news, information, and services for over 105 years. *Billboard* is more than just a trade publication; rather, it's a unique chronicle of the music, video, and home entertainment industries. The company's mission is "To provide maximum new information in the timeliest possible fashion to help our readers do better business. Moreover, since our audience includes a wealth of experts we aim to offer them surprising and insightful advance knowledge they couldn't possibly locate anywhere else."[5]

TABLE 7-1   *Billboard* Readership Demographics

AGE	%	SEX
18-24	6%	Male 69%
25-34	32%	Female 30%
33-44	27%	n/a
45-54	26%	n/a
55+	9%	n/a

TABLE 7-2   1999 Readership Survey, Harvey Research, ABC Statement

INDUSTRY	% RESPONDING	TOTAL READERS
Record companies, manufacturers of hardware, studios	29%	43,500
Retailers, distributors, mass merchandisers	25%	37,500
Schools, colleges, students, faculty, library, music fans, and audiophiles	15%	22,500
Radio personnel, including program and music directors	8%	12,000
Recording artists, performers, attorneys, agents, and managers	8%	12,000
Music publishers, songwriters, and related fields	4%	6,000
Journalists, PR organizations, agencies, etc.	3%	4,500

---

5. *Billboard* Editor's Statement, 1999. *Billboard* is a registered trademark and all material is copyrighted. Permission to reuse material must be obtained from publisher, VNU Business Media, Inc.

TABLE 7-2   1999 Readership Survey, Harvey Research, ABC Statement

INDUSTRY	% RESPONDING	TOTAL READERS
Buyers of talent	3%	4,500
Others allied to the field	3%	4,500
Miscellaneous	2%	3,000

Audience: *Billboard* has an international audience with re ders in over 110   countries. *Billboard* brings the "Bible" of music and entertainment to the industry with top-notch news and reporting of cutting-edge reviews, as well as the most respected charts for retailers, record company executives, and artists.

Interesting *Billboard* Facts:

Of the 150,000 readers of *Billboard*:

- 13% spend more than 40 nights per year in a hotel (average 21 nights for all readers).
- 54% have purchased audio equipment in the last year or plan to purchase audio equipment in the coming year.
- 23% take 10 or more airline trips per year.
- 52% have purchased computer equipment in the last year or plan to purchase computer equipment in the coming year.
- 46% use a cellular phone with an average monthly bill of $183. 00.29% have bought or leased a luxury car in the last year or intend to buy or lease a luxury car in the coming year.

1998 readership survey compiled by Harvey Research.[6]

Billboard Branding (Pre-Internet):

- *Billboard* magazine: Weekly global coverage reaches over 150,000 readers in 110 countries. The music and entertainment industries' authoritative voice.
- *Billboard* conferences: Hosted by *Billboard*'s expert editors, these major conferences bring industry leaders together to exchange opinions and network.
- *Billboard* directories: *Billboard* Music Group offers directories providing essential information on every facet of the

---

6.   1999 Readership Survey, Harvey Research, ABC Statement. *Billboard* is a registered trademark and all material is copyrighted. Permission to reuse material must be obtained from publisher, VNU Business Media, Inc.

industry—the "definitive" who's who for the entire music and entertainment world.

■ *Billboard* entertainment marketing: Drawing on an international name and logo, *Billboard* Entertainment Marketing develops powerful licensing opportunities, including world-class partnerships with Fox's top-rated *Billboard* Music Awards Show and ABC's American Country Countdown.

■ Extensions of the brand: Targeted publications include *Amusement Business*, which is the premier publication for the live entertainment and amusement industries; *Musician*, which addresses the needs of today's active musicians; and *Music & Media*, the leading pan-European trade for weekly radio and music industries.

Moving the *Billboard* Brand Online: *Billboard* possesses a powerful brand name. With a century of brand equity, the company was able to move the brand online to face new challenges and meet new successes. It was the brand name that was a major part of the process, making the Web a "no-brainer." *Billboard* was able to leverage the brand on the Internet, not only as a business-to-business (B2B) product, but also as a business-to-consumer (B2C) product. The Web afforded *Billboard* the opportunity to extend its reach to the consumer market with ease.

Challenges in the Transition to an Online Brand:

■ Utilizing the WWW as a viable communication channel, and providing content that is consistent with offline brand communication.

■ Evolving with technology to sell customers.

■ Incorporating the Internet into an integrated online and offline marketing campaign.

■ Achieving an ROI for *Billboard*'s Internet venture.

■ Conquering the fear of copyright holders. Similar to MP3 issues, music is based on IP and you cannot be a publisher and disrespect IP.

■ Overcoming unknown barriers with technology that "pop up" unexpectedly along the way.

Strategies and Outcome: *Billboard* actually started online as a dial-up site developed to download software, where users could dial up into proprietary software systems. The Internet at this point was a means of distribution that was cost-effective and had tremendous reach. Then, with the evolution of the WWW, companies were quickly learning that Web site technology was a way to sell customers. Suddenly, the Internet enabled *Billboard* to have a much larger branding opportunity. However, it was always the underlying notion that whether offline or online, the brand carried tremendous power in and of itself. The Web, to *Billboard*, proved to be a viable communications channel. Now, *Billboard* was experiencing audience growth and reach like never before, with female audiences increasing tremendously. On the Internet, *Billboard* does not target a particular market, rather, on the ubiquitous Web, it focuses on a diversified pop culture—the people who follow music follow *Billboard.* The *Billboard* Web site (*www.billboard.com*) takes brand content online with interactive experiences beyond charts and articles. The Web allows *Billboard* to have areas of multimedia for audiences to enjoy. Never before have the *Billboard* charts had sound clips accompanying them. The Web site also brings *Billboard* videos to its audience. At times, *Billboard* faced slight glitches with technology, such as having a radio show that had to change from "streaming" to "on-demand." Sure, it can be frustrating, but it's always better to catch these glitches early on, before they are noticeable enough among audiences and could quite possibly damage the online brand.

The power of content from industry experts and the multimedia experience on the site leverage the power of the brand in cyber space. Was the transition ever a concern for the *Billboard* print publication? Would there be cannibalization of the offline brand? These are always concerns, but for *Billboard* more so than with tertiary audiences. With clever marketing strategies to drive traffic between print *Billboard* and online Billboard.com, the issue is minimized. For example, the Billboard.com URL is added to the folio of all the magazine's pages.

In addition to *Billboard* Internet audiences enjoying the site, the *Billboard* weekly publication is still considered the "Bible," with everything based on the magazine. At the same time, *Billboard* is considered the top music information source on the Web. The site is trafficked with over 8 million monthly page views and more than 1.6 million monthly visits. It did not take long for *Billboard* online to become established as the industry's best source of Internet information and the "hot" destination for loyal *Billboard* followers worldwide. As a result, audiences expect the Web site to be current and up-to-date—an attribute of the *Billboard* brand. This attribute is reinforced on the Web with a site that is updated twice daily to maintain the brand's image. *Billboard* online gives visitors access to historical archives (10 years of past *Billboard* articles and 40 years of past *Billboard* charts), concert reviews, album previews, online conference registration, and a tour of the search database. In addition to constantly updating information, *Billboard* regularly augments its design, although initially it exhibited a skillful approach in building a Web site that was user-friendly and allowed visitors to navigate easily. The Web site content, of course, is fresh and always pertinent to the industry (consistent communication with the offline *Billboard* brand).

As a result of *Billboard* 's transition online, there are various opportunities for professionals in the music industry to create a Web page and profile an artist on the *Billboard* site. An icon on the home page, with album cover graphics, is prominently displayed to reach millions of consumers. These feature pages allow artists to display album reviews, images, and artist information, links to the record label site, retail information, sound and video clips, and touring and appearance dates. In addition, the *Billboard Bulletin*, the daily calendar that concentrates on the essentials of industry news, is also found online (by fax as well) to provide the "scoop" that the well-informed industry executive needs to know. Via the Internet, global business learns about executive moves, the latest labels, artist signings, and retail activity.

Billboard, through the power of its brand, has made the transition to the Internet smoothly and successfully. The brand continues to thrive and fulfill audience expectations in the music industry by maintaining its position as the premier source of music and entertainment news, information, and services. *Billboard* fully utilizes the Internet with its tremendous power to communicate the brand—expanding services to loyal followers as well as gaining new audience reach. *Billboard* is able to satisfy its objectives both online and offline:

"*Billboard* analyzes and interprets the present while both anticipating and helping shape the future. We are lonely in our high ideals, determined in our high standards, and dedicated to the excellence of a form of newsgathering that has its own news making momentum. There is only one worthy adjective for what we [*Billboard*] do and it's our name: We cover our international beat the *Billboard* way."

SUMMARY

As a universal language, music opens the door to the entire spectrum of demography, and is found in every sector of the entertainment industry. Whether it appears as a movie soundtrack, a live event, over the airwaves or the Internet, through recordings, or pulsing through an arena as the local team comes out on the court, music serves as both a marketing tool and a marketed medium, driving a multi-billion-dollar industry.

FOR FURTHER READING

Books

1. Brabec, Jeffrey and Todd Brabec, *Music, Money, and Success: The Insider's Guide to the Music Industry* (New York, NY: Simon & Schuster, 1994).

2. Burgess, James, *The Art of Record Production* (New York, NY: Omnibus Press, 1999)

3. Dannen, Frederic, *Hit Men: Power Brokers & Fast Money Inside the Music Business* (New York, NY: Vintage, 1991).

4. Garofalo, Reebee, *Rockin' Out: Popular Music in the USA* (Boston, MA: Allyn & Bacon, 1997).

5. Krasilovsky, M. William, Sidney Shemel, and John Gross, *This Business of Music, 8/E* (New York, NY: Watson-Guptill, 2000).

6. Lathrop, Tad and Jim Pettigrew, *This Business of Music Marketing and Promotion* (New York, NY: Billboard Books, 1999).

7. Lendt, Chris K., *Kiss and Sell: The Making of a Supergroup* (New York, NY: Watson-Guptill, 1997).

8. Passman, Donald S. and Randy Glass, *All You Need to Know About the Music Business* (New York, NY: Simon & Schuster, 1997).

Magazines to Devour

1. *Billboard*, BPI Publishing

2. *Electronic Media*

8 SPORTS

OVERVIEW

I f ever there was a medium that allowed its viewers to imagine themselves as participants, acting out their hopes, dreams, fears, and aspirations, it is sports. Since the earliest times, populations—entire civilizations, for that matter—have entertained themselves by watching bigger, faster, stronger, and wilier members of their community beat up on the guys next door in some way other than declaring full-fledged war—and viewers have paid for the privilege.

Of course, as long as that privilege was being paid for, someone needed to promote the event to drive the revenue. Thus, sports marketing was born, eventually incorporating media, advertising and communications, promotions and special events, and sponsor relations. As revenues increased, the sports industry—most importantly, the athletes themselves, in terms of financial compensation—recognized that they had moved beyond what once might have been considered pure competition into the realm of entertainment.

Sports underscore both the importance of marketing to build "wannasee" and the power of branding—even in a live medium where the outcome is unpredictable, keeping us on the edges of our seats most of the time. Sports participants—and the targets of sports marketing—range from weekend amateurs, to college players, to professionals and their entourages. But, sports marketing is highly targeted to and dependent on the passive observer, the guy or gal sitting on the couch, daydreaming of what he or she could—or might have—do or done, whether on the high school basketball court, the professional football field, or the once-proud bastion of amateur sports, the Olympics.

While there have always been purists who have decried the commercialization of sports, sporting events have always entertained participants. In today's world, the line between sport and entertainment has grown even fuzzier.

SPORTAINMENT

Recently, *Variety* magazine published an article developed jointly by its staff and the staff of a sports industry trade magazine, *Sports Business*, entitled "Sportainment," defining a newly named sub-sector of the entertainment industry. It is interesting to review the highlights as we come to understand why sports and entertainment marketing are viable partners and allies, and on occasion, competitors.

How did the marriage of sport and entertainment come to be? It isn't simply from the ability of sport to deliver tremendous live, PPV, and TV audiences. The connection between the viewer and the medium is much tighter than that of a simple participant/viewer scenario. Perhaps the answer lies in the appeal of sports stars—often the same as that of fan worship for movie stars, the heroes as real or celluloid. Sports stars are wealthy and larger than life; they move around the world, live in palatial homes, dress to kill, and are allowed enormous latitude in their excesses. Or maybe it's the link between entertainment personalities and sports. Just view the sea of faces at the edge of NBA games in major entertainment cities and you will see Woody Allen, Spike Lee, Jack Nicholson, Melanie Griffith, Steven Speilberg, and many of the entertainment industry's biggest business executives.

Interestingly enough, sports can succeed without *ever* being entertainment. For a TV show, play, or film to work, it has to be planned and crafted to deliver a particular result—to make the audience laugh, cry, or simply gasp. Sport competitions are different—there are no certainties; the audience attends for different reasons. You wouldn't move your finger to the remote to watch *Friends* if there hadn't been a laugh for five weeks, but try applying that logic to the fans of a failing football team in the midst of a bad season. Sports fans buy their tickets and turn up week in and week out. They don't want to be entertained as much as share an experience. They want to be there when history is created, to cheer and cry with each other.

They can too, because sports are a step closer to real life than pure entertainment. Sports are pure unscripted theater, and that is what sets them apart. As the National Football League knows only too well, on any given Sunday, anything can happen—and often does. What unites sports and traditional entertainment are their abilities, in different ways, to enthrall the public and create an all-absorbing parallel universe that viewers can live in for a few hours before returning, albeit reluctantly, to the real world.

THE KEY C'S

If we were to separate the elements of the sports industry—particularly the business and marketing of this entertainment sector—we would divide them between *content* (the activity or event itself) and *conduit* (the medium by which it is presented, be it live, TV, cable, PPV, or over the Internet). *Consumption* is as complex as any aspect of the entertainment industry since it is segmented by type of sport, gender of spectator, and even socio-economic factors.

Convergence occurs when successful movies are based on sports, such as *The Paper Lion, Tin Cup, Bull Durham, Field of Dreams, Rudy, Remember the Titans, The Natural, The Mighty Ducks*, and many others. Sports-based electronic games have been very successful. Radio sports talk shows draw a very loyal listener base. Books about games provide content for the development of other sectors, including TV series and theatrical releases, as well as just plain reading enjoyment for hardcore sports fans.

Now let's move on to the specifics: the targets of sports marketing.

MAJOR LEAGUE SPORTS

Each of the principle ball sports followed by the public shares a common structure. Each includes the *leagues*, run by commissioners and their staffs; the *franchises*, which are also known as *teams*; and the *players*, who are hired, fired, or richly compensated by the *owners*, who are governed by *contracts* and require *rules* to set the parameters for the competitions.

MAJOR LEAGUE BASEBALL (MLB)

The first baseball team to field professional players was the Cincinnati Red Stockings in 1869. In 1867, eight professional teams formed the National League. Competing leagues sprang up and folded, but Ban Johnson's Western League seized on franchise territories abandoned by the National League in 1900 and began luring National League players with higher salaries. Renamed the American League, it also began drawing away fans. The two leagues agreed to join forces in 1903 by having their champions meet in the World Series.

The sport flourished until the Black Sox Scandal of 1919, in which eight Chicago White Sox players were accused of taking bribes to throw the World Series. In 1921, the owners hired Judge Kennesaw Mountain Landis as baseball's first Commissioner to clean up the game's image. After a period of time in which the owners enjoyed almost total control of the game, players' rights discussions began, resulting in the following actions:

- The players formed the Major League Baseball Players' Association (MLBPA) in 1954.
- The players signed the first collective bargaining agreement with the owners in 1968.
- The players called their first strike in 1972, a 13-day walkout for an improved pension plan.
- The players won the right to free agency in 1976.
- The players staged another seven-week strike in 1981, which interrupted the season.

Salary increases slowed and the free agent market dried up in the mid-1980s, prompting the MLBPA to sue the owners for collusion. The owners agreed to a settlement of $280 million in 1990. Baseball's eighth Commissioner, Fay Vincent, resigned in 1992 after the owners effectively removed all power from the Commissioner's office. An executive council of owners led by Milwaukee Brewers' owner Bud Selig took control.

Prompted by the owners' decision to unilaterally restrict free agency and withdraw salary arbitration, the players started a 232-day strike. However, play resumed in 1995 when the owners and the MLBPA approved a new collective-bargaining agreement. Selig stepped down from the Brewers in 1998 to become the game's ninth Commissioner.

Having alienated countless fans, baseball was resuscitated in 1998 by Mark McGwire and Sammy Sosa as they pursued Roger Maris' 37-year-old single-season 61-home run record. Later that year, MLB signed a new six-year, $800 million TV contract with ESPN.

Sweeping changes took place in 2000 when owners who had voted the previous year to eliminate the American and National League offices (centralizing power with the Commissioner's office) also voted to restore the "best interests of baseball" powers to the Commissioner, giving Selig full authority to redistribute wealth, block trades, and levy fines on teams and players for inappropriate behavior. MLB also won a major financial achievement when Fox Entertainment agreed to pay $2.5 billion for exclusive rights to televise the All-Star Game and all post-season competitions through 2006.

Today, MLB is composed of 30 teams in 28 cities. These teams are all independently owned, but follow the rules and organization of the league. The league itself is divided into two leagues, the American and National Leagues. The champions of each league face each other every October in the World Series. Teams play 162 games in a season that lasts from April to October. Spring training is held in March, when the teams play games against each other in addition to practicing for the regular season.

A significant portion of the American male population has personal experience with baseball, having played t-ball, Little League, Pony League, or high school and college ball. The itch doesn't go away either, as witnessed by countless adult softball leagues. All the background and interest make baseball America's most attended sport, with about 70 million in attendance each year, since they play the most games and have some of the larger venues. The highest salary in the league belongs to Texas Rangers' shortstop, Alex Rodríguez, who earns $22 million a year.

MLB highlights its stars yearly, in the MLB All-Star Game that is held in mid-season, usually at the beginning of July. The All-Star

Game brings together the best players from each team to play in a National League versus American League match-up.

Players in the MLB usually come from an extensive minor league system of teams that are either affiliated with the major league teams or are independent. Affiliates contract with MLB teams for coaches, players, and salaries, while paying their own stadium fees, marketing costs, and travel and housing costs. Independents have no affiliation with the Major League.

Baseball is seen as the least expensive sport to attend as cheap bleacher tickets can still be found. Over 130 million people (62.7%) claim to be baseball fans, and fans aged 18–49 make up 60% of baseball's attendees. However, as teams continue to move into new, expensive, state-of-the-art stadiums, ticket prices continue to rise.

NATIONAL BASKETBALL ASSOCIATION (NBA)

Dr. James Naismith, a physical education teacher at the International YMCA Training School in Springfield, Massachusetts, invented basketball in 1891. Naismith nailed peach baskets at both ends of the gym, gave his students a soccer ball, and one of the world's most popular sports was born. Initially, the game was considered to be too rough, thus it was limited to armories, gymnasiums, and dance halls. To pay the rent for the use of the hall, teams began charging spectators fees for admission and the leftover cash was divided between the teams.

In 1949, the Basketball Association of America merged with the Midwestern National Basketball League to form the 17-team National Basketball Association (NBA). The sport received an unexpected boost when a point-shaving scandal rocked college basketball, making the pros look relatively clean. Basketball gained additional popularity in 1954, when the league introduced the 24-second shot clock, which sped up the game and increased scoring.

In 1976, the NBA merged with the American Basketball League. Basketball superstars, including Magic Johnson and Michael Jordan, helped the sport overcome the many fringe issues that created fan apathy, including drugs, racial backlash, and violence. And then along came one person that almost single-handedly brought the sport to the level of popularity it enjoys today: David Stern.

Stern, the longest-running Commissioner of any league, seemed to have a marketing savvy and a gift for finding the right solution to each problem. He understood that sports in the new generation of sports fans needed the excitement, involvement, and passion of an engaging entertainment experience. He understood the value of sponsorships, licensing, merchandising, and network television, and went after these deals with an extraordinary sense of commitment and the aid of a very savvy marketing executive, Rick Welt, Executive Vice President of the NBA.

Today's NBA is made up of 29 teams in 28 cities. The teams are divided into two conferences, Eastern and Western, and play each other for the NBA championship in June. The regular season lasts from October to June, with each team playing 82 games. NBA attendance is around 20 million people per season. In 1996, the average player salary for the NBA reached $2 million dollars, while the player minimum was at $250,000. However, players with star appeal, like Michael Jordan, demonstrated that revenues from product endorsements could be far greater than an already significant salary.

Basketball has become one of the more expensive sports to attend. Average ticket prices ranged from $35 to $92 for the 2000–2001 season. For example, in the 2000–2001 season, the cost of taking a family of four to a New York Knicks game was almost $470. Even less expensive teams still approach almost $200 for a family of four. These prices limit basketball attendance to those who can better afford it.

The NBA All-Star Game is played mid-season, usually in February. Most NBA players come to the league out of college or from abroad; however, the trend of players entering out of high school has led to a development league being created. The National Basketball Development League (NBDL) began its inaugural season on November 16, 2001.

SMALLER SALARIES, BIGGER DREAMS: THE WOMEN'S NATIONAL BASKETBALL ASSOCIATION (WNBA)

While NBA players are raking in the big bucks, their sisters in the Women's National Basketball Association (WNBA) are not—but it hasn't affected the growing popularity of this league. The WNBA is not the first effort at presenting professional women's basketball; the first attempt came about in the late 1970s—well before its time. In fact, the WNBA may be a perfect example of how important entertainment marketing can be. The earlier effort depended almost solely on grassroots marketing, and as such, was never taken seriously by the media, most of whom did their best to laugh it out of existence.

However, today's WNBA is a marketer's dream, a league that takes full advantage of the rising popularity of women's sports. Fed by Title IX, a government decree that came about in the late 1970s and mandated equal access and funding for women's sports, this audience is made up of young—and not so young—women who enjoy the thrill of watching people of their own gender compete on a national, televised level. While the WNBA cannot come close to matching the revenues of its brother league yet, it offers an exciting, fast-paced alternative to men's basketball, which at times can seem more like a rerun of *Land of the Giants*. More important to the subject matter of this book, there is a growing revenue stream from TV rights for the national championship, licensed products, sponsorships, and the rest of the assorted effluvia that makes sports the big business they are today.

NATIONAL FOOTBALL LEAGUE (NFL)

Descending from the English game of rugby, American football was developed in the late 1800s by Walter Camp, a player from Yale University who is generally considered the "Father of American Football." He is credited with beginning play from scrimmage, the numerical assessment of goals and tries, the restriction of play to 11 men per side, set plays, and strategy features which have led to the development of the game played today.

In 1920, the American Professional Football Association was formally organized to begin play. Jim Thorpe of Canton was elected APFA President and the membership fee was set at $100 per franchise. The original teams were:

- Canton Bulldogs
- Cleveland Tigers
- Dayton Triangles
- Akron Professionals
- Rochester (NY) Jeffersons
- Rock Island Independents
- Muncie Flyers
- Decatur Staleys
- Chicago Cardinals
- Hammond Pros

Over the next two years, teams came and went, and the original league folded and was reorganized. In 1922, the APFA changed its name to the National Football League. In the 1930s, the league had settled in 10 teams. The level of interest in the sport remained regional until 1958, when that year's championship game, the first to be televised nationally, kept audiences riveted with an overtime victory by the Baltimore Colts over the Giants. In 1962, the NFL signed its first league-wide television contract with CBS for $4.65 million. In 1966, NFL Commissioner Pete Rozelle negotiated a deal to combine the American Football League with the NFL, with the championship game between the two titled the Super Bowl.

Football's popularity exploded during the 1970s, helped by the rise of franchise dynasties. During the 1990s, the league expanded into 30 teams. The NFL made plans for new expansion in 1999, awarding a franchise to Robert McNair of Houston, who paid a record $700 million franchise fee and $310 million for a new stadium. In 2001, the NFL struck a four-year, $300 million deal with Sportsline.com, CBS, and AOL to operate and promote the league's NFL.com Web site.

Today's NFL is made up of 31 franchises, with the 32nd set to join the league in 2002 as the Houston Texans. Currently, the teams play in two conferences, the American Football Conference (AFC) and the National Football Conference (NFC). As of 2002, the games will be played in eight divisions with four teams each. The Commissioner of the NFL is Paul Tagliabue. Each team plays 16 regular-season games between late August and January, culminating in the Super Bowl, which is played at the end of January. The NFL equivalent of the All-Star Game is the Pro Bowl, which is played in Hawaii at the end of each season. Most NFL players enter the league from college, or from NFL Europe, the Canadian Football League, or the Arena Football League.

Attendance for the 2000 season ranged from 1.1 million for the Washington Redskins to 54,000 for the Arizona Cardinals. Salaries in the NFL are dependent on the salary cap, which is the absolute maximum each club may spend on player salaries in a capped year. The cap is set each year at a specified percentage of the expected NFL gross team revenue for the next year, as determined by the NFL's auditors. For the year 2001, the salary cap was approximately $67.4 million. The top salary for 2001 was the $11.35 million the Jacksonville Jaguars paid to Mark Brunell.

One of the most pressing political issues facing the NFL today is the conduct of its players. In the past few years, numerous players have been arrested on drug charges, murder, or domestic abuse, forcing the NFL to institute stringent policies against drug and alcohol use.

National Hockey League (NHL)

The NHL traces its heritage to 1893, when the Stanley Cup (donated by Lord Stanley, Governor General of Canada) was first awarded to the Montreal Amateur Athletic Association hockey club of the Amateur Hockey Association of Canada. The National Hockey Association (NHA) was the first professional league to award the Cup (a large silver chalice with a new layer added each year, passed to the winning team and engraved with the names of that team's players) in 1910.

In 1917, Frank Calder, a British scholar and former sports journalist who came to Canada to be a soccer player, decided to keep the NHA's teams intact, rename the organization the NHL, and appoint himself President. The league consisted of four teams that played a 22-game schedule. The NHL added its first U.S. team in 1925, when the Boston Bruins joined the league.

The 1920s saw continued expansion, but the NHL remained amorphous as many teams joined up and dropped out during the decade. Hordes of players went to World War II, forcing the NHL to field teams whose players were too young, too old, or barely able to skate. The league almost shut down, but the Canadian government encouraged play to continue, claiming it boosted national morale.

The NHL, after representing a small number of teams for many years, launched its largest expansion in league history in 1967, when six U.S.-based franchises joined up. The league expanded to 21 teams in 1979 by absorbing its rival professional league, the World Hockey Association. U.S. interest in the sport stagnated for many years, however, as it was largely considered a Canadian sport and its reputation for brutal violence turned off many fans. The NHL tried to put an end to its slugfest image by implementing new rules in 1992, reducing violent play and emphasizing a quicker game based on skill and style.

Team owners instituted a player lockout in 1994, but their goal of implementing a salary cap was not very successful. In 1997, the NHL added four new expansion teams (Atlanta, Columbus, Ohio, Minnesota, and Nashville), introducing them over a four-year period.

The league's plan to boost popularity by using professional players in the 1998 Winter Olympic games in Nagano, Japan, was thwarted by limited, late-night coverage. Later that year, NHL team owners agreed to a $600 million, five-year television contract with The Walt Disney Company's ABC and ESPN, starting with the 2000–2001 season. In 2000, as part of a plan to bring its entire Internet business under the NHL roof, the league bought IBM's interest in NHL Interactive CyberEnterprises for $10 million.

Today's NHL is organized into 30 teams, 24 in the U.S. and 6 in Canada. The Commissioner of the league is Gary Bettman. There are two conferences, the Western and the Eastern, with three divisions each. Each team plays 82 regular-season games in a season lasting from September to June.

Attendance for the 2000–2001 season reached record levels with over 20 million attending, with an average of 16,000+ per game. The average payroll per team for the same season was over $34 million, with an average salary of $1.4 million. The three teams with the highest payrolls are the New York Rangers, the Detroit Red Wings, and the Colorado Avalanche. The NHL All-Star Game is played in mid-season, usually in late January. Both blue-collar and white-collar workers attend hockey, but high ticket prices do set some limitations on who can attend games.

The major political issue facing the NHL right now is the decline of the Canadian teams, which are all struggling in the smaller Canadian market and seem to be on the verge of bankruptcy. There is a movement to relocate the teams to the U.S. so that they can take advantage of the larger American market. However, many see this as an attempt to take Canada's national sport out of Canada and are very strongly against it.

THE IMPACT OF MARKETING

The four major sports leagues have become much more aggressive in the marketing of their product of late. The leagues have found new opportunities to exploit teams, players, league history, venues, and memorabilia in ways not imagined just a few years ago.

The two biggest drivers of income both for the leagues and the franchise owners are television rights and ticket sales. The changing nature of the television industry in the last two decades has led to spiraling rights revenue for leagues and teams. Teams now have local broadcasting revenue deals—often with local cable sports channels—that bring in millions of dollars. In some cases, notably baseball, the local rights fees paid to the teams are incredibly substantial. The large amount of money to be made from local television revenue prompted the merger of baseball's New York Yankees and basketball's

New Jersey Nets into one entity, for the purpose of launching a new local cable sports channel to show the teams' games.

However, teams in large markets make substantially more revenue from local television than do teams in smaller metropolitan areas. Teams have found this money so difficult to share that MLB owners have considered folding two struggling franchises rather than finding a way to share this local television revenue more equally among the teams. The aggressive pursuit of local television dollars led to the hoarding of money by owners in large televisions markets, even to the detriment of the sport as a whole.

The other method to substantially increase revenue year-over-year is moving a team into a new stadium, whether it is in the team's current city or in a different one. A new stadium (or a substantially renovated one) provides owners additional streams of revenue, such as the collection of personal seat licenses, which are purchased so that the holder of the license holds the right to purchase season tickets for a particular seat. Other new income streams come from additional tiers of seating and a larger number of luxury boxes. New stadiums also provide opportunities to sell naming rights to corporations. These multi-million-dollar deals generally last between 10 and 30 years, and can cost companies substantial annual sums every year. The largest deal to-date is Reliant Energy's 30-year, $300 million deal for the naming rights to the new stadium for the 2002 NFL expansion team, the Houston Texans.

In stadiums, arenas, and ballparks, all owners have access to the same techniques and strategies to increase revenue from fans who attend games. The leagues' teams have exploited the entertainment expense tax breaks for corporations by offering large companies luxury boxes, or enclosed rooms that oversee the action with amenities such as catered food, bars, individual tables and chairs, and even conference capabilities such as voice and data ports.

To drive individual fans and families to games without lowering prices, teams have become extremely adept at ticket promotions. Teams partner with companies to provide branded products that are given free to "qualified" ticket holders. A team schedule magnet sponsored by Budweiser, for instance, might be given away to the first 20,000 fans who are over the age of 21 at a baseball game.

In addition to the free magnets, caps, and mini-pennants that have become staples of the promotional scene, teams are finding new promotional items to spark fan interest, such as the retrospective (retro) bobblehead doll. The bobblehead doll features an oversized head of a team player that "bobbles" on an undersized body. These dolls, first popular in the 1950s, have had enormous success in driving attendance at games where tickets have traditionally been less desirable. If the bobblehead craze is similar to the Beanie Baby craze that preceded it, bobbleheads will be able to substantially drive attendance for a year or two, and then will fade in popularity, necessitating teams and leagues to discover the next big promotional craze.

Although promotions are one of the oldest forms of advertising, they are extremely effective in improving the experience a customer has when attending a sporting event. They also serve as a constant reminder of that enjoyable occasion and more specifically, of the sponsors or teams connected to that event. This tactic indirectly helps to promote the brand image of the teams or companies involved, and increases the likelihood of returning customers.

Outside of creating revenue by catering to those who attend and watch games, the leagues have been much more aggressive at exploiting other revenue streams. The biggest expansion in these outside revenues is the exploitation of naming rights deals for team stadiums and arenas. A corporation signs a contract, agreeing to pay millions of dollars for a set number of years, for the right to have the team's venue carry the corporation's name. For example, the Denver Broncos will get $120 million over the next 20 years to have their new facility carry the name of mutual fund manager Invesco. This is despite the fact that the facility incorporates the name of the team's previous stadium in the new stadium's name, "The Invesco Field at Mile High."

Teams have also introduced new products to increase merchandise sales. One of the bigger changes is the introduction of a third "alternate" uniform that can be worn for either home or away games. These alternate uniforms are usually restricted, so that they are worn only a certain number of times a season, or on certain days. The Chicago White Sox, for example, have a retro alternate uniform that mimics their 1920 uniform, but is only worn for Sunday ballgames at their home stadium. This is another product that people, especially kids, will buy if they are loyal to that team.

For the student of the modern-day sports business, and to understand the complete strategy of marketing sports, one of the best books on this subject is Mathew D. Shank's *Sports Marketing, A Strategic Perspective*, now in its second edition. It is equally effective as a textbook and an industry executive handbook.

A WORLDWIDE ATTRACTION

Sports presentations speak a global language. The NFL has a strong international television presence with 182 countries and territories carrying broadcasts—many on Disney-owned ESPN. The fact that NFL Europe is building credibility only adds to the sport's visibility. MLB is broadcast throughout the world, and is especially popular in Latin American countries. Many broadcasters—including ESPN International, Fox Sports Americas, and Televisa—offer several packages that include the All-Star Game, divisional and league championships, and the World Series. The July 2000 All-Star Game in Atlanta was seen in 200 countries and was shown live as far away as Australia and South Korea.

The NBA is currently seen in 205 countries—with Malta and Kazakhstan recently signing up—on 129 broadcasters, while play-by-play can be heard in 42 languages, including Maltese, Flemish, and Tagalog. The NBA's Sacramento Kings and Minnesota Timberwolves opened their regular-season schedules in Japan. NBA.com TV, launched in November, is a 24-hour channel that looks at games in progress, statistics, highlights, and re-transmissions of classic games. *Inside Stuff*, the NBA's weekly feature show, is translated into 15 different languages, with a local host for each version.

Heidi Ueberroth, Senior Vice President of International TV and Business Development for NBA Entertainment, says the sport appeals to worldwide audiences because of several key factors:

- There is universal popularity for both the sport and its players: Kobe Bryant, Vince Carter, and Kevin Garnett are all huge stars around the world. (As a matter of fact, Vince Carter was on magazine covers in Hong Kong before he ever appeared in a game on TV there.)
- The action of broadcast sports is easy to follow, regardless of language.
- Basketball is the fastest growing participation sport, especially with youth. The fact that the NBA has brought the game overseas has also helped popularize the sport. Last season alone, the NBA scheduled games in Israel, Milan, Italy, Mexico City, and Tokyo.

These same factors apply to each of the major sports, opening new inroads to foreign populations for marketers.

Having established themselves on television, sports have now taken their games to the Internet. Last September, high-speed broadband Internet telecasts were available in real time in the Netherlands, Austria, and Singapore, through video on-demand (VOD) and near-VOD services.

The compelling nature of sports is perfect for the global reach of the Internet, according to key sources. According to Nadine Gelberg, Director of the Sports and Entertainment Practice at Harris Interactive, the category is just beginning to reach its prime. "Even with their successes," says Gelberg, "sports sites have been slow to capitalize on the Net's potential." Gelberg believes that sports e-commerce has great potential for growth. "Being a fan is a very active experience," says Brenda Spoonemore, Vice President of NBA Internet Services. "It's yelling at the TV and wanting to buy the uniform of your favorite team. There's kind of a self-selective process going on, and the people we get are already participators. It fits with the Internet as an active experience."

Developments in media technology are challenging the very fabric of athletic competition and the revenues associated with sports. Digital TV and the Internet have the ability to change the way revenues are generated, which may lead to the wealthiest franchises getting even wealthier. League structures that control popular professional sports in the U.S. are very rigid, and the impact of the Internet is yet to be fully realized. While leagues can control the "blackout" of undersold games in North American markets, the same is not currently true when using the Internet.

THE STRIKES: MARKETING BACKLASH

Among the many issues, crises, and unpredictable occasions that create havoc for the sports marketing executive, the one that generates true panic is a players strike. When well-paid, well-perked athletes decide to strike for increased pay, it becomes a strong negative image for everyone involved. Players strikes typically evoke little sympathy from fans, for many are already paying ever-higher prices for stadium tickets—not to mention the monthly cable bill and PPV charges.

The result can be backlash from fans economically blackballing the teams and the leagues, voting with their pocketbooks and staying home. Empty ballparks and equally dark basketball stadiums resulted when MLB and the NBA struck and refused to play during their respective seasons. Irate fans were not easily diffused when some of the wealthier players publicly suggested that alimony for several wives and upkeep on million-dollar mansions or collections of luxury cars made their current seven- or eight-figure salaries inadequate.

Given that the base definition of the marketing function involves the sale of tickets, merchandise, season subscriptions, sports cable subscriptions, PPV sports events, and other sponsorship relationships, bad press of this kind can be somewhat challenging—and have far-reaching consequences.

Consider filmed entertainment (movies or broadcast/cable): If the stars were to strike (as is frequently threatened by the Screen Actor's Guild or Screen Writer's Guild), more than filming would stop. The fan magazines, the award shows, the theaters, the video stores, the soundtracks, the gossip columns, and all the professional services so dependent on these entities would go into hiatus. Imagine if you can, lawyers, agents, business managers, advertising agencies, publicists, media planning and buying firms, as well as the media themselves, all "at liberty."

Strikes in the world of sports have the same ripple effect, but perhaps with longer-lasting effects. Sports fans tend to be some of the most loyal consumers, but at the same time, the ever-widening gap between rich and poor can lead to a situation in which the fan stops identifying with the team—and therefore stops supporting it with his or her dollars. This situation is exacerbated by the free agency that has fed the player payroll over the last several decades, as the constant change of players, often for bigger contracts elsewhere, leaves little "team" left to root for.

Today's marketers must be aware of this constantly changing landscape and work hard to promote the binding ties that keep fans attached to their teams. Given the fact that revenues, especially from cable rights, keep increasing, chances are very good that the labor/management issue will not soon resolve itself.

THERE'S NO SIN IN SYNERGY

Perhaps the best evidence of sports convergence with entertainment can be found in the increasing ownership of sports media, and sports teams themselves, by the entertainment conglomerates. The dollars generated by sports, as well as the synergistic opportunities, have not been lost on the "Big Boys." Sports programs are spread across the networks; ESPN and its spin-off, ESPN2, can be found on cable.

But, the relationship of sports to entertainment does not end merely at the conduit level. Disney has an 80% share in ESPN, and has extended the brand into the highly successful ESPN Zone restaurants/sports bars that are springing up across the U.S. Digging deeper, Disney also owns two sports franchises, the Mighty Ducks (hockey) and the Anaheim Angels (baseball). The importance of these business units to Disney can be clearly seen in the fact that the company decided to forego gambling onboard its cruise ships—a multi-million-dollar revenue stream—due to the stipulation that owners of sports franchises cannot be involved in gambling. Walt Disney World is the spring training home of the Atlanta Braves baseball team, as well as the Walt Disney World Speedway, a mile-long NASCAR track that also serves as a base of operations for the Richard Petty Driving Experience, which allows racing fans to get behind the wheel of a Winston Cup stock car.

Disney, like Viacom, which owns the Los Angeles Dodgers baseball franchise through its Fox Entertainment Group, understands the power of connecting the public's fascination with competition to other corporate objectives such as increased attendance at theme parks and the halo effect that can spread from the fan's attitude toward a team and its celebrity players—not to mention the possible convergence between a team and content for films TV, books, and the like. While the movie *The Mighty Ducks* in no way represents the professional athletes who play under that name as they pass the puck on the Anaheim ice, the repetition of the name—the brand—goes a long way in supporting both concepts.

NON-LEAGUE SPORTS

The four major league sports are not alone in their ability to attract an extremely loyal fan base. A wide variety of alternatives exist in today's competition-hungry world.

PROFESSIONAL WRESTLING: SPORTS OR ENTERTAINMENT?

Modern professional wrestling is derived from the classical form of the wrestling sport, but it became Americanized through carnivals and barnstormers after the Civil War. Today, the professional wrestling that appeals to countless millions of fans worldwide relies on a different set of choreographed rules and departures from the original format. Body-slamming, head-locking, chair-throwing combinations provide a unique rendition of sports spectacular and entertainment extravaganza.

Wrestling's first superstar was Ed "Strangler" Lewis, competing in the early 1920s. The Great Depression brought an end to Strangler Ed's career and a downturn in the fortunes of the sport, as finances and market basket concerns restricted the disposable income available for enjoyment. However, by the early 1930s several wrestling matches with major stars of the time drew significant crowds, resulting in ticket sales of $100,000 at various venues, including Yankee Stadium in New York and Wrigley Field in Chicago.

Wrestling was an inexpensive form of programming and was soon available in over 50 television markets as a new audience of older fans was content to be entertained and amused by the daily antics of the wrestlers, including Gorgeous George, a wrestling personality of the 1950s who gained wide audience appeal through mass television exposure. When regular family television fare added Lucy, Milton Berle, Ed Sullivan, Jackie Gleason, and other regular programs, wrestling was again eclipsed.

It was not until Vince McMahon acquired control of the World Wrestling Federation (WWF), the professional wrestling enterprise of the late 1980s, that the sport regained its prominence and rose to unprecedented success. The simultaneous growth of cable and the ability to reach a large targeted audience via ESPN or other male audience networks helped the WWF build an integrated media and entertainment company, headquartered in Stamford, Connecticut.

Outside the U.S., the UK is the WWF's chief market, although the growth there is being repeated more or less worldwide. Wrestling has evolved from being sports entertainment to an athletic soap opera, with an ever-changing story line and different characters. It's a soap that British pay broadcaster Sky considered worth $35 million over the course of its new five-year deal, even though its territory is also covered by a terrestrial agreement with Channel 4.

NASCAR

Stock car racing is one of the fastest growing spectator sports in the U.S. From its slightly illegal beginnings—early stock car drivers were bootleggers who gathered together to show off their souped up autos, built to outrun government "revenuers"—to its current popularity, NASCAR has steadily built a following that defies stereotypes.

The first NASCAR-sanctioned stock car race was staged on the Daytona Beach, Florida road course on February 15, 1948. The first season champion was Red Byron, who won 11 races and collected $1,250 in post-season awards for winning the championship. Compare that to today's champions, who earn millions of dollars, both for winning and in sponsorship fees.

Possibly the best evidence of NASCAR's popularity—and acceptance by big entertainment—is the new NASCAR track at Walt Disney World in Florida. Disney, the premier entertainment marketer of our time, understands that NASCAR is no longer small potatoes, and that playing to the racing crowd can build incremental sales in theme park visits among an extremely loyal audience.

EXTREME SPORTS

No longer satisfied with a casual game of catch on a Saturday afternoon, Americans—especially the youth market—have been turning to extreme sports. With these sports, Americans attempt to satisfy their need to thrill-seek and take risks, under the guise of a sport. Such extreme sports are snowboarding, ice climbing, skateboarding, paragliding, and Building, Antennae, Span, Earth (BASE) jumping. According to *Time* magazine, "The rising popularity of extreme sports bespeaks an eagerness on the part of millions of Americans to participate in activities closer to the metaphorical edge, where danger, skill and fear combine to give weekend warriors and professional athletes alike a sense of pushing out personal boundaries."[1]

The number of participants in these sports has increased monumentally as the American population chooses to create its own risks in a country that is relatively stable. According to American Sports Data Inc., a consulting firm, snowboarding has grown 113% in five years and now has nearly 5.5 million participants. Similarly, mountain biking, skateboarding, and scuba diving have all seen record numbers.

Historically, one of America's defining characteristics has always been risk. The U.S. is a country founded by risk-takers fed up with the English crown and expanded by pioneers—a word that seems utterly American. Extreme sports athletes claim that the sports make them feel very much alive; however, the irony is that many of them actually get hurt. In 1997, the U.S. Consumer Products Safety Commission reported that 48,000 Americans were admitted to hospital emergency rooms with skateboarding-related injuries. In addi-

---

1. *Time* magazine, September 6, 1999, p. 28+.

tion, snowboarding emergency room visits were up 31%, and mountain climbing incidents were up 20%. According to every statistical measure available, Americans are participating in and injuring themselves through adventure sports at an unprecedented rate.

NOT-SO-EXTREME SPORTS

Of course, there is more to the world of sports than big leagues and big risks. Americans have been in love with the outdoors since the first explorers gasped at the wide-open spaces and purple mountain's majesty. Today, more than ever, hunting, fishing, and camping capture the imagination of a population that perhaps feels a tiny bit caught up in the urban or suburban lifestyle. (To what else can we attribute the popularity of sports utility vehicles (SUVs), those behemoth four-wheel-drive vehicles that eventually wind up on the used car lot, that four-wheel-drive mechanism still as pristine as the day it left the showroom floor?)

These sports generate a significant amount of marketing revenue. While the variety of other-than-league sports is far too wide to cover in this book, there is one excellent example that illustrates the point perfectly.

CASE IN POINT: WHOSE LINE IS IT ANYWAY?

If you turn on your television on a Saturday morning and click your way to the TNN station, you're liable to end up being entertained by two men in a fishing boat. The boat may well be a Ranger or a Cajun boat, the rods could be made by Shimano or Berkeley, the reels might be manufactured by Garcia or Penn, and the lures used may well be made by the Culprit or Fred Arbogast companies. Sound like a foreign language? Not to worry—the host is sure to mention the manufacturer sooner or later during the action-oriented show. No, you're not watching an infomercial; these are legitimate shows, with hosts whose names are household words to a certain enthusiastic following. Names like Bill Dance, Jimmy Houston, Rolland Martin, or Hank Parker are accompanied by their pal for the day, ranging from Hank Williams, Jr., to Terry Bradshaw, to Garth Brooks.

What you're getting a peek at is just one facet of a multi-billion-dollar-a-year part of entertainment on a grassroots level. Fishing alone brought in $37.8 billion in 1996, according to the American Sport Fishing Association's study funded by the U.S. Fish and Wildlife Service.[2] In fact, the annual spending by the 20% of Americans who angle, according to the study, is responsible for the following:

- A nationwide economic impact of $108.4 billion
- 1.2 million jobs (about 1% of America's entire civilian labor force)
- Related spending in travel and tourism, location-based entertainment (LBE), and a host of other entertainment areas covered in this book

The entertainment marketing of these television shows reaches viewers to whom the content has become a staple. It reaches across the mainstream of America, to an audience that probably watches more fishing shows than PBS. The merchandise that drives the entertainment, in this case, gets its 15 minutes of fame from trade shows attended by thousands of vendors, from shows open to the public in almost every major city, and from the over 600 organizations within the sport fishing industry, such as BASS, a national organization that hosts contests and television shows, and—surprise, surprise—promotes new tackle and techniques. Fishing alone supports about 2,400 wholesalers and distributors, 6,000 fishing tackle shops, 3,800 sporting goods stores, 1,000 marine dealers, and more than 6,000 other retailers. The fishing phenomenon is, like other sports, going global too. Witness the formation of the European Fishing Tackle Trade Association (EFTTA).[3]

Factor in the need for hotels, motels, food, campers, boats—and even first aid, on occasion—and the web of economic impact is huge. You may never see Bill Dance on-stage with U2, but to a significant part of America, he's a star, influencing people to buy whatever he says, right down to their Hanes underwear.

TIGER, TIGER, BURNING BRIGHT

Finally, it would be impossible to talk about sports marketing without mentioning Tiger Woods. While golf has been an increasingly popular pastime (there are some who will argue the point regarding its status as a sport, but tell that to the guy who just walked 36 holes), for years it has been thought of as a primarily white-guy activity.

Then came Tiger. Bursting onto the scene, Woods provides those who handle marketing for professional golf a bonanza. He is loaded

---

2. See *www.asafishing.org/statistics*. The study was made under Cooperative Grant Agreement No. 14-048-009-1237.

3. See *www.martex.co.uk*

with talent, and has already proven that he knows what to do with it with his incredible string of victories. He is young, dynamic, and very articulate. He is attractive, and his racial heritage (Asian and African-American) brings a refreshing diversity to the golf scene. Woods has something for everyone—and for a lot of everyones who never had much interest in golf.

In short, Woods has given golf entrée into several previously untouched demographic segments, and marketers are salivating. Woods has already joined Michael Jordan in Nike's pantheon of sports celebrities, and now exhibits the Nike "swoosh" on everything from his hat to his golf balls. His presence in the golf tour has led to an unheard of event in sports TV—Sunday golf actually outdrawing televised NBA games—not an audience demographic one might have associated with golf in earlier days.

Tiger is hot—and he's only getting started. It remains to be seen how his presence will continue to affect the game. One aspect of that presence is already clear: Like Serena and Venus Williams in the previously highly white world of tennis, Tiger provides a role model to young athletes who have been sorely lacking in same, from an ethnic/racial perspective. Above and beyond the bonus of those great big markets just waiting to be opened, the aspirational value of the presence of new faces in old established sports will keep those products vibrant and exciting.

Like baseball and fishing, golf is a sport in which many Americans—male and female, and of all ethnic backgrounds—now participate. It's a market that can continue to grow, and the flame of Tiger, Tiger burning bright has lit part of the way.

Sports and the marketing of the entertainment value of sports are highly dependent on the aspirational value of the content—and nothing typifies aspiration better than the granddaddy of couch potato sports: the Olympics.

THE OLYMPIC CHALLENGE

Ah, the Olympics: the height of sports purity, of dedication to competition for competition's sake, of sportsmanship. The Olympics are the easiest event in the world to market, full of national pride and global goodwill, presided over by a group of dedicated individuals, intent on furthering nothing but the squeaky-clean image of this renowned event.

A wonderful image, but lately it has been quite questionable. The International Olympic Committee (IOC) has been wracked for the past few years by a wide-ranging payoff scandal that revealed a culture based on back-scratching—you want the Olympics in your city, you give my nephew a job. Or, as in the case of Kevin Gosper, the IOC Vice President whose 1993 Utah ski vacation figured into investigations surrounding gift-giving in the awarding of the 2002 Winter Games to Salt Lake City, it was give my daughter the honor of being the first Australian to carry the Olympic torch for the Sydney Games.

Part of the difficulty in changing the IOC is in the makeup of the committee. Members represent the IOC in their countries—not the other way around. And while membership criteria have changed—there are now active athletes in the IOC—the term limits are not consistent between new members and old. Those active athletes can only hold the position for eight years; compare that to the 20 that Juan Samaranch has served.

The IOC has never been squeaky-clean, starting with the decision to limit the games to amateurs, which had more to do with the aversion of 19th Century aristocrats to competing with the working classes than sports purity. And then there was the string of Olympiads from 1936 (Germany), 1940 (Japan), and 1944 (Italy)—most interesting, given the makeup of the Axis during World War II. Then came the ongoing allegations of under-the-table payments to athletes—from both the U.S. and USSR—and, of course, the question of muscle-enhancing drug use.

Finally, there is the controversial element of allowing paid professionals to compete in the Olympics. While there are those who will argue the point that certain world powers have been paying their Olympians forever, the introduction of elements such as the U.S. basketball "Dream Teams," comprised of the top NBA players, has taken a little of the shine off the aspirational quality of the Games. It has, however, served marketers well, extending the reach of the Olympics into already established TV audiences not previously interested in the Games.

Despite that, the athletes make the Games; no doubt they will again. Still, while cheering, it's best to know what the Olympics are, and what they aren't.

SPORTS ONLINE: TODAY'S TECHNOLOGIES

Traditional marketing methods are losing their grip on customers at an alarming rate, mainly because of the vast technological changes of the past decade. Computer-generated images and the use the Internet have had a great impact on sports marketing and will continue to do so in the future—and still more change is on the way.

One of the newest technologies to hit the sports market is virtual technology. For example, viewers may see a logo for Coca-Cola pop up during a televised baseball game on the wall behind home plate. The purpose of this is to advertise while the game is being broadcast. The people at the stadium do not see it, but it is virtually implanted onto the screen for the small-screen viewer—typically a much larger audience. This type of marketing can be a cheaper form of advertising; additionally, the product can be changed inning-by-inning—minute-by-minute if desired. The viewers focusing on home plate action are forever focused on the message—unlike commercials that are broadcast between innings.

Another form of virtual marketing is interactive sports. For example, OradNet Inc.'s new TOPlay[tm] Soccer creates an interactive 3D graphics representation of actual soccer matches that can be viewed by fans online. Fans have control of how they view a soccer match, from zooming in and out of plays to watching the game through the eyes of their favorite player. They can also view replays in slow motion from any angle.

This represents a new category of immersive sports media. Immersive sports not only let fans enjoy games in a new way, but also create valuable new marketing opportunities for sports content providers, including virtual advertising and e-commerce possibilities that do not compete with traditional broadcast revenue models. One of the chief avenues for innovation lies in the area of information, which sports fans crave.

INFORMATION SOURCES

Sports news, statistics, analysis, schedules, and prices: all of this information can now be found online. The most popular type of information source online is the news service. These are large repositories, mostly Web sites, with the same types of sports news, graphics, and design found in a daily newspaper. Unlike a paper, however, they can by updated many times daily. Two of the most popular sites are ESPN.com and CBS SportsLine. These commercial undertakings charge fees of about $5 a month for their advanced service. ESPN.com, CBS SportsLine, and the Boston Globe Sports Pages are prime examples of how newspapers and sports magazines will look when most households have fast Internet connections and sleek, high-contrast, paper-like displays.

The high cost and hassle of newsprint distribution make online distribution an attractive option for publishers. These Internet news services, which have a familiar feel because they are laid out much like newspapers, solve some of the problems associated with traditional newspaper and broadcast news. The amount of news presented is no longer directly determined by advertising space or available airtime (although it is indirectly determined by advertising through staff size). Moreover, layout constraints are less likely to limit content, and all news can be recorded "for the record" and left online for search and reference.

Services like ESPN.com have hired talented writers because they know that users prefer fewer, more personal, and highly engaging articles over hundreds of AP wire summaries. People want stores that entice them and grab their attention. Sports fans are looking for writers who have a feel of the sport, knowledge of its history, a clear understanding of local personalities and rules, and a rapport with the fans.

Currently, these online services do not provide much community news, but such information is a power draw: news about a next-door neighbor who won a national title in some rare sport is generally considered more exciting by the sports fan than 95% of more mainstream national sports news. Why? Because local news personally connects a fan to the action (even if the fan has never met the neighbor) and it provides a potentially useful social tie to the fan's community.

Expanding online services like ESPN.com to provide community-based stories will require large distributed staffs, unlike automatic sports article generation programs like Sportswriter, which do not provide the type of depth and analysis fans expect. These new news services are attracting customers because of their novelty, timeliness, and depth of resources. However, until better displays and fast home access materialize, these services will need more innovative services to steal leisure time away from convenient, inexpensive newspapers.

In addition to news, the popular information-based sports services provide play-by-play descriptions of sporting events. ESPN.com, for instance, has football "drive charts" and basketball "shot charts." These graphics diagrammatically show where and when the action took place, second by second. This type of detail, seldom found in newspapers due to space limitations, is being used to entice information-starved fans to pay monthly membership fees. Live audio of some NBA basketball games and sports radio stations are already making their way onto the Internet, as are highlight video clips and special interactive video demonstrations (e.g., *Sports Illustrated's* online interactive baseball map).

Once a fan has news and play-by-play, he or she may want scores and statistics. Selling sports stats is already a multi-million-dollar industry. Several CD-ROM software packages like Microsoft's *Complete Baseball* now provide online repositories that update the software's stats daily, charging $1.25 per day. Companies like Stats, Inc. provide details like the number of running back "stuffs" and umpire call tendencies, which are available instantly for a $30 registration fee and $.25 per minute online charges. All of the major sports services are overflowing with statistical information; ESPN's Scoreline charges $.95 a minute for scores, and Motorola's sports beeper that reports on baseball games in progress costs about $50 per month. Now, some online services are even providing customizable, real-time scrolling Java scoreboards.

The amount of sports information being distributed online is accelerating. Over 2500 sports-related Web pages currently exist, and they are estimated to grow to about 10,000 by 2004. All four major leagues have Web sites that provide up-to-date information and will be used to solidify fan loyalty and add incremental revenue. In addition, teams have their own individual Web sites, providing fans with game schedules, ticket information, and opportunities to buy team and player merchandise.

The information available to the growing number of fans, direct to adults online or their PC-enabled children, includes statistics and current news that is frequently more current than the traditional magazine and newspaper media. This technology connection helps maintain avid fan loyalty and has begun to locate new sports enthusiasts.

While gaining a virtual spectator audience, and still part of the consumption factor, sports via the Internet are missing the emotional punch of on-site, at-the-venue thrills and crowd intensity. At a minimum, even the close-ups of television angles and camcorder on-the-field intimacy, as portrayed on weekend television, overwhelm the antiseptic online sports experience.

SUMMARY

From the major leagues to soccer, golf, polo, tennis, bowling, fly fishing—nearly any sport imaginable—the parameters of sports and their place in the integrated marketing of entertainment content have only just begun. The loyal fan base of each sport is a ready and willing target for a wide variety of sponsorship opportunities, promotions, and tie-ins, with products for the health-conscious, as well as those not normally associated with the hale and hearty. Most important, sports offer an inroad to all ages, races, socio-economics, and genders.

FOR FURTHER READING

BOOKS

1. Carter, David, *Keeping Score: An Inside Look at Sports Marketing* (Central Point, OR: PSI Research, Oasis Press, 1996).

MAGAZINE ARTICLES

1. CNN/Sports Illustrated Web site, "Baseball Millionaires," April 4, 2001.

2. CNN/Sports Illustrated Web site, "The NFL Salary Cap for 2001."

3. "Jordan Mania is Sweeping the NBA," *The Washington Post*, October 6, 2001.

4. Green, Aaron D., "Owning the Team," *The Sporting News*, Issue 58, 1997.

5. Sanomir, Richard, "NBA and AOL Discussing New Network," *The New York Times*, November 14, 2001.

6. Hyman, Mark, "How Bad is the NBA Hurting," *Business Week*, May 7, 2001.

7. Cassiday, Hilary, "Sports, Athletes, Sponsors Return with Focus on Supporting Nation," *Brandweek*, October 14, 2001.

WEB SITES

1. ESPN.com, "Owners Vote for Contraction," November 6, 2001.

2. ESPN.com, "National Football League Statistics."

3. National Basketball Development League, *www.nbdl.com*

4. National Basketball Players Association, "About Us" guide. *www.nbpa.com*

5. National Hockey League, NHL.com, "2001 Season Preview."

6. Hoovers Online Company Profiles, Hoovers.com, (NBA, NFL, MBL, NHL).

9 TRAVEL AND TOURISM

OVERVIEW

To some, the terms "travel" and "leisure" have absolutely no business being anywhere near one another in a sentence. To these people, the concept of travel is fraught with missed airplanes, fleabag hotels, and skies that never offer anything but a constant downpour—not very reflective of a leisurely getaway. Fact is, many of us have had those infamous experiences that flavor our dinner conversations with new acquaintances and old travel partners. But in spite of the little glitches here and there, the public still seems willing to pack their bags and get onboard—heading to hotels, resorts, theme parks, ski slopes, islands, cruise ships, music halls, theaters, casinos, and sports stadiums—thanks to great marketing and promotion, and the fact that most destinations offer the wonderful experience they promise.

PROMISING PARADISE

Marketing to prospective tourists is an exciting, highly volatile, incredibly creative, and extremely rewarding pursuit that offers enormous financial returns when it is done well. However, it has its challenges, among them:

- The number of constituencies that must pass judgment on the strategy and tactics, including advertising, PR, and promotions.
- Subjective evaluation by management with little or no experience in marketing or the ability to judge the merits of effective advertising.
- The need to react to many external and uncontrollable issues, including economics, crime, poverty, violence, and political instability.

The marketing of travel and tourism requires a plan that allows not only for the instantaneous decision by those who are actively looking for somewhere to go—now—but also to those who may simply be window-shopping, creating a fantasy for a later day. Done correctly, marketing will entice both these parties. But enticement, as in any situation, is only half the battle. Once the happy traveler reaches his or her destination, the dream must be delivered to build not only repeat visitation (the soul of the travel industry), but great recommendations to friends and family. This level of satisfaction is only achieved when the guest arrives with clear expectations. But they need to GET those expectations met, too—not just arrive with them. Exceeding those expectations is a bonus; failing to meet them will often ignite a wildfire of negative word of mouth.

EXPERIENCE MEETS EXPECTATION

To match experience with expectation, marketers must understand the strengths and weaknesses of their product to get the right guest to the right destination. Research is intended to identify the lifestyle of the prospective vacationer for the product, assess the discretionary budget required to pay for the trip, match expectations with core advantages, and recognize the media considered most frequently by the target customer as credible sources of vacation information. Simply put, not every traveler wants to spend a week at the Ritz-Carlton®—some may prefer a grass shack at the edge of the beach, where loud Hawaiian shirts are *de rigueur*. The challenge to each location is to constantly secure its share of the vacation pocket-book.

The key to, and complexity of, marketing destinations is that the guest expects a consistent, unchanging experience, while the destination itself can be under fire from any number of variables—weather, strikes, change in the value of the dollar, political upheaval, rise and fall of crime rates, you name it. This creates a constant stream of challenges to the marketing team. This is the great difference between marketing travel and other types of entertainment, which, barring a sore throat for Bruce Springsteen or stale popcorn for *Titanic*, remains relatively consistent. This challenge can become even greater when locations are linked in the process of developing travel packages. At certain times in the political climate, an Antiquities and History tour offering Greece and Israel can provide travelers with a marvelous overview of the growth of the Humanities. At other times, certain parts of the tour might present a rather different picture, focusing more on potential inhumanities. However, when planned carefully and presented properly, package tours and multi-destination trips can offer the marketer a much wider target market, and travelers a wonderful value. While price and promotion are important in building a destination marketing plan, equally critical is positioning. In the very competitive arena of travel and leisure, a location's image and its halo effect are critical elements of differentiation.

POSITIONING

Travel destinations fall into one of three basic images: positive, negative, or neutral. Many locations enjoy positive positioning due to movies and the media consistently celebrating their positive attributes—think Paris or Rome. Others may not be so fortunate; travel packages to Afghanistan may be a tough sell in the early part of the 21st Century. Subjective as these images may be, it is important to consider them when preparing a marketing plan, for if the image is basically negative, no amount of expensive marketing strategies will be cost-effective. Unfortunately, the image may never be resolved or improved, even if it is due to a misperception or some perceived flaw.

If, on the other hand, the image is neutral, the game is wide open. This *tabula rasa* (blank slate) offers a huge opportunity to build on. For years, the island of Aruba, the city of Philadelphia, and the town of San Louis Obispo had little or no image. Marketing their strengths and adding to their infrastructure enabled them to become destinations of choice. Aruba became known for rain-free holidays and easy access to casinos. Philadelphia created events like "The Book and The Cook," 10 days of best-of-show house tours, and an expanded promotion of the most successful flower show outside of Chelsea Gardens, England. And, no interested traveler would dare to miss the Hearst Castle when passing through the otherwise sleepy town of San Louis Obispo.

THE IMPORTANCE OF INTEGRATION

When addressing positioning, integrated marketing communications become important in creating message consistency and affordable impact on the consumer's decision-making process—both conscious and unconscious. At every level, the standard of excellence in achieving the desired positioning for a location requires working with the same strategy, the same goals, and the same presentation of the image in every media and at every contact point with all audiences. This is imperative when trying to expand the consumer base or to reposition an existing destination. A great example of this is Las Vegas. Once known as "Sin City," Las Vegas actually used the lingering whiff of adult-oriented entertainment to build itself into one of the primary convention markets in the county. However, its effort to broaden its base by promoting itself as a center of family entertainment almost backfired, when adults started to avoid the locations on the Strip that offered child-oriented activities. Las Vegas has quietly returned to its roots in the last few years, refocusing on its image as a theme park for adults.

An umbrella image and individual tactical outreach—with individual emotional motivators—may not have an immediate impact, but they help to implant an image for future planning. Advertising, direct marketing travel agent communications, PR, booklets, brochures, contests, and hospitality messages must be consistent, utilizing repetition to build a strong message. It is then that delivery on the promise is important. To sustain tourism growth, the destination must also market the program internally as well as externally. If the store clerks, hotel staff, restaurant waiters, tour guides, and thousands of locals who derive their income from tourism are resentful, feel put upon, dislike meeting and greeting visitors, or are sending out negative interchanges based on culture, politics, race, or religion, the marketing plan is doomed.

A recent show on the Travel Channel described a successful marketing program on behalf of Paradise Island. Nassau, the Bahamas, seeks to promote itself by simply connecting visitors to the island with residents over dinner or lunch at their homes. It is an exchange that wins points for internal marketing savvy, and gains promoters on both sides of the equation. The residents display pride in their home country and provide information about culture, food, politics, and places to go that only insiders would know. The visitors leave with a deeper level of real understanding and appreciation of the visit. They make new friends and spread the word when they get back home.

ON THE ROAD

Whatever motivates the choice, travel and tourism—integrated with the hospitality industry—represent the second largest employer in the U.S. (over 12 million jobs) and a total revenue stream of over $500 billion per year. With more leisure time and disposable income than ever, the American traveling public is a prime market for the tourism industry. In an arena that is crowded and competitive, knowing the potential motivators for the target market is crucial.

Typically, the desire to travel stems from one of three motivators:

- The wish to visit someplace exotic or different
- Stimulation and the gathering of new knowledge
- The pursuit of a hobby

In any case, *good marketing is the promise of customer satisfaction*—and with travel, that satisfaction often comes from achieving an escape from the guest's day-to-day life. While films, books, and even software games respond to the desires, wants, or needs of the customer to feel as if he or she has gone to some faraway place— mental transportation—the travel and tourism business is all about actually going there. The segment is best described as the business of providing a vacation, holiday, and general get-away—a true escape for the purposes of relaxation, leisure activity, and possibly some form of personal renewal. Marketing and sales efforts must be designed to motivate consumers to select the service and experience providers that best tantalize with descriptions of convenience, location, amenities, sports and recreation, emotional and physical assets, and packages that are priced well.

BUILDING THE PLAN

Once the motivator most closely associated with the potential consumers of a product or destination is identified, the plan to reach those consumers should be built on the traditional basics: research, strategy, and marketing to their desires.

TRAVEL RESEARCH

Every sector of the travel and leisure industry requires information to plan its communications campaign and identify its target audience, and each has a particular approach to gathering and evaluating that data. Conde Nast does continuing surveys with its readership. Credit card companies, especially American Express, invest heavily in research and tourism marketing to capture discretionary budgets for vacation travel. The magazines people read/use for travel information send out reporters to compile editorial and visual content that hopefully qualifies and reinforces the image their advertisers present. Every hotel, cruise line, travel agency, and time-share company of substance has a visitor survey that gauges customer satisfaction, complaints, and attributes that make for positive or negative reactions. Advertising agencies use leading research firms to gain insights into the positioning, slogan, and image that best represents an idealized version of the site being sold. Even the smallest of locations, once they have identified the type of tourist that is attracted to their location, may do some rough, inexpensive focus group research to gain responses to proposed ads and radio commercials.

There are also numerous travel consultants—usually former convention bureau executives or marketing directors for destinations, airlines, and hotel chains—who are prepared to offer their services to prepare research. Travel agents, now under pressure to prove their relevance as consumers turn to the Internet for information and travel bookings, rely on the American Society of Travel Agents (ASTA), which has developed proprietary studies over the years.

In addition, there are academic journals that offer thoughtful approaches to researching the needs and wants of the potential consumer. *The Journal of Travel Research* and the more recently established *Journal of Vacation Marketing* (*JVM*), from Henry Stewart Publications in London, provide considerable support for travel research methodology. Some of the research papers presented in *JVM* include: "Evaluating Vacation Destinations Brochure Images", by Annette Pritchard and Nigel Morgan; "How to Develop a Strong Hotel Branding Strategy with a Weak Branding Budget," by Hugh Taylor; and "Methods Used by Airlines to Determine Ticket Prices," by Janice Chapman.

The best research of a destination is done through an actual site visit. One of the perks of the travel and leisure industry is what is known as a "fam trip"—a familiarization trip, offered to qualified professionals to initiate them into the unique attractions and characteristics of a particular destination. This intra-industry marketing tool—a respected and classic motivation and appreciation reward system—is often offered at no cost to travel agents, travel writers, and marketing professionals. There may occasionally be a small fee attached, to weed out those who might be more interested in their own travel than creating a unique selling proposition for the destination.

One special note: in doing site research on more exotic locations—or those where there are potential issues of danger or unpleasant surprises—researchers may want to bring a professional guide or tour leader along to prevent mishaps. In addition, marketing professionals must define carefully and fully how destinations deal with travelers of varying abilities, a consumer segment with very special needs.

STRATEGY

The most successful programs over the years have been those that utilized an effective integrated marketing communications strategy. The marketing and advertising budgets of most destinations are modest. Only a few, such as Las Vegas and Orlando, have the $30 to $50 million annual budget funded by the very destination attractions that will benefit. Sales tax, hotel tax, and restaurant and bar taxes all have a local component that goes directly to support the marketing effort.

On a scale of 1–10 on a volume meter, the noise each location competes against hovers somewhere around 12. The cities, states, hotels, motels, theme parks, and other facilities competing for a portion of the discretionary dollar spent over $500 billion dollars worldwide to broadcast their message in 1999.

A portion of that budget is directed at individuals, families, and groups planning their holidays and vacations. Just as important—if not more so—are the dollars spent attracting and maintaining events that draw traffic, such as the Olympics, the Super Bowl, beauty pageants, golf tournaments, major conventions, and significant cultural events. To successfully deliver the message, marketers (as always) must rely on differentiation.

CREATING AN IDENTITY

To be a draw for tourism, a city (large or small) must have a focus, an identity. Say the words "New Orleans," and pictures of Bourbon Street, the French Quarter, Mardi Gras, and great Cajun and Creole food spring to mind. Every destination that wants to compete for attention and the discretionary vacation budget eventually strives for the marketing equivalent of a selling proposition or unique sales claim. They range from the simple "Virginia is for Lovers," to the extreme for New York as "The Entertainment Capital of the World," to the sublime such as "Paris, the City of Lights."

Cities with a successful tourist trade almost always share certain attributes:

- Extensive and varied lodging accommodations
- A variety of dining choices, including a unique regional cuisine
- Shopping
- Wide selection of activities for all ages

But above all is at least one identifying characteristic that makes the city—big or small—worth a trip: its own unique personality. The challenge to the travel and leisure marketing professional is to find that voice, then shout it to the world through product branding, market positioning, and delivering on guests' expectations. A few examples of U.S. destinations that have done this successfully by focusing on entertainment follow.

NASHVILLE, TN

Nashville was still a relatively sleepy regional city when the Grand Ol' Opry first started broadcasting out of Ryman Auditorium. The sounds emanating from radios across the hills and hollers of Tennessee lured many a picker and grinner, their eyes focused on stardom. Before long, acts such as Minnie Pearl, Patsy Cline, and Hank Williams found a national following, which unleashed a river a talent that flowed right toward the source, creating the "Country Music Capital of the World." The city spawned spanking-new music studios that recorded the Nashville sound and bus and truck tours that created a national craving for the down-home stars, live and in-person. It wasn't long before television realized the potential of that audience, and The Nashville Network (TNN) was born.

Today, country music holds the attention of millions of fans, and the acts that grace the stage of Ryman are now as likely to be electrified as acoustic. TNN, started by Gaylord Entertainment (a Nashville-based media company), sold out to CBS in the 1990s, and is now a part of the CBS/Viacom empire. With a broader base of aficionados and a wider broadcasting distribution network, country music now provides the media conglomerate with a way to leverage a unique and growing audience. That audience is lured to Nashville not only by the music, but through the ongoing and consistent marketing of the city as a destination.

Along with the traditional methods of destination marketing (including niche magazines that feature editorials on Nashville and country music stars, as well as ads from major attractions in the city), Nashville has a strong showcase in the Country Music Awards, which give the viewer a great sense of the attractions in the city. Additionally, the Country Music Association (CMA), which markets country music stars as an important ingredient in contemporary brand promotions, sponsorships, and licensing arrangements, sponsors a three-day conference every year in Nashville for opinion leaders and marketing professionals. Visitors see the sites, hear performances from the best entertainers, taste the food, learn to two-step and line-dance, and enjoy the hospitality and warmth of the city. And in the interim, they spend money at the local retail shops, buying tee-shirts, Stetsons, and boots—which they, in all likelihood, will never wear once they get home.

Nashville has also realized that a large population of tourists thinking about visiting music destinations has a choice of cities that feature that attraction. Many of these folks just want to hear great music, from blues, to country, to gospel. In the spirit of co-opeti-tion—in which natural competitors draw strength form one another by creating mass to drive visitation—Nashville joined New Orleans and Memphis to form a marketing package called The U.S. Music Trail Tour. Also included in that partnership is a tiny town in Missouri that has become one of the powerhouse destinations of the music-loving community...

BRANSON, MO

High in the hills of Southern Missouri, in the middle of the Ozarks, sits a town of 1,400 full-time residents that attracts six million people per year. Branson, Missouri has become a destination of choice for visitors from a rectangular slice of America that runs north to Minneapolis, east to Chicago, west to cities all across Texas, and south to Arkansas. This town, with infrastructure problems, poor road systems, few motels—certainly no five-star hotels—and no management or marketing staff, has earned the right to be called the "Largest Live Country Music Center in America." There is no gambling, no late-night hours in the few bars, and the focus is on squeaky-clean fun. Yet Branson boasts more theater seats than Broadway, and more all-star and live theater presentations than any entertainment center in the world—at lower ticket prices. So who comes to Branson, how are they reached, and why do they bother?

Branson is an example of the primacy of proper targeting of age, religion, race, and socio-economic demographics. Every single week, 10 months per year, buses, vans, and shuttles arrive with visitors who fall into the following demographic categories: average age of 60-plus, retired, high school education, mostly blue collar occupations, generally white Christians who enjoy packaged vacations. They purchase five or six nights of $15 tickets, head to the all-you-can-eat buffets, target the discount shopping, and revel in the chance to talk to the performers whose names light up the marquees of Branson.

These entertainers—which most younger audiences have never heard of and the over-50s thought had disappeared—either own their own $12 million state-of-the-art theaters or have naming and exclusive performance rights with long-term contracts. Andy Williams, Jim Stafford, Tony Orlando, Bobby Vinton, John Davidson, Kenny Rogers, Yakov Smirnoff, Wayne Newton, Charlie Pride, and many others have established shows with 30-piece orchestras, name guest performers, expensive costumes, and talented dancers and singers. The shows boast well-prepared choreography, scene transitions, and seasonal concept changes. Many of the theaters have satellite hook-ups to produce their own radio shows and link programs onto the Internet.

Tour parking lot after huge parking lot, and the geographic dispersion of the Branson customers becomes clear. Those who come by car are mostly from within a day's drive of the destination, including all the neighboring states: Texas, Missouri, Arkansas, and the eastern border states of Tennessee and Kentucky. The nature of the cars speaks to the audience demographics: late-model pick-up trucks, mini-vans, Chevrolets, Fords, Pontiacs, and the occasional Cadillac or Lincoln Town Car.

But those parking lots only tell part of the story. Those credit cards from Illinois, Minnesota, Nebraska, the Dakotas, and other distant locations get to Branson due to its marketing success. The fleet of huge, 40-ton buses parked discretely at the edge of each theater represents access for well over 65% of the visitors. For 30 years, the bus companies have actively marketed in their own geographic areas, and are definitely responsible for the origins of the early visitors and today's long-distance audience.

The roots of this entertainment phenomenon are in a theme park, Silver Dollar City, which ranks third in the nation for annual visitation. As the park developed its following and people became familiar with Branson, the entertainment offering increased, taking advantage of a visitor population that was left with little to do after theme park closing hours. As the selection of venues grew, the city leadership decided to form a Branson Marketing Committee, operating separately from the Chamber of Commerce. They named an experienced marketing executive as the Director of the Marketing Committee to work with all the theater, motel, restaurant, and themed attractions, who in turn hired an experienced PR professional. The PR plan was to get a major story about this unique location placed nationally, and in 1990, the town was featured on *20/20*: primetime television. The phones began to ring off the hook in the town, and within the next year, over one million visitors came to enjoy the entertainment.

Several ad agencies were hired, including Bozell, Jacobs, Kenyon & Eckhardt, who prepared TV commercials and magazine ads. But the real corker was the next PR effort, which brought Regis and Kathie Lee to the town's major theater, the 4000-seat Grand Plaza. The nationally broadcast show stayed for one week, and the national exposure of the town's entertainment venues grew tourism to over three million, competing aggressively with Nashville, Myrtle Beach, Memphis, and Pigeon Forge (home of Dollywood)—destinations that also provide live country music.

However, Branson leaders knew that entertainment and PR alone would not build repeat visitation. Guests expected better services, and Branson provided them: improved roads, more access points, new five-star hotels, better restaurants, and more attractions. The town now boasts 44 theaters, a three-screen IMAX, fabulous new shows, hundreds of new condominiums, and several golf courses. The time-share operators have moved in, offering three nights for $99 in a two-bedroom townhome, just for listening to a pitch for the purchase of a time-share ownership.

The long-sought goal of six million annual visitors was accomplished by bringing in the Radio City Rockettes for regular Christmas shows and the globally televised Miss USA Contest for a full week in the spring. This certainly gives new meaning to the industry description of a successful show: this is one long-running hit that really does "have legs."

AUSTIN, TX

Visitors arriving at Austin's Bergstrom International Airport are greeted with signs in the jetways and banners across the airport lobby that make the claim that Austin is "The Live Music Capital of America." Does the city hold any actual crown not already claimed by Nashville and Branson? No, but that doesn't keep it from making a concerted effort to pitch to the perceptions of potential visitors. At night in Austin, it's the live music that makes the beat go on.

The city of Austin didn't awaken one morning to realize its own potential for garnering more tourist dollars. As one of the fastest growing cities in America, greater Austin, with over a million people, is driven chiefly by a large university (University of Texas), a large community college (Austin Community College), and software and hardware manufacturers like Dell Computer, Motorola, IBM, and AMD. Many graduating students decide to stay and work in the city, while others are recruited from silicon hubs like San Jose, Phoenix, and Boston. In fact, this business traffic caused American Airlines to add regular non-stop flights to and from these technologically based cities.

The average Austin resident and business visitor is young, educated, and ready to be entertained, and Austin's Sixth Street is the place he or she heads. Much like Bourbon Street in New Orleans, this area is a strip of music nightclubs and restaurants featuring jazz, rock, blues, country, and other varied forms of entertainment. The city, quite aware of the destination's strength, located its new Convention Center as near to this center of entertainment as possible; some software companies located their casual-dress, long-hours offices nearby so their employees could take advantage of entertainment breaks.

The *Austin Chronicle*, a free weekly tabloid that wins its advertising with its thorough handling of entertainment, lists over 180 active venues where, on any night, a music fan can find live music being played. These range from open-mike bars to bookstores/coffeeshops, full-scale nightclubs specializing in blues, rock, and country, to huge venues featuring national and international roadshows. On any given night, it's possible to catch Jimmy LaFave at the Cactus Café, Toni Price at the Continental Club, Bobby "Blue" Bland at Antone's, or U2 at Palmer Auditorium. The city's daily newspaper, *The Austin American Statesman*, has a regular Thursday insert, *Xlent*, that covers nothing but entertainment, particularly live music.

Each year, the city celebrates its self-proclaimed status by hosting a week-long music festival, South by Southwest (SXSW). The festival brings thousands of visitors to the city, and presents an opportunity for performers to be discovered by agents and producers. And in the synergistic tradition discussed throughout this book, this entertainment event has spawned a sister SXSW film festival.

BIG CITIES, BIG CHALLENGES

There are locations throughout the world that have become self-propelled marketing machines—cities that are so intimately connected with entertainment that it would seem that marketing these destinations would be a slam dunk. However, the question of "guest perception" has certainly affected the two premier entertainment cities of the U.S.: Los Angeles (specifically, Hollywood) and New York. Over the last decade, each of these destinations has dealt with removing the reality to meet the expectation.

HOLLYWOOD

Mention the initials "LA," and entertainment junkies around the world will immediately conjure up visuals of palm trees, Beverly Hills, sunny beaches, and movie stars. More specifically, they target Hollywood. From the fifty-foot-high letters in the Hollywood Hills to the pressed-in-cement footprints outside of Mann's—originally Grauman's—Chinese Theater, the images and icons of Hollywood are burned into minds around the globe. In fact, "Hollywood" is one of the most widely recognized brands in the world. Mention the word anywhere, and anyone who has ever seen a movie, whether in a 1,000-seat state-of-the-art theater or projected onto a bed sheet, will know what you are talking about—at least how *they* perceive it.

And that is the perplexing part of the Hollywood brand. In the words of Dorothy Parker, when it comes to Hollywood, there is no "there" there—at least the "there" so many visitors seem to expect. Visitors to Los Angeles have often left disappointed, searching for Hollywood and Vine, and finding nothing but a nondescript street corner. No stars hanging out, no Schwab's drugstore, no famous producers looking for new starlets. Just a decaying side of town, often worked by hustlers. The studios themselves are not in Hollywood.

So, what do you do with such an incredibly well-recognized brand? Give it a place to live.

That has been at the heart of the Hollywood and Highland development project, which has been on the drawing board and under construction for nearly 10 years. In the early 1990s, a team of developers, marketing experts, architects, and designers put their profit-driven heads together and realized that there was lightning here to be caught in a bottle. Their answer to creating the "there" is a mixed-use destination that will offer retail, restaurants, and Hollywood imagery to the droves of visitors looking for somewhere to make their memory of this legendary place. In a master stroke of marketing genius, the keystone of the development will be the new home of the Academy of Motion Picture Arts and Sciences: Oscar's house. Beginning in 2002, the Oscars will be broadcast yearly from Hollywood and Highland, further cementing the location firmly in the minds of people searching for the "there."

NEW YORK

New York labored under a similar problem. Times Square, the so-called "Crossroads of the World," had disintegrated into a gathering place for pimps, prostitutes, hustlers, drug addicts, muggers, and assorted other non-tourist types. But still the tourists came, looking for the bright lights and crowds, the sailors kissing women on VE Day, the smoking Camel billboard, in other words, the imagery that had been burned into their collective consciousness over the decades.

In a fabulously successful clean-up campaign, the powers that be grabbed hold of Times Square in the last decade of the 20th Century and took a 180-degree turn back toward glamour. The first things to go were the triple-X porno shops; next on the list were the denizens who lined the streets. Then the developers moved in, taking the once-grand vaudeville houses—now housing only the sleaziest of porno films—and restoring them to their former grandeur. Chief among these was the New Amsterdam Theater. Say what you like about the appearance of Disney in Times Square—and born and bred New Yorkers who liked the grit of 42nd Street have a *lot* to say—the team at Disney Development did an outstanding job refurbishing one of Florenz Ziegfield's stomping grounds. Today, Times Square gleams, all scrubbed and sparkling, with a breathtaking selection of entertainment destinations—in short, a terrific "there" in a city that is the most "some" and the most glorious "where" in the world.

Both of these cities enjoy the benefits of not only the marketing done by their Chambers of Commerce—New York in particular has a very successful program luring new businesses to the city—but from continued exposure through various forms of media and entertainment. Additionally, they are outstanding examples of recognizing the need to keep guests' expectations satisfied through continued redevelopment and refurbishment.

DYNAMICS OF TRAVEL AND TOURISM MARKETING

Earlier in the 20th Century, "getting there is half the fun" became a slogan of the tourism industry. While many of today's travelers can certainly complain about the layovers, cancelled flights, and missed connections created by the airlines' "hubbing" system, the journey is still as important as the destination. Today's traveler has an astounding array of choices when it comes to creating his or her travel package, and with the introduction of the Internet, the dynamics of the travel industry are in flux now more than ever.

TA TA TO THE TRAVEL AGENT?

As the travel and hospitality industry boomed with the increases in disposable time and discretionary income, travel agencies became important partners to airlines, railroads, bus companies, cruise lines, hotels, resorts, and theme parks. A travel agent was the sole source supplier for the American dream of going on the road. Housed in offices across the country, in chains such as American Express, Carlson Wagonlit, Ask Mr. Foster, and Liberty Travel, travel agents created dream packages for the adventure-bound.

A free service for the traveler, agencies collected their revenues from the modes of travel and destinations themselves. Their marketing campaigns—full-color spreads in the Sunday travel sections, complete with photos of sandy beaches and international landmarks—helped fuel the desires of the traveling public, and were an important part of the overall marketing of the industry. The packages the agencies offered—so many nights of hotel rooms, cheap airfares, and meal plans made travel affordable for the general public.

However, as the economics of travel began to change, so did the travel agency industry. The deregulation of the airlines, fueling price-cutting wars, began to erode the profit margins at giants such as United, American, Delta, Pan Am, Eastern, and TWA, and saw the rise and fall of smaller airlines such as People's Express, Republic, and Ozark. Many of these smaller airlines, primarily regional carriers, were sucked into the maw of the larger players, creating an industry that is now primarily concentrated in the hands of a few giants, such as United, American, and Continental.

A few renegades—Southwest and Virgin, for instance—have succeeded, but the fortunes of this industry have had a huge impact on travel agencies as airlines have struggled to find ways to cut costs. One cost-cutting measure was to decrease the fees paid to the agencies. Agents tightened their belts, sat down at their computers, and continued to price out the best packages they could for their clients—little knowing, in the mid 1990s, that they were staring straight into the screen of the device that might bring about their ultimate downfall: the computer.

The rise of the Internet brought huge changes to an industry already focused on shrinking margins. As computer-savvy travelers began to explore the destinations of the Information Superhighway, they came across Web sites such as Travelocity and Expedia—the 21st Century version of the travel agency. These sites synergized with airlines, hotel chains, and rental car companies to create packages to meet and beat the pricing offered at agencies—without the need for the consumer to leave his or her home. Consumers could now plug directly into timetables and ticketing, sidestepping the agency middleman. As the airline industry began to realize that this was in fact a paradigm shift in how consumers booked their travel, they jumped onboard with sites such as Orbitz, forming co-opetive networks with other airlines to offer tickets directly to the traveler. Direct connection with the consumer now meant that the fees previously paid to the agencies were a non-issue, removing a critical revenue stream from that industry.

While there are still thousands of travelers more comfortable with the face-to-face connection offered by agents, the travel agency industry is currently struggling to hold its own. In some cases, what was once a free service is now a fee service, with the agencies tacking a price on their service package. The outcome of this shift remains to be seen, but one critical component of the marketing of the industry may be facing extinction. After all, a key benefit of the agencies in the overall health of the industry has been their ability to spin the dream of the destination while opening new vistas to travelers. That dream-spinning has contributed mightily to the overall marketing of the industry.

With a generation of consumers now reaching the age that can travel—on their own, away from parents—travel agencies will continue to feel the impact of the Internet. The "Echo Baby Boomers"— the children of the original Boomers—are entirely comfortable with computer connections, and Web sites are an easy reference for them. Web sites, of course, demand their own form of marketing. How will the consumer find such a site if he or she isn't aware of it? While search engines such as Google and Ask Jeeves are helpful, the Internet—following the collapse of the dot-bomb explosion—is discovering that it is not a world unto its own. Sites such as the ones previously mentioned are now utilizing traditional media campaigns to drive hits; in addition, many of them offer links to Web sites developed by the destinations themselves, offering an even fuller view to the consumer. These days, it is not surprising to find some of the smallest bed and breakfast inns providing 360-degree visits to their sites, including panoramic views of antique-filled rooms, a view of the hearty country breakfast offered, prices by season, and quality information about things to do in the area. However, all of these sites also recognize that there is a growing need for security reassurance regarding credit card and personal information needed to conclude the transaction.

RELATIONSHIP MARKETING

Keep in mind that the final success in this industry is based on the customer's experience with the product. Therefore, there is a heavy emphasis on relationship marketing in this industry, promoting the personal touches and hassle-free services offered by the particular modes of travel and destinations.

INTRA-INDUSTRY TRADE SHOWS
AND ASSOCIATIONS

There are associations and trade shows for every segment of the travel industry—destinations market to the individual traveler(s), to travel agents, and to business planners looking for potential conference sites and rewards for their sales force or executives.

An excellent example of the diverse nature of the travel industry is the Incentive Travel & Meeting Executives Show (IT&ME), which focuses on what is known as "incentive travel"—rewards for a busy sales force, harried employees, or top executives. IT&ME has been held for 29 years at Chicago's McCormick Place, usually in October, part of the so-called "shoulder season"—a less busy part of the year—for most destinations. Originally called "The Motivation Show," its objective is to act as a marketplace for the diverse products within the tourism industry, including premiums, incentives, business gifts, and incentive travel services. The show exhibits more than 2,500 suppliers of merchandise and travel services, representing the service categories of more than 60 countries. Representatives of major hotel chains, accredited tour operators, and travel companies specializing in incentive travel, chambers of commerce, and individual resorts—all of these can be found at IT&ME, which attracts over 40,000 potential decision-makers in the field of incentive travel.

Trade fairs such as this have become an integral part of connecting consumer with industry experts, as well as furthering the education of not only the destinations, but the market as well. Seminars and workshops are scheduled throughout the course of the three-day show, covering subjects such as "Incentive Program Basics," "Consumer Promotion Tactics, Motivation Strategies, and Trends," and "Meeting and Incentive Travel Planning Essentials." Shows such as IT&ME are also an excellent place for novices in the travel and leisure industry to get a handle on how the industry markets itself.

The Society of Incentive & Travel Executives (SITE) is an association whose membership is made up of business professionals dedicated to the recognition and development of motivational and performance improvement strategies, of which travel is a key component. SITE serves as a networking and educational opportunity for its members, with a variety of local chapters, conferences, and one main conference held each year in an incentive destination such as Las Vegas, Hong Kong, or London.

Another key association in the industry is the American Society of Travel Agents (ASTA), the world's largest association of travel professionals. Over 26,000 travel agents and the companies whose products they sell—such as tours, cruises, hotels, and car rentals—are members of ASTA, which also serves as the advocate for travel agents, the travel industry, and the traveling public. ASTA benefits its membership through representation in industry and government affairs, providing education and training, and by identifying and meeting the needs of the traveling public. Reflecting ASTA's stance on the necessity of travel agents, their current motto is: "Without ASTA, you are on your own." Cheery thought.

ASTA was originally founded in 1931 as the American Steamship and Tourist Agents Association, changing its name later to reflect the more universal scope of the travel industry. ASTA's current initiatives focus on fighting for travel agents and for the traveling public. ASTA also sponsors a World Travel Congress, offering exposure for industry suppliers.

The Cruise Lines International Association (CLIA) is the spokesgroup and lightening rod for criticism regarding lapses by member cruise companies. The association also contributes strongly to generic information on the pleasures and positive attributes of cruising in an attempt to increase the audiences for this experience. They organize special trade shows where companies can gather, talk about new techniques in every aspect of running a line, and showcase new, successful marketing offers and packages. Cruisefest, which runs in conjunction with ASTA, offers opportunities for travel industry professionals to network and benefit from seminars and workshops. Since Cruisefest is typically held in ports such as Miami or Vancouver, industry professionals also have the opportunity to tour some of the latest cruise ships afloat.

Each of these associations also publishes its own newsletters and magazines, available not only to the industry, but to the traveling public.

CUDDLING THE CONSUMER

Relationship marketing must extend well beyond the intra-industry efforts. While courting the industry professionals who assist travelers in making decisions is critical, reaching out directly to the consumer is paramount. After all, when push comes to shove, it's the traveler who will be standing in line in front of the ticket counter or checking in at the hotel—not the agent or Webmaster.

COME FLY WITH ME

Since the latter half of the 20th Century, some of the most effective promotions developed within the travel and tourism sector have been the frequent flier and hotel reward programs offering points in exchange for miles flown and nights booked. These programs, once the exclusive province of airlines and hotels, have now synergized in a variety of ways. Today's consumer can now accumulate points in frequent flier programs through the use of branded credit cards, long-distance minutes, and any number of unique offerings.

However, these programs have grown almost too popular, resulting in the originators changing the rules. While the initial rewards offered by industry giants such as United or American offered free flights, hotel rooms, and car rentals, the typical reward program has now scaled back perceptibly. The free flights now have a variety of restrictions and mileage amounts tacked on, dependent on when you fly; the free hotel rooms are a thing of the past, with the only offer a 50% reduction in price. Given that the price they are reducing is the "rack rate"—the non-discounted price for a room—travelers can often get better rates by simply calling the hotel and asking for whatever promotional price might be in effect that night. Free car rentals have now evolved into upgrades or 50% reductions, though there are still some rental chains offering a free day. For the long-time member of frequent flier programs, these changes can leave a bad taste, causing fliers to switch brands. Rule number one in creating these kinds of programs should always be: "The consumer isn't stupid"—they recognize when something previously rewarded has been taken away, and they tend not to like it.

BRANDING BEDS

Major hotels chains have successfully built national—and, in many cases, global—brands with strong, persuasive marketing, customer loyalty programs, and constant upgrading of their facilities. The desire to stamp "you are special/we are unique" on these establishments has resulted in efforts such as unique room décor (fish bowls in every room at the Royalton Hotel in New York; tables and chairs welded in the middle of the pool at the Delano in Miami), rewiring every room for high-speed Internet hook-up, and extraordinary promotions combining airlines, shopping, and restaurants. Web-based reservations, 1-800 access from anywhere in the world, and attention given to the leading travel agencies have paid dividends and built room occupancy to its highest level ever.

The Hyatt chain, founded by Chicago's Pritzker family; the Westin group, built by Dallas-based Trammel Crowe; the Sheratons; Ian Schrager's growing chain of fabulous one-of-a-kind hotels; and the Starwood group, with their chic W boutique hotels, are all part of the explosion in branding hotels and using the product management techniques of extending the line and building sub-brands to cater to a diverse audience base—in effect something for everyone. Even Disney and Universal, who, for a period of time were willing to place visitors to their entertainment parks in other properties, hired leading architects to fashion hotels that reflect popular themes, appeal to their primarily family audiences, support their major brands, and enhance the total experience of being in Orlando, Anaheim, Paris, or Tokyo.

CASE IN POINT: MARRIOTT INTERNATIONAL

The consistent, branded loyalty "heads in beds" winner is Marriott International Inc., a leading worldwide hospitality company that traces its heritage to a small root beer stand opened in Washington, D.C. in 1927 by J. Willard and Alice S. Marriott. Today, Marriott International has nearly 2,100 lodging properties, located in 50 states and 59 countries and territories. Bill Marriott, Jr. and his father have constructed and expertly managed a wide spectrum of hospitality properties including hotels, motels, all-suites, vacation resorts, and time-share clubs. From the highest end—the J. W. Marriott or Marriott Marquis—to the motel categories of Courtyard, Fairfield, and the ever-consistent Residence Inn by Marriott, the company demonstrates "best of breed" in each category. Marriott has done this through a careful separation of amenities, pricing, and marketing approaches, even though their properties often co-exist in contiguous locations. The Marriott chain has built the most diverse audience brand and line extensions ever launched in the hospitality sector.

Marriott's success is due in some part to their focus on relationship marketing. One example is how Marriott courts frequent travelers, whether business or regular vacationer, and ensures they are well-rewarded. The chain understands that these travelers represent the mainstay of the travel and tourism industry as defined by the 80/20 rule: 20% of the guest population represents 80% of their sales revenue. To entice repeat visitation of that all-important 20%, Marriot offers the industry staples of reward programs built on frequency of stays, frequent flyer synergy programs, their own newsletter, and relationships with credit card and telephone companies, which support the accumulation of miles/points. However, they have also offered unique tie-ins such as an arrangement with E-trade, an online broker, which awards traders with points good toward a free night's stay. Now under discussion is the option to convert existing Marriott points into E-trade cash. (United Air Lines is another partnership with E-trade, demonstrating another example of marketing synergy in the battle for building and maintaining customers.)

Marriott, along with many other hotel chains, uses constant repetition of newspaper ads in travel sections throughout the country, sponsors TV commercials to reinforce the ambiance of the brand and the romance factor, and carefully markets to travel agents, with glossy, expensive booklets and brochures, window posters, and familiarization trips for high sales producers.

ADVERTISING, PUBLICITY, AND PROMOTION

Travel and tourism form a very specialized niche in the marketing world. Most communication consultants or advertising executives who have managed multi-million-dollar budgets for leading packaged goods companies, automotive brands, and leading retail chains have no understanding at all of this major category. The marketing managers of hotel chains, resorts, island destinations, cities, countries, cruise lines, leisure airline travel, and ski slopes tend to seek out specialized boutiques with prior experience. Thus, the chicken and egg syndrome is alive and well in this segment, with the inevitable musical chairs as one specialized agency loses Jamaica and picks up Barbados, or the loss of Delta is replaced by the arrival of United Airlines. While this keeps the game in the family, there is very little innovation or breakthrough creativity as the marketing offers are recycled, and the "beauty shots" of sand, sea, and sky all seem to look like one another.

Additionally, agencies must work hard to overcome the occasional or perpetual problems of crime, anti-Americanism, terrorism, typhoons, monsoons, and government instability. Advertising and marketing budgets are often cut or eliminated for a period of time, until the new government cabinet or long-suffering local business community decides to run a "come back to Paradise" campaign. Then, the PR machinery begins to spin stories about the reduction of the pre-existing problem, and how peace and safety have returned.

AGENCIES

There is a certain expertise and desire to break new ground that is in the heart and soul of every ad agency creative director or founder. While it may sometimes seem difficult to be truly innovative in the marketing of travel, the professionals who populate this sector occasionally find intriguing ways to do so. Those best equipped to do so often come from the travel industry, or have trained at universities specializing in the practice like the Cornell University Hotel Management School and the Culinary Institute of America (CIA) in upstate New York, which are both accredited schools in the industry. In addition, some agencies sponsor client research, analyze and evaluate the results, and make intelligent recommendations. Most notable are several agencies in Florida, including Crispin/Porter, Pepperdine, and Yessawich.

Analyzing every single advertising and PR relationship within the travel industry would be mind-numbing, but it is interesting to see the nature of some of these relationships and where they have been stable—and where they have changed with the velocity of a busy hotel's revolving door.

Grey Advertising—specifically, Grey Travel and Entertainment—helped to launch the Celebrity Cruise Line with print and radio advertising only, on a budget of $7 million. Then the Celebrity client went to a travel boutique, where they experimented with television advertising using the slogan "Let us exceed your expectations" and a budget of over $10 million. In mid-2000, Grey picked up the Renaissance Cruises account, primarily a direct-to-the-consumer advertiser with a budget of nearly $50 million.

The Island of Jamaica tourism account split its advertising and PR services between two companies, one of which was Young & Rubicam (Y&R). When Jamaica left Y&R, they consolidated their integrated marketing communications at FooteCone&Belding, which had recently lost the Bermuda account to Doyle Dane & Bernbach (DDB). DDB at one time handled the Jamaica tourism account along with the air carriers to the destination, Jamaican and American Airlines.

It's best to update your scorecard on the players and their professional communications agencies in any given season frequently, as moves are made as often as government cabinets change and marketing directors are replaced. No new broom sweeps cleaner than the tourism advertising business. However, on occasion, there is an exception; a grateful Cayman Islands, with a small marketing budget, has retained the services of one small ad agency for at least 12 years.

ALTERNATIVE DESTINATIONS

Travel and tourism extend well beyond the boundaries of cities, national parks, and hotel beds. Adventure is the soul of travel, and many consumers are interested in experiencing destinations that offer them something other than the standard cityscape or hotel room.

CRUISES

If you knew your average customer was over 65 years of age, the cost of a new ship was over $250 million, your competition was building new ships at the rate of one per year, the percentage of the U.S. population that had ever cruised was under 4%, and the business model was based on those same senior citizens taking more cruises, would you worry? The cruise industry did. Along with those statistics, the industry also suffered from the perceptions that there was too much so-so food, too much motion on the ocean, not enough diverse activities, and cruising was too expensive. Facing a crisis, cruise lines became proactive, successfully changing the product and growing the industry.

In a nutshell, they took a leaf from the Disney leisure experience to make it more magical and appealing, then they encouraged the CLIA to do some comprehensive research. Finally, they implemented the research recommendations and began to plan out their future with a marketing perspective. The cruise industry went through a major metamorphosis. The major cruise companies retrofitted their ships with new amenities, or built new ships based on the market research, which presented what consumers needed to make a sea vacation a "must do" experience. A marketing miracle was in progress. By 1998, the world cruise market was composed of about 2,225 ships, over 10 million cruise passengers had filled the berths, and a good percentage considered their cruise to be one of their best vacation experiences and would definitely book again, as reported by the CLIA[1].

CASE IN POINT: CRUISE LINE

Carnival Cruise Line was the first in the cruise industry to utilize the powers of marketing and audience identification for their company. Carnival's in-residence marketing wizard, Robert Dickerson, saw the future and began to cater to the new customer. The potential for changing the demographics of the cruise customer from 100% senior citizen retirees to a mix of couples with children, young single adults, and empty nesters, all with time and disposable income on-hand, reflected the greatest potential for the future sustainability of the industry.

Carnival took the risk and made the decision to attract the youngest possible audience that could afford a budget vacation with certain specific offerings. This 25- to 35-year-old population was identified as wanting a reasonably priced, all-inclusive vacation, far from home, that might represent the kind of freedom and relaxed fun they remembered from their college Spring Break days. This consisted of plenty of beer, dancing, gambling, no stuffy dress code, parties all day and night, comfort food with no pretensions, unrestricted coupling, and exotic ports of call, at one complete price. A snapshot of the young, casually-dressed crowd, some carrying cases of beer or beverage coolers, boarding a typical Carnival Cruise ship filled to capacity with this new customer, confirmed that the marketing promise of the "Fun Ship" was exactly what was required. Even the occasional "cruise to nowhere"—six or seven days out to sea in calm Caribbean water with 24-hour festivities and no port of call—appealed to this group.

Carnival's success alerted the rest of the industry to the business potential of shifting their product and marketing toward a variety of audience targets, including the middle-aged, more affluent customer. The results of the marketing research were casinos, libraries fully stocked with current bestsellers, movie videos, electronic games, spas, gyms, hairdressers, fashion shops, skeet shooting, and golf on deck. On the very newest mammoth ships, guests now find multiple communal hot tubs, rock climbing walls and ice skating rinks, and full-dress Broadway-style shows in fully appointed nightclubs. Who cares about the destination or ports of call when a whole world of entertainment and leisure is right inside the ship, with no packing or unpacking, cabs, or reservations needed? To many, cruising is the

---

1. Annual Report for BT Alex, Brown Research, by Robin Farley. Used with permission.

ideal vacation—and a marketer's perfect offer. Thousands now willingly heed Celebrity Cruises' call to "let us exceed your expectations" or the Princess Cruises' successful theme: "Come join the original Love Boat." From under 4% ever cruised, the industry research matrix shows an increase to over 10% of a younger audience, fully prepared to repeat their vacation onboard a ship.

Ever-increasing success led Carnival to recognize the importance of brands and the inability of one cruise line brand to provide everything for everyone. Carnival's management team purchased the Holland American line to market luxury cruising to the affluent vacationer, and then bought the Windjammer sailing ship line to provide a more unique and authentic sailing experience for a more limited passenger list.

As a final note, possibly the best example of the importance of branding in cruising is the arrival of the Disney Cruise Line. Investing over a billion dollars in two brand-new ships, purposely built for the mantra of a "seamless guest experience," Disney's venture into cruising is an unqualified success, luring not only families with children, but senior citizens and singles as well. Consumers who align themselves with the Disney brand have very high expectations that they will have a comfortable, safe, entertainment-filled experience, and Disney has parlayed this brand equity into a business that is actually pulling from the first-time cruiser demographic.

Part of Disney's success in the market was a strategy that called for creating specific spaces and programs for children. Given that Disney recognized that childless couples and singles would think of Disney Cruise Line as a floating playroom, the company created a revolutionary program that would draw children to their own cruising experience, while creating a level of guilt-free comfort for their parents. Disney's Oceaneer Adventure, custom tailored to specific age groups, has been successful in meeting the goals of the company and the expectations of all their cruising guests.

THE ALL-INCLUSIVE

In a period when cost was more important than comfort, one leisure company was created to serve up exotic locales for consumers in Europe who were on tight post-war budgets and in need of a getaway. Club Med, originated by a French company, provided a complete one-week vacation for one inclusive cost. This eliminated any concern about constant payments for additional services, the fear of running out of money, or not being able to pay the bills after the vacation was over. They offered the middle-class French family—and later the European family—a complete holiday experience at a remote beach at extremely low prices, made affordable by providing very basic amenities. The accommodations were usually family-sized tents, with outdoor showers, shared bathrooms, and family-style dining, usually in a tin hut—rustic, but in a warm climate with little or no rain.

The marketing concept was simple and eminently successful: "One price for a complete vacation for the whole family." There were always several young, attractive male or female general organizers (GOs), who were in charge of the sports activities during the day and the entertainment in the evening. These adult camps or clubs were usually accessible by car or train.

This is a far cry from today's modern Club Med. Under the same management, but with a new generation of marketing executives, today's Club Med serves up a streamlined and upscale offering in handsome, comfortable bungalows, with hotel-style cuisine, and state-of-the-art sports equipment, managed by the always helpful GO. Club Med can now be found at exclusive beach locations all over the world, accessible by plane and then car, bus, or van.

The marketing proposition is still the same, appealing to a similar family-oriented, budget-conscious consumer. The advertising presents "$699 and up for plane, accommodations, all meals, beer & wine, most sports—all you need to go into your pocket for is to shake out the sand." The closing promise or positioning line is "Renew—Club Med." In addition to making a very persuasive marketing offer, the facilities deliver exactly what is promised and expected, resulting in a firm relationship with a great number of loyalists and returnees.

However, in a period of sales downturn, Club Med discovered through research that the Club had gotten a reputation as a "swinger's paradise," with nude sunbathing and licentious behavior as the main attractions. Management quickly changed whatever was driving that perception, since the desire was to stick with a family-oriented business, a much more sustainable and attractive model.

But one man's pain is another's pleasure. In this case, the latter man was an entrepreneur and appliance retailer named Butch Stewart, who gave birth to the next level of "all-inclusive," the beach resort: Sandals, on the Caribbean island of Jamaica. His offer of plane, luxury hotel, gourmet meals, cocktails, and sports all for $1000 to $1800 per person (with couples prices at a promotional offering during off-season periods) brought capacity crowds from major metropolitan cities. The chain expanded to other islands in the Caribbean and was imitated by the Hedonism chain; soon, other all-inclusive resorts followed as it became a vacation rage. These resorts have even managed to avoid the liability of real or perceived dangers from local crime, due to their nature of being self-contained and secure worlds. Clearly, in this case, an industry was reinvented by a marketing idea, supported by the needs it fulfilled for the target audience: conveyance, one price, quality, and reliability.

TIME SHARE—COMING OF AGE

At the beginning, time-share marketing appealed to those Americans who wanted the dream of a two-week vacation, not in a hotel or motel, but in place they could own. The attraction of a fully-furnished one- or two-bedroom apartment, with kitchen, swimming pool, picnic tables and barbeque, in close proximity to a tourism destination like Miami, Orlando, or Tampa, made for easy selling. However, most of the sales were to gullible, lower middle-income purchasers, who were duped into buying a share of a motel for one or two weeks for their lifetime ownership, making time-shares a shady business at minimum.

In a discussion of place and relationship marketing, this was a low-class sale at its most highly skilled, with glossy booklets, special deals for early confirmations, and unique financing at exorbitant rates. All this was under the stewardship of commissioned salespeople applying high-pressure tactics, weaving stories of the opportunity and nature of the units, without a twinge of conscience or moral restraint—*Glengarry Glen Ross* in Bermuda shorts.

The truth behind the pitch was a requirement of 10% down, a monthly payment at very high interest rates, no market for the promise of easy resale, and an annual maintenance with accelerating costs. Worst of all, the time-shares were usually old motel properties, with cheap and tacky décor and furniture, poor management and infrequent maintenance. The new owners were left feeling victimized, with little of the glorious vacation for their hard-earned investment. Often this was exacerbated when the property went bankrupt, leaving the owners with all the responsibility.

The other selling point was the "exchange privilege"—the thrill of being able to trade two weeks in Orlando for another destination like California, Arizona, New Orleans, or even New York. Unfortunately, in the early years of this marketing concept, exchanges were difficult, cumbersome, and often unrealized. Since the concept grew rapidly and unsuspecting purchasers became a large group, the complaints became thunderous. The Attorney General stepped in, along with many state officials responsible for preventing consumer abuse.

Fast forward to the present, to a remarkable change in the time-share environment. Leading hotel brands have entered the field, providing credibility and a reassurance that previously did not exist. Unfortunately, the marketing executives assigned to rebuild the image first had to wipe out 20 years of bad press and wholesale bilking of the public. The worst challenge in marketing is to reverse a negative or shady image. The best opportunity is when there is no image—not even a positive halo effect—in this case, the brand can be built from the ground up in a guided process.

In the last eight years, Marriott, Hyatt, Disney, Sheraton, and Westin have all entered the time-share market, and have named this special hospitality product the Vacation Club. This time period has also seen the development of two major exchange companies, Interval International and RCI, which handle the time-share exchange process. Both exchange companies issue books with small photos of possible exchange properties all over the world. The books list and display about 1,200 to 1,300 properties in many U.S. vacation spots, with as many as five or ten in locations such as Orlando or Southern California. There is roughly a $100 charge for making an exchange, which covers administrative costs.

Consumers still have some difficulty getting exactly which exchange they want, but flexibility, certain special marketing bonuses, and trading in points earned with hotel partners enable owners to take advantage of the program. Time-sharing has overcome its past and become a vacation marketing miracle. In fact, many resort developers are now creating properties especially designed for time-share purposes—they then rent out any excess "inventory" as condos.

CONDOS

A final note to affirm that brands are important in every part of the travel and tourism industry, and that smart marketing can overcome even a potential implosion like that facing the time-share in its early history: the Four Seasons and Ritz-Carlton, two of the premier hotel chains in America, have begun to build and offer luxury condominiums at prices that exceed $100,000 for a four-week lifetime ownership. The first ones have been built in Carlsbad and Laguna, California, Hawaii, and Scottsdale, Arizona, near existing or newly renovated flagship hotels in their chains. The marketing is careful, complex, and includes branding reassurance, along with access to existing Four Seasons and Ritz Carlton properties. As these leading chains expand to Europe, the new-economy wealthy will be able to have homes in many destinations, without the responsibility of care-taking.

THEME PARKS

In the early 1950s, the current king of animation, Walt Disney, grew dismayed by the lack of venues he could take his young family to for an outing. Amusement parks of the time were relatively shady places, hangouts for teenagers and con artists. Recognizing that opportunity was the soul of innovation, Disney decided to take a shot at creating the kind of amusement park families could enjoy. Thus the dream of Disneyland began—and with it, today's multi-billion-dollar theme park industry.

Walt Disney's first attempts to establish his dream were initially laughed at, frowned upon, and refused financing. In an interesting twist of fate that would come full circle decades later when the Walt Disney Company would purchase the broadcasting network, ABC backed his idea, giving him the funds needed to create Disneyland, the first in the empire that now includes Walt Disney World in Orlando, Euro Disney, Tokyo Disneyland, and soon, Disney Hong Kong. The Disney theme park empire has also underwritten the moves of Michael Eisner, leveraging the brand's equity into every-thing from retail outlets, to software, to Broadway theaters.

Theme parks are a destination for a wide swath of the interna-tional public, offering a vacation the entire family can enjoy. But more than that, from a marketing perspective, they are a self-pro-pelled marketing machine for the brand. Visitors to Disney proper-ties spend their days and nights completely enfolded in the brand, interacting with story lines and characters, and being led out of each attraction through a retail outlet, packed with Disney merchandise to remind them of their trip. In a perfect example of synergy, new releases from the Disney studios become attractions at the parks, driving visitation; the park experience drives trust in the Disney brand, promoting future releases in all sectors of the company's busi-ness.

Furthermore, Disney has also perfected the concept of synergy partners, including other major brands through various deals in which the company shares in revenue while offering the halo effect of their own brand's goodwill. Whether in the thinly disguised trade fair that is the Innoventions pavilion in Epcot, where brands such as Xerox promote their own innovative new products, to the ever-present Kodak film outlets, Disney brings consumers face to face with products aplenty. However, families are happy to be a part of the promotion process, as Disney's world-famous eye for operational detail assures them of a safe, memory-filled experience.

While Disneyland and Walt Disney World are paeans to the most famous animated characters in the world, Universal Studios pays homage to the movies—Universal movies. Located in Los Angeles, Orlando, and Japan, Universal Studios is another example of synergy between the silver screen and the entertainment-hungry consumer. When sitting in a seat in a dark room with 300 strangers isn't enough, Universal offers you the opportunity to sit in a specially designed tram, surrounded by animatronics, and get tossed around with 16 strangers in a motion-based simulator—don't just see the movie, ride it. And while you're at it, stay in a hotel on the property, visit the retail shops, and eat in the restaurants.

These two park concepts have spawned an entire industry of attractions that can best be described as amusement parks on growth hormones. With their cousins—Six Flags, Paramount Parks, Dollywood, Silver Dollar City and the rest—theme parks offer a day's or week's worth of entertainment to a public that wants to do more than just ride a roller coaster.

As an industry, theme parks are one of the largest employers in the country, and are rapidly spreading throughout the world. The main association for the industry, the International Association of Amusement Parks and Attractions (IAAPA), holds a yearly show that covers over one million square feet of exhibit hall space, drawing over 50,000 attendees over a four-day period.

B2C marketing for the industry is accomplished through the use of all forms of media; B2B marketing is accomplished through yearly trade events such as IAAPA, as well industry magazines, chief among them *Entertainment Management* and *Fun World*.

VIVA LAS VEGAS...ATLANTIC CITY AND RENO, TOO!

And speaking of fun worlds...been to Las Vegas lately?

If you haven't, you're missing the greatest theme park for adults ever created. Las Vegas offers reproductions of Paris, New York, Venice, and Monte Carlo—all in the form of casino resorts—exploding volcanoes, pirate ship battles, a roller coaster atop one of the highest towers in the Southwest—and, oh yes, entertainers, one-armed bandits, high-stakes gambling, free drinks, dancing girls, and whales.

Whales?

Anyone who's been to a big casino has seen the areas separated by velvet rope where folks go to play in high-stakes games. Who are these people? They're "whales"—in short, the big fish that casinos carefully cultivate through complimentary ("comped") rooms, flights, and food. Whales are part of the dream of Las Vegas, where everyone who is willing to plunk down a few dollars at the blackjack tables dreams of hitting it big and being invited behind those velvet ropes.

Comping is part of the people skills most essential to marketing casinos. Gambling venues, like all other entities of the travel and tourism business, know that they can't please everyone, but that they need to build and maintain repeat business. Comping is just one of the tools in that customer orientation. The Luxor in Las Vegas, as an example, has a block of 300 rooms set aside for comping on weekdays, and as many as 500 rooms it can comp on a weekend.

The entertainment marketing strategy for casinos has escalated from free shows in the lounge for anyone who could stand at the bar and pay for a few drinks to competition between casinos for name artists. It was rumored that Frank Sinatra received a share in one of the older casinos to guarantee his appearance there each year, which brought in the high rollers. This would increase the take at the tables well above the cost of the talent. Barbra Streisand was paid $10 million plus a percentage of the supplementary income to perform one night, New Year's Eve of the new millennium, at the MGM Grand—but the traffic into the casino that night, one must assume, certainly helped defray that expense.

Most marketers understand that getting new customers is more expensive than retaining repeat ones. This is certainly true for casinos. According to a study by the Forum Company, the cost of retaining a loyal customer is only 20% of the cost of attracting a new one.[2] The needs, wants, and desires of people drawn to a gambling environment must be motivated by more than an attractive price on an airline ticket to get there. The marketing mix must reflect the fundamental components of product, price, and distribution.

---

2.   Sellers, Patricia, "Getting Customers to Love You," *Fortune Magazine*, March 13, 1989.

Consider how Las Vegas, Atlantic City, Reno, and other cities known for games of chance have expanded their targeting from the desires of individuals to embrace larger markets, including the associations discussed throughout this chapter. All of those members need somewhere to go when gathering en masse, and Las Vegas has built a great part of its business on welcoming them to this once-tiny desert town. Las Vegas holds the distinction of having the most hotel and motel rooms available of any city in America—more than Orlando, one of the other national leaders in this category. The city's hospitality capabilities, coupled with an excellent airport, have led the Convention Bureau to become one of the most proactive in America. Hardly a week goes by that nametag-wearing crowds aren't seen milling to and from the Convention Center.

Aside from the city's unified effort to attract tourists, which includes arrangements with airlines serving Las Vegas to offer frequent discount flights to the city, the casinos themselves systematically market to audiences through the use of clubs, tournaments, headliner acts, and other special events. While casinos typically employ outside marketing agencies to act on their behalf, the successful casinos, large or small, all have a readily identifiable "hook" that helps generate customer satisfaction relationships with new and regular patrons. The Luxor, for instance, with its striking pyramid architecture and Egyptian motif interior, draws 60% to 65% of its revenue from its slot machines. So, one logical on-site marketing tool is a slot club. The Luxor's is called the Gold Chamber, and most members are a result of a focused advertising campaign aimed at $500-a-day slot players. Casino studies show that the average repeat customer belongs to as many as 6–12 slot clubs across the nation.

The Luxor also uses direct mail campaigns in addition to advertising to obtain regulars. In addition, the casino employs casino hosts, each of whom is responsible for 250 regular customers. Every guest at the Luxor gets a letter within three days of his or her visit; a host is responsible for keeping in touch with each of his or her 250 regulars at least once every three months. For instance, if a player hits a jackpot, the player also receives an Egyptian good luck pin. All of this attention and communication go toward maintaining a customer base, and the goal is to make them feel needed and wanted.[3]

---

3.   For more detail, see the thorough coverage in: Rudd, Denis P. and Lincoln H. Marshall, *Introduction to Casino & Gaming Operations*, 2/E (Englewood Cliffs, NJ: Prentice Hall, 2000).

Harrah's Casinos transcend the one-of-a-kind status of the Luxor with casinos in almost every major gambling city in America. Promus Companies, the parent company, uses product bundling and the comping of rooms and meals to encourage its customer base. Bruce Rowe, the Director of Gaming Information Technology Development at Promus, says, "We are in the adult entertainment business; our main product offering is gambling and there are many components that support it, such as hotels, entertainment facilities, and restaurants."[4]

Casinos across America, at locations like Lake Tahoe, Laughlin, Reno, Atlantic City, and New Orleans (riverboat casinos), focus on individual identity hooks as well as concerted marketing efforts aimed at building and maintaining customer bases. Many even offer free courses to encourage the skills aspect of gaming, whether a person wishes to know more about slots, cards, dice, or roulette. Like much of the hospitality industry, gaming operations are people-oriented businesses; they require strong communications from PR departments and promotional support from the entire company.

Smaller gaming houses and casinos do the same things on a smaller scale. There are clubs, tournaments, and bundling events like Valentine's Day special packages and New Year's Eve special packages. There are some casinos that have learned that the way to a customer's heart is through the stomach. A trip down any casino strip will reveal signs offering free drinks, inexpensive steak dinners, or, in one Las Vegas casino's case, there is even the offer of a one-pound hot dog for only 99 cents—an attraction that not only brings repeat customers, but had enough sizzle to merit coverage in a PBS special on the great hot dog spots of America.

INDIAN CASINOS

The Indian Gaming Regulatory Act, passed by Congress in 1988, first permitted legal gambling by Indian tribes in their home states. By 1993, the National Indian Gaming Commission had finalized rules for the casino, bingo, and/or other gambling venues available at about one-third of the 557 federally recognized Native American reservations. The need for revenue first drove the formation of such locations, and a test case in Florida in 1979, when the Seminole tribe had a prize that exceeded the state lottery total, paved the way.

---

4.   Philip Kotler, John Bowen, and James Maken, *Marketing for Hospitality and Tourism, Second Edition*; Prentice Hall, 1999. Page 436.

Success stories from Minnesota to Connecticut have helped increase the number of Class III facilities (those able to offer the full array of casino games). The marketing attraction is in part geographical, since Indian casinos exist in 29 states, as well as the altruistic sense of contributing the revenues from gaming to the national white buffalo of the Indian tribes.

A case in point is the Foxwood Resort and Casino in Ledyard, CT, operated by the Mashantucket-Pequot tribe, which was one of the first to offer the kind of glitz available at the Nevada or Atlantic City casinos. Here, the state of Connecticut has taken an active part in helping with the marketing, since 25% of the income from the 4,000 slot machines alone accounted for $100 million in revenue for the state in 2000. Connecticut has also signed a similar compact with the Mohegans in an extension of the agreement with the Pequots.

SUMMARY

Travel and tourism are integral to the entertainment industry, providing the destinations that showcase entertainers, as well as offering relaxing getaways that are a form of entertainment in themselves.

The success of this sector of the entertainment industry has also created a trickle-down effect to the local marketplace, which has launched an entirely new form of marketing: the phenomenon of experiential branding.

FOR FURTHER READING

BOOKS

1. Cook, Bruce, *The Town That Country Built: Welcome to Branson, Missouri* (New York, NY: Avon, 1993).

2. Davidoff, Philip G. and Doris S. Davidoff, *Sales and Marketing for Travel and Tourism*, 2/E (Englewood Cliffs, NJ: Prentice Hall, 1994).

3. Dickinson, Bob, Andy Vladimir, Robert H. Dickinson, and Andrew N. Vladimir, *Selling the Sea: An Inside Look at the Cruise Industry* (New York, NY: Wiley, 1996).

4. Early, Pete, *Super Casino: Inside the "New" Las Vegas* (New York,

NY: Bantam Books, 2000).

5. Feiler, Bruce S., *Dreaming Out Loud: Garth Brooks, Wynona Judd, Wade Hayes and the Changing Face of Nashville* (New York, NY: Avon, 1998).

6. Kotler, Philip, John Bowen, and James Makens, *Marketing for Hospitality and Tourism, 2/E* (Englewood Cliffs, NJ: Prentice Hall, 1999).

7. Leopold, Craig and Richard W. Oliver, *Honkey Tonk: The Amazing Story of the Nashville Predators* (Nashville, TN: Thomas Nelson, 2000).

8. Pecora, Norma Odom, *The Business of Children's Entertainment* (New York/London: Guilford Press, 1998).

9. Rudd, Denis P. and Lincoln H. Marshall, *Introduction to Casino & Gaming Operations, 2/E* (Englewood Cliffs, NJ: Prentice Hall, 2000).

10. Semer-Purzycki, Jeanne and Robert H Purzycki, *Sails for Profit: A Complete Guide to Selling and Booking Cruise Travel* (Englewood Cliffs, NJ: Prentice Hall, 1999).

11. Schickel, Richard, *The Disney Version: The Life, Times, Art & Commerce of Walt Disney* (Chicago, IL: Ivan R. Dee, 1997).

12. Thomas, Bob, *Building a Company: Roy O. Disney and the Creation of an Entertainment Empire* (New York, NY: Hyperion, 1999).

Magazines to Devour

1. *Byways*

2. *Conde Nast Traveler*

3. *National Geographic Traveler*

4. *Roads to Adventure*

10 LOCATION-BASED ENTERTAINMENT AND EXPERIENTIAL BRANDING

OVERVIEW

Increases in disposable income and discretionary time have opened the doors to all sectors of the entertainment industry, with each of them doing their best to grab the consumer's time and money. This book has focused on how entertainment marketing has helped accomplish that goal. However, as the entertainment industry takes a bigger slice of the income pie, other industries are peering under the tent to see what all the hubbub is about. Suddenly, the rest of the world seems to have realized that a great experience—the heart of entertainment—can do a lot more than fill discretionary time. It can also entice consumers, grabbing their interest and building their brand loyalty.

In this chapter, we'll take a look at the growth in certain sectors of the out-of home entertainment industry—and how entertainment made the move from message to medium in marketing.

LOCATION-BASED ENTERTAINMENT

Remember "cocooning"? Remember the pundits of the 1980s and 1990s who predicted that most of humankind, tired of working themselves to the bone, never setting eyes on their loved ones, slaving to get that food on the table, were going to march themselves into the living room, armed with videotapes, microwave popcorn, and their beverage of choice, plop themselves in front of that cable-fed home theater with 60" screen, surround–sound, and four-head VCR with stop action for special effects, settle into that lounge chair, surrounded by the ones they loved, and never venture out into the real world again until the next work minute? Remember cocooning and how everyone was going to stay tucked in nice and comfy at home? Oh, woe was the *out*-of-home entertainment industry to the prophets of the late 20th Century!

Guess what? It seems as though there was a slight miscalculation. It appears that the same species that invited Fred and Wilma out for a night by the tribal fire, that crowded the Globe Theater to sneak a peak at Will Shakespeare's latest scratchings, and that found a nickel or two in the midst of the greatest depression the world has ever seen to spend on a movie just didn't want to prop those legs up in the old recliner for very long after all. Lo and behold, it seems as though the vast array of home entertainment equipment sold in the last decade may have only served to up the ante in the public's demand to be entertained everywhere they go.

This increased desire for sensory stimulation is everywhere we look. Been to a professional basketball game lately? No longer do the players simply run onto the court, possibly greeted by Dallas Cowboy Cheerleader clones. Nope. Now they sprint onto the floor in the spotlight, strobes flashing, bass-line pumping, INDOOR FIREWORKS BLASTING! Local newspapers? No staid, grand old "Gray Lady" anymore; she's been replaced by four-color photos, one-page stories, charts, graphs, and sidebars all ablaze in quick, colorful eyebites, a circus in print. Clothing? Niketown, with shoes, clothes, multimedia projection and full size basketball court! Airports? TVs in the waiting areas to relieve the boredom (and sell the product). Food courts, childrens play areas and retail shops that outdo local malls! And the local mall? Festival marketplaces! Mall of America, with seven acres of Camp Snoopy!

All of this is driven by the fact that humans are generally gregarious by nature. We want to rub shoulders with each other, for a million different reasons. And if we can rub shoulders, eat dinner, see a movie, and pick up a new pair of jeans, all in the same fell swoop, well that's even better, because the prophets were partially right. We don't have much free time, and we do want to spend some portion of it with our family. We just seem to want a choice between the lounge chair and a public venue—but it better be a GREAT public venue, one that entertains, edu-tains, and, most likely, eat-ertains.

This is not front-page, stop-the-presses news. In the last two decades, our desire for entertainment has fed not only the theme and amusement park industry, but has spun off smaller, locally based endeavors as well. Fueled by such prognosticators as *Entrepreneur* magazine, family and children's entertainment centers (FECs and CECs) appeared on (and in many cases, disappeared from) what seemed to be every corner lot and strip mall in the country.

AMUSEMENTS COME OF AGE

Typically, FECs took the form of multi-attraction-driven destinations, including everything from miniature golf and go-karts to video games, motion-based simulators, laser tag, and redemption games (which did not promise a trip to heaven; they spit out tickets, which could be redeemed for trinkets based on the number of points scored).

FECs capitalized on what was being called the "Echo Baby Boom," the rise in birth rate associated with Boomers having off-spring. Because many of those Boomers waited until later in life to have children, their child-bearing coincided with that of the 20-something people who also were in a family way, creating a larger generation than the Boomers themselves.

Families, hungry for things to do together, swarmed to these facilities. However, in time, teenagers often took over, which left some parents uncomfortable with bringing their children to the FEC. Several entrepreneurs saw opportunity in this trend, and soon a new niche was born: the children's entertainment center (CEC). CECs typically focused on a large, soft, modular play system, resembling a gerbil cage on steroids, surrounded by the same redemption games found in FECs. Food, in the form of pizza and hot dogs, was also offered.

These facilities multiplied like rabbits, the most prolific being Discovery Zone, which reached a peak at over 300 locations. Chuck E. Cheese was another entrant in the race; while the attraction offering was similar, Chuck E. Cheese included one other element that seemed to help repeat visitation at the parental level: beer. Since most children are not given access to the family car, Chuck E. Cheese understood that something had to bring parents back time after time. The strategy apparently worked. Discovery Zone, poorly managed and too thinly spread, collapsed in bankruptcy; Chuck E. Cheese continues to pack them in.

In general, though, parents eventually took a look around and realized that there were other destinations in the neighborhood that could offer a more educational experience to their kids—museums and heritage destinations—and off they went, in search of something the kids could get some value out of. However, now the children seemed to need more than a wax Indian standing over a stuffed buffalo or the world's largest ball of tinfoil. "AHA!!" said the entrepreneur and design community. We can't simply educate them!! We need to entertain them while they learn!! Thus was born the concept of "edu-tainment," a trend that has spread like butter on hot popcorn, eventually finding its way into the corporate plant tours and retail establishments we will discuss in the next section.

ENTER THE BIG BOYS

Investors in these FEC and CEC projects ranged from moms and pops and downsized corporate executives to high rollers such as McDonald's Corporation and Blockbuster Video. As the shakeout of the me-toos occurred, the number of small investors thinned down considerably. However, the intent of both the successful and not-so-successful projects was not lost on some very big players.

These investors included the biggest names in retail, restaurant, and real-estate development. And, of course, there was the entertainment community. With an eye on leveraging brand equity, creating outposts for products, and increasing brand awareness, entertainment companies such as MCA Universal, Sega, Sony, SKG Dream-Works, and Disney investigated new ways to combine the entertainment experience with location-based products. With years of experience in inviting the public in and coaxing the dollars out, these players brought some intriguing new destinations to cities around the U.S., and, in some cases, the world.

However, unlike the FECs of the last decade, these giants paid more attention to the retail mall model, creating location-based entertainment (LBE) products to combine with other synergistic and often competing venues. LBEs took the traditional paradigm of the FEC—coin-operated amusements, video games, and food—and blew this segment into the 21st Century. Examples, usually designed with the 18–34 set in mind, include Dave and Buster's, which is essentially a high-quality sports bar/restaurant surrounded by adult-level redemption games and billiards, and its clone, Jillian's. Disney jumped onboard in Orlando and Chicago with DisneyQuest, their version of an indoor amusement park, featuring Disney-related activities based on animation, as well as custom-designed virtual rides. Sega, best known for coin-op games, partnered with MCA Universal and SKG DreamWorks to create GameWorks, a concept that combined food and entertainment with a high-end range of games and experience simulation, packaged in a highly themed environment built to look like the inside of an old factory.

By combining large-scale retail, food, entertainment, and attraction elements in environments that screamed WOW, real-estate developers attempted to create new destinations known as urban entertainment centers (UECs). Like the retailers who leased space in malls, these companies thought they could find strength in numbers. UECs were created through "co-opetition": businesses creating new ecosystems by working together to optimize the opportunities in locations ranging from the Cleveland waterfront to Coconut Grove. The goal was to draw partners into the business mix that could provide elements that may have been missing in a particular venture—and to drive repeat visitation into the retail stores that were part of the mix.

Again, as in retail mall development, UECs also featured at least one anchor tenant to encourage initial and repeat visitation. Cineplexes (and megaplexes) were the most common anchor. The reason for this was simple: With the vast machinery of Hollywood turning out new "software" (movies) every week, a cinema provided the best vehicle for repeat visitation. Clustered together, the right combination of what may have previously been stand-alone venues attracted a greater number of visitors than each might have been able to draw on its own.

The end result of this combination of venues was a mega-destination of interest not only to the local community, but to tourists as well, increasing the geographic draw far beyond the typical 30-minute drive time most stand-alone entertainment centers used as an outside boundary. Additional benefits of clustering included an increased length of stay, extended appeal into dayparts that may not have been particularly strong for a stand-alone, and the ability to find better uses for under-performing space.

Some of these developments did well, mostly those that focused primarily on eating and seeing a movie, such as CocoWalk, in Coconut Grove, Florida. With a 16-screen multiplex theater and restaurants ranging from the Baja Beach Club, to Fat Tuesday, to Howl at the Moon Saloon, plus 28 retail shops, CocoWalk offers South Florida residents a destination that is a natural for repeat visitation and increased length of stay. The atmosphere of this center on a normal night is that of one big festive party; on any night that focuses on a major sporting event, such as the Super Bowl, it is beyond description. People have *fun* there.

Another example of a relatively successful UEC is CityWalk, located at Universal Studios in Burbank and Orlando. CityWalk is a destination attraction that includes a variety of full sit-down restaurants, live music venues, retail shopping—although mostly of the something-to-remember-the-trip-by variety—and a multiplex.

CityWalk, however, is different from other UECs as it helps to draw people to its partner, Universal Studios theme park—and that difference, and the success of the CityWalk effort, captured the attention of entertainment brands not traditionally known for having local entertainment destinations. One of these brands—Sony—realized that it could strengthen its brand image by creating a destination that not only offered a high-gear entertainment experience, but also tied its products to that experience, cementing Sony as the entertainment brand of choice in the guest's mind.

CASE IN POINT: SONY METREON

Sony Metreon, located in San Francisco, is an urban entertainment destination that was informed by CityWalk and the success of the Sony theater across from Lincoln Center in New York City. Lincoln Center itself is an entertainment destination, with the Metropolitan Opera, the New York Philharmonic, the New York City Ballet, several movie screens, and a variety of upscale shopping and dining experiences, all within a few square blocks. Businesses in the area feed off one another's synergy in much the same way a mall would, with the exception being that the desired product—or experience— is entertainment. Sony Development looked at the traffic in the area while considering a new approach in the development of a Sony the-ater-based project in a still-pioneering area of San Francisco.

Additionally, the Sony Wonder installation in New York (where visitors could have a hands-on experience of editing video and music, among other attractions), featuring Sony equipment, had proven to be a significant tourist draw. The same was true for a simi-lar installation in Chicago; most important, neither of these destina-tions actually sold Sony products. Instead, they acted as a brand-driven experience that afforded guests the opportunity to taste new technology.

The Metreon project came off the drawing board as a destination that would not only drive per-visit revenue, but would also strengthen Sony's image as the leading developer of new entertain-ment technology. To increase the chances of success for this second goal, Sony Development focused on a different approach. While other retail-oriented destinations were using a recipe that called for movie screens, dining, and retail, Sony included the movies, but chose to underscore the entertainment component by including a unique blend of other attractions—a strategy that also keyed in on the company's desire to reach a multitude of age groups.

Instead of the typical retail stores seen in most urban entertain-ment destinations, Sony included the following:

- For families and younger children, a children's entertainment attraction based on Maurice Sendak's classic *Where the Wild Things Are* allows visitors to actually live the experience of the book, taking guests through a series of games and experi-ences that closely follow the story line. One of the critical fac-tors in developing children's entertainment is creating an attraction that will drive repeat visitation—bringing the fam-ily and their dollars back to the site more than once every few years. Basing this attraction on a story that children can eas-ily ask for on a nightly basis allows for continued visitation— and keeps boredom at bay.

- For the 18- to 34-year-old market, Airtight Garage offers a sur-real setting where the works of Jean "Moebius" Giraud have inspired interactive games that are unique to Metreon, includ-ing HyperBowl®, which allows guest to "bowl" down the streets of San Francisco, through the trees of Yosemite, or across the deck of a rocking pirate ship.

■ The dining component—critical in driving repeatability and length of stay in experience-driven entertainment destinations—offers a wide variety of choices, including the Night Kitchen (again inspired by Sendak) and A Taste of San Francisco (five popular Bay Area restaurants).

Metreon, however, is also designed as an *experiential branding* destination, and Sony has taken a full swing at exposing guests to their new technologies. The retail component includes:

■ Sony Style, which allows visitors to investigate Sony electronics in a no-pressure living room environment, from TVs and handy cams to audio at Music 101^{TM}.

■ PlayStation®, a hands-on game store, offering new titles and expert tips.

Additional experience-driven retail includes:

■ Discovery Channel Store: Destination San Francisco^{TM}, an interactive and educational store.

■ Digital Solutions, a technology store that offers the latest in computer games and computer hardware, as well as digital audio equipment and portable devices. Portal One^{TM}, which offers gaming accessories, anime, and urban gear.

Metreon inhabits a 350,000 square foot space and cost $85 million. The center received 150,000 visitors in its first five days. The challenge will be to keep attendance up, as many destination attractions suffer from a drop-off once the novelty factor wears off. However, the variety of experiences offered seems to be a good mix for supporting this branding effort.

OFF THE STREETS AND INTO THE MALL

Concurrent with the development of projects such as Metreon, retail mall developers were taking note of the visitation patterns of LBEs. Always interested in finding new ways to draw traffic into the climate-controlled byways of America's new main streets, developers such as the Mills Corporation—whose gigantic outlet shopping destinations were beginning to spring up outside of major urban areas—began to see entertainment as a driver for repeat visitation.

Entertainment in malls was not a new idea; developers had been including movie theaters in their projects for years. But now they became intrigued by the prospect of creating a greater length of stay with the patrons who might just duck in for a movie then leave. And, while the LBE/UEC trend was certainly feeding the interest of developers, one project had caught their attention, big time—a retail project on the Las Vegas Strip.

CASE IN POINT: THE FORUM SHOPS

The Forum Shops were originally planned as a strategy to keep guests within the confines of Caesar's casino during those moments when they weren't gambling or attending shows. Given that Caesar's was the finest example of themed casinos on the Strip at that time— 1992—the retail area was designed to match the resort's story line and level of luxury.

On the luxury end, developers shot for the ambience of Rodeo Drive, Madison Avenue, and the Via Condotti. On the thematic side, the plan called for an experience that would keep Caesar's guests entertained—and provide a reason for guests of other casinos to venture out to Caesar's. Given that pulling people from the tables at Vegas was a bit of a chore at that time, the developer realized the experience would have to be something special.

The answer to the experience question took the form of a destination that has become a classic in the retailing world. The Forum Shops, which have now gone through two additional expansions, is a fantasy recreation of an ancient Roman streetscape, complete with arches, columns, and a sky that grows dim for "evening" and brighter for "daytime." But those thematic elements are nothing compared to the fountains, laser shows, animatronic Bacchus, Roman Great Hall, Atlantis fountain, 50,000-gallon aquarium, and a myriad of other show elements that keep the traffic pouring in.

45,000 to 50,000 guests visit this center every day, with a peak day of over 81,000. Annual visitation is nearly 20 million per year— compare that to Orlando's Universal Studios' visitation of 5.4 million. And these visitors spend money; the Forum Shops average over $1,300 in sales per square foot, the highest in the retail industry. Most significant, the Forum Shops are now considered one of the top tourist destinations in Las Vegas, with every one of those tourists a potential customer, either of the stores or the restaurants that line the Roman streets.

The Forum Shops were not the first to bring entertainment into the retail mix, but they certainly set a very high standard—one that most destinations could not hope to reach because the foot traffic simply wasn't available to feed the retailers. This type of technology-driven "shopper-tainment" works best in tourist destinations. However, the local mall down the street began to take advantage of the same principles by incorporating events that not only drew customers to their sites, but also created an environment that offered more than just a retail opportunity.

As the entertainment component began to take on more importance, destinations such as Ontario Mills outside of Los Angeles were planned with entertainment "districts." In the case of the Ontario project, this included a GameWorks, a Dave and Buster's, and a concept called the American Wilderness Experience—along with the requisite movie screens. The project successfully demonstrated the draw of entertainment, building visitation, and increasing the time the customer stayed in the mall.

"Entertainment retail" became a buzzword in the industry and a trend all over the country. Additional projects within the UEC framework are destinations such as Kansas City's Power & Light District, Chicago's Navy Pier and Marina City-area developments, and Circle City in Indianapolis. Washington, D.C.'s MCI sports arena is attached to a UEC that includes a three-level Discovery Store, developed by the Discovery Channel. And of course, 42nd Street, once the most notorious red-light district in New York, is awash in Disney, Madame Tussaud's Wax Museum, Broadway City (a large arcade), and an ESPN Zone (a sports-themed restaurant, also owned by Disney).

THE PARTY'S OVER?

So, a happy ending for LBE and entertainment retail? Not exactly. More than anything else, these high-end UECs raised the bar in terms of facility development. Once the "Big Boys" appeared, each new project was challenged by the next guy in town. Operators were faced with the climbing costs of keeping up with the Joneses, and finally, the LBEs reached the point of no return: basically, the investment was too high to achieve the expected returns.

The reason for the fall was simple. How many of us have visited malls across the country, only to realize once inside whatever architectural jewel may house the stores and food court, the stores were exactly the same as the ones in the mall back home? The malling of America brought the Gap, Banana Republic, the Nature Company, the Body Shop, J. Crew, and assorted other standards to every neighborhood in the U.S. There is, of course, a reason for this: Customers want these products, and when successfully marketed, customers need these products. But very few people actually need to play video games or virtual reality. Therefore, the expected hordes of players failed to show up at most of the over-budgeted projects—at least for any sustained period of time.

The lack of sustained visitation was also affected by the fact that, other than the grossly expensive theming packages that dressed up the environments, what filled the floors in one entertainment venue was no different from the next—each concept was drawing on the same suppliers of video games and coin-operated amusements, so most destinations offered the same goods as the local mom-and-pop store down the street—hopefully with a higher "cool" factor. But cool only goes so far in keeping the guest satisfied.

Many of the products pushed into the marketplace were long on promise, but short on delivery—regardless of the behemoth company or major superstar behind them. Most of the concepts went through incredibly difficult shakeout periods, trying to reframe the food/attraction mix to meet the demands of the particular market. And, as a final stroke of the ax, the home PC market skyrocketed with games, driven by bigger, faster, better computers that quickly offered the same—if not better—graphics as the destination-based games.

All in all, the LBE industry missed the mark and found many concepts plunging over the cliffs of bankruptcy. Hundreds of millions of dollars of investment went by the wayside. While concepts such as Dave and Buster's have hung on successfully, DisneyQuest Chicago closed its doors (the Orlando location, fed by Walt Disney World, remains open for the time being).

EXPERIENTIAL BRANDING

As the entertainment pieces of the destinations began to suffer their economic fates, the payoff for the retail users of such destinations began to suffer. The desire to include actual entertainment destinations began to fall off. However, one lesson from the trend stayed intact: Customers were drawn to the overall experience that entertainment created—the "something different," the excitement, the stimulation. Over in the amplified world of marketing, brand managers were taking notes. And thus, the concept of experiential branding was born.

STRIKE UP THE BRAND

The 20th Century saw the birth of "The Brand" as the keystone of consumer outreach. This somewhat ephemeral concept grew in importance throughout the last century to the point where people not only believed the brand message—they actually volunteered to display it on their person, paying for the privilege.

In theory, brands establish an identity by association with meaningful ideas, values, and a quality position that people can readily understand. In other words, "I know it, I trust it, and it fits my particular take on life." During the evolution of branding, to fully entice the consumer, differentiation was key: create unique selling propositions that would translate into immediate benefits for the customer—"If I put that stuff in my hair, I'll be the sexiest man alive; if I use the other brand, I'll just look greasy."

Traditionally, marketing professionals would then march the brand out to the public through the use of print or broadcast advertising—utilizing actors, spokespeople, or clever copy to lock the brand into the consumer's consciousness. This might be done through humor; it might be done through a more serious approach—whatever worked with the brand and the image the client wanted to project. In any case, the message was delivered through the traditional media outlets appropriate to the campaign. Finally, the brand was then attached to as many products as possible.

The success of the traditional format is exemplified by our memories of jingles, commercials, and icons that remained long after the impression was made. In some cases, the slogan itself became part of the vernacular—"I can't believe I ate the whole thing" and "Where's the beef"—while the product itself was forgotten (Alka-Seltzer and Wendy's, respectively). Eventually, no matter how popular the slogan—or the product—the message became just another combination of words that meant nothing to a distant generation. Consider "Quick, Henry the Flit" or "Moxie." Nothing coming to mind? That's not a surprise.

INCREASED CHALLENGES FOR DEVELOPING AND MAINTAINING A BRAND

The traditional marketing/advertising approach to brand-building has run into challenges as technology has expanded the media that can be utilized to promote a brand. Consumers are bombarded with over $160 billion in advertising spending[1]—in the form of over 3,000 messages per day. Brand messages can now be seen on shopping carts, grocery store floors, luggage carousels at airports, subway tunnel walls—and plastered all over the clothing worn by a major portion of the 18- to 34-year-old set. Additionally, an increasingly skeptical public, highly sensitized to advertising in any form, also presents a challenge to brand-building (although this supposed "skepticism" does raise a few questions in light of the clothing choices mentioned previously).

And then there's the competition. As the Big Boys seek new ways to extend their equity, names not previously associated with particular products appear and give old-timers (and young upstarts) a run for their money.

Consider Caterpillar, long known for heavy earth-moving equipment. Some genius decided to extend the brand to work clothing, and the next thing you know, Caterpillar workboots are giving Timberland fits. And the use of the Internet—the hot, new, rapid-response medium—gets the message out there faster than ever before. Sustained differentiation then becomes a difficult task and brand loyalty actually suffers. According to some surveys, only 43% of consumers report being brand loyal—down 11% in just two years.[2]

This difficulty in sustaining the brand message is coming at the same time that brands are taking on even more importance to consumers. Distrust of businesses, political figures, financial institutions, or job/financial security has left much of the public searching for touchstones they can believe in. At the same time, the traditional fulfillers of the touchstone role—churches, the state, the community—have fallen on hard times. The isolation of the modern world has taken a swipe at much of what older generations took for granted in creating and maintaining their own identities.[3]

---

1. Morgan, Adam, *Eating the Big Fish* (John Wiley & Sons, Inc. 1999).

2. The Roper Reports 2000 Annual Presentation, "*Kinnected* The Movement to Connection: Technology, Relations, Brands," New York, NY, 2000.

3. Forrester Research, *Brand Impact of Experiential Marketing Case Studies*, Cambridge, MA, November 1999.

This phenomenon has opened the door for some brands—those with strong, clear identities—to step into this gap in the belief system. These brands actually help consumers define themselves. In short, people have formed emotional attachments to brands, exemplifying a confidence that is transferred to the consumer as they take on the brand's identity, enhancing their self image: I wear, therefore I am. Savvy marketers can utilize this emotional attachment to extend the brand into seemingly unrelated products and services. After all, what does a mouse have to do with software? Before leaping to the obvious conclusion, consider one specific mouse—Mickey—and one specific product niche—interactive software for children. While one might not normally tie the Disney name to computers, the strong connection with children and family helps make the idea saleable— in a very big way. In short, the successful brand becomes an icon for the consumer, with greater meaning than just a product.

How does a brand build itself into a cultural icon at a time when getting a message to the consumer is increasingly difficult? How can marketers overcome the clutter and the me-tooism of the competition? Most important, how does the brand truly come alive for the consumer so that it becomes ingrained? The answer lies in bringing the brand to life so that consumers can connect with it, claim it as part of their lifestyle. To do this, marketers are finding that tying the brand to an entertainment-driven experience—one that creates a pleasant memory or educational offering—can be very successful in today's entertainment-oriented world. If this is accomplished successfully, these brands connect with the consumer as human—not just as product user.

This "experiential branding" takes the core values of the brand and introduces them into an actual environment—one that gives the visitor a visceral experience of what the brand means and offers. *Experiential branding is the intersection of entertainment and marketing.*

The concept first hit the retail side of branding with individual brands. Manufacturers such as Nike (with Niketown) have discovered the power of exhibiting their product in environments that include merchandising approaches combining museum-like exhibits, state-of-the-art audio-visual technology, online interfaces, and themed décor to support—but not define or overpower—the brand image. While Niketown offers product for sale, it does not necessarily compete with other retail partners in the area that also offer their merchandise; instead, these hip facilities act as yet another marketing effort for local retailers, by promoting the brand image.

But, experiential branding has now moved outside the boundaries of the consumer arena, burrowing deeper into the brand psyche. The two most important manifestations of the trend are in corporate heritage centers and corporate attractions.

Mr. Brand, Meet Mr. Experience

Companies around the world have used an educational approach in rudimentary fashion through the traditional plant tour; however, today's marketers have extended that approach into what can best be described as a corporate theme park or attraction. These experiences are typically site-specific, which includes both "brick-and-mortar" destinations and special events; they may also join in "co-opetition" with other brands to provide mass and stimulate visitation.

According to Gregory Beck, AIA, a leading New York-based designer of brand attractions, these destinations—also referred to as "heritage centers"—"demonstrate the theme park-like benefits of engaging people by having them experience the brand story—a mantra that has recently sent many companies in search of their "roots." In developing these scripts, it is often not only about the products themselves, but the values that they represent. In other words, it's usually not about *performance*, but about the *emotional* attributes of a product or service. The brand character of Swatch watches, for example, is not about "time," and Nike's retail attractions are definitely not about sneakers. (The Swiss company speaks about "irreverence, passion, provocation," while Niketowns represent "assertive life/style theaters.") Both companies also sponsor Olympic and special-event pavilions noted for their clever environmental narrative.

These new attractions, created as high-touch sensory experiences, are often seen as the leading edge of a 'brand narrative' that speaks over many channels. Today, marketing strategies are designed as a sophisticated choir of environmental, online, print, and broadcast voices. As a result, corporate attractions are taking on additional significance, becoming virtual homes that can be revisited through the Internet, and a focal point for special events. Ultimately, they may be the only tangible expression of the brand itself.

"Our mission is to speak clearly across all of our brands, in unified voice, with clear brand channels," says George H. Ladyman, Jr., Vice President for AOL/Time Warner in New York. The recently merged AOL/Time Warner conglomerate has created a multi-venue branding challenge. "We are currently evaluating our physical brand presence worldwide, including a flagship attraction in our new headquarters building in Columbus Circle [Manhattan]. Our goal is to focus on the consumer in an informative, entertaining, and engaging way." Ladyman, former Vice President of Design for Six Flags Theme Parks and Managing Director of CUH2A Entertainment, oversees a guest venue network across all AOL/Time Warner properties, reflecting a new presence of attraction-based management in traditional media boardrooms. [4]

Brand attractions also hold the promise for achieving a "sweet spot" among the four elements that define compelling guest experiences. As identified by authors B. Joseph Pine and James Gilmore, these attractions can *entertain* and *educate* while providing an *esthetic* and *escapist* experience. [5] (In fact, Pine and Gilmore take the concept of experiential branding one step further, postulating that today, every business is a stage and every employee a cast member—a theory that has worked for Disney for years, and is now moving into the marketplace.) Combining all four of these elements results in powerful communication "place-events," which will theoretically rise above the 3000-messages-per-day clutter.

CASE IN POINT: THE BRAND AS CORPORATE ATTRACTION—CEREAL CITY

Up until a few years ago, young families could pack up the brood and show up on the doorstep of the local factory for a plant tour. For no charge, moms and dads could entertain and educate their children with everything from huge bulldozers to paper-making. Lumber mills, breweries, chocolate factories, auto plants, newspapers, and dairies all offered tours. Parents could pat themselves on the back for teaching their kids; kids walked out wide-eyed, with samples to take to show and tell.

Over the last 10 years, insurance, liability, and security issues have forced many of these businesses to get out of the tour business—at least within the walls of the actual plant. However, market-

---

4.   *Entertainment Management Magazine,* "Corporate Attractions: Entertainment Reinvents Brand Storytelling." Gregory Beck, AIA, March 2001.

5.   Gilmore, James H. and Joseph B. Pine, *The Experience Economy: Work Is Theatre & Every Business a Stage* (Boston: Harvard Business School Press, 1999).

ing professionals have not allowed the concept to disappear—far from it. Today's corporations are turning to new approaches that actually increase the brand experience, utilizing all the bells and whistles that today's technology can afford them. Such is the basis of Kellogg's Cereal City USA, a facility that snaps, crackles, and pops with entertainment.

Located in Battle Creek, Michigan, a town whose name lingers in the backs of those Baby-Boomer brains subjected to thousands of hours of Saturday morning cartoons, Kellogg's Cereal City USA is an excellent example of the successful melding of entertainment, education, and marketing. And, although the Kellogg's brand is certainly firmly implanted on the facility, the attraction possesses enough historical information to keep it from toppling into a "big commercial" feeling.

Unlike The World of Coca-Cola or Hershey's Chocolate World, Kellogg's Cereal City USA is not owned and operated by the company whose brand is featured. Instead, it is owned by a non-profit organization, the Heritage Center Foundation, organized five years ago to respond to the public's demand for a replacement for the Kellogg's plant tours closed in 1986.

The first bit of business facing the Foundation was the question of what the replacement venue should actually feature. While part of the population may think of corn flakes in conjunction with the words "Battle Creek," the city's cereal history is actually rooted in another long-ago attraction that once lured visitors from around the world, the Battle Creek Sanitarium. Owned and operated by Dr. John Harvey Kellogg, the sanitarium was a mecca for health enthusiasts of the late 19th to early 20th Centuries. The history of the facility, the town itself, and the health craze that fueled the growth of both entities are all-important parts of the overall story. So, with that in mind, the Heritage Center Foundation created an attraction that focuses on all of these factors, combining exhibits, theaters, interactive play areas, food, and retail into a treasure trove of stealth marketing.

This experiential branding effort mirrors the right brain-left brain differences between the two brothers who started the cereal craze. Dr. John Harvey Kellogg focused on nutrition and the importance of a healthy regimen; Will Keith Kellogg tirelessly promoted the brand, creating new marketing techniques that incorporated psychology and entertainment, changing the course of PR and advertising. From the silo-themed glockenspiel, featuring hourly performances by an animatronic Tony the Tiger™, Snap! Crackle!

and Pop!, and Toucan Sam, to the three major themed areas and numerous interactive and educational exhibits and theaters, Kellogg's Cereal City USA combines the seriousness of Dr. John with the whiz-bang marketing of Will Keith.

AN HISTORICAL PERSPECTIVE

A key element of Kellogg's Cereal City USA is the Historical Timeline, told through a series of museum-quality interactive exhibits and a theatrical presentation, *The Cereal Bowl of America*. Guests are presented with an overview of the Battle Creek Sanitarium, a health resort operated by Dr. John Harvey Kellogg, and featuring a vegetarian diet that focused on grain-based foods. An accident in the kitchen led to the discovery of corn flakes, and soon this new cereal product was all the rage. Considering that up to this point, Americans typically started their mornings off with heavy, fat-based foods, corn flakes quickly found not only a following, but also a very competitive marketplace. Not long after the initial success of Kellogg's product, a former visitor to the sanitarium, C. W. Post, started his own cereal business in Battle Creek, followed by scores of other suppliers; this led to the sobriquet "Cereal City." Presented in a richly themed theater, *The Cereal Bowl of America* tells this tale through the eyes of a Battle Creek historian named Duff.

But, Kellogg's did more than change the eating habits of the country. Another innovative theater experience, *A Bowl Full of Dreams*, tells the story of Will Keith "W.K." Kellogg, an early marketing genius. W.K. introduced his product to the public through the use of methods that are now considered basic principles of marketing. He was one of the first to use premiums to sell the product, either through "send in the boxtop" promotions or by including prizes in the cereal box itself. A philanthropist as well as promoter, W.K. demanded that the premiums placed in cereal boxes during the Depression be something of value to children during a time when money for luxuries was scarce. Kellogg also introduced the idea of using "civic spokespeople," or celebrities, to push the product, including Wild Bill Hickock, Andy Devine, Captain Kangaroo, and Superman. In fact, Kellogg's promotion of his product followed the arc of entertainment, from radio, to TV (especially during Saturday morning cartoons), and now to an experiential branding center, Kellogg's Cereal City USA itself.

Finally, keeping up with entertainment trends, *The Best to You Revue* ties the history of the town, the industry, and the star itself, cereal, together. Audience members are "transformed" to the size of a salt shaker on the breakfast table of a Michigan farmhouse and are told the whole entertaining tale through the use of oversized props, animation, and familiar Kellogg's characters.

Having been introduced to the background of the town and the company, guests can take a "tour" through the second of the three major themed areas, the Cereal Production Line. Taking the place of the popular factory tours discontinued in 1986, this production line provides guests with a look at every aspect of cereal production. In a video tour led by "Mr. Grit," guests see the control room, the cooking room, the flaking rolls, the toasting ovens, and the packaging area. The area includes the sounds and smells of the real thing. To complete the overall experience, guests are provided with a warm serving of corn flakes.

A GRAIN OF FUN

Once their curiosity and senses have been satisfied, guests may then move on to the interactive heart of the attraction: Cereal City. The third of the three major themed areas, Cereal City is where active experience takes the place of the more passive theatrical revues. Described as an "exploratorium," Cereal City offers a variety of experiences for guests of all ages, including:

- Dig 'Em's Diner, a trivia-based computer game focusing on the nutrition of cereal
- The Digestive Fun House, where guests can use interactive exhibits to learn about the digestive system, complete with sound and light
- A sketch and color area that allows guests to experience first-hand how cereal characters are developed
- Tony and Tony Jr.'s Table Top Hop, where kids slide from a giant cereal box into oversized soft Froot Loops and up and over nets surrounded by a huge milk carton A "meet and greet" area for Tony the Tiger, Cereal City's official mascot

Since Kellogg's Cereal City USA estimates the typical length of stay to be two-and-one-half to three hours, the facility also contains a food and beverage area to serve the needs of hungry guests. The 115-seat Red Onion Grill provides a variety of lunch and dinner choices, including deli sandwiches, pizza, burgers, and salads, and features an extensive cereal premium collection exhibit. Modeled after a diner of the early 20th Century, the Red Onion Grill gets its name from a diner that was located near the Battle Creek Sanitarium.

ADDITIONAL REVENUE STREAMS

Finally, guests are directed to the last stop for any present-day experience—the factory store. This retail venue offers Cereal City USA and Kellogg's character merchandise, from Kellogg's Cereal City USA jackets and tee-shirts, to Tony the Tiger stuffed animals and keychains, to a variety of souvenirs with Kellogg's character likenesses. Kellogg's Cereal City USA also offers its interactive experience for special events after hours. Catered receptions, including Tony the Tiger as host, can be held in the atrium of the facility. The entire facility, including the exhibits and theaters, is also available to private groups. Additionally, the facility is available for a range of other events, including organizational meetings, group outings, company picnics, and birthday parties.

THE ECONOMICS OF EXPERIENCE

Advertising is typically measured in cost per thousand (CPM) impressions. Traditional advertising offers a high CPM—imagine the number of impressions delivered by a full-page ad in *The New York Times* and compare that to the in-depth experience a visitor has with the Kellogg's brand at Cereal City, where the length of stay averages two-and-one-half hours. While the cost of an experiential brand destination might run into the millions—or multi-millions—the quality of the experience delivered and pleasant association with the brand that serves as the take-home message can be highly effective.

Additionally, experiential branding can often afford an opportunity to create synergy with other brands, extending the power of the experience to other strategic partners. This cannot only drive greater visitation due to the desire of the consumer to "taste" several experiences within one venue, but it can also defray costs by splitting the development expense.

Cereal City demonstrates several of the opportunities that experiential branding offers to marketers. Experiential branding:

■ Creates an atmosphere that demonstrates actual "see, feel, touch" product values in a consumer-friendly interactive environment.

■ Creates an environment in which the consumer has a complete, sensual experience, locking in pleasant memories that are subconsciously associated with the brand.

■ Presents a strong image to investors and the financial community, demonstrating a full commitment to brand support.

■ Offers an environment/platform for brand introductions and extensions.

One other important side-effect of experiential branding, especially when done in close proximity to the actual geographic location of the corporation's employees—such as brand attractions/heritage centers—is that the corporation can inspire excitement about the brand and company in its own employees, serving to boost morale and inspire company pride. In an age where the entry-level age demographic seems to place a high level of importance on "cool," an experiential branding strategy can be another arrow in the recruiter's quiver.

That same image of cutting-edge experience can also successfully promote a brand when utilized to create an attraction that invites the consumer to more fully understand what the brand stands for.

BRINGING THE BRAND TO LIFE

Experiential branding requires an approach that goes beyond traditional brand development. It is more than logos and packaging, spot ads, and PR. Developing a destination that will bring a brand to life requires a team that understands the technology required—and one that also understands the pitfalls of facility operation.

The biggest abyss facing marketers interested in this approach is the possibility of creating a monster that only sucks money from the bottom line. This happens when the destination:

■ Relies too much on expensive technology, assuming that it is only the "gee whiz" that is important to the customer. Gee whiz lasts one or two trips. An experiential branding attraction will fail if it cannot drive repeat visitation. This was what led to the eventual downfall of the themed restaurant craze that hit in the late 1990s—the sites were fun, once or twice. Unless the food itself was great—which typically it wasn't—the customer only came once or twice, then moved on.

- Cannot be easily or affordably "refreshed," that is, changed out to allow for new guest experiences.
- Becomes a nightmare to operate, both from the staffing and product presentation perspectives. If the destination requires too many people to operate, the profits disappear from the bottom line. If guests become confused—traffic patterns are too complex; the environment becomes too crowded—they won't return.
- Ignores the importance of staff training and motivation. All the technology investment in the world will not pay off if, in the end, the guest's final memory of the place is an encounter with a slack-jawed employee too interested in chatting on the phone to answer a question. The staff must be a part of the entire experience of the brand, matching the brand values, whether the product is shooting for hip, traditional, historic, or simply entertaining.
- Does not offer the guest something of value. Consumers are quick to recognize that which is no more than one big commercial, with nothing in it for them. The experience must entertain and/or educate.

To avoid these problems, marketers working toward a brand experience must begin the process by utilizing experts in the areas of retail design, technology, and operations. These experts should be brought in at the very beginning, while the brainstorming is occurring. While roadblocks should not be put in the way of the creative process—"we can't do that because"—the process does need to be informed by the realities of budget, availability, and operation. Most important, the marketing team must take into account the experience afforded by these professionals in their work on other projects. There are many projects that have inspired marketers to jump on the me-too bandwagon that are being kept afloat simply for reasons of ego—not because they are actually accomplishing the goals of the brand.

In creating a successful project, there are 11 basic stages the team will go through to reach their final goal.

THE 11 STAGES OF PROJECT DEVELOPMENT

The following guidelines have been amended from *Project Development Guidelines for the Themed Entertainment Industry*[6], a guide developed by the Themed Entertainment Association, an organization made up of professionals in the experiential branding and LBE industry.

These steps are offered to provide a roadmap for marketers interested in developing brands outside the usual and customary presentations, who may not be familiar with the processes involved. Experiential branding can be a very powerful tool, but only if developed correctly, with all the complexities of a fully operational consumer destination carefully considered. While most marketing professionals may not wind up in the trenches of location development, they should be aware of the challenges these types of installations present. Thus, the following information is presented as an introductory overview.

The process of developing a project can be expressed in 11 distinct stages under the following four major headings:

A. The Master Plan and Program (Stages I and II)
B. The Design Process (Stages III, IV, V, and VI)
C. The Implementation Process (Stages VII and VIII)
D. The Pre-, Grand, and Post-Opening (Stages IX, X, and XI)

The first two stages culminate with the project's Master Plan. The nine stages that follow the Master Plan address the complete design and implementation processes that are required for a project's development.

In establishing descriptions for the 11 stages of project development, the Standards Development Committee discovered that the various definitions of a Project Master Plan have no common basis. To an architect, a Master Plan might be a site plan; to a show designer, a Master Plan might include storyboards for a show or attraction; and to an economist, a Master Plan might mean developing a demographic analysis. While all of these definitions are valid in describing various Master Plan components, a true Master Plan must

---

6. *Project Development Guidelines for the Themed Entertainment Industry, Second Edition.* © The Themed Entertainment Association, 1995.

completely address all of the issues required to develop the Owner's/ Developer's Project Program. This therefore becomes our starting point for the Project Development Guidelines.

A. THE MASTER PLAN AND PROGRAM

1. *Master Plan Organization and Project Program:* At this stage, the project's goals and scope are formulated and documented while the project team is chosen and its tasks are delineated. The delivery of clear goals that define the scope, nature, size, financial parameters, schedule milestones, and target audience, as well as the creation of planning and development strategies, will establish the Project Program.

2. *Preliminary Concept Design:* Preliminary Concept Designs are developed for major project components to address the attitude, scope, and nature of the project. The issues addressed include not only the conceptual design, but the economic and operational guidelines as well. The conceptual design developed at this stage is based on the Owner's/Developer's Project Program.

B. DESIGN PROCESS

1. *Final Concept Design:* The Final Concept Design covers all project disciplines carried forward to a level of detail sufficient for understanding the project's scope to determine the requirements of all disciplines needed to design and develop the project. Verification of the Final Concept Design against all major components of the Project Program will complete the project's Master Plan.

2. *Schematic Design:* This stage develops the design "scheme" to a level of detail that identifies the sizing and interfaces required to bridge between the various component elements and project disciplines.

3. *Design Development:* This stage develops the design to a level of detail that accurately describes the project. Generally, this includes detailed strategies and specifications, as well as design documentation describing the show, architectural, and site elements that support the project's design intent.

4. *Production and Construction Documents:* This stage develops all Production and Construction Documents, which the consultants, vendors, and contractors need to implement

the project. It can include developing plans, specifications, drawings, scripts, storyboards, and other detailed information that will support and delineate the production and construction bid documents. Verification of the Production and Construction Documents against all major components of the Project Program will complete the project's Design Process.

C. IMPLEMENTATION PROCESS

1. *Production and Construction:* This stage deals with the bidding, negotiation, and subsequent production and construction of all components for the show.
2. *Show Installation:* Show Installation covers the installation, termination, testing, and programming of all components and equipment directly related to the show system and technologies proposed for the Project Program. All show systems are tested during this stage to ensure they will meet the Project Program requirements as set forth in the Master Plan.

D. PRE-, GRAND, AND POST-OPENING

1. *Pre-Opening:* The Pre-Opening stage covers the training of operations/maintenance personnel, the establishment of operations and maintenance procedures, the loading of operations furniture, fixtures, and equipment, and the stocking of all inventory required for operation.
2. *Grand Opening:* The Grand Opening is the culmination of the entire project's development. It is also the official opening and presentation of a fully operational and completely finished product to the general public.
3. *Rehabilitation/Expansion:* The Rehabilitation/Expansion stage begins when an infusion of new ideas and/or updated processes, thematic content, or additional components are required to maintain a project's viability. When requirements include new facilities, a major rehabilitation of existing elements, or any other major additions or alterations, the process then becomes a new and separate project and must again address the 11 stage of project development.

SUCCESS STORY

In general, there are several common elements among successful experiential branding projects. They include:

- The project must demonstrate the knowledge of the brand from both the company's and the customer's perspective, otherwise the consumer's expectations may not match the end result.
- The project must educate, enhance, and entertain, and be presented within an aesthetic that supports the brand image.
- The project cannot stand alone; it must be supported within a traditional framework of advertising and promotion.
- The project should be located in an area that can draw from tourist as well as local traffic. Co-opetition with other attractions can also be helpful.
- The project must be able to be refreshed within the boundaries of a realistic budget to do so.

SUMMARY

Entertainment, as demonstrated within each chapter of this book, has a significant role in today's world. While it stands alone as a consumable product, it can also be used to create brand loyalty, while also offering a platform for brand extensions. However, when entertainment is used as a device for brand building, marketers must take into account the need to create experiences that will resonate within the consumer by combining traditional marketing approaches with the lessons learned from the development and operation of stand-alone entertainment venues. Otherwise, the brand runs the risk of creating a negative experience that will ultimately affect the brand itself.

FOR FURTHER READING

BOOKS

1. Gilmore, James H. and Joseph B. Pine, *The Experience Economy: Work Is Theatre & Every Business a Stage* (Boston: Harvard Business School Press, 1999).

2. Morgan, Adam, *Eating the Big Fish* (New York: John Wiley & Sons, Inc. ,1999).

3. *Project Development Guidelines for the Themed Entertainment Industry, Second Edition* (Burbank, CA: The Themed Entertainment Association, 1999).

MAGAZINES TO DEVOUR

1. *Entertainment Management*

2. *The EZone Newsletter*

11 CHANGES AND CHALLENGES

OVERVIEW

As today's world economy shifts and shakes, raising the standard of living in some countries, lowering it in others, entertainment tags along, offering the newly leisured a place to go, directed to a facility, a screen, a station, a team, or a publication by the same force that moves the industry in the U.S.: the power of marketing. But marketers face new challenges in this global entertainment economy. Aspects of those changes have already been touched on in the coverage of the various segments, but now we will revisit them on the global stage.

GOING GLOBAL

Why has the entertainment marketing revolution exploded across the globe into a multi-billion-dollar industry? Everywhere we turn, remote spots—whether in the heart of Africa, up the Amazon River Basin, or in the wide Outback of Australia—draw the modern-day marketers in search of riches and new revenue frontiers. Any traveler to faraway lands is struck by how cultures seem to be melding together—how folks everywhere don jeans or ties or the fashions seen in American movies and television. Entertainment as an industry is expanding at a phenomenal rate.

Some of this expansion can be attributed to a changing economic model, as financing for much of the new content comes from foreign sources, eager to participate. Some of these tremors are a result of the direct, positive impact on the bottom line of transnational media and entertainment corporations that include Disney, AOL/Time Warner, Bertelsmann, Sony, Vivendi/Universal, News Corp, CBS/Viacom, GE/NBC, and allied communications giants like WPP, Omnicom, Interpublic Group, Havas, Publicis, and Dentsu.

Only a few decades ago, entertainment revenues were divided into 90% domestic and 10% international. By the early 1990s, this formula had changed to dollar for dollar. The cause of the global entertainment revolution was a strategy that started slowly and gained momentum fed by local consumption patterns—the development, marketing, and promotion of local talent, local content, ethnic music, country-specific pop stars—and some backlash against the spread and domination of American culture. The new cry became "think global—act local" as consumers looked for their own customs, culture, lyrics, language, and humor.

Up until now, the largest impact of the spread of entertainment globalization has been the shift from government ownership, support, and domination of the television networks, film, and music production companies, publishing/media organizations, and Internet portals. The growth of each of these sectors has benefited from both the multinational media conglomerates, as well as aggressive entrepreneurial efforts in countries around the world. Their combined push to introduce the conduit and the content to new audiences has created a plethora of new marketing opportunities. As those sectors have blossomed, so have the marketing expenditures associated with each.

MARKETING IN THE NEW MILLENNIUM

The issues facing entertainment marketing can be roughly split into two areas of discussion: *That was then* and *this is now*. The *"then"* is what up until now served as state-of-the-art technology and conduit—until the appearance of the Internet, digital technology, and satellite transmissions. The *"now"* discussion, thanks to screamingly fast changes in technology, may change the entire picture in a very short period of time. The marketing of entertainment, from this point on, will be affected more than ever by the means of distribution, international laws and treaties, and the continued development of technology.

Rather than partake in a country-by-country discussion of what great ad or clever technique has been used recently to promote any of the entertainment sectors, this last section will focus on the issues that may serve to steal the thunder from the marketing effort. We'll wrap up with a cursory overview of the state of the industry around the globe.

THE CHALLENGE OF CHANGE

In their simplest forms, all of the entertainment content covered in this book—movies, network broadcast and cable TV, radio, publishing, sports, and electronic games—uses technology for dissemination to create revenue streams. The marketing function serves to make the consumer aware of the specific forms of conduit so that consumption—the cash transaction—can take place. If the dissemination of the content undergoes change, so do the functions—and the practices—of marketing. Today, that dissemination is facing huge changes, all stemming from the Pandora's box of the globalization of entertainment, and the technologies used to facilitate that trend.

There are three issues that are causing waves of concern throughout the entertainment industry:

- The challenge of upholding intellectual property (IP) laws (copyrights) internationally
- The changing patterns of distribution due to new technology
- The piracy of content

All three of these issues have their roots in the ever-increasing ease in which content can be cross-platformed, not only by the originators, but by individuals who may have less-than-legal uses for the content.

STABILIZING THE GLOBAL
MARKETING ENVIRONMENT

As discussed in Chapter 1, IP is the key to the entire entertainment industry. IP is divided into two categories: industrial property, which includes inventions (patents), trademarks, industrial designs, and geographic indications of source; and copyright, which includes literary and artistic works such as novels, poems and plays, films, musical works, artistic works such as drawings, paintings, photographs, sculptures, and architectural designs. Rights related to copyright include those of performing artists in their performances, producers of phonograms in their recordings, and those of broadcasters in their radio and television programs.[1]

Copyright is what protects the ownership of creative properties—and without ownership, there can be no *protectable* revenue stream. If IP laws are not consistent—if there is not a stable environment for the marketing of IP— the international trade of entertainment is gravely threatened. For copyright laws to do their job, however, they must be consistent from jurisdiction to jurisdiction. It's one thing to protect one's property at home in the good old US of A, and quite another to do the same in a far-off corner of the globe, where the legal system may not operate in quite the same way.

The good news is that copyright is a concern everywhere, to any company producing content that can be recreated across media platforms. Given that, the legal entities of over 170 countries around the world have formed the World Intellectual Property Organization (WIPO), an alliance that focuses on maintaining the rights of content owners around the world. The WIPO carries out many tasks related to the protection of IP rights, such as administering international treaties, assisting governments, organizations, and the private sector, monitoring developments in the field, and harmonizing and simplifying relevant rules and practices. The WIPO recognizes that rapid and wide-ranging technological change, particularly in the fields of information technology and the Internet, is the greatest challenge facing IP today.

While this may not stop the neighborhood hacker from downloading content from the Internet, it is beginning to have serious impact on the organizations that are putting that content up on the

---

1.   World Intellectual Property Organization, *About Intellectual Property* (*www.wipo.org/about-ip/en/*), 2001.

Web. Major busts of far-flung operations have occurred throughout 2001, with more underway.

DIGITAL DREAMS

Much has been made of the impact of the Internet on the world in general. This new form of communication has spread its tentacles in a hundred different directions, from the simplest of instant messages to the crushing effect of the fall of the dot-com stocks. And it's true—the Internet will play a significant role in e-commerce and communication well into the 21st Century—in one form or another. But the biggest change facing the entertainment universe is digital technology, a breakthrough that offers incredible opportunity—and very serious challenges.

Digital technology is already readily available in the marketplace; it is the basis for the clear sound of CDs and the additional content found on DVDs. But this is small potatoes in comparison to the potential use of digital distribution. Digitized content can be transmitted quickly, cheaply, and efficiently—once the technology has been put in place. That "once" is no small consideration; at an average of $100K per movie screen to upgrade to digital reception, the industry is looking at a several billion dollar investment—and everyone in the industry is busy pointing fingers at one another to determine just who should pay for it.

Exhibitors say the distributors; the distributors say the exhibitors; but no one denies the potential revenue ramifications down the line. Movie theaters that are refurbished to receive digital transmission can be utilized for more than just movie viewing; the same distribution system can provide "butts in the seats" for special events—rock concerts and videoconferencing, for example—increasing daypart usage. In terms of movies themselves, the quality of the image will no longer be dependent on the quality of the print—not to mention that the prints themselves will cease to exist. This alone will add up to a tremendous cost savings for the studios, not only in distribution, but also in marketing. Consider the following example:

DIGITIZING FOR DOLLARS

Studio A is a leader in international theatrical film distribution, which includes its own film products, international acquisitions of other studios' material, and co-productions in other parts of the world. They operate a far-flung empire, operating in 50 countries with 25 direct distribution offices. However, they are concerned with the cost of disseminating their publicity and marketing materials—including media kits and movie trailers—to the field.

For example, for a top release, the studio must produce 35mm color key sets from an original transparency, then produce and ship multiple sets. For one release alone, this could mean 300 sets going to 60 different locations. The cost of this process stretches into the millions, especially when shipping is taken into account. Given that it takes anywhere from three to four weeks to get the publicity materials out to the field, start to finish, time also becomes a large factor. However, if the studio changes its approach to accommodate digital distribution, it can reduce the up-front expenditure as well as the time it takes to complete the process.

Rather than set up yet another department to handle the process, the studio chooses to hire a third-party company to provide an international portal for various media, going directly to media houses in various territories. By doing this, the studio can now:

- Distribute and control text files to authorized representatives and approved media
- Provide generic captioning of the materials, which can be manipulated by authorized users to translate captions into other languages
- Upload both text and image files
- Provide unlimited—but fully trackable—downloading of materials by approved media, without the cost of additional kits
- Maintain the security of the files through live tracking of who has downloaded what and when
- Receive 24-hour technical support from the third party's client support team
- Plan and facilitate tighter deadlines for the release of material

The studio has now added value to its original system in terms of access, speed, security, quality, efficiency, archiving, and material management. This added value has a direct impact on the ROI. Even with the cost of implementing the system, based on past expenditures, the studio generates an ROI in the double digits—and has the added benefit of all the other stated values.

On the trailer end, the studio was traditionally creating analog tapes in digibeta and Beta SP formats. Those tapes would be shipped to the territories in a rough-cut format to gather feedback for production. This usually involved three iterations of the trailer—each a separate tape, with separate shipping costs. By shifting to a Quick-time format, the cost of shipping is eliminated, and the turnaround time for feedback collapses from several days to as little as four to five hours. In addition, the final cut could be stored digitally, which would allow for cross-platform usage, from Web sites to interactive CDs. Once again, considerable cost savings as well as increased speed and efficiency are the results.[2]

This example of the use of digitization is very clear-cut, and does little to affect traditional processes in any negative way. However, the larger use of digital content, in the form of film distribution, has a ripple effect that restructures the traditional distribution system of movies and related spin-off products from a release window basis to a transaction basis.

DIGITIZED DISTRIBUTION

The traditional distribution schedule for a major release is as follows: The first window is the theater release. Approximately six months after the theatrical release, the film moves to video/DVD release; nine months later it moves to PPV; twelve months later it shifts to subscription cable services, such as HBO or Showtime; and after eighteen months, it shows up on ad-supported network and cable stations. Each of these release windows has an associated marketing effort tied to it.

However, according to some experts, the use of digital media will lay the foundation for video on-demand (VOD), which will allow the consumer the flexibility of getting a film when he or she wants it, rather than waiting for release windows. This will have a significant impact on the revenue streams associated with each of these distribution channels—video/DVD rental, PPV, subscription cable, and ad-supported broadcast. To control the revenue flow—to keep VOD from cutting into the orderly structure already in place—the theory supposes that the distribution system will change to a transaction base. The releases will be staggered by a schedule that determines when the film will be available for consumption *by transaction*. Those transactions would include (post-theatrical release):

■ *Sales transactions (six months post-theatrical release)*: VHS/DVD sales; VOD rights purchase (consumer buys lifetime rights to VOD of a particular film)

---

2.   Information from "Economic Case Studies in Cross-Media Publishing," as presented at the SeyboldSF Conference, 2001.

- *Rental transactions (nine months)*: VHS/DVD rental; VOD/
  PPV viewing (consumer pays for unlimited viewing of a particular film within a specific timeframe)
- *Subscription transactions (twelve months)*: VHS/DVD, VOD,
  and movie channel subscriptions (consumer pays a monthly
  subscription fee)
- *Ad-supported transactions*: Ad-supported VOD and cable;
  network TV[3]

Again, the shift to this new distribution model would affect traditional marketing. More importantly, as this transaction model can
apply to other forms of media as well, as they become cross-platformed—the release of e-books online versus in print (or POD); VOD
sporting events via both broadcast and Webcast—this new approach
would stretch across entertainment sectors.

In conclusion, the digitization of media allows for new market
and distribution approaches. However, not all of these approaches
will be legal, which leads us to the third challenge facing marketers
and the industry at large: piracy.

PIRACY

Digital content has its advantages, but unfortunately, it also
exacerbates an already serious problem facing the entertainment
industry. The Motion Picture Association of America (MPAA) and its
international counterpart, the Motion Picture Association (MPA),
estimate that the U.S. motion picture industry loses in excess of $3
billion annually in potential worldwide revenue due to piracy. Due to
the difficulty in calculating Internet piracy losses, these figures are
NOT currently included in overall loss estimates. However, it is safe
to assume Internet losses cause untold additional damages to the
industry.[4]

As with IP issues, piracy affects every area of the distribution of
entertainment media, and has a related impact on marketing
efforts—specifically, undermining the revenues needed to launch

---

3. Forrester Research, Inc., *Movie Distribution's New Era*, March 2001.

4. The Motion Picture Association of America
   (*www.mpaa.org/anti-piracy/*).

marketing programs, as well as to produce the content itself. Pirate operations have none of the expenses associated with original production—the MPAA estimates that the average $55 million film has an associated marketing cost of $27 million—they simply ride on the coattails of the efforts and reap the rewards. Four out of ten movies never recoup their original investment.

To recoup such enormous investments, the industry relies on the carefully planned sequential release of movies described in the previous section. When piracy of a film occurs at any point in the release sequence, all subsequent markets governed by the release windows are negatively affected.

One real-world example of piracy's devastating impact on the legitimate marketplace is with the 1999 release of the film *Star Wars: Episode 1–The Phantom Menace*. Pirate copies of the film (created by using camcorders in U.S. theaters) flooded the Asian marketplace while the film was still in U.S. theatrical distribution. When the film opened legitimately in Asian theaters, attendance was far below expectations. In addition, home entertainment retailers lost vital business in the home video window due to the availability of pirated copies. In this case, piracy affected legitimate theatrical distributors, exhibitors, and local businesses.[5]

It is no surprise that the MPAA encourages foreign governments to abide by, and fully implement, important agreements such as those described in the previous section discussing WIPO treaties.

TYPES OF PIRACY[6]

Piracy takes many forms, depending on the medium. The most prevalent examples are as follows:

Optical Disc Piracy. Optical Disc Piracy involves laser discs (LDs), video compact discs (VCDs), and DVDs. The greatest challenge in the piracy of this type of medium is the fact that the duplicated item is as clear as the original—as opposed to the murky quality of a VHS tape reproduced from a tape shot in a theater with a camcorder. Plus, they are inexpensive to reproduce and can be churned out quickly.

---

5. The Motion Picture Association of America
    (*www.mpaa.org/anti-piracy/*).

6. The Motion Picture Association of America
    (*www.mpaa.org/anti-piracy/*).

Internet Piracy. Internet piracy involves the unauthorized use of copyrighted motion pictures. This includes the sale, trade, lease, distribution, uploading for transmission, transmission, or public performance of a motion picture online without the consent of the motion picture's copyright owner.

Downloadable Media . Downloadable media are the digital files that allow for motion pictures to be compressed and uploaded for direct download onto a computer. Downloadable media formats are used to illegally offer and distribute motion pictures to other Internet users, by directing consumers to sites where a movie can be accessed and downloaded.

Hard Goods . Hard goods piracy refers to the illegal sale, distribution, and/or trading of copies of motion pictures in any non-downloadable media format, including videocassettes, LDs, and DVDs. These hard goods are typically sold on Web sites, online auction sites, and via spamming (email solicitations).

Streaming Media. Streaming media is delivered to online users in real time. Like hard goods and downloadable media, streaming copyrighted content can only be done with the express authorization of the copyright holder.

Circumvention Devices. A circumvention device is exactly what it sounds like: any device that allows someone to secure copyrighted content by circumventing content protection devices. This includes encrypted software put in films, videos, and discs. Again, these devices allow for perfect digital copies to be created from the original, then distributed illegally.

Videocassette Piracy. Videocassette piracy is the illegal duplication, distribution, rental, or sale of copyrighted videocassettes. Produced in illicit duplicating facilities, or "laboratories," these copies are distributed through swap meets, cooperating video dealers, and street vendors.

Camcording. Refers to the use of hand-held video cameras to record motion picture films off of theater screens. The tape is then copied onto blank videocassettes and optical discs for illegal distribution. These copies are not only distributed in the U.S., but are also often shipped overseas before the release of the film in foreign theaters.

Screeners. Refers to illegal copies that are sometimes made from legitimate advance copies used for screening and marketing purposes. Screeners were a specific focus of raids on pirate organizations in late 2001.

Back-to-Back Copying. Yes, you may be in violation of piracy laws if you've ever connected two VCRs and copied an original video onto a blank cassette.

Theatrical Print Theft. This is the rarest type of theft. It involves the theft of a 35- or 16mm film for the purpose of making illegal copies. This allows for relatively high-quality videotape, which then serves as the master for the duplication of unauthorized videocassettes.

Signal Theft. Signal theft is the act of illegally tapping into cable TV systems or receiving unauthorized satellite signals. It also includes illegally tampered cable decoders or satellite descramblers. This type of theft is particularly onerous when committed by cable or broadcast TV operators that pirate satellite signals of programs not licensed by a particular country and then re-transmit them.

Broadcast Piracy. Broadcast piracy occurs on over-the-air broadcasts. The illegal act is the on-air broadcasting of a bootleg videocassette of a film or the airing of legitimate films or television programs without permission from the copyright holder.

Public Performance. Unauthorized public performances occur when an institution or commercial establishment shows a tape or film to its members or customers without receiving permission from the copyright owner. This is not dependent on the charging of a fee from members or customers.

Parallel Importation. Parallel importation refers to the importation of goods authorized for manufacture or distribution in the exporting country, but which is imported without express authority of the copyright or trademark owner. Parallel importation is legal, or at least looser, in some countries. A prime example is Australia, whose release date for first-run movies is months out from the U.S. release. Australia recently liberalized its parallel import laws on movies. Unfortunately, this undercuts exhibitors in that country, as consumers may be able to purchase regionally coded DVDs before broad theatrical release.

THE GLOBAL SNAPSHOT

An in-depth investigation of each country of the world and their entertainment/media structures would fill an entire shelf at the local library. For the purpose of this book, the following example is included to provide a taste of the global scene, not a complete overview. Pay special attention to the influences of government control and the development of content/focus on conduit.

We begin with Canada and Mexico, who both share a border with the U.S. and are co-signers of the North American Fair Trade Act (NAFTA).

NORTH AMERICA: CANADA

Canadians feel very strongly about establishing and maintaining a separate identity from the U.S., even though the Canadian economy is closely integrated with that of the U.S.

The technology of Canadian media and entertainment is very similar to that found in the U.S. The Canadian Broadcasting Corporation (CBC) is Canada's national public broadcaster. It was created in 1936 through an act of Parliament that was concerned about the growing American influence in radio. The CBC operates both English-language and French-language national television networks. Both languages are broadcast on two separate channels: one with regular programming and one with all-news programming. There are also two private national television networks: CTV and Global Television.

Currently, the CBC reaches its international markets via five avenues:

- Radio Canada International
- Sale of television programs
- CBC Web sites
- Newsworld International

The fifth avenue, TV5, is a globally distributed, French-language, general-interest network, created in 1985. TV5's region-specific programming reaches 120 million homes via six satellites, covering Europe, Quebec, Africa, Latin America and the Caribbean, the Orient, the U.S., and Asia.

Canada's largest piracy problem has been in the area of software. Finally on the decline, estimates of lost revenue were running as high as $450 million per year.

CENTRAL AMERICA: MEXICO

Mexico is also similar to the U.S. in terms of its conduit base, with more than 300 TV stations and 25.6 million TVs. However, from that market, one broadcaster, Grupo Televisa SA de CV (Televisa), holds a nearly 90% share. Unlike Canada, this primary provider is not a government-owned entity, and therefore operates under a more marketing-driven mandate than the CBC.

Televisa has interests in the following businesses:

- Television production and broadcasting
- Pay television programming
- Direct-to-home satellite services
- Cable television
- International distribution of television programming
- Feature film production and distribution
- Publishing and publishing distribution
- Music recording and distribution
- Radio production and broadcasting
- Professional sports and show business promotions
- An Internet portal, EsMas.com
- An equity interest in Univision Com, Inc., a U.S. Spanish-language television broadcaster that commands an 84% share of Spanish broadcasting within the U.S.
- A 51% stake in a joint venture with Cablevision and a 60% stake in Innova, which operates the SKY direct-to-home satellite known as Sky Latin America

Televisa is the heavyweight in Spanish-language television: it produces, broadcasts, and distributes Spanish-language television programs to 85 countries throughout North and South America and Europe, with its main international outlets being the U.S., Spain, and other Latin American countries.

Copyright piracy remains a major problem in Mexico, with U.S. industry loss estimates remaining high. Pirated sound recordings and videocassettes are widely available throughout Mexico. The International Intellectual Property Alliance (IIPA) estimates that trade losses due to copyright piracy in Mexico totaled $469 million in 1998; figures for 1999 and 2000 are not yet available. The Business Software Alliance, a trade association representing the packaged software industry, estimates that the Mexican piracy rate in 1999 was 56%, which resulted in losses of approximately $134 million. The International Federation of the Phonographic Industry, a music trade association, estimates the piracy rate for music in Mexico to be approximately 40%.[7]

SOUTH AMERICA: BRAZIL

Globo Cabo, a holding company based in Sao Paulo, is the largest operator of cable television in Brazil, serving 1.5 million subscribers with over 6.5 million homes passed in 67 cities of Brazil. Impressive, considering there are only 1.8 million total subscribers in the entire country.

In July 2000, Globo Cabo acquired VICOM, a privately held company with over 3,000 ground-based satellite transponders in Brazil. The company explored ways to exploit synergies between its extensive urban cable network and VICOM's vast satellite network. The company also collaborated with Microsoft to develop a broadband Internet platform in Brazil. Microsoft bought a 9.6% stake in the company and together they launched Virtua, a high-speed residential broadband service. Virtua is available exclusively to their cable TV subscribers. The company is also investigating broadband offerings to facilitate the convergence of interactive and digital TV.

Globo also has an edge in the area of content. The parent holding company has interests in newspapers, magazines, and TV; this provides a cornucopia of content to be leveraged across the board. Additionally, the Globo network, through Globo TV International, is beamed from Brazil to a myriad of countries. Household penetration is split into two groups of nations: the U.S., Australia, and most South and Central American countries are home to numerous Brazilian expatriates; the second group of nations, such as Portugal, Angola, and Mozambique, share Portuguese as its common language and are equally receptive to the programming.

Video piracy continues to be the main source of piracy in Latin America. Brazil, the largest market in the region, also has one of the highest piracy rates, with piracy losses topping $120 million in 1999. It is the position of the MPA that the Brazilian government has, to date, demonstrated inadequate commitment and attention toward protection of IP rights. [8]

---

7.   Office of the United States Trade Representative, *Foreign Trade Barriers: Mexico* (*www.ustr.gov/html/2001_mexico.pdf*).

In many countries in the region, piracy is linked to organized crime, thus complicating both investigation and enforcement. Signal theft is also common in the region, while Internet piracy has not yet posed a real threat due to lack of bandwidth in the region.

EUROPE: GERMANY

Germany's major player, Kirch Holdings, participates in each stage of the entertainment value chain. Kirch's major competencies are its vast library of content, stronghold on sports entertainment, position of leadership in German television broadcasting, content production, and technological know-how.

Kirch Media currently manages Kirch's license trading, film technology, free television channels and program production, and ProSiebenSat1 Media, Germany's largest listed media group. Kirch's library includes the licensing rights to 63,000 hours of programming. Through its co-production and financing arrangements with American studios, Kirch owns the German-language rights to 70% of Hollywood films. Kirch Media also has long-term licensing arrangements with several American movie and television companies, including Sony, Viacom, Universal, Warner Bros., Disney, Polygram, and Spelling Entertainment. Kirch PayTV provides and markets digital and PPV programming to the German-speaking market. Kirch also extended Rupert Murdoch's News Corp's BSkyB a 24% ownership stake in Kirch PayTV, to fund its expansion into digital television.

Kirch has also made a point of acquiring the rights to popular sporting events, such as European soccer league games and the celebrated World Cup tournaments. The company also owns the rights to the annual European soccer tournament (UEFA Cup), in addition to ice hockey, boxing, basketball, golf, and tennis matches. Their new connection with Formula One motor racing presents another opportunity; last season, 17 races of Formula One were broadcast to an audience of over 5 billion.

Better enforcement of existing German legislation has led to a decline in piracy in all areas except the Internet.

---

8. The Motion Picture Association of America
    (*www.mpaa.org/anti-piracy/*).

THE MIDDLE EAST: ISRAEL

Television is a government tool in Israel, established in 1967, the year of the Six Days War between Israel and its neighboring Arab countries. Israeli television was first broadcast by Channel One, overseen and administered by the Israel Broadcasting Authority, which retains control of the channel today.

According to the Israel Broadcasting Authority Law, the Authority's responsibilities rest in three main areas:

- To broadcast television (and radio) as a public service
- To broadcast educational and entertainment programs, as well as information in the areas of social, economic, monetary, cultural, scientific, and arts policy
- To ensure that the broadcast gives suitable expression to various opinions, and transmits reliable information

Today, Channel One is divided into two divisions. The first, the News Division, directs news, sports, special local and overseas broadcasts, and current affairs magazines. The second, the Program Division, is made up of five departments. They include the documentary department, entertainment department, drama department, children's and youth department, and the Israel heritage department.

Channel Two was created in 1993. Unlike Channel One, Channel Two is funded by the sale of on-air advertising. Channel Two is not entirely separate from the government, however. Educational TV, a branch of the Ministry of Education, has been incorporated into Channel Two and is supported by government funds.

Israel's Arab population is not neglected. Channel Three, which is also government owned, is a satellite/cable-only channel that broadcasts news and entertainment in Arabic or with Arabic subtitles. The content includes cultural and sports programs, news features, and "open studio," live broadcasts. Channel Three can be picked up in all Middle Eastern countries, North Africa, the Persian Gulf, and some southern European nations.

On the cable front, Israel has three major operators: Golden Channels, Matav, and Tevel. In the areas of music and film, while Israel has some domestic production, most content is imported from the U.S. Israeli film production is subsidized by government funds, but not enough moviegoers watch Israeli movies to finance further productions. Both advertisers and consumers prefer imported content from satellite; no Israeli programming extends beyond Israeli borders.

Israel's lack of trans-national development in entertainment may offer a monstrous opportunity for the Israeli entertainment industry. However, the opportunity for marketers remains to be seen, both from cultural and political perspectives. Middle East unrest continues to depress the opportunities available in the entertainment marketing sector. Additionally, the Middle East has not been known for strict sentencing for copyright violations.

INDIA

An overview of the global entertainment and media scene—even a cursory one—would not be complete without mention of India, especially due to the overwhelming success of the Indian cinema industry known as Bollywood. The term is a derivation of combining Hollywood with Bombay, the center of Indian film production.

Indian cinema has produced over 27,000 feature films and thousands of documentary short films, in 52 different languages; today, India makes almost 800 feature films every year, making it the largest film-producing country in the world. These films are distributed worldwide, to an audience that eagerly awaits each new release featuring a raft of popular stars.

On the TV scene, the big player in today's India is ZEE TV. The channel turned India's mostly staid TV industry on its head with its forward-looking philosophy. ZEE TV provides viewers with innovative programs: talk shows, game shows, discussion, situation comedies, and dramas, broadcast in Hindi—created by Indians for Indians. ZEE TV also continues to serve the needs of India's myriad linguistic groups (there are 15 major languages spoken in India) by producing a variety of shows in different languages.

STAR TV, which pioneered satellite television in Asia, became ZEE's partner in India on December 1993, when STAR purchased 50% of Asia Today LTD, the Hong Kong-based broadcaster of ZEE TV. ZEE TV is now watched daily by an average of 180 million viewers across the world, and meets the primetime requirements of both the Eastern and Pacific time zones. Aimed at serving the needs of South Asians living abroad, the channel airs 24 hours a day.

On the cable TV scene, a government effort to clean up private broadcasters has resulted in the banning of tobacco and alcohol advertisements, "adult shows," and advertisements containing references that might offend religious sentiments. The government-controlled channel Doordarshan does not broadcast such advertisements.

The Indian entertainment industry has the potential to grow by 27% in the next five years according to a preliminary report prepared by the Confederation of Indian Industry (CII).[9] The report forecasts growth of 31% for television, 21% for films, 55% for music, and 55% for radio. However, the report suggests specific recommendations to counter piracy. Anti-piracy laws should be made stricter and should be coupled with continuing emphasis on increased public condemnation of piracy. The report suggests a joint effort between the Indian film and music industries.

ASIA: JAPAN

Nihon Hosokyokai, or Japan Broadcasting Corporation (NHK), the only TV/radio broadcasting station authorized by law to provide universal services, operates five channels. Two are terrestrial channels: one provides news, movies, dramas, sports, and entertainment; the other supplies educational programs. The remaining three channels are DBS channels, offering, respectively, sports/news, old movies, and HDTV broadcasts.

On the cable front, Japan's notoriously rigid isolationist practices have worked against the full development of cable TV. Between the fact that the government has limited the number of channels and the practice of limiting foreign ownership of stations to 33% (just recently increased from 20%), there are hurdles facing MSOs in this market. Additionally, Japanese consumers are still in a mindset similar to that of American consumers in the early days of cable; they believe there is enough programming available for free, and that cable is too expensive.

From a piracy perspective, the Japanese market suffers from an influx of pirated films emanating from Vietnam. Vietnam's government-owned film distributor routinely disseminates illegal copies of foreign films; however, action by the MPA and Japanese government has slowed this problem.

ASIA: CHINA

Conducting business in China is one of the biggest challenges—and opportunities—facing western countries today. In the midst of a

---

9.   *Anti Piracy Laws Enforcement Key For Indian Entertainment Industry* (*www.indiaexpress.com/news/entertainment/20011106-0.html*), November 6, 2001.

struggle for political control, combined with the opening of trade and some investment, the Chinese entertainment industry is searching for a path. With its roots in the propaganda past, as well as art house films stressing traditional Chinese values and mores, the Chinese film industry is as much an opportunity and challenge as anything else in this intriguing economy.

In 1999, the Chinese government announced it would permit foreign companies to collaborate with domestic companies to make movies and manufacture moviemaking and recording equipment. This not only affected the production of movies, but the content as well. Violence and sex have long been targets of censorship in Chinese-made movies, but that is slowly changing as foreign sensibilities become involved in the process—for better or for worse remains to be seen. In the meantime, it is estimated that about 60% of all movies to be shown in China will be domestic productions.

However, piracy has been a problem in China—and continues to be. At times, the figures released by the government have suggested that the piracy rate was running as high as 90%. There were large-scale imports of pirated products from surrounding areas and the number of production lines in-country had also increased. However, the government will be obliged to take more determined enforcement actions against pirates after the official WTO accession of China.

The Chinese cable industry is big—100 million cable TV users—but supposedly totally homegrown. Supposedly, because many foreigners have struck deals with China's local cable operators, who have merrily ignored the central government's ban on the same. However, it appears that a crackdown may be on its way. In any case, foreign entertainment marketers have yet to see what the outcome will be, and who will be able to take advantage of any opportunities that may present themselves.

SUMMARY

Entertainment marketing, once primarily the domain of U.S.-based studios, has expanded into all sectors of the entertainment industry around the world. As technology joins discretionary time and disposable income in creating a global marketplace eager to consume entertainment products, today's marketing professionals must be aware of a variety of new challenges and opportunities. The continued development of content and conduit around the world creates an increasingly competitive entertainment economy, filled with consumers who have almost instantaneous access—either legally or illegally—to product. Marketing professionals must learn how to harness today's technologies to create new strategies for product roll-out and maintenance.

12 CONCLUSION: WHERE DO WE GO FROM HERE?

As evidenced by the preceding chapters, there seems to be very little that might cause the entertainment industry to stop dead in its tracks. It has continued to grow throughout the last century in spite of—and perhaps due to—worldwide economic depression and recession, global and regional warfare, an increase in the cost of events, and not-so-fabulous publicity over strikes and scandals. In short, the entertainment industry continues to gain momentum, creating challenges and opportunities as it grows.

However, our world is in the throes of yet another transformation, the most wide-reaching since the Industrial Revolution, which changed our way of life forever. The Technology Revolution will do the same, and entertainment, in many ways, will be leading the charge. Why? Because entertainment today covers not only what we do with our free time, but, as we have discussed, how we approach work, information gathering, dissemination of news, and, yes, the use of our discretionary income. If nothing else, the use of entertainment—or what some may call the experience—has permeated our society in ways P.T. Barnum might have been applauding, loudly.

Entertainment marketers can best be prepared for the future by following the traditional journalistic practice of asking themselves who, what, why, where, and when.

WHO: THE AUDIENCE

Most critical in the discussion of the future audience of entertainment marketing is who the audience will be. And, since we are talking about the future, it's a pretty safe bet to say that the audience will be made up of a generation that is playing video games before they can read—those toddlers whose eye-hand coordination amazes their parents, and whose single-minded focus on flashing electronic images is mind-blowing in their ability to comprehend the complexity of the levels and goals of *Mario Brothers* before they can tie their shoes—which of course, they don't have to do, thanks to Velcro™.

Most important in the discussion of the coming generation of consumers is the consideration that these people are stunningly more comfortable with technology than their parents; that their understanding of the world around them, and how to communicate and receive/search for information, is exponentially greater than ours—because they will have never lived within the boundaries of snail-mail, slow downloads, incomprehensible MS-DOS commands, or telephones screwed to the wall. They will not consider their communication and entertainment environments fixed; they will understand that they can have what they want, when they want, how they want.

Because this flexibility will be a permanent fixture in their lives, they will become even more of a moving target to marketers than their parents were. They will expect more from their entertainment because their lives are about constant visual stimulation. They will, in turn, need more to be prompted to turn their attention to specific events and experiences. They will keep marketers on their toes when it comes to understanding what they want, what they would like to need, and how they demand to be informed.

WHAT: TECHNOLOGY AND TRENDS

Throughout our discussion, we have attempted to provide a cursory overview of the technology that is shaping the world of entertainment (and therefore entertainment marketing); "attempted" because the lifespan of technology today is similar to that of the tsetse flies that are born and die daily in laboratories around the world. It is nearly impossible to be totally current with these changes, because the old technologies of research, writing, and editing are bound by the pace of human ability—it requires huge amounts of time and energy to create a text, formulated from ideas and concepts. And in that time, new technologies are born and die, leaving their imprint on the advances that follow. In the time it took to write this book, the dot-com boom turned into the dot-com bomb, opening new doors in our minds about how we can connect with one another, and new expectations of how the businesses involved in that new economy might profit—and ultimately succeed or fail. Is it possible to sit here today and predict with any certainty that telephony or cable or DBS will truly be the wave of the future? How can it be, when less than a decade ago, the thought of PCs in nearly 50% of U.S. homes was considered far-reaching—far, as in decades ahead?

Entertainment marketers will need to be even more technologically savvy than their audiences, for they will need to create the concepts, molded to the audiences and their technologies, that will carry messages to consumers—consumers who could possibly continue to have more disposable income at an earlier age than ever before, if the current trend is any indication.

And then there is the question of what is entertainment—at one time, it was reading, then it was reading and radio, then reading, radio, and movies, and then the NBA, extreme sports, the WWF, *Myst*, MPEGS—it never stops. We cannot forecast what the next generation will consider entertainment, because it will be built around the precepts of their own experience of the world. But more and more often, it will be marketing professionals who will create those concepts, because entertainment not only takes the audience away from its humdrum world, it sells. It sells through name recognition, sponsorship, and product tie-ins. It is the sneak attack. It is the road to the subconscious, reaching the consumer while the consumer is happy, relaxed, alert, or excited, tying the message directly to the memory of a pleasant experience—regardless if pleasant means adrenaline-produced or serotonin-stimulated.

WHY: THE MORE THINGS CHANGE...

Dare we say it again? Disposable income. Discretionary time. Tired of those yet? If so, good—because they aren't the only reasons the entertainment trend will continue.

To broach this topic, we need to return to the fact that entertainment is the number-two export of the biggest economy in the world, the U.S. Like it or not, our culture has continued to affect that of the world around us over the last century, *primarily* through our entertainment exports.[1] People around the globe have been exposed to the so-called American "way of life," and have developed their expectations of what they will find here through their experience of our entertainment (ask anyone, including fellow U.S. citizens, who have come to New York and tried to rent an apartment like the ones they've viewed on *Friends, Seinfeld,* or *Mad About You*). In many ways, it has also affected how they may view their own cultures, their own opportunities, and their own economies.

The breakthroughs of the western world—the Cola Wars, McDonalds on the Champs Elysee, Starbucks in the Forbidden City—happened as an aftermath of the populations of those countries becoming aware of the products initially through entertainment, then having the opportunity to take part in consuming them, thanks to the corporate desire to build international revenue streams. It is this last factor that will be the predominant force in the growth of entertainment and entertainment marketing. Like it or not, capitalism is winning. Like it or not, capitalists will continue to pursue new frontiers. And, like it or not, those new frontiers will continue to provide fertile pastures for the global media conglomerates that have products that everyone, everywhere seems to want— escape from the right now of reality. After all, what was the first mass activity of Afghanis in Kandahar upon liberation from the Taliban? They went straight to the movie theater—no women allowed, but straight to the movie theater, nonetheless.

Entertainment marketing will continue to be an incredibly intriguing opportunity as we move forward into a new global economy, through a highway formed by new technology. And for marketing—the creation of a product that answers a previously unstated need of a mass audience—will continue to plot the course for corporations. And entertainment is the second greatest opiate of the masses.

---

1.   Please note the use of the word "*culture*," as opposed to "*politics*," "*economy*," "*power balance*," or any other term that might best be covered in and by other sources.

WHERE: WHERE DO YOU WANT IT?

So now we have the who—the global population; the what—the technology; the why—revenue streams. Where? Everywhere. Anywhere. Where do you want it? Gobi Desert? No problem. Rainforests of the Amazon? Be right with you. Polar icecap? Been there, done that. Technology makes it possible; the desire of multinational conglomerates makes it probable; and synergy, mentioned throughout this book, makes it pervasive.

The ability to create content that can be delivered through a multitude of resources—the conversion to digital transmission—will continue to create new avenues for the multiplexing of the message. While it may not (yet) be all forms in all places (because, after all, we do have to wait for the world to catch up in terms of the technology's availability), we will continue to see the message delivered in every format possible. Whether it's product placement on the screen, courtesy of an international movie blockbuster, or a tie-in in Red Square with the Happy Meal toy at McDonald's, or the digital placement of a corporate logo on the backstop of the World Series baseball stadium, or the premise of a novel featuring a brand name thanks to a healthy fee, or the downloading of yesterday's episode of *ER* via your satellite cell phone while you meditate on the Taj Mahal, or the broadcast of MegaHitBand, live from Wembley Stadium, sponsored by MasterCard, entertainment is moving everywhere, all the time.

Marshall McLuhan once stated that "the medium is the massage"[2]; in other words, that the medium was every bit as important—in some cases, more so—as the content itself. In fact, the medium might actually create new ways for the message to be interpreted and interwoven into our lives, our businesses, our sciences, and our culture. At no time in history has this ever seemed more true, thanks to the global reach of technology and the global push of business. Sometimes it seems as though everything we watch, read, download, or listen to exists primarily to be used as a marketing medium.

However—and this is a BIG however—do not expect that this fertile heyday will last. As the world around us becomes more familiar—as the sights we see at home become more and more like the sights we see elsewhere, whether it is the full-size replica of the Eiffel

---

2. McLuhan, Marshall and Quentin Fiore, *The Medium Is the Massage* (New York, NY: Bantam Books, Inc, 1967).

Tower in Las Vegas or the Burger King in an English village—the consumer will begin to react and respond. A need for authenticity will begin to push the audience toward that which is *not* the same, that which delivers a more creative answer to an unstated need. Creativity and innovation will continue to be important—maybe more so. That is, of course, until someone discovers what a hot concept it is, brands it, puts a teenage boy-band spokesperson in front of it, franchises it, and slaps it down on the streets of Amsterdam.

WHEN: GET ONBOARD

The changes that will affect entertainment marketing are happening now, in the technologies, the audiences, the multinational corporations, and the international desire to know more, right now. Marketing professionals who desire to become part of the entertainment phenomenon are challenged to more clearly understand the world around them and the tools with which they can reach the consumer—as they always have been.

For as long as humankind has gathered around the community fire to rub elbows, entertainment has been part of the draw. We thrive on the opportunity to drop our day-to-day troubles, experience new sensations, broaden our interests, and learn something new. Today's entertainment industry offers all of this and more, launching an entertainment marketing revolution from its home base of the U.S. to every corner of the world.

However, the ever-expanding role of technology as both a conduit and a tool of convergence is creating new challenges for the industry. Today's entertainment business far outdistances any geographic boundaries, and must rely on courts outside the U.S. to maintain a healthy marketing environment by upholding IP laws and treaties. Fortunately, the presence of entrepreneurs and governments active in the growth of the global entertainment industry helps maintain the necessary balance.

As marketing professionals take hold of this phenomenon and become part of entertainment's $500 billion worldwide economy, they must keep in mind that what sells entertainment *is* entertainment. From the three-minute mini-movie shown as a trailer, to the driving beat of the radio ad's soundtrack, to the indoor fireworks at a basketball arena, to retail brands promoted through virtual experiences, to Web sites that tie each and every medium together, consumers connect with those messages that most massage their desire to be swept away.

In the tradition of P.T. Barnum, whether it's movies, publishing, broadcast TV, cable, sports, electronic games, travel and hospitality, or experiential branding, in the smallest market or the furthest stretch of the Outback, the marketer's job is to entice the consumers into the tent—give them what they've come for—and give them the tastes, the sights, and the sounds they crave—the experience of entertainment.

INDEX

A

"A" films, 7

A&E, 114

A&R (Artist & Repertoire) professional, 192

ABC, 75
  programming, 66
  soap opera supermarket magazines, 80

ABC Unlimited, 30

Absolute Power, 144

AC Nielsen companies, 26

Academy of Motion Picture Arts and Sciences (AMPAS), 246

Ad-supported transactions, 304

Advance Publications, magazines, 159

Advertising, 13
  budget, 42–43
  cable television, for book genres, 143–44
  magazines, 160
  newspaper, 52–53
  travel/tourism, 254–56

Affiliates, 69

African-American audience, 112–13

Aguilera, Christina, 189

A.I., 57

Airplay, 173–75

All-inclusive concept, 258–60

Allen, Woody, 206

Altavista.com, 96, 161

Alternate travel destinations, 256–67
  all-inclusive resorts, 258–60

Carnival Cruise Line case study, 257–58
  casino resorts, 263–66
  condos, 261–62
  cruises, 256–58
  Indian casinos, 266–67
  theme parks, 262–63
  time shares, 260–61

Amazon.com, 96, 182
  populist reviews at, 139

AMC, 44

American Airlines, 248

American Bookseller's Association (ABA), 132, 136

American Federation of Musicians (AF of M), 171

American Federation of Television and Radio Artists (AFTRA), 171

American Movie Classics, 115

American Society of Composers, Authors and Publishers (ASCAP), 171

American Society of Travel Agents (ASTA), 238, 250

Americana radio, 94–95
  subgroups, 95

Angelika Theater (New York City), 62

Anthony award, 141

Anthony, Marc, 186

AOL, 126, 163

AOL/Time Warner, 126, 298

Arbitron, 26

Arista Records Inc., and MP3.com, 195

Armageddon:
  movie tie-in, 55

soundtrack, 191
Armstrong, Louis, 191
Artisan, 61
Artist's Coalition, 171
Arts & Entertainment (A&E), 87, 104
Aruba, 236
Asia, 314-15
Ask Jeeves, 249
Asymmetric digital subscriber line
  (ADSL) model, 89–90
AT&T, 121, 126
Atlantic City, NJ, 263–66
Atlantic Recordings Corp., 190
  and MP3.com, 195
Audience, 318
Austin, TX, 244–45
  music venues, 245
  Sixth Street, 244
  South by Southwest (SXSW), 245
Author as brand, 143–44
Avengers, The, 51–52
Average book buyer, 134–35
Average quarter-hour ratings (AQH), 92

B

"B" films, 7
B2B marketing, 263
B2C marketing, 263
Back-to-back copying, 307
Backlist sales, books, 138
Backstreet Boys, 197
Baja Beach Club, 274
Baker & Taylor, 147–48
Barnes & Noble, 10, 135, 147, 153
Baywatch, 83
Beck, George, 283
Behind-the-scenes professionals, 48–50
  executive producer, 49
  in-house studio producer, 49–50
  president of marketing, 49
  senior independent producer, 49
  studio president/CEO/chairman, 50
Benchley, Peter, 48
Bergstresser, Charles M., 155
Bertelsmann AG, 149, 298
  BMG and EMI Group, and MP3.com,
    195
BET, *See* Black Entertainment Televi-
  sion (BET):

Big Box retailers, 135
Big Night, The, 34
Billboard:
  audience, 200
  Billboard Bulletin, 203
  brand name, 198
  challenges in the transition to an
    online brand, 201
  company mission, 198
  facts about, 200
  moving the brand online, 201
  pre-Internet branding, 200–201
  strategies/outcome, 201–3
Billboard.com case study, 198–203
Biography, 114
Black Entertainment Television (BET),
  74, 112–13, 120
  Black Star Power, 179
Black urban music, 187
Blackboard Jungle, The, 144
Blair Witch Project, The, 61
Blakely, Mike, 173
Bland, Bobby "Blue," 245
Block, Adam, 191
Blockbuster Video, 118–19, 272
Bloomberg via DIRECTV, 111
BMG Direct, 181
BMG Entertainment, 165, 172, 197
Bobblehead doll, 216–17
Bocelli, Andreas, 188
Bogus request scam, 175
Bonnycastle, Richard, 131–32
Book release, 136
Booker Prize, 141
Books:
  average book buyer, 134–35
  content acquisition, 149–50
  digital content, impact on publish-
    ing, 151
  distribution channels, 135
  electronic publishers, 151
  electronic publishing (e-publishing),
    152–54
  forecasting, 133–34
  genre, 130–31
  genre subcategories, 131
  hardback versus paperback, 132–33
  long discount, 147
  marketing, 136–47

author as marketer, 142
backlist sales, 138
blurbs, 139
book awards, 141
book fairs, 136
book release, 136
branding the genre and the author, 142–44
direct marketing, 137–38
movie tie-ins, 144
reviews, 138–39
sales calls, 136–37
mass-market books, 130
mergers and acquisitions, 148–50
at mid-twentieth century, 148–49
Open e-Book Standard (OEB), 153
print-on-demand (POD) publishers, 151
readers, 133–34
remaindered titles, 148
revenue, 149
romance publishing, 131–32
self-publishing, 151–52
small publishers, 150–51
sub-rights divisions, 149–50
trade books, 130, 134
vanity presses, 152
Borders, 135
Boston Globe Sports Pages, 229
Bowie, David, 177
Box office revenue, 43–45
Bozell, Jacobs, Kenyon & Eckhardt, 243
Bradshaw, Terry, 224
Brand attractions, 284
Brand extension, 114–16
Branding, 16–18
Branson, MO, 242–44
Silver Dollar City, 243
Branson, Richard, 180
Bravo, 104, 114–15
Brazil, 310-11
Bressler, Richard, 193
British music audiences, 197
British Telecom, and asymmetric digital subscriber line (ADSL) model, 89–90
Broadcast Music Inc. (BMI), 171
Broadcast piracy, 307
Broadcast.com, 96
Bronfman, Edgar, 197

Bronson, Harold, 190
Brooks & Dunn, 186
Brooks, Garth, 184, 186, 224
Brosnan, Pierce, 42
Brothers McMullen, The, 116, 118
Brubeck, Dave, 191
Bryant, Kobe, 218
Budget:
advertising, 42–43
marketing, 23
Bull Durham, 207
BUMA, 171–72
Burger, Paul, 189
Burnstein, Cliff, 195
Business Software Alliance, 309-10

C

"C" films, 7
Cable Cox Communications, 121, 126
Cable dishes, 124–25
Cable operators, selling up, 120
Cable Tactical And Marketing (CTAM) conference, 124
Cable television, 101, 107–9
advertising, for book genres, 143–44
basic cable, 102–19
brand extension, 114–16
cable carriage, 119–21
cable cooperatives, 123–24
cable operators, 121–22
cable programmers, 121
conduit, 104
conduit marketing, 121
content, 104
demographics, 74
early cable marketing, 103–4
early marketing efforts, 104–5
independent film, 116–19
industry growth, 107–10
Telecommunications Act of 1996, 107–9
and marketing, 22–23
marketing reach/segmentation, 111–19
adults ages 25-45, 112
children, 111
executive/family with financial interests, 111

males 18-49, 112
minority reach, 112–13
teenagers, 111
women, 111
marketing strategy, 114–15, 121
multiple-system operators (MSOs), 103–4
near-video on-demand (NVOD), 107
new channels, 120
new TV technology, 125–27
convergence, 126
digital TV, 126–27
interactive television, 126
pay-per-view (PPV), 106–7
premium cable channels, 105–6
subscribers, 120
search for, 122–24
universal audience, 115–16
viewer subscriptions, 102
Cable Television Advertising Bureau, 102
Cablevision, 103, 121, 126
Caldecott Medal, 141
Calder, Frank, 214
Camcording, 306
Camp, Walter, 212
Canada, 308-9
Canadian Broadcasting Corporation (CBC), 308
Canal+, 198
Capital Cities/ABC, 158, 159
Capitol Records Inc., and MP3.com, 195
Carnival Cruise Line case study, 257–58
Carreras, Jose, 187
Carroll, Ed, 115
Carter, Vince, 218
Cartoon Network, 119
Caruso, Enrico, 188
Case, Steve, 109–10
Casino resorts, 263–66
comping, 264
entertainment marketing strategy, 264
new customers, attracting, 264
Cayman Islands, 255
CBS, 75, 159
early programming, 66

programming, 66–67
promotions, 80
tie-in programs, 80
CBS SportsLine, 229
CBS/Viacom, 14–15. 298
CD Radio, 98
CDNow.com, 182
CDs, 172, 182–83, 301
Cegetel, 198
Celebrity Cruise Line, 255
Cereal City USA case study, 284–88
Charlotte Church case study, 188–89
Cheers, 78–79
Chermayeff, Ivan, 15
Chicken Soup for the Soul, 141
Children's entertainment centers (FECs), 271–72
China, 314-15
Chinese music audiences, 196
Christian/gospel music, 189–90
Chuck E. Cheese, 272
Cider House Rules, The (Irving), 138
Cinemax, 105
Circle Awards, 141
Circle City, Indianapolis, 278
Circulation:
magazines, 160
newspapers, 156
Circumvention devices, 306
Citizen Kane, 155
CityWalk, 274
Clark, Helen, 196
Clark, Mary Higgins, 154
Clickradio.com, 193
Clinton, William ("Bill") Jefferson, 179
Cloning programs/formats, 79
Club Med, 258–59
CNBC, 143
CNN, 104, 119
CNNfn, 111, 119
Coca-Cola, 26
CocoWalk, 274
Collins, Joseph, 109
Collins, Ltd., 14
Columbia House, 181
Columbia Records division, Sony, 185
Comanche Dawn, 173

Comcast, 103, 126
Community Antenna Television (CATV)., 103
Complete Baseball (Microsoft), 230
Condos, 261–62
Conduit, 2, 7–11
    defined, 2
    sports, 207
Conley, John, 151
Consumption, 2, 11–12
    defined, 2
    sports, 207
Content, 2–7
    copyright, 5–6
    defined, 2
    perishability of product, 3
    production, 6–7
    sports, 207
    talent, 3
    technology, 3
Continental Airlines, 248
Contracts, 5–6
Convergence, 2, 12–13, 126
    defined, 2
    sports, 207
Copyright, 5–6, 300
Cornell University Hotel Management School, 255
Cosby Show, The, 82, 84
Costner, Kevin, 46
Country Club Plaza (Kansas City), 8
Country Music Association (CMA), 186, 241
Country Music Television's (CMT's) Great American Country, 179
Cox Communications, 103
Cox Enterprises, 158, 160
Cox, James M., 155
Craig, George, 14–15
Creative idea, 3, 4–5
    content, 3, 4–5
Creative Labs Nomad, 194
Crispo, Elvis, 187
Cross-marketing, electronic games, 164–65
Cross-promotion, music, 186
Crowsnest Book, 154
Cruise Lines International Association (CLIA), 250, 256

Cruise, Tom, 144, 191
Cruises, 256–58
Crystal, Billy, 56
CTV (Canada), 308
Culinary Institute of America (CIA), 255

D

"D" films, 7
Dailey, Janet, 143
Daley, Bob, 39
Dance, Bill, 224–25
Dave and Buster's, 273
Davidson, John, 242
Davis, Miles, 191
DDBWorldwide, 29
De Young, Charles and Michael, 155
Deal-making, 33–34
Decision making:
    categories of decisions, 24
    large decisions, 25
    no decision at all, 25
    small decisions, 24
Delano hotel, Miami, 250
Delta Airlines, 248
Demographics, 73–74
    cable television, 74
    network television, 73–74
    Nielsen ratings, 73–74
Dentsu, 298
Denver Broncos, 217
Denver, John, 188
Design Development stage, 292
Designated Market Area (DMA), defined, 72
DeVito, Danny, 144
Diamond Multimedia Rio 500, 194
Digital content, impact on publishing, 151
Digital subscriber lines (DSL), 163
Digital technology, 301
Digital TV, 126–27
Digitized distribution, 303–4
Diller, Barry, 36–37, 39
Dion, Celine, 192
Direct broadcast satellite (DBS), 101
    viewer subscriptions, 102
Direct marketing, books, 137–38
Direct marketing catalogs, 11
DIRECTV, 125

Discounters, music, 180
Discovery Channel, 87
Discovery Store, 278
Discovery Zone, 272
Disney, 4, 15–16, 29, 30, 37–38, 120, 150, 220–21, 272–73
Disney Channel, 105
Disney theme park empire, 262–63
DisneyQuest, 273
Disney's Oceaneer Adventure, 258
Distribution channels:
  books, 135
  electronic games, 166
Dixie Chick case study, 184–85
Dollywood, 263
Domestic Box Office (DBO), 43
Domingo, Placido, 187–88
Dore, Kathy, 115
Doubleday, 148
Dow, Charles H., 155
Dow Jones & Co., 158
Downloadable media, 306
Doyle Dane & Bernbach (DDB), 255
Drew Carey Show, The, 88–90
DVDs, 127, 301

E

E!, 83
E-Toys, 11
Eastern Airlines, 248
Eastwood, Clint, 144
"Echo Baby Boomers," 249
Edgar award, 141
EDI-Neilsen, 26
Eisner, Michael, 4, 15, 37–40, 109
El Norte, 116
Electron Press, 153–54
Electronic Arts, Inc., 163
Electronic games, 162–66
  cross-marketing, 164–65
  GameCube, 163
  and marketing, 23
  marketing hurdles, 165
  new channels of distribution, 166
  Nintendo, 163
  revenue, 162
  Sony Playstation2, 163
  Tandy games, 163
  targeting the market, 164

Electronic publishers, 151
Electronic publishing (e-publishing), 152–54
EMI, 172
Eminem, 197
Encore, 105
English Patient, The, 54
Entertainment:
  four C's of, 2–13
    conduit, 2, 7–11
    consumption, 2, 11–12
    content, 2–7
    convergence, 2, 12–13
Entertainment agencies:
  outside, role of, 28–30
Entertainment hierarchy, three P's of, 19–40
Entertainment industry:
  early history of, 21–22
  and marketing, 22–23
Entertainment marketing:
  basics of, 1–18
  books, 136–47
  cable television, 101, 107–9
  content, 2-7, 207
  demographics, 73-74
  electronic games, 162–66
  experiential branding, 279–94
  extreme sports, 223–24, 319
  future of, 317–23
  going global, 298
  independent films, 58–63
  Internet radio, 96–97
  location-based entertainment (LBE), 270–79
  major league sports, 208–15
  music, 182–86
  network television, 65–81
  newspapers, 156–58
  public broadcasting, 85–87
  radio, 90–99, 173–75
  sports, 215–21
  travel/tourism, 234–56
Entertainment marketing team:
  complex structure of, 27
  outside agency, role of, 28–30
  tailoring, 26–30
  titles, 27
"Entertainment retail," 278

Entertainment Tonight, 83
Entrepreneur magazine, 270–79
ER, 78
Erin Brockovich, 197
ESPN, 74, 112, 115, 143, 218, 220–21
ESPN International, 218
ESPN Zone, 15–16
ESPN.com, 229–30
Estefan, Gloria, 187
Europe, 311
European Fishing Tackle Trade Association (EFTTA), 225
Evening at the Pops, 86
Evergreen products, 48
E.W. Scripps newspaper group, 158
"Exchange privilege," time shares, 260–61
Executive producer, 49
Expedia, 248
Experiential branding, 279–94
    brand message, sustaining, 281–82
    brand vs. experience, 283–84
    bringing the brand to life, 289–90
    defined, 282
    developing and maintaining a brand, 280–83
    economics of experience, 288–89
    project development stages, 291–94
        design process, 292–93
        implementation process, 293
        master plan and program, 292
        pre-, grand, and post-opening, 293
Extreme sports, 223–24, 319
    defined, 223
    and risk, 223–24

F

Fall launching season, network television, 80
Family entertainment centers (FECs), 271–72
Fashion industry, and entertainment product, 16
Fast food industry, and sponsorship, 16–17
Fat Tuesday, 274
Fatbrain, 154
Federal Communications Commission (FCC), 66

Federal Trade Commission (FTC), 110
Ferron, Carrie, 132–33
Field of Dreams, 207
Final Concept Design, 292
First-run programs, 83
Fishing, 224–25
Fleming, Ian, 143
Fly album (Dixie Chicks), 185
Food Network, 143
Foos, Richard, 190
FooteCone&Belding, 255
Ford, Harrison, 54, 144
Forecasting, books, 133–34
Forum Shops, 277–78
Four C's of entertainment, 2–13
Four Seasons, 261–62
Four Weddings and a Funeral, 116
Fox Entertainment Group, 67, 75, 221
    major studio production volume, cuts in, 60
Fox Family, 115
Fox, Michael J., 82
Fox News, 120
Foxwood Resort and Casino (Ledyard, CT), 266
Friends, 78, 320
Full Monty, The, 58, 116, 118
FutureSell: Radio's Niche Marketing Revolution (Herweg/Herweg), 94

G

GameCube, 163
Gannett Co., 159
Gannett, Frank E., 155, 157
Gannett newspaper group, 156–58
Garnett, Kevin, 218
Gavin magazine, 95
Gaylord Digital, 185
Gaylord Entertainment, 186, 241
Geffen, David, 39
Gelberg, Nadine, 219
GEMA, 171–72
General Cinemas, 44, 62
General Electric, 159
General Electric/NBC, 159
Genre, 130–31
    as brand, 142–43
    subcategories, 131
Gent, Chris, 198

George Strait Country Music Festival, 185

German music audiences, 196

Germany, 311

Get Music, 197

Gilmore, James, 284

Glassbook, 154

Global entertainment revolution, 298

Global marketing environment, stabilizing, 300–301

Global music market, 195–98
 Vivendi Universal, 197–98

Global Television (Canada), 308

Globo Cabo (Brazil), 310

Gnutella, 165

Goldberg, Whoopi, 56

Golden Eagle Romances, 131

Golden Eye, 42–43

Google, 161, 249

Gorgeous George, 222

Gospel Music Association (GMA), 190

Gottlieb, Steve, 190

Grafton, Sue, 143

Grand Ol' Opry, 240

Grand Opening stage, 293

Grass-roots efforts of self-promotion, 34

Grey Advertising, 29, 255

Griffith, Melanie, 206

Grisham, John, 133, 135, 144

Grossman, Lawrence, 86

Grupo Televisa SA de CV (Televisa), 309

GSD&M, 185

Gulf & Western, 14

H

Halo effect, 78–79

Hanks, Tom, 46, 57

Hard goods piracy, 306

Hardback versus paperback, 132–33

Harlequin Romances, 131–32, 144

Harper & Row, 148, 149

HarperCollins Publishers, 14–15

Harrah's Casinos, 266

Hatch, Orrin, 109–10

Havas, 298

HBO, 105, 119, 124–25

HDTV, 87–88

He Touched Me: The Gospel Music of Elvis Presley, 190

Hearst Castle, 236

Hearst Corporation, 159

Hearst newspaper group, 156, 158

Hearst, William Randolph, 155

Hedonism chain, 260

Hercules, 83

Hero album (Michael Jackson), 185

Herweg, Ashley Page, 94

Herweg, Godfrey W., 94

Herzog, Brad, 140

Hewlett-Packard Jornada 540, 194

High concept, 46–48
 no-high-concept films vs., 48

Hispanic segment, 112–13

History Channel, 87, 114

Hit Men: Power Brokers & Fast Money Inside the Music Business (Dannen), 174

HMV, 181

Holiday, Billy, 191

Hollywood/Los Angeles, 245–46
 Hollywood and Highland development project, 246
 Mann's Chinese Theater, 245

Hoop Dreams, 116

Horizontal cross-plugs, 77

Household rating, defined, 73

Households using television (HUT), 75
 defined, 73

Houston, Jimmy, 224

Houston, Whitney, 192

Howl at the Moon Saloon, 274

I

IDs, 77

IFC Films, 119

IFC Productions, 119

Iger, Robert, 109–10

Iglesia, Enrique, 187

Il Postino, 118

Imprints, and marketing, 23

Imus, Don, 140

In-flight movies, 58

In-house studio producer, 49–50

Incentive Travel & Meeting Executives Show (IT&ME), 250

InCourt, 119

Independent Film Channel (IFC), 105–6, 117, 119

Independent films, 58–63
    and cable television, 116–19
    independent screens, 62
    and Internet, 61–62
    marketing, 59–61
    movie fans, 62–63
    movie posters, 62
    and movie tie-ins, 61
    and word of mouth, 61
Independents, 69, 172
India, 313-14
Indian casinos, 266–67
Indian Gaming Regulatory Act, 266
Ingrams wholesalers, 147–48
Inside Stuff, 218
Intellectual property (IP), 5–6, 300
    music, 170–71
International Olympic Committee
    (IOC), 226–27
Interactive television, 126
Interactive Week, 161
International Association of Amusement
    Parks and Attractions (IAAPA), 263
International Federation of the Phono-
    graphic Industry, 319
International Intellectual Property Alli-
ance (IIPA), 309
International Joint Music Venture
    (IMJV), 171
Internet, 57
    and the entertainment industry, 301
    and independent films, 61–62
    and movie marketing, 57
    and the travel/tourism, 248
    wannasee, 57
Internet piracy, 306
Internet radio, 96–97
    advantages of, 96
    driving force in, 96–97
    marketing, 97
Internet TV, 127
Interpublic Group, 298
Intra-industry marketing, 77–78
Irving, John, 138
Israel, 312-13
    Israel Broadcasting Authority Law,
    312
iUniverse, 153

J

Jackson, Michael, 185
Jagger, Mick, 177
Jamaica, 255
Japan, 314
Japan Broadcasting Corporation (NHK),
    314
Japanese music labels, 196
Jaws/Jaws2, 48
Jeopardy, 78
".Jewel boxes," 183
Jillian's, 273
John, Elton, 197
Johnson, Robert, 112–13, 186
Jones, Edward D., 155
Jones, George, 155, 164
Journal of Vacation Marketing (JVM),
    238–39
Journal of Travel Research, 238

K

Katzenberg, Jeffrey, 38, 40
Kellogg's Cereal City USA, 284–88
Kerbango.com, 96
Key demographics, 73–74
KFAN, 95
KHYI, 95
King, Stephen, 133, 135, 143, 154
Kirch Holdings (Germany), 311
Kiss tour case study, 176–78
Knight-Ridder, 158, 160
Koontz, Dean, 143
Koplovitz, Kay, 115
KPIG, 95

L

La Scala (Milan), 188
Lack, John, 178
Ladyman, George H. Jr., 283–84
LaFave, Jimmy, 245
L'Amour, Louis, 143
Large decisions, 25
Las Vegas, NV, 236, 263–66
Latin music, 186–87
Latin Music Awards, 187
Laydown, 135
Le Carre, John, 143

Leaders, 31–32
Learning Channel, 87
Lebowitz, Steve, 191
Lee, Spike, 206
Legacy division (Sony Entertainment/
  Columbia Music), 191
Leonard, Elmore, 143
Lerner, John, 198
Letterman, David, 56
Levin, Gerald, 38–39, 109
Levine, James, 188
Levy, Alan, 182
Lewis, Ed "Strangler," 222
Liberate Technologies, 126
Liberty Records, 180
Licensing, 16–18
Licensing programming, 84
Life is Beautiful, 57
Lifetime, 74, 143
Lillith Fair, 185
Lippman, Laura, 132–33
Liquor industry, and sponsorship, 16–17
Listen.com, 193
Live music, 175–79
  Kiss tour case study, 176–78
  megatours, 176–78
Local television ratings, 26
Local television stations:
  affiliates, 69
  independents, 69–70
  local programming, 70–71
  owned and operated (O&O), 68–69
Location-based entertainment (LBE),
  270–79
  Cereal City USA case study, 284–88
  decline of, 278–79
  entertainment in malls, 277–78
  Sony Metreon case study, 274–76
Loews Cineplex Entertainment, 62
Long discount, 147
Los Angeles Times' book review, 139
Los Angeles Times, on the Internet, 158
Lost in Space, movie tie-in, 55
Lowenstein, Douglas, 162
Ludlum, John, 143
Lukk, Tiiu, 42
Luxor, Las Vegas, 265

M

Macavity, 141
Mad About You, 320
Madonna, 33
Magazines:
  advertising, 160
  circulation, 160
  and marketing, 22
  number published, 159–60
  "zines," 161–62
Major League Baseball (MLB), 208–10
  All-Star Game, 209–10
  composition of, 209
  first Commissioner, 208
  history of, 208
  strikes, 220
  ticket sales/prices, 210
Major league sports, 208–15
  Major League Baseball (MLB), 208–10
  National Basketball Association
    (NBA), 210–11, 319
  National Football League (NFL), 212–
    13
  National Hockey League (NHL), 214–
    15
  Women's National Basketball Associa-
    tion (WNBA), 211–12
Major studio production volume, cuts in,
  60
Mall entertainment, 277–78
  Forum Shops, 277–78
Marketing:
  books, 136–47
    author as marketer, 142
    backlist sales, 138
    blurbs, 139
    book awards, 141
    book fairs, 136
    book release, 136
    branding the genre and the author,
      142–44
    direct marketing, 137–38
    movie tie-ins, 144
    radio interviews, 140–41
    reviews, 138–39
    sales calls, 136–37
    TV talk-show circuit, 139–40
  challenge of change, 299

defined, 13
and entertainment industry, 22–23
global marketing environment, stabilizing, 300–301
music, 182–86
    CDs, 182–83
    cross-promotion, 186
    Dixie Chick case study, 184–85
    personalities, 184
sports, 215–21
    backlash, 219–20
    international sports presentations, 218–19
    Olympics, 226–27
    revenue, 215–17
    sports-entertainment synergy, 220–21
    television rights, 215
    ticket sales, 215
    Woods, Tiger, 225–26
travel/tourism, 234–56
    customer satisfaction promise, 237
    integration, 236–37
    matching experience with expectation, 234–35
    positioning, 235–36
    strategy, 239–40
    travel research, 238–39
Marketing manager, radio station, 91
Marketing plan, 59
Mario Brothers. 318
Marriott, Bill Jr., 253
Marriott, J. Willard and Alice S., 253
Martha Stewart Living Show, The, 84
Martin, Ricky, 184, 186
Martin, Rolland, 224
Martin, Steve, 56
MasAskill, Chris, 154
M*A*S*H, 78–79, 115
Mass-market books, 130
McBain, Ed, 144
McCann Erickson, 29
McClatchy, James, 155
McDonald's Corporation, 272
McGraw Hill, 148
McGraw, Tim, 185
McGwire, Mark, 209
MCI sports arena (Washington, D.C.),
278
McLuhan, Marshall, 321
McMurty, Larry, 143
Megaplexing, 8–9
Megastore market, music, 180–81
Megatours, 176–78
Mehta, Zubin, 188
Merchandising, 16–18
Meredith Corporation, 159
Mergers and acquisitions, books, 148–50
Messier, Jean-Marie, 197
Meta-tags, 97
Metallica, 194–95
Metro area, defined, 73
Metro-Cable Marketing Co-Op, 123
Metropolitan Opera House (NYC), 188
Mexico, 309-10
MGA Universal, 272
Middle East, 312-14
MIFED, 77
Mighty Ducks, The, 207, 221
Mightywords.com, 154
Miller, Paul, 157
Minnesota Timberwolves, 218
MIPCOM, 77
Mira Romance, 131
Miramax, 29, 54, 57
Mission Impossible soundtrack, 191
Mod Squad, The , movie tie-in, 55
Moguls, 34–40
    Diller, Barry, 36–37
    Eisner, Michael, 37–38
    Levin, Gerald, 38–39
    Ovitz, Michael, 39–40
Motion Picture Association of America (MPA), 304
Motion Picture Association of America (MPAA), 304
Motion Picture Experts Group (MPEG) files, 193, 318-19
Motorola's DCT-5000, 126
Movers and shakers, 30–35
    deal-making, 33–34
    leaders, 31–32
    moguls, 34–40
Movie fans, independent films, 62–63
Movie marketing, 41–64
    behind-the-scenes professionals, 48–50

executive producer, 49
in-house studio producer, 49–50
president of marketing, 49
senior independent producer, 49
studio president/CEO/chairman,
50
independent films, 58–63
risk, 45–50
high concept, 46–48
wannasee:
creating, 50–58
in-flight movies, 58
Internet, 57
movie tie-ins, 55
movie trailers, 53–54
Moviefone, 56
newspaper advertising, 52–53
Oscars, 56–57
sneak previews, 51–52
television commercials, 52
test screenings, 51
Movie performance, accurate prediction
of, 48
Movie posters, independent films, 62
Movie tie-ins, 55
and independent films, 61
Movie trailers, 53–54, 77
Moviefone, 56
MP3, 97, 179, 193–94
MP3.com, 193
Instant Listening Service, 195
MSN TV, 88–90
MSNBC, 111
MTV, 74, 178–79, 184
mtvi (mtv.com), 179
Mulan movie tie-in, 55
Multi-attraction-driven destinations,
FECs as, 271–72
Multi-channel multipoint distribution
service (MMDS), 101
Munsey, Frank, 155
Murder, She Wrote, 115
Murdoch, Rupert, 14–15, 36–37, 149,
311
Music, 169–204
A&R (Artist & Repertoire) profes-
sional, 170
airplay, 173–75
Billboard.com case study, 198–203

bogus request scam, 175
content, 170–72
development process, 170
global music market, 195–98
Vivendi Universal, 197–98
intellectual property (IP), 170–72
labels, 172–73
independents, 172
private labels, 173
live music, 175–79
Kiss tour case study, 176–78
megatours, 176–78
marketing, 182–86
CDs, 182–83
cross-promotion, 186
Dixie Chick case study, 184–85
personalities, 184
MTV, 178–79
music videos, 178–79
niches, 186–92
black urban music, 187
Charlotte Church case study, 188–
89
Christian/gospel music, 189–90
Latin music, 186–87
opera, 187–88
repackaging/compilations, 190–91
soundtracks, 191–92
payola, 174
piracy, 194–95
retail distribution, 179–82
discounters, 180
megastore market, 180–81
music clubs, 180–81
revenue, 180
rights, 170–72
technology trends, 192–95
Music Choice, 97
Music clubs, 180–81
Music Managers Forum, 171
Music videos, 178–79
MusicCountry.com, 185
Musicland, 180
Myst, 319

N

Naismith, Dr. James, 210
Napster, 97, 165, 194–95
NARM (National Association of Record-

ing Manufacturers), 172
NASCAR, 222–23
Nashville Cable Network, 186
Nashville Network (TNN), 241
Nashville, TN, 240–41
Nassau, the Bahamas, 237
National Academy of Recording Arts and
Sciences (NARAS), 171
National Association of Television Pro-
gramming Executives (NATPE), 77
National Basketball Association (NBA),
210–11, 319
history of, 210–11
ticket prices, 211
National Basketball Development
League (NBDL), 211
National Book Award, 141
National Book Critics Award, 141
National Enquirer, 157
National Football League (NFL), 207,
212–13
attendance, 213
franchises, 213
history of, 212–13
original teams, 212
player conduct, 213
National Geographic Specials, 86
National Hockey League (NHL), 214–15
attendance, 215
decline of Canadian teams, 215
history of, 214–15
teams, 215
National Record Mart, 180
Natural, The, 207
Navy Pier and Marina City-area developments (Chicago), 278
NBC, 75
early programming, 66
movie company, lack of, 80
programming, 66–68
netLibrary, 154
Network self-promotion, 75–76
Network television, 65–81
ABC, programming, 66
CBS:
early programming, 66
programming, 66–67
cloning programs/formats, 79
demographics, 73–74

fall launching season, 80
local television stations, 68–71
affiliates, 69
independents, 69–70
local programming, 70–71
owned and operated (O&O), 68–
69
as mass-reach medium, 66
movie-based strategies, 80–81
NBC:
early programming, 66
movie company, lack of, 80
programming, 66–68
newer networks, 67–68
promotion and marketing, 75–81
horizontal cross-plugs, 77
intra-industry marketing, 77–78
network self-promotion, 75–76
on-air self-promotion, 76–77
relationship marketing and the
halo effect, 78–79
standard cross-plugs, 77
vertical cross-plugs, 77
ratings, 26
TV ratings, 71–75
Neuharth, Al, 157
New TV technology:
convergence, 126
digital TV, 126–27
interactive television, 126
New York, 246–47
New York Times, 157
New York Times' book review, 138–39
New York Times Co., 158, 159
New Zealand music audiences, 196
Newberry Medal, 141
NewsCorp., 14, 36, 298, 311
magazines, 159
Newspaper advertising, 52–53
Newspapers:
competitive environment, changing,
156–57
on the Internet, 158
media moguls, 155
newspaper groups, 157–58
revenue, 156
Newton, Wayne, 242
Niches:
music, 186–92

black urban music, 187
Charlotte Church case study, 188–89
Christian/gospel music, 189–90
Latin music, 186–87
opera, 187–88
repackaging/compilations, 190–91
soundtracks, 191–92
Nichols, J. C., 8
Nicholson, Jack, 206
Nielsen, Arthur C. Sr., 71
Nielsen ratings, 71–75
Designated Market Area (DMA), 72
household rating, 73
households using television (HUT), 73
how they work, 71–72
key demographics, 73–74
key terms, 72–73
metro area, 73
rating, 73
share, 73
sweeps, 72
time slots, 74–75
Nihon Hosokyokai, 314
Niketown, 282
Nintendo, 163
Nobel Prize in Literature, 141
Nokia Corp., 164
Non-commercially driven broadcasting, 85–87
public broadcasting, 85–87
Non-league sports, 221–27
extreme sports, 223–24, 319
NASCAR, 222–23
not-so-extreme sports, 223–24
professional wrestling, 221–22
Non-traditional revenue sources (NRS), 91
North America, 308-10
Not-so-extreme sports, 223–24
Nova, 86
N'Sync, 184, 197
NTT DoCoMo's iMode, 164

O

Off-net programs, 82
Olympics, 226–27
Omnicom, 298

On-air self-promotion, 76–77
On-demand video sysems, 58
1-800-OKCable, 123–24
Ontario Mills, 278
Open e-Book Standard (OEB), 153
Open TV, 126
Opera, 187–88
Oprah, 83
Optical disc piracy, 305
Oracle, 126
OradNet Inc., 228
Orbitz, 248
Orlando, Tony, 242
Oscars, 56–57
Otis, Harrison Gray, 155
Outside agency, role of, 28–30
Ovitz, Michael, 38, 39–40
Owned and operated (O&O) stations, 70–71
Ozark Airlines, 248

P

Padden, Preston, 110
Pan Am, 248
Paper Lion, The, 207
Parallel importation, 307
Paramount Communications, 14, 149
Paramount Parks, 263
Parker, Hank, 224
Parsons, Richard, 109, 110
Parton, Dolly, 192
Pavarotti, Luciano, 187
Pax, 68
Payola, 174
PC Magazine, 161
Peanut Press, 154
Pelican Brief, 144
PEN/Faulkner Award, 141
Penzler, Otto, 143
People/power/players, 19–40
decision making, 23–26
categories of decisions, 24
large decisions, 25
no decision at all, 25
and research, 25–26
small decisions, 24
entertainment industry
early history of, 21–22
and marketing, 22–23

entertainment marketing team, tailoring, 26–30
molding the message, 20–23
movers and shakers, 30–35
deal-making, 33–34
leaders, 31–32
moguls, 34–35
and research, 25–26
People's Express, 248
Perfect Storm, The, 54
Performing Rights Society (PRS), 172
Perishability of product, 3
Personalities, marketing, 184
Philadelphia, PA, 236
Pine, B. Joseph, 284
Piracy, 304–7
music, 194–95
types of, 305–7
back-to-back copying, 307
broadcast piracy, 307
camcording, 306
circumvention devices, 306
downloadable media, 306
hard goods piracy, 306
Internet piracy, 306
optical disc piracy, 305
parallel importation, 307
screeners, 307
signal theft, 307
streaming media piracy, 306
theatrical print theft, 307
unauthorized public performances, 307
videocassette piracy, 306
Pittman, Bob, 163
Pittman, Robert, 178
Playboy Channel, 106
Polygram, 311
Populist reviews, 139
Postman, The, 58
Power & Light District (Kansas City), 278
PPB (printing, paper, binding), 133
Pre-Opening stage, 293
Preliminary Concept Design, 292
Premier entertainment cities, 245–47
Hollywood/Los Angeles, 245–46
New York, 246–47
Premium cable channels, 105–6

President of marketing, 49
Presley, Elvis, 190
Price, Toni, 245
Pride, Charlie, 242
Primestar, 125
Print-on-demand (POD) publishers, 151
Prints and advertising (P&A) budget, 41–42
Private labels, 173
Product diversification, 26
Product tie-ins, 55
Production and Construction Documents stage, 292–93
Production and Construction stage, 293
Production, and content, 6–7
Professional wrestling, 221–22
Project Development Guidelines for the Themed Entertainment Industry, 291
Promotion director, radio station, 91
Promotions, 77
CBS, 80
radio, 92
Public broadcasting, 85–87
branding, 86–87
maintaining/expanding viewership, 87
pop-ups, 87
signaling value, 86
Public relations, 13
Public service announcements (PSAs), 76
Publicis, 298
Publicists, 142
Publishing industry, 129–67
books, 130–54
average book buyer, 134–35
character as brand, 146–47
content acquisition, 149–50
digital content, impact on publishing, 151
distribution channels, 135
electronic publishers, 151
electronic publishing (e-publishing), 152–54
forecasting, 133–34
genre, 130–31
genre subcategories, 131
hardback versus paperback, 132–33

Harry Potter, 146–47
long discount, 147
marketing, 136–47
mass-market books, 130
mergers and acquisitions, 148–50
at mid-twentieth century, 148–49
Open e-Book Standard (OEB), 153
print-on-demand (POD) publishers, 151
readers, 133–34
remaindered titles, 148
revenue, 149
romance publishing, 131–32
self-publishing, 151–52
small publishers, 150–51
sub-rights divisions, 149–50
trade books, 130, 134, 147–48
vanity presses, 152
changing publishing environment, 147–54
electronic games, 162–66
cross-marketing, 164–65
GameCube, 163
marketing hurdles, 165
new channels of distribution, 166
new game frontiers, 163
Nintendo, 163
revenue, 162
Sony Playstation2, 163
Tandy games, 163
targeting the market, 164
magazines, 159–62
advertising, 160
circulation, 160
number published, 159–60
"zines," 161–62
and marketing, 23
newspapers, 155–59
above-the-fold section, 156
competitive environment, changing, 156–57
on the Internet, 158
media moguls, 155
newspaper groups, 157–58
revenue, 156
Pulitzer, Joseph, 155
Pullium, Eugene C., 155
Pulp Fiction, 118

R

Rabbani, Ethisham, 165
Radio, 90–98, 91–99, 173–75
airplay, 173–75
Americana radio, 94–95
audio diversity, 92–93
commercial radio stations in America, by format (chart), 93
Internet radio, 96–97
advantages of, 96
driving force in, 96–97
marketing, 97
and marketing, 23
promotions, 92
radio marketing basics, 91–95
revenue, 174
satellite radio, 98
target niches, identifying, 94
on TV, 97
Rainmaker, The, 144
Random House, 148, 153
Rating, defined, 73
Raymond, Henry J., 155
Readers, 133–34
Reader's Digest Association, magazines, 159
Real.com, 193
Recording Industry Association of America (RIAA), 171
Redford, Robert, 46, 116–17
Reed Elsevier, magazines, 159
Reed, Rex, 34
Regal Cinemas, 9
Rehabilitation/Expansion stage, 293
Relationship marketing:
travel/tourism, 249–54
courting the consumer, 251
frequent flier programs, 252
hotel "brands," 252–53
hotel reward programs, 252
intra-industry trade shows and associations, 250–51
Marriott International case study, 253–54
Relationship marketing and the halo effect, 78–79
Remaindered titles, 148
Remember the Titans, 207

Reno, 265
Renshaw, Simon, 184
Rental transactions, 304
Repackaging/compilations, music, 190–91
Republic Airlines, 248
Retail distribution:
    music, 179–82
        discounters, 180
        megastore market, 180–81
        music clubs, 180–81
        revenue, 180
Retail distribution of films, 7–11
Revenue:
    electronic games, 162
    music, 180
    radio, 174
    sports, 215–17
Reviews, books, 138–39
Rhino Records, 172, 190–91
Riding the Bullet (King), 154
Rights, music, 170–72
Risk, high concept, 46–48
Ritz-Carlton, 234, 261–62
Roberts, Julia, 46, 144
Roberts, Nora, 143
Rocket eBook, 154
Rogers, Kenny, 192, 242
Romance Channel, 143
Romance publishing, 131–32, 142
Roseanne, 82
Ross, Steve, 38, 39
Royal Philips Electronics, 182–83
Royalton Hotel, New York, 250
R.R. Donnelley & Sons, 151
Rudy, 207
Rush, Geoffrey, 118
Ryan, Meg, 57
Ryman Auditorium, 239

S

Saatchi & Saatchi, 29
SACEM, 171–72
Sacramento Kings, 218
Sales transactions, 303
Sam Goody, 180
San Luis Obispo, CA, 236
Sandals, 259–60
Satellite radio, 98

Scheider, Roy, 48
Schematic Design, 292
Schlesinger, Dr. Laura, 140
Schroders, 35
SciFi Channel, 116
Scour exchange, 193
Screeners, 307
Scripps, Edward W., 155
SDTV, 127
Seagram Company, Ltd., 197–98
Search engines, 161–62
Secret History, The, 133
Sega, 272
SegaNet, 163
SegaofAmerica, 163
Seinfeld, 78–79, 320
Self-publishing, 151–52
Self-Publishing Magazine, 152
Selig, Bud, 209
Selling programming, 84
Semel, Richard, 39
Senior independent producer, 49
Sex, Lies, and Videotape, 59, 116
Shalit, Jonathan, 189
Shamus, 141
Shank, Mathew D., 217
Share, defined, 73
Share of audience research system, 26
Sheen, Charlie, 82
Sheinberg, Sid, 39
Shine, 116, 118
Shooting Gallery, The, 62
Shopping centers, 8
Show Installation stage, 293
Showtime, 105, 125
Signal theft, 307
Silhouette Romances, 131–32, 144–45
    distribution, 144–45
    licensing agreements, 145
    marketing strategy, 144–45
    retail sales, 145
    Silhouette Desire, 145
    Silhouette First Love, 145
    Silhouette Intimate Moments, 145
    Special Edition, 145
Silver Dollar City, 243, 263
Simon & Schuster, 14, 144, 148, 150, 154, 164–65
Sinatra, Frank, 191

Six Flags, 263
SKG DreamWorks, 272–73
Sleepless in Seattle, 57
   soundtrack, 191
Small decisions, 24
Small publishers, 150–51
Small Publishers Association of North
   America (SPAN), 150
Smirnoff, Yakov, 242
Smith, Jeff, 191
Smith, Liz, 34
Smithsonian Magazine, 161
Sneak previews, 51–52
Snyder, Richard, 144
Soap opera supermarket magazines, 80
Society of Incentive & Travel Executives
   (SITE), 250
Soderbergh, Steven, 116
Soft drink beverage industry, and spon-
   sorship, 16–17
Softbook Press, 154
Sony, 272, 298, 311
Sony Loews, 44
Sony Metreon case study, 274–76
Sony Music Entertainment, 165, 172,
   186
   and MP3.com, 195
Sony Playstation2, 163
Sosa, Sammy, 209
Soundtracks, 191–92
South America, 310–11
Spears, Britney, 189, 197
Spec's Music, 180
Spelling Entertainment, 311
Spezializtz, 196
Spice, 106
Spielberg, Steven, 39, 46, 48, 57, 206
Spin City, 82
Sponsorship, 16–18
Sportainment, 206–7
Sports, 205–32
   conduit, 207
   consumption, 207
   content, 207
   convergence, 207
   fishing, 224–25
   Major League Baseball (MLB), strikes,
      220
   major league sports, 208–15

Major League Baseball (MLB),
   208–10
National Basketball Association
   (NBA), 210–11
National Football League (NFL),
   212–13
National Hockey League (NHL),
   214–15
Women's National Basketball Association (WNBA), 211–12
marketing, 215–21
   backlash, 219–20
   international sports presenta-
      tions, 218–19
   Olympics, 226–27
   revenue, 215–16
   sports-entertainment synergy,
      220–21
   television rights, 215
   ticket sales, 215
   Woods, Tiger, 225–26
non-league sports, 221–27
   extreme sports, 223–24, 319
   NASCAR, 222–23
   not-so-extreme sports, 223–24
   professional wrestling, 221–22
Sportainment, 206–7
technology trends, 228–31
   information sources, 228–31
Sports Illustrated, 119
*Sports Marketing: A Strategic Perspec-
   tive* (Shank), 217
Sports venues, and marketing, 23
Sportswriter, 229
Spring House, 190
Stafford, Jim, 242
Standard cross-plugs, 77
Starbucks Coffee, 118
Starz, 105
Stats Inc., 230
Steeple Hill Romances, 131
Stern, David, 210
Stern, Howard, 140
Streaming media piracy, 306
Streisand, Barbra, 33
Strikes, Major League Baseball (MLB),
   220
Strips, 84
Studio A, 301–3

Studio model, 59
Studio president/CEO/chairman, 50
Sub-rights divisions, 149–50
Subscription transactions, 304
Sun Microsystems, 126
Sundance Channel, 105, 117–19
Sundance Cinemas, 62
Sundance Film Festival, 116–18
Sundance Institute, 116
Super center concept, 8–9
Sutherland, Sam, 189
Sweeps, 72
Syndication, 81–85
    barter, 85
    cash deals, 84–85
    first-run programs, 83
    off-net programs, 82
    selling/licensing programming, 84
    stripping, 84
    syndicated product in auction, 83–84
Synergy, 15

T

Talent, 3
Tandy games, 163
Tartt, Donna, 133
TBS, 115
TCI, 103, 126
Techno-geeks, 102
Technology:
    and content, 3
    and trends, 318-19
Technology-based distribution, 9–10
Technology Revolution, 317
Technology trends, music, 192–95
Teens/young adult market segment, 45,
    55, 57
Tele-Communications, Inc., 159
Telecommunications Act of 1996, 107–
    9, 123
Television commercials, 52
Television networks, and marketing, 22
Television ratings, 26
Television technology, 87–90
    HDTV, 87–88
    MSN TV, 88–90
    TiVo, 90
Tent pole film, 48
Test screenings, 51

Theatrical print theft, 307
Theme parks, 262–63
    Disney theme park empire, 262–63
    and marketing, 23
    Universal Studios, 263
There's Something about Mary, 58
Thomson Corp.:
    magazines, 159
    newspapers, 158
Thorpe, Jim, 212
Time shares, 260–61
Time slots, 74–75
Time spent listening (TSL), 92
Time Warner, 103, 121, 150
    Cable, 119-20, 121
    magazines, 159
    WarnerElectraArista Music (WEA),
    172
Time Warner-Disney conflict, 109–10
Times Mirror, 158
Times Square (New York City), 246–47
Tin Cup, 207
Titanic, 57
TiVo, 90
TMC (The Movie Channel), 105
TNT, 115
TOPlay Soccer, 228
Tourism, *See* Travel/tourism
Tower Records, 180
Toys 'R' Us, 11
Trade books, 130, 134, 147–48
    long discount, 147
Trade fairs, 250
Trailers, 53–54
Trans World Entertainment, 180
Travel agents/agencies:
    and the economics of travel, 248
    online, 248–49
Travel Channel, 237
Travel consultants, 238
Travel packages, 235
Travel/tourism, 233–68
    advertising/publicity/promotion, 254–
    56
        agencies, 255–56
    alternate destinations, 256–67
    all-inclusive concept, 258–60
    Carnival Cruise Line case study,
        257–58

casino resorts, 263–66
condos, 261–62
cruises, 256–58
Indian casinos, 266–67
theme parks, 262–63
time shares, 260–61
creating an identity, 240–47
Austin, TX, 244–45
Branson, MO, 242–44
Nashville, TN, 240–41
"fam trip", 239
frequent flier programs, 252
hotel "brands", 252–53
hotel reward programs, 252
and the Internet, 248
marketing, 234–56
customer satisfaction promise, 237
dynamics of, 247–49
integration, 236–37
matching experience with expectation, 234–35
positioning, 235–36
strategy, 239–40
travel research, 238–39
Marriott International case study, 253–54
premier entertainment cities, 245–47
Hollywood/Los Angeles, 245–46
New York, 246–47
relationship marketing, 249–54
courting the consumer, 251
frequent flier programs, 252
hotel "brands," 252–53
hotel reward programs, 252
intra-industry trade shows and associations, 250–51
Marriott International case study, 253–54
tourism growth, sustaining, 236
travel agents/agencies, 238, 247–48
travel motivators, 237
Travelocity, 248
Travolta, John, 33–34
Trebek, Alex, 78
Tribune (Chicago) newspaper group, 158
Trip to Bountiful, The, 116
Tucci, Stanley, 34

Turner Broadcasting, 160
Turner Broadcasting System (TBS), 104
Turner, Ted, 39
TV5 (Canada), 308
TV ratings, 71–75
TV talk-show circuit, and books, 139–40
TVRO, 124–25
TVT, 172
TWA, 248
Twain, Shania, 197
TWBA, 29
2001:A Space Odyssey soundtrack, 191

U

U2, 245
Ueberroth, Heidi, 218
Unauthorized public performances, 307
United Airlines, 248
Universal Music Group, 172
Internet strategy, 197
Universal Studios, 263, 311
major studio production volume, cuts in, 60
UPN, 67–68, 75
Urban entertainment centers (UECs), 273
U.S. Film Festival, 116
U.S. Music Trail Tour, 241
U.S. Satellite Broadcasting (USSB), 118
USA Network, 115–16, 197
USA Today, 157
USSB, 125

V

Vacation Club, 261
Vanity presses, 152
Vertical cross-plugs, 77
VH-1, 178, 184
Viacom, 114, 120, 150, 159, 311
and Black Entertainment Television (BET), 113–14
Video-on-demand (VOD), 126, 303
Videocassette piracy, 306
Vincent, Fay, 208–9
Vinton, Bobby, 242
Virgin Mega-Stores, 181
Virgin Records, 180–81
Vivendi Universal, 197–98, 298

Vizzavi, 198
Vodafone, 198
Voice of an Angel in Concert, 189

W

Wal-Mart, 11
Wall Street Journal, 157
Walt Disney Studies:
 major studio production volume, cuts
  in, 60
Wannasee:
 creating, 50–58
 in-flight movies, 58
 Internet, 57
 movie tie-ins, 55
 movie trailers, 53–54
 Moviefone, 56
 newspaper advertising, 52–53
 Oscars, 56–57
 sneak previews, 51–52
 television commercials, 52
 test screenings, 51
Warner Amex Cable, 178
Warner Bros., 29, 51–52, 54, 311
 major studio production volume, cuts
  in, 60
Warner Cable, 119–20
Warner Music Group, 195
 and MP3.com, 195
WarnerElectraArista Music (WEA), 172
WarnerElectraAtlantic (WEA), 39
WarnerMusic, 172
Washington Post newspaper group, 158
Wasserman, Lew, 39
WB, 67, 75
Wells, Frank, 39
Western Media, 29
Westinghouse, 150
What Lies Beneath, 54
Wherehouse, 180
Wide Open Spaces album (Dixie
 Chicks), 185

Wild Wild West, 51
Williams, Andy, 242
Williams, Hank Jr., 224
Williams, John, 191
Williams, Lucinda, 173
Winfrey, Oprah, 140
Wireless Application Protocol (WAP),
 164
Women's National Basketball Associa-
 tion (WNBA), 211–12
Woods, Tiger, 225–26
Word, 190
Word of mouth, and independent films,
 61
Work for hire, 5–6
Work product, 5–6
World Intellectual Property Organiza-
 tion (WIPO), 300
World Wrestling Federation (WWF),
 222, 319
WPP, 298
Wrestling, 221–22
Wyatt, Justin, 46

X

Xena: Warrior Princess, 83
Xlibris, 153
XM Radio, 98

Y

Yahoo.com, 96, 161
Yearwood, Trisha, 186
Young & Rubicam (Y&R), 29, 113,255

Z

Zappa, Frank, 177
ZEE TV (India), 313
Ziff Davis Publishing, magazines, 159
"Zines," 161–62
Zomba Group, 197

The *Financial Times* delivers a world of business news.

Use the Risk-Free Trial Voucher below!

To stay ahead in today's business world you need to be well-informed on a daily basis. And not just on the national level. You need a news source that closely monitors the entire world of business, and then delivers it in a concise, quick-read format.

With the *Financial Times* you get the major stories from every region of the world. Reports found nowhere else. You get business, management, politics, economics, technology and more.

Now you can try the *Financial Times* for 4 weeks, absolutely risk free. And better yet, if you wish to continue receiving the *Financial Times* you'll get great savings off the regular subscription rate. Just use the voucher below.

8 reasons why you should read the Financial Times for 4 weeks RISK-FREE!

To help you stay current with significant
developments in the world economy ...
and to assist you to make informed business
decisions — the Financial Times brings you:

❶ Fast, meaningful overviews of international affairs ... plus daily
briefings on major world news.

❷ Perceptive coverage of economic, business, financial and political
developments with special focus on emerging markets.

❸ More international business news than any other publication.

❹ Sophisticated financial analysis and commentary on world market
activity plus stock quotes from over 30 countries.

❺ Reports on international companies and a section on global investing.

❻ Specialized pages on management, marketing, advertising and
technological innovations from all parts of the world.

❼ Highly valued single-topic special reports (over 200 annually)
on countries, industries, investment opportunities, technology and more.

❽ The Saturday Weekend FT section — a globetrotter's guide to
leisure-time activities around the world: the arts, fine dining, travel,
sports and more.

For Special Offer See Over

FT FINANCIAL TIMES
World business newspaper

8 reasons why you should read the Financial Times for 4 weeks RISK-FREE!

To help you stay current with significant
developments in the world economy ...
and to assist you to make informed business
decisions — the Financial Times brings you:

❶ Fast, meaningful overviews of international affairs ... plus daily briefings on major world news.

❷ Perceptive coverage of economic, business, financial and political developments with special focus on emerging markets.

❸ More international business news than any other publication.

❹ Sophisticated financial analysis and commentary on world market activity plus stock quotes from over 30 countries.

❺ Reports on international companies and a section on global investing.

❻ Specialized pages on management, marketing, advertising and technological innovations from all parts of the world.

❼ Highly valued single-topic special reports (over 200 annually) on countries, industries, investment opportunities, technology and more.

❽ The Saturday Weekend FT section — a globetrotter's guide to leisure-time activities around the world: the arts, fine dining, travel, sports and more.

For Special Offer See Over

FT FINANCIAL TIMES
World business newspaper

The *Financial Times* delivers
a world of business news.

Use the Risk-Free Trial Voucher below!

To stay ahead in today's business world you need to be well-informed on a daily basis. And not just on the national level. You need a news source that closely monitors the entire world of business, and then delivers it in a concise, quick-read format.

With the *Financial Times* you get the major stories from every region of the world. Reports found nowhere else. You get business, management, politics, economics, technology and more.

Now you can try the *Financial Times* for 4 weeks, absolutely risk free. And better yet, if you wish to continue receiving the *Financial Times* you'll get great savings off the regular subscription rate. Just use the voucher below.